The Rise and Fall of Corporate Social Responsibility

Corporate social responsibility was one of the most consequential business trends of the twentieth century. Having spent decades burnishing reputations as both great places to work and generous philanthropists, large corporations suddenly abandoned their commitment to their communities and employees during the 1980s and 1990s, indicated by declining job security, health insurance, and corporate giving.

Douglas M. Eichar argues that for most of the twentieth century, the benevolence of large corporations functioned to stave off government regulations and unions, as corporations voluntarily adopted more progressive workplace practices or made philanthropic contributions. Eichar contends that as governmental and union threats to managerial prerogatives withered toward the century's end, so did corporate social responsibility. Today, with shareholder value as their beacon, large corporations have shred their social contract with their employees, decimated unions, avoided taxes, and engaged in all manner of risky practices and corrupt politics.

This book is the first to cover the entire history of twentieth-century corporate social responsibility. It provides a valuable perspective from which to revisit the debate concerning the public purpose of large corporations. It also offers new ideas that may transform the public debate about regulating larger corporations.

Douglas M. Eichar is an Associate Professor and Chair of the Department of Sociology and Criminal Justice at the University of Hartford, USA.

The Rise and Fall of Corporate Social Responsibility

Douglas M. Eichar

Routledge
Taylor & Francis Group

NEW YORK AND LONDON

First published 2015
By Transaction Publishers, New Jersey, USA

Published 2017
by Routledge
711 Third Avenue, New York, NY 10017

and by Routledge
2 Park Square, Milton Park, Abingdon, Oxon, OX14 4RN

Routledge is an imprint of the Taylor & Francis Group, an informa business

Library of Congress Cataloging-in-Publication Data
A catalog record for this book has been requested

ISBN: 978-1-4128-5690-4 (hbk)
ISBN: 978-1-4128-6520-3 (pbk)
ISBN: 978-1-315-11007-3 (ebk)

Typeset in Warnock Pro
by Apex CoVantage, LLC

To Nick, Andy, Chris and Sue

Contents

Preface

The beginning of the twenty-first century witnessed the appearance of a vanguard of large corporations showcasing their efforts to act as good corporate citizens. Starbucks sells coffee made of beans that have the "Fair Trade" label, certifying that family farmers grew them and were paid a fair price. Method offers cleaning products that won't harm the environment. The Gap sells sweaters made of cotton that was not picked by children or coerced adults. Nike stipulates that the workers who make their running shoes are paid at least the minimum wage that is locally mandated.

These efforts comprise what is generally understood as corporate social responsibility (CSR): corporations offering goods and services produced and delivered in accordance with a set of socially responsible standards and practices that have been voluntarily adopted. There are a variety of outcomes that are encouraged by those who have adopted socially responsible practices in recent years. Chief among these, as the examples above illustrate, are environmental sustainability and better working conditions for workers in developing countries.

Advocacy of this new CSR reflects a strong faith in the market. The assumption is that with more and more educated consumers looking to spend in ways consistent with their values, an emergent market for virtue has eliminated the tension that previously existed between maximizing profits and being socially responsible in the conduct of business. In short, CSR is viewed as good for business. With good corporate citizens like Starbucks and Nike serving as beacons for other corporations to follow, the new CSR holds out the promise that corporate irresponsibility can be overcome naturally, and without more stringent interventions.

This should sound familiar. The roots of CSR are as deep as those of the large corporation itself. The two emerged in tandem. But when those in the twentieth-century vanguard of large corporations discussed the social responsibilities of businesses, they were not referring to environmental sustainability or workers in developing countries. Instead, they were discussing practices that would benefit their chief stakeholders: their employees and the local communities in which they resided. Then, too, there was the strong hope that corporations could voluntarily solve problems—many of which they helped create, like employment insecurity and local poverty resulting from low wages.

The Rise and Fall of Corporate Social Responsibility tells the story of this original incarnation of CSR. Like proponents today, those who took the corporate high road in the last century justified their socially responsible practices on the basis that they were good for business. Some were convinced that satisfied and secure workers were more productive, while others targeted the growing numbers of conscientious consumers who preferred to give their business to companies with good reputations for treating their employees well and helping their local communities. As CSR grew over the course of several decades, the promise of corporate voluntarism translated into an increasing dependence upon large corporations to provide things like health insurance and private pensions to their employees, and a growing reliance upon corporate philanthropy to help local communities sustain civic institutions and address local problems.

During the waning years of the twentieth century, however, many large corporations abandoned the high road to profitability. The promise of CSR was rapidly replaced by the lowered expectations that corporations should do whatever it takes to raise shareholder value. These expectations were met with weakened commitments to workers and communities. Corporations shed socially responsible practices, whether it was job security and health insurance for employees, or philanthropy for communities. The swiftness of the fall of the first version of CSR was matched by the starkness of the change in orientation.

In light of all of the positive attention that the new CSR has attracted, and because many hold high hopes that problems will be voluntarily solved as the trend grows, this would seem to be a perfect time to reexamine the rise and fall history of CSR's original form. The problem with socially responsible practices that are voluntarily offered is just that, they are voluntary; they can be readily withdrawn, well before the targeted problems they are meant to address are solved. This book serves as a cautionary tale.

—

This book was many years in the making. I would first of all like to thank my sons, Nick, Andy, and Chris, for their support, as well as their understanding of why I seemed to be in my study all of the time. I would also like to thank my friend and colleague Warren Goldstein for his encouragement over the years and the critical feedback that he provided. Last, I would like to thank my wife, Sue, whose love and support helped to sustain me. As my tough and careful editor, she did not make my writing life easy, but she made this a better book.

1

Introduction

The Rise and Fall of Corporate Social Responsibility

In 1917, working conditions at General Electric plants made the company a fertile ground for union organizers. Whether it was skilled machinists upset by efforts to deskill their craft through scientific management, or assembly line workers disgruntled by speed-ups on the line, many workers had already expressed their dismay by quitting. The company had an annual turnover rate of over 100 percent. In July of the following year the radical International Workers of the World (IWW) led the labor force of the company's Lynn, Massachusetts plant on a bitter strike.[1]

Owen Young, then the company's general counsel, sent his personal representative, Atherton Brownell, to Lynn to report on what he saw. Brownell characterized the strikers as a coalition of "Socialists, the Russian Labor Union, the IWW., the anarchists, the Bolsheviks, and the more radical men in the established labor unions." By November, the company experienced strikes at its factories in Fort Wayne, Indiana; Erie, Pennsylvania; and Pittsfield, Massachusetts. Not long afterwards, Brownell advised Young that in order to offset the influence of "the more radical element," the company needed a new approach to its workers that would mold them into "an articulate body that would stand solidly against unnecessary and harmful labor disturbances and continued friction"—in other words, unions.[2]

When Young assumed the position of chairman in 1922, he, along with the company's new president, Gerald Swope, began to experiment with personnel policies designed to nurture employee loyalty, and most importantly, avoid unions. Included in the mix were life insurance, company health care, mortgage assistance, and worker grievance boards. These are examples of *socially responsible practices*, in which a corporation's mode of operation is consistent with broader social goals like job security, workplace safety, or environmental sustainability.

Of course, whether in 1922 or today, these personnel practices could have been stipulated in a union contract (*negotiated responsibility*). They could have also been more strongly secured through government regulations (*mandated responsibility*). What GE attempted to demonstrate was that a corporation could voluntarily adopt such practices (*voluntary responsibility*). Today, this voluntary approach is referred to as *corporate social responsibility* (CSR), and GE was a paragon of its original form that focused on the treatment of employees.

In fact, CSR can be traced back to the nineteenth century, when large corporations burst onto the economic scene. Though many Americans marveled at what they saw, many also looked on with alarm. These included small merchants who worried that they might be crushed by the predatory practices of companies such as Standard Oil, as well as craftsmen distressed by the prospect of losing both their craft and independence as wage laborers working for companies like Carnegie Steel. Rising consternation coalesced into a broad array of demands for reform, ranging from antitrust to laws regulating the workplace to the right of workers to be represented by unions. As quickly as it came on the scene, the large corporation became a contested institution.

Corporate owners fought to preserve what they considered the main prerogative of ownership: unhindered decision making. Their resistance wore two faces. The first and most visible was the stern face of hard-nosed, sometimes bare-knuckled politics and violence, like a Rockefeller lobbyist bribing a state legislator or some of Carnegie's men wielding clubs against strikers. But resistance showed a friendly face as well. Though clearly in the minority, employers like Proctor and Gamble and National Cash Register voluntarily adopted more humane workplace practices and gave generously to their local communities. Concerned that demands for reforms might gain traction and naked resistance might engender even greater hostility, these owners hoped to keep government and unions at bay by showing that both were unnecessary. Thus was born CSR.

From the end of the nineteenth century, CSR grew gradually, both in the number of large corporations that adopted its practices and in the variety of practices that came to signify the trend. The original, central forms of CSR targeted corporations' chief stakeholder, their employees. Known first as *welfare work*, analysts eventually settled upon the label of *welfare capitalism*. As CSR practices expanded to include other stakeholders, especially the cities in which businesses operated, CSR developed the second front of *corporate philanthropy*. This version of CSR, the combination of welfare capitalism and corporate philanthropy, constituted one of the most consequential business trends of the twentieth century.

When GE joined the trend in the 1920s, it quickly became a leader. Over the course of the next several decades, GE's commitment broadened to include the schools, hospitals, and other institutions within the local communities like Schenectady, where the company resided. Alongside this growing package of personnel practices and philanthropic commitments, Young and Swope also fashioned a CSR philosophy. Contrasting the orientation of his generation of corporate managers with that of the first generation of entrepreneurial founders, Young stated, "Today, when the corporation has become an institution, the duty of management is no longer solely to the investor."[3] In a speech on "The Responsibilities of Modern Industry," Swope's appraisal of constituencies to whom the corporation owed a duty listed the public first and the stockholder last, with workers in between. Later in his career, Swope moved workers ahead of the public.[4]

Just as GE was representative of the rise of CSR, it also came to symbolize its fall. This dramatic turn of events occurred during the reign of Jack Welch, who assumed the positions of president and CEO in 1981. To his many fans, Welch was a business hero who spectacularly increased the price of the company's stock during his twenty years atop the firm. To his many critics, however, Welch was a corporate villain who had earned the epithet of "Neutron Jack"—a CEO whose explosive decisions destroyed the jobs of thousands of employees, while leaving the buildings intact. In just his first four years at the helm, he took a workforce of 411,000 and eliminated over 100,000 jobs, achieved largely by the closing of seventy-three plants and facilities. For the rest of his tenure, payroll was kept at 300,000, in part by an annual appraisal system, dubbed by some as "management by stress." Each year GE's 85,000 managers and professionals were graded on a five-point scale, and the bottom 10 percent were dismissed.[5]

This orientation to employees was consistent with Welch's business philosophy, which, frequently couched in sports metaphors, centered on winning: "winning's good. Winning is what it's all about. . . . You like to be in the football locker room that lost, or won?" An intensely competitive man, Welch pointed to his involvement in youth sports as a formative influence. It followed that "the team that fields the best players wins the game . . . when you don't you lose." Not averse to alternative metaphors, Welch also characterized his perennial job cuts as "weeding the garden" and "refining the gene pool."[6]

The Young-Swope and Welch eras serve as the beginning and ending chapters of employee and community-centered CSR at GE. But this story of the slow, apparently durable growth of CSR, followed by its rapid decline in the 1980s and 1990s, played out at countless other American corporations. In the latter years of the twentieth century, millions of jobs were eliminated, as the words "downsizing" and "restructuring" entered the American lexicon. While layoffs were nothing new to the American economy, it was noteworthy that the list of those issuing pink slips included CSR stalwarts for the first time. Eastman Kodak Company had been a pioneer in employee-friendly practices as far back as 1897. It came to be known for its generous array of benefits, which regularly grew over many years, and it was not uncommon for two or three generations in the same family to be employed in the same plant. In 1986, however, the company announced that it would cut 10 percent of its workforce. Despite the typically thin profit margins of the retail industry, Sears Roebuck had distinguished itself for decades by offering its workers improvements in everything from profit sharing and fringe benefits to secure jobs and the chance of promotion. But in 1992 it announced that it would cut over 43,000 jobs on top of the 21,000 it had already eliminated in 1991. The giants of the insurance industry, companies like Aetna, Travelers, Equitable Life, and John Hancock, who had collectively built a reputation of benevolent paternalism toward their workers over the course of many years, announced thousands of layoffs in 1991. Finally, in 1993, after seventy-nine years of extending virtual lifetime employment to its employees, IBM announced it would eliminate 25,000 jobs. Not only did this wave of downsizing wreak havoc in the lives of those who lost their jobs, but the communities that bore the brunt of the layoffs, like Schenectady (General Electric) and Hartford (Aetna, Travelers), were devastated as well.[7]

Looking back over the last quarter of the twentieth century, downsizing constituted but the leading edge of an across the board decline in the original forms of CSR, as indicted in a raft of trends that by the beginning of the new century had become firmly established patterns. These include:

- A decline in job security. Between 1983 and 2000, the median number of years with one's current employer declined by over 25 percent for men between the ages of thirty-five and sixty-four (by over 33 percent for men fifty-five to sixty-four).[8]

- The number of workers in less secure, "alternative employment arrangements" (independent contractors, on-call workers, temp workers, and contract company workers) increased during this period and stood at 9.3 percent of workers in 1999.[9]
- The share of low-wage jobs—those that pay wages at or below the poverty line increased from 1979 to 1999 and represented more than 25 percent of all jobs.[10]
- A decline in health insurance as a fringe benefit. For full-time employees of large and medium size corporations, the percentage covered by employer provided health insurance declined from 97 percent in 1980 to 67 percent in 2000.[11]
- A shift in who bears the risks for pensions. For full-time employees of large and medium-size corporations, the percentage covered by a "defined benefit" pension—those that guarantee a fixed payment in retirement based upon wages and years of service—declined from 84 percent to 36 percent between 1980 and 2000.[12]
- Corporate philanthropy, as a percentage of profits, declined by 50 percent between 1987 and 2002.[13]
- The sharp increase in the 1980s and 1990s in the use of offshore tax sheltering schemes—shifting assets or headquarters to places like Bermuda—cost the US Treasury an estimated $50 billion a year in corporate tax revenue. While corporations paid 21 percent of all taxes in 1980, by 2001 they only paid 13 percent.[14]

CSR: The Friendly Face of Resistance

Conventional wisdom points the finger at global competition as the cause of the decline in this twentieth-century form of CSR. Up until the 1970s, most major American industries were oligopolies, with each controlled by a handful of large, bureaucratic corporations. For example, in the automobile industry there were the mammoths of General Motors, Ford, and Chrysler, while U.S. Steel and Bethlehem Steel dominated the steel industry. Because they faced little domestic competition, and little international competition, due to devastation of competitor nation economies as a result of World War II, American businesses were able to enjoy profit margins high enough to underwrite their CSR practices. But without competition, the argument goes, these corporate giants became progressively inefficient and slow to change. They were therefore ill adapted for the new environment of global competition that appeared during the decade of the 1970s. Unable to compete, and with declining profit margins, large corporations abandoned CSR because they could no longer afford it.

This conventional narrative suffers from two problems, one comparative and one historical. The comparative problem is that, hit by the same global economic tsunami and forced to be as vigilant in keeping costs down, large corporations in most European countries did not abandon the socially responsible practices that benefited their employees and their communities. The historical problem is that CSR had survived and even grown during earlier economic crises, including the Great Depression.[15]

To illustrate the comparative problem further, at the same time that American workers were experiencing the effects of downsizing and the loss of benefits, German workers retained their health coverage, and French workers mostly remained in secure jobs; the massive downsizings that devastate communities did not occur. Of course, German and French employers may have abandoned CSR like their American brethren had they been participants in the trend; they were not, or at least not to the extent of American employers. The reason that European workers and communities fared better was because the constituent features comprising CSR were not left to the caprice of employers. Instead, items like health care and pensions were protected by strong governments (in the form of regulations and welfare provisions) and strong unions, and these could not be readily abandoned. In contrast, CSR, because it constituted a voluntary set of practices, was vulnerable to abandonment by management when economic times got tough.

It is important then to understand CSR in relation to a country's political economy and labor relations. The comparative question becomes why American regulations and unions were weak, while CSR was strong. To understand the decline of CSR, it is necessary to understand its rise and prominence before the 1980s, or why, in short, the United States came to depend so heavily upon an institution that was so inherently vulnerable.

One possible answer is that CSR represented the efforts of corporate leaders to fill the void of missing welfare provisions left by a deeply rooted political culture characterized by a weak state and weak unions. But this would be a charitable view of American corporate history at best. While some large corporations did step in to fill a void, it was one they had fought to create. The truth is that American corporations, in comparison to their European counterparts, had for the better part of a century done a far better job of keeping both government and unions at bay.

A better approach to understanding America's dependence on corporations' voluntary measures is to consider the common problem that all societies face as large corporations begin to dominate the economic landscape. On the one hand, these enterprises generate great wealth and employ a large percentage of the labor force, thus representing tremendous assets for societies as they struggle to meet the needs of their citizens. On the other hand, large corporations concentrate power, and their large size gives them the capacity for doing great harm, ranging from the exploitation of employees to the fouling of the environment.

As a result of the array of problems left in its wake, the large corporation has historically been a controversial, contested institution. The socially responsible policies and practices that are most often associated with CSR, like the provision of health insurance, the availability of safe products, or environmentally sustainable modes of production, are best understood as the outcome of struggles that pit the heads of corporations attempting to protect the prerogatives of ownership against reformers attempting to both control large corporations and tether them to broader social purposes. These struggles, then, determine the balance between the private and public purposes of corporations.

There are three main pathways to engendering any set of socially responsible practices (the public purpose) among corporations. The most effective among these, what can be called *mandated responsibility*, are government regulations, which, in turn, have two types. *Social regulations* mandate socially responsible outcomes, including rules that govern working conditions, employment, discharge of pollutants, and consumer safety standards, among others. Sometimes social regulations mandate that corporations assume a role in delivering *welfare state* goods, such as health insurance, pensions, or unemployment insurance. Government may also attempt to secure the public purpose of corporations through *economic regulations* that give society influence over economic decisions (publicly owned corporations, regulatory commissions) or control their size (antitrust).

The second pathway is through union contracts, what can be called *negotiated responsibility*. Here, responsible practices are stipulated in union contracts. These can include a variety of workplace and personnel conditions, such as working conditions, the provision of health insurance and pensions, and the use of seniority in promotion and layoff decisions.

The third pathway is through the voluntary provision by corporate management, or what can be called *voluntary responsibility*. Though CSR is not the only path to the goal of corporations acting in a socially responsible fashion, the book keeps to the convention of using CSR to refer to the last path: socially responsible practices that are voluntarily adopted by corporations.

Where reformers gain the upper hand in these contests with corporations, societies come to rely more heavily upon mandated and negotiated responsibility (regulations and union contracts) to ensure socially responsible practices. Where the resistance of corporate owners wins out, societies ultimately rely upon voluntary responsibility (CSR). Though these are never as robust as the practices rendered by regulations or contracts, CSR can range from the sporadic—as when individual owners have a philosophical commitment, when consumer demand is sufficient to encourage it, or when it is necessary to attract skilled workers—to the more extensive, when they become a tool for fending off challenges from reformers.[16]

The outcomes of these contests between reformers and corporations vary by the particular practice being contested, and they vary over time, as the relative strength of each side shifts. As a result, each society has a distinctive *regulatory structure* for tethering large corporations, comprising a different mix of government regulations (both social and economic), union contracts, and CSR. Broadly speaking, in Europe this conflict resulted in a more resilient structure of both strong government regulations and unions, and less reliance upon CSR (strong mandated responsibility, strong negotiated responsibility, weak CSR). In the United States, however, large corporations were more successful in avoiding both government regulations and unions. Not only did their hard-edged forms of resistance remain effective, but as CSR became the more visible, if not dominant, face of that resistance, a critical mass of politicians and workers were also convinced that neither stronger regulations nor more unions were needed. As a result, America's regulatory structure became heavily reliant upon the voluntary adoption of socially responsible practices (weak mandated responsibility, weak negotiated responsibility, strong CSR).

If resistance, and the resulting differences in regulatory structures are central to understanding the comparative problem with the conventional explanation of CSR's decline, what about the historical problem: why did CSR decline when it did? The durability of CSR ultimately depended upon the strength of its catalyst: demands for reform. As long as owners and managers felt threatened by the prospect of regulations and unions, CSR was not only viable, but it grew stronger. By the 1980s, however, the legitimacy of the large corporation was unchallenged. It was no longer a contested institution. As its catalyst withered, so did CSR. This, then, explains why CSR declined during the economic struggles of the 1980s and early 1990s, and not during earlier economic crises when the large corporation was still was a target for reformers' demands.

Reengaging the Debate

The heart of this book tells the story of the rise and fall of CSR in the twentieth century. But this story is nested within a broader story: the rise of large corporations in the United States, the demands for reform they inspired, and the resistance of their owners and managers to society's efforts to control them. Since CSR needs to be understood in relation to the country's entire regulatory structure for large corporations (mandated responsibility, negotiated responsibility, voluntary responsibility), the book has a triadic structure, in which changes in political economy, labor relations, and CSR are reviewed and knitted together.

The history of CSR, and its part in the nation's regulatory structure during the last century, provides a valuable angle from which to revisit what was once an animated debate in America: what is the role of corporations, and what should we expect from them? From their birth as economic organizations in the nineteenth century, Americans expressed great ambivalence toward large corporations. Many marveled at the sheer scale of these enterprises, from the architectural feats of their buildings to the magnificent machines that resided within them. And Americans were certainly impressed by the products that left the building, from cheap textiles to train engines.

But these behemoths, especially as personified by the founding "robber barons" of the period, were also feared. Because they greatly expanded the category of wage labor, many saw them as a threat to the republican virtue of independence as exemplified by yeoman farmers and master craftsmen. Indeed, after reading accounts of early factories in England, where a new class of wage earners worked and lived in wretched conditions, some expressed alarm even before they made their first appearance on our shores. In 1785 Thomas Jefferson wrote that factory work brings dependence, which, in turn, "begets subservience and venality, suffocates the germ of virtue, and prepares fit tools for the designs of ambition."[17] Others worried more that the central value of equality was threatened by the extremes of wealth and poverty produced by an economic system dominated by large corporations. Over time, still other critics charged that large corporations corrupted the very foundations of democracy. These "private governments" not only bribed politicians, they also represented a growing sphere of private decisions that had deleterious public effects, whether these involved a business closing its doors and putting hundreds out of work, or a factory contaminating a local lake with its sludge. Those more devoted to capitalism itself expressed the concern that the great power that these enterprises exercised in crushing small businesses and setting prices undermined the economic system's guarantor, competition.

This concern was matched by discussions of what should be done. Should large corporations be broken up and destroyed, with small-scale production and competition "restored?" Or should corporations be regulated? Or should they be expected to assume some set of social responsibilities commensurate with the privileges extended to the corporate form of organization? In the course of their history many critics have gained prominence in the answers that they provided. Among others there have been Edward Bellamy, who proposed nationalization of corporations, Louis Brandeis, who advocated antitrust, and Ralph Nader, who suggested the federal chartering of corporations.

Though the debate concerning corporations lasted for well over one hundred years, and while it was at times quite heated, it is largely quiet now. The dominance of large corporations is no longer much challenged, but instead has come to assume the character of those things that we take for granted. It is now largely accepted that corporations have no other purpose but to serve the private interests of their shareholders.

A quick review of the evidence at the beginning of the twenty-first century would show that the original forms of CSR, welfare capitalism and community-based corporate philanthropy, have continued to decline. Coupled with examples of corporate scandal that seemingly abound, the large corporation appears unmoored from public purpose. The time is therefore ripe for revisiting the history of efforts to connect large corporations to broader social goals.

A Preview

Chapter 2 focuses upon those events and forces that helped lay the groundwork for the country's regulatory structure. The setting for the birth of CSR was the turmoil of the rapid industrialization of the late nineteenth century. During this period, the emergence of capitalism on a grand scale and the growing dominance of large enterprises were not settled affairs. Challengers included trade unionists, socialists, populists, utopians, anarchists, and grangers, and especially antimonopolists, all of whom articulated alternative pathways ranging from socialism to nationalization to independent regulatory commissions. Collectively, challengers, and the reforms they proposed, contributed to an atmosphere of possibility and unsettledness, and a fear on the part of big-business owners that what might be marginal could grow into something substantial.

Against those demanding reforms and regulations, owners fought ferociously to protect what they considered as the inalienable preroga- tive of decision making without any restraints. Influencing the outcome of these early contests was the nation's *political economy*, used in the book to refer to the relative power of the business and government sectors of society. In the United States, the government is congenitally predisposed toward slow growth as a result of its federalist structure, separation of powers, and abundant checks and balances. Consequently, government was no match for corporations as they quickly grew at the end of the nineteenth century to nearly unimaginable size. The result was a lopsided political economy in which corporations dominated the federal government.

To begin with, the owners of large corporations were able to repel most efforts at imposing social regulations. However, an antimonopoly coalition of merchants, small farmers, and workers helped win passage of both the Interstate Commerce Act (1883) and the Sherman Antitrust Act (1890). These economic regulations set America upon a path of using antitrust enforcement and independent regulatory commissions to regulate large corporations. Instead of directly regulating the size of corporations, these approaches were guided by the faith that if fair competition in the marketplace was preserved, small enterprises would prevail against large corporations.

The faith in these economic regulations turned out to be misplaced, as corporations effectively resisted their implementation. As a result, large corporations continued to grow larger. Of course, there are many economic, political, and historically specific reasons that corporations got larger in the United States. As a review of these is well beyond the scope of this book, attention will be focused instead on the role of *governance structures*. These are practices that corporations devise in an attempt to contain or mitigate economic competition—and which in the United States tended to produce larger enterprises. Chapter 2 will illustrate their creative, if at times ethically challenged, use by John D. Rockefeller as he built Standard Oil.

Viewing these endeavors side by side, corporations not only attempted to control their political environment (i.e., resisting both social and economic regulations), they also attempted to control their economic environment. The successes that corporations experienced in both pursuits contributed to an increasingly lopsided political economy. And, of course, the more lopsided it became, the better able corporations were to further resist mandated responsibility.

The heads of big business also took advantage of their concentrated power to wage what was frequently a violent, and usually successful, campaign against labor unions. One result was that few workers were covered by union contracts. Another was the style of unionism that could withstand the assault of business. The business unionism of the American Federation of Labor's first leader, Samuel Gompers, survived, while the political unionism of the Knights of Labor, which sought greater power for workers and reform of the larger economy, perished. The early result, then, was that the second pillar of America's regulatory structure, negotiated responsibility, was weak.

But some owners recognized that this no-holds-barred display of might, while expedient, also fueled the flames of opposition. Power needed a friendly face. Displays of CSR, then, became a shield to ward off the demands of both workers and the state, and a staff to project a benevolent, legitimate power. A review of the histories of corporations such as Proctor and Gamble and National Cash Register shows that a key reason for adopting humane work practices was the desire to keep encroaching unions out of their workplaces. Similarly, a desire to preempt government action led employers to adopt socially responsible practices both at the workplace and beyond in the form of corporate philanthropy. Of course, these practices required an investment of resources, which not all businesses could afford. It was the combination of larger size and the effectiveness of governance structures that gave participating corporations the wherewithal in the form of steady profits to fund CSR practices.

In sum, not only were the initial pathways of the nation's regulations, unions, and CSR established by the end of the nineteenth century, a dynamic relationship among them was established: the stronger the threats of regulations or unions, the stronger the CSR response of large corporations. Chapters 3–6 trace both the gradual articulation of these pathways and the evolution of their interrelationships by chronologically reviewing the ideological, political, and labor challenges to large corporations that arose. Each of these chapters is composed of three main sections corresponding to the three pillars of America's regulatory structure: first, struggles in the political economy that pitted ever-growing corporations against ideological and political challengers that resulted in mandated responsibility; second, battles between owners and unions that produced negotiated responsibility; and third, the growth in CSR that was stimulated by threats posed by the potential of regulations and unions.

Chapter 3 covers the Progressive Era, chapter 4 the 1920s, chapter 5 the Great Depression and World War II, and chapter 6 the postwar period up through the mid-1960s. Each chapter highlights critical junctures in our political economy and labor relations when events such as merger waves, war, government expansion, labor strikes, economic growth, and economic depression engendered challenges to the large corporation that threatened to shift the balance of power between government and business on the one hand, and unions and employers on the other.

At these critical junctures, challengers illuminated stronger mandated and negotiated pathways for controlling large corporations. But the ability to explore these alternatives throughout these decades was conditioned by one constant: American corporations continued to grow bigger and more powerful, and, as a result, America's political economy remained decisively tilted toward business power. Therefore, at these junctures, the leaders of major corporations generally prevailed in the major challenges to their power, and the doors to these alternatives were closed. However, large corporations could not prevail in completely preventing the growth of government or unions; as these grew, so did the threats to managerial prerogatives to which corporations responded with greater CSR. But the growth of both government and unions was not accompanied by the full acceptance of either institution. The dynamic tension that made the structure work was thus unstable.

The growth of these pathways culminated in the decade of the mid-1960s through the mid-1970s, when America's regulatory structure reached its peak of effectiveness, the subject of chapter 7. This was a period when the main challengers to corporate power shifted from unions to civil rights leaders, women's groups, consumer advocates, and environmentalists, and where challengers came to insist upon regulation rather than the voluntary social responsibility of corporate managers. The result was a series of laws that aimed at regulating the workplace, consumer safety, and the environment. The apparatus of collective bargaining also grew to maturity, and unions were using it to negotiate contracts with bigger and better compensation packages that featured expansive health care and pension benefits. As the threat of mandates and unions grew, so did the voluntary practices of employers, whether in the form of employment security or philanthropic efforts to confront social problems. America's pattern of weak regulations, weak unions and strong CSR seemed at the tipping point where stronger regulations and unions would be fully established, and the need for CSR would diminish.

Slow in the making, CSR experienced a rapid decline at the century's end, the subject of chapter 8. The increasing globalization of the economy and the declining profits that ensued triggered a number of changes that revealed the vulnerability of the regulatory structure's pillars in a lopsided political economy. First, the slide of the American economy during the 1970s became a fertile ground for the business community to mount an attack upon government in general, and regulations of corporations in particular. This environment also helped spawn the Reagan Revolution of the 1980s and its attempt to reset the regulatory clock. Second, as mandates faltered, so did unions. Without institutional power or political cover, unions became a tempting target for cost reductions as profits were squeezed. As a result, unions entered a tailspin of concession bargaining, lost certification elections (and decertification), and declining rates of unionization. CSR was now vulnerable, as the threat of government and unions diminished. Its decline became rapid when a movement of corporate raiders and shareholder activists successfully demanded that corporations be oriented exclusively to raising shareholder value. As corporate social responsibility was not part of the new equation, it came to be sacrificed on the altar of profits.

In chapter 9 an effort will then attempt to reengage the debate concerning large corporations by exploring how best to re-tether them to larger social purposes. Attention will be focused first on the emergence of the "new CSR" of the twenty-first century. Targeting a new set of stakeholders and beneficiaries, there has been a proliferating number of corporations attempting to, among other things, develop environmentally sustainable production methods and products, and establish a set of standards to improve working conditions for workers in the developing countries that supply many corporations with their products and services. Examples include Starbucks selling coffee with the Fair Trade label, Whole Foods promoting the reduction of consumption of nonrenewable resources, and Method Products selling only environmentally safe products.

There is certainly nothing wrong in encouraging these voluntary efforts. In fact, the original incarnation of CSR that this book examines suggests that there is every reason to believe that it will produce some good results. However, *The Rise and Fall of Corporate Social Responsibility* serves as a cautionary tale here, as it presents even stronger evidence that supports the conclusion that excessive reliance upon such voluntary measures will fall far short of the goal of re-tethering corporations to broader social purposes. Ultimately, greater social responsibility on the part of corporations will be forthcoming only when they are once again contested ideologically. The book ends by offering a set of proposals for building a more resilient regulatory structure. For government, these include family-friendly workplace regulations, federal incorporation, and using the purse strings of government to engender socially responsible practices for contractors. For unions, these include changes in labor law and the establishment of work councils. Should such a regulatory structure be built, the decline of CSR will no longer be a sign of large corporations unmoored from society's grasp, but instead an indicator that society relies little upon voluntary measures to ensure that corporations act in socially responsible ways.

Notes

1. Ronald W. Schatz, *The Electrical Workers: A History of Labor at General Electric and Westinghouse* (Urbana, Illinois: University of Illinois Press, 1983), chapter 2.
2. Ibid., 37, 22.
3. Ibid., 15.
4. David Loth, *Swope of G.E.: The Story of Gerald Swope and General Electric in American Business* (New York: Simon and Schuster, 1958), 162.
5. Jack Welch, with John A. Byrne, *Jack: Straight from the Gut* (New York: Warner Business Books, 2001); Carol Hymowitz and Matt Murray, "General Electric's Welch Discusses His Ideas on Motivating Employees," *Wall Street Journal*, June 21, 1999.
6. Hymowitz and Murray, "General Electric's Welch Discusses His Ideas"; Steve Denning, "Don't Blame Green for GE's Problems," *Forbes*, March 1, 2011, http://www.forbes.com/sites/stevedenning/2011/03/01/dont-blame-green-for-ges-problems/.
7. New York Times, *The Downsizing of America: Millions of Americans are Losing Good Jobs. This is Their Story* (New York: Times Books, 1996); *Business Week*, "The Pain of Downsizing," *Business Week*, May 8, 1994.
8. United States Department of Labor, Bureau of Labor Statistics, "Employee Tenure in 2000," August 2000, http://www.bls.gov/news.release/history/tenure_08292000.txt. (Since men's labor force was relatively stable during this period, only men's data are reported here).
9. Marissa DiNatale, "Characteristics of and Preference for Alternative Work Arrangements," *Monthly Labor Review* 124, no. 3 (March 2001): 28.
10. Lawrence Mishel, Jared Bernstein, and John Schmitt, *The State of Working America: 2000/2001* (Ithaca, New York: ILR Press, 2001), 130.

11. Employee Benefit Research Institute, "Employee Databook on Employee Benefits, chapter 4: Participation in Employee Benefits Programs," Employee Benefits Research Institute, updated July 2008, http://www.ebri.org/pdf/publications/books/databook/DB.Chapter%2004.pdf.

12. Ibid.; There was a corresponding rise in firms offering "defined contribution" pensions, those where employers make contributions each year (to which employees can often add), and where retirement income depends on the success of an individual's investments.

13. Michael E. Porter and Mark R. Kramer, "The Competitive Advantage of Corporate Philanthropy," in *Harvard Business Review on Corporate Responsibility* (Boston: Harvard Business School Press, 2003), 28.

14. Robert S. McIntyre, Director of Citizens for Tax Justice, hearing before the Committee on the Budget, United States House of Representatives, Waste, Fraud, and Abuse in Federal Mandatory Programs, Serial No. 108–9, June 18, 2003, http://www.ctj.org/html/corp0603.htm; Leonard Wiener, "The Tax Man Goeth," *U.S. News and World Report* 133, no. 7 (August 19, 2002).

15. Though CSR programs were cut during the first years of the Depression, they grew substantially in the latter years of the downturn—see Chapter 5.

16. The claim that CSR is a form of resistance to unions and regulations has deep roots. Early union organizers were particularly concerned about what they saw as the union-avoidance function of CSR workplace initiatives. Contemporary analyses that make similar claims include Sanford M. Jacoby's *Modern Manors: Welfare Capitalism Since the New Deal*, Princeton, New Jersey: Princeton University Press, 1997, and Andrea Tone's *The Business of Benevolence: Industrial Paternalism in Progressive America*, Ithaca, New York: Cornell University Press, 1997.

17. Thomas Jefferson, "The Present State of Manufacturers," (1785), in *The Philosophy of Manufacturers: Early Debates Over Industrialization in the United States*, eds. Michael Brewster Folsom and Steven D. Lubar (Cambridge, Massachusetts: The MIT Press, 1982), 17.

2

The End of the Nineteenth Century: Regulatory Pathways are Set

Mandated Responsibility

Growth of Large Corporations: The Rise of the Behemoth

Though the large corporation made an antebellum appearance in both textiles and railroads, it was the post-Civil War period that witnessed its full arrival on the economic scene. Improvements in transportation and communication connected a far-flung set of territories and created a large national market. Technological innovation helped to bring about whole new industries. The combination of national markets and new industries created an abundance of opportunities for budding entrepreneurs who enthusiastically embraced the competition and joined the fray. But once engaged in economic battle, some came to regard competition as a problem that required a solution. This is illustrated well in the case of the refinery industry and in the actions of John D. Rockefeller.

The refinery business was typical of many of the new industries born to the technological innovations of early industrialization. The capital required to enter the field was low, and legions of investors rushed in after oil was discovered in Titusville, Pennsylvania, in 1859. As the supply of oil expanded, gluts developed from overproduction and prices entered a deflationary spiral where many investors went under. One of the surviving firms was located in Cleveland, Ohio, and went by the name Andrews, Clark and Company. One of its partners was Rockefeller.

After buying out his main partner in 1865, Rockefeller embarked upon a strategy of rapid growth that involved bringing in new partners and taking out loans. By the late 1860s, however, overproduction and volatile prices remained a problem in the oil industry. This did not sit well with this driven young man from a small town in western New York. As an intensely pious man, Rockefeller viewed business through a religious lens and assigned transcendent purpose to his business practices. Not only did he perceive the disorder of the oil industry as morally repulsive, he identified the culprit as "ruinous competition."[1] It became his calling to create order out of chaos by replacing competition with cooperation.[2] He pursued this objective with a missionary's zeal, but with methods that would forever gain him infamy.

One of the first efforts to lower the competitive heat in the oil industry involved an attempt to coordinate the actions of the industry's businesses. The cartel, or pool, consists of an agreement among an industry's firms to set quotas and prices, and range from informal "gentlemen's agreements" to formal contracts. After 1860 pools became quite common in the US economy, and as diverse as the Steel Rail Pool, Wall Paper Association, Upholsterers' Felt Association, Gunpowder Manufacturers' Association, and the Michigan Salt Association.[3] In 1872 Rockefeller took the lead in forming the National Refiners' Association, which would maintain higher prices by assigning quotas to its members, thus limiting production. Later in the year, the refiners' association signed the so-called Treaty of Titusville with the Petroleum Producers' Association, agreeing to pay higher prices to producers in exchange for production limits.

But as was true of most efforts at establishing pools in the United States, both agreements soon crumbled. The common problem was that cartel agreements were voluntary, and thus not legally binding, since state courts tended to view them as criminal conspiracies. In the case of the refiners' agreement, nonmembers of the association became "free riders" who could enjoy the higher prices while not being bound by a quota. As far as the Treaty of Titusville was concerned, because the tremendous expanse of the American market made the monitoring of compliance nearly impossible, cheating became common.[4]

The inability to coordinate the relations among competing firms convinced Rockefeller that cartel agreements were essentially "ropes of sand," and reinforced his efforts to find other routes to containing competition. For example, as he established himself as one of the larger refiners, Rockefeller was instrumental in the expansion of a practice that would gain him his first notoriety. Beginning with an agreement with the Lake Shore Railroad in 1868, he received a preferential rate in the shipment of crude oil. The incentive on the part of Rockefeller was clear, since these discounts, known at the time as "rebates," gave him a competitive advantage over his rivals who would have to pay the regular, higher rates. The incentive on the part of Lake Shore and other railroads was to achieve regular and substantial freight traffic at a time that they also struggled to survive in a highly competitive industry. It did not take long, however, before Rockefeller was in the position to dictate the terms of rebates to the various railroads.[5]

Rebates also proved to be a useful cudgel in convincing competitors to sell out to the newly incorporated (1870) Standard Oil Company. In what became known as the "Cleveland Massacre," Rockefeller was able to take over twenty-two of his twenty-six Cleveland competitors after rumors spread of an agreement, ultimately short-lived, with the Pennsylvania Railroad. As with everything else that he did, Rockefeller became a master in the art of mergers, or horizontal integration. By 1877 he was so successful in his efforts that he controlled 90 percent of the oil refined in America.[6]

While he contained the competition in the refinery industry, Rockefeller was still subject to the vagaries of competition at the retail level of distribution and at the point of production. To deal with this problem, Standard Oil was also in the vanguard of developing vertical integration, where control is sought over the raw materials needed for production or outlets for distribution. To gain control over production, Rockefeller purchased oil-producing properties in the late 1880s, and within a few years, Standard Oil was extracting 25 percent of the nation's crude. In order to guarantee an outlet for his oil, he used "predatory pricing," selling oil below cost door to door in order to "persuade" storekeepers to carry Standard kerosene exclusively.[7] Rockefeller's success did not go unnoticed. Whether it was Swift Brothers & Company purchasing refrigerated cars for its meat products, or Carnegie Steel acquiring iron-ore deposits, vertical integration began to spread throughout American industry.[8]

This brief review constitutes only a short list of Rockefeller's organizational innovations, both legal and unscrupulous, that produced a very large enterprise. As a result, the rise of Standard Oil is often used as a case study to explain the rise of large corporations at the end of the nineteenth century. The most influential theory is that of business historian Alfred Chandler. In *The Visible Hand*, Chandler asserts that the key to understanding the advantage of bigness is efficiency. As companies grew, they achieved economies of scale that allowed them to out-perform smaller, less efficient competitors.[9]

In recent years, however, a number of sociologists and historians have challenged the efficiency theory of large corporations, claiming that they were in no way inevitable. Instead of efficiency, these analysts offer alternative explanations that rely upon factors such as contingency, institutionalization, and power. The sketch of Standard Oil's history highlights how contingent factors help explain bigness. For example, where cartels withstood legal challenge, as was true in countries like Germany and Austria, smaller businesses could fashion enforceable agreements.[10] Once bigness began to spread, it was "institutionalized," becoming the accepted or preferred way of conducting business. Other actors, whether judges or bankers or politicians, then facilitated the form taking hold, by way of beneficial court rulings, preferential loan treatment, or favorable laws.[11]

Given its importance in understanding America's regulatory structure, this book underlines the importance of power. If greater efficiency was the result, it usually was not the cause of bigness. As the case of Standard Oil illustrates, power was exercised to eliminate rivals. One of the myths of nineteenth-century capitalism in America is that its familiar icons, like Rockefeller, comprised a group of rugged individualists committed to the game of economic competition. But while most of these early capitalists accepted competition when it allowed them to enter an industry, most worked diligently to contain or eliminate it once they were established. The reason for this is that competition, especially when it is intense, is prone to overproduction, declining profits, price wars, and bankruptcies. This problem becomes more serious as corporations get bigger and there is more to lose.

Historical experience suggests two broad solutions for this "problem of competition." The first is to beat the competition by cutting costs, especially labor costs—a topic of a later section. The second solution is to limit the competition by what are sometimes called *governance structures*, like cartels and both horizontal and vertical integration. These constitute an important part of the overall efforts of owners to control, or rationalize their economic environments, and thus reduce risk.[12] In short, instead of assuming that less efficient firms lost out and got swallowed up by the more efficient, the example of Standard Oil supports the conclusion that those with greater power were in a position to ruthlessly destroy the competition, whether the latter were inefficient or not. And, of course, as corporations like Standard Oil got bigger, the power to contain competition grew as well.

—

Though the causes of large corporations are still debated—a debate that will not be entered into here—what is beyond dispute is that, regardless of their origins, corporations quickly became a contested institution. On the one hand, they inspired awe, as large enterprises tended to house the large machines that served as testimony to America's technological greatness. Beginning in the 1870s, however, large corporations became targets for many who questioned the legitimacy of large-scale enterprises. Out of these challenges emerged a broad array of reform proposals.

Ideological and Political Challenges: Antimonopolists, Socialists, etc.

"At the heart of the Industrial Revolution of the eighteenth century there was an almost miraculous improvement in the tools of production, which was accompanied by a catastrophic dislocation of the lives of the common people."[13] While Karl Polanyi was describing the "great transformation" that took place in English cities, he could as easily have been describing US cities in post-Civil War America. But what he ascribed generally to the Industrial Revolution was really the byproduct of three concurrent revolutions: industrialization, capitalism, and urbanization. The impact of these revolutionary waves was to topple traditional social arrangements. The congeries of social problems left in their combined wake included mounting unemployment, poverty, hunger, homelessness, disease, and crime.

Every decade or so these problems reached crisis proportions during the troughs of business cycles, which were nowhere close to being tamed during the more laissez faire capitalism of the nineteenth century. During these periods, survival became a daily struggle, and emergent social arrangements seemed anything but viable. Arguably, the worst depression in the nation's history began in 1873 and lasted for sixty-five months—still a record. For the nation as a whole, eighteen thousand mostly small businesses went under in just the first two years. Estimates of the level of unemployment reached at its nadir range from one-quarter to one-third of the workforce. By 1877, 40 percent of Americans worked for only six or seven months out of the year, and as few as 20 percent worked regularly.[14]

As society was being turned upside down, and as many Americans experienced uncertainty and insecurity, the country witnessed an eruption of intense protests that challenged its evolving economic system, featuring farmer organizations, labor unions, third parties, and a variety of other associations and movements. Since large corporations were beginning to become more prominent, and as they came to symbolize this new system and the problems it generated, they were frequently the targets of protesters who advocated a wide variety of reforms.

Many of these challengers drew upon an indigenous tradition of antimonopolism in forging their attack upon corporations. The roots of this tradition can be found in the generation before the Civil War, when America's congenital fear of concentrated power targeted two institutions. One was the Second Bank of the United States, which, in fact, was a privately held bank that functioned as the depository of the federal government's revenue. The other was the granting of special charters by states, which was the predominant means of incorporation in most states. The indictment of these institutions featured two main charges. First, the investors and stockholders of both institutions were seen as recipients of special privileges, which violated the American values of fairness and equal opportunity. Second, both institutions were seen as inherently corrupt; for example, it was not unusual for special charters to be granted in exchange for political support and contributions.

After the war, it was the large corporation that became the target of antimonopoly sentiments, and antimonopolism emerged as the ideological font for many of the attacks upon corporations. Farmers, small merchants, and skilled craftsmen all viewed the emerging large corporations as recipients of unfair advantage, such as the rebates they received from the railroads. The power that they wielded politically to influence legislation through lobbyists, contributions, and bribes created the impression that they were inherently corrupt as well. But large corporations were also viewed as a direct threat to the republican ideal of an independent citizenry. After all, farmers, merchants, and craftsmen were united by a "producerist" ethos, in which they were directly responsible for the products that they produced and sold. As a result, each group felt that the concentrated power of these large establishments threatened their highly valued independence— this became an important new charge, added to the antimonopoly indictment.[15] It is important to note that during this period, "monopoly" was typically not used narrowly to refer to a single corporation in control of an entire industry. Instead, it was synonymous with the corporation itself.

In the vanguard of protests were farmers organized as the Grange. Originally founded as a social and educational organization, Grangers soon focused their energies upon challenging the growing practice of railroad rebates. Complaining that these were the products of corrupt, backroom deals that unfairly privileged large corporations like Standard Oil, farmers advocated for the regulation of railroads.[16] Early on this translated into calls for regulatory commissions at the state level that would regulate rail rates, in order to ensure that all could fairly compete.

Agrarian discontent soon broadened, as farmers began to feel the full impact of market forces and worried about declining political fortunes in the face of urbanization. The chief source of this discontent was the persistently low prices for farm commodities in the years following the Civil War. While some of this was due to supply outstripping demand, farmers came to blame large banks and the gold standard for high interest rates that made farm credit hard to obtain. Farmers thus became a key constituency of political parties that advocated increasing the money supply. This was viewed as not only breaking the hold of financial monopolies, but the key to lowering interest rates, which would give farmers access to the capital they would need to compete—the ensuing inflation would also raise farm prices and lower debt. Prominent among these "financial antimonopoly" parties was the Greenback Party, which elected 14 Representatives to Congress in 1878.[17]

Small businessmen and merchants were also frightened by the implications of consolidation, which by the early 1880s had become more visible. Since they viewed their success as rooted in local markets and the result of vigorous, but fair, competition, they were naturally alarmed when they read about the ruthless tactics used by Standard Oil to destroy the competition. Especially influential was an 1881 *Atlantic Monthly* article by Henry Demarest Lloyd that helped to make Standard Oil a lightening rod for criticism of big business.[18] Not long afterwards, New York merchants took the lead in forming the National Anti-Monopoly League. Though dissolved in 1883, it became the New York state chapter of the National Anti-Monopoly Organization that pushed for antitrust legislation that would abolish trusts and restore competition.[19]

The challenge to big business from workers at the workplace itself will be the focus of a later section. Here it can be noted that many of the skilled craftsmen, artisans, and mechanics—the main constituency of early unions—acted politically upon worries that the wage dependence associated with large corporations represented a distinct threat to their autonomy.[20] As a result, these workers sometimes offered at least tacit support to the political efforts of farmers and merchants to control corporations. At other times, worker worries translated into active support for the antimonopoly efforts of unions themselves. One of the most important of these unions was the Knights of Labor (KOL), whose 1878 political platform called for the elimination of the wage system in order to remove the danger of wage dependence. The employment system of large corporations would then be replaced by a new system of cooperatives that would restore worker autonomy.[21]

Farmers, merchants, and workers thus had their own favored solutions to the problem of corporations (regulatory commissions, antitrust, and worker cooperatives, respectively). However, each drew from the same antimonopoly well. Ultimately, then, antimonopolism represented a cross-class ideology, the main strain of which sought to abolish large corporations through economic regulations. Significantly, however, while this coalition of interests rejected the corporation as a legitimate economic entity, it did not reject America's growing market economy. Indeed, each constituent group embraced competition, the defining feature of capitalist economies. Of course, at this point in time, it was the moral meaning of competition (competition as a guarantor of fairness and independence) that resonated more than its economic meaning (competition as a guarantor of economic efficiency).

While most antimonopolists focused their efforts on eliminating corporations, other challengers sought to reform them through social regulations in the hopes of mandating greater social responsibility on the part of corporation owners. Almost all of these efforts were focused at the state level, and hundreds of legislative proposals were offered in the last quarter of the nineteenth century. These included efforts to limit child labor, forbid the hiring of women for dangerous occupations, require payment of wages in lawful money (as opposed to script), stipulate the time of payment, and require safety and sanitation inspections. The most popular reform proposals, however, were those that attempted to limit the hours of work. Of particular importance was the campaign to mandate an eight-hour day, with hundreds of eight-hour leagues forming in the years immediately following the end of the Civil War.[22]

The rationales offered in support of these reforms were varied. Many reformers drew from the same ideological planks of antimonopolism, viewing corporations as privileged, corrupt, and threatening to American values. This group constituted what came to be the reformist strain of antimonopolism. Others, however, simply invoked the need to protect women and children. In some cases, the underlying rationale was more novel. For example, the most influential advocate of the eight-hour day was Ira Steward, a Boston trade unionist. Steward argued that with greater leisure time, workers would develop new desires. Since workers would demand the same pay for their reduced hours, increased consumer demand stemming from these new desires would lead to an expansion of production and a corresponding reduction in costs—in essence, a regeneration of capitalist society.[23]

Other opponents of corporations felt that the only way to reform corporations socially was to redirect them economically. This could be accomplished with public ownership of corporations, which by the late 1880s gained traction as a solution to the problem of big business. Some of this was due to the popularity of newspaperman Edward Bellamy's novel *Looking Backward, 2000–1887*, published in 1888. The book depicts a utopian America in the year 2000, in which the problems of 1887, most connected to the rise of large corporations, have vanished. Paradoxically, the key to this transformation was big business itself. Bellamy was in many ways in the vanguard of those who, while alarmed by large corporations, saw them as economically inevitable. The trick was to somehow socialize the benefits of these giants. In Bellamy's utopia, this involved collective ownership, as he proposed the nationalization of industry where the state would be the sole monopoly and employer. The popularity of Bellamy's scheme was reflected in the 150 Nationalist clubs that were organized in twenty-seven states by 1890 and by the one million copies of the book sold by the early 1890s. Advocacy of this reform was also reflected in the formation of the National League for Promoting the Public Ownership of Monopolies, a group of prominent social reformers who pushed for the public ownership of "natural monopolies," like public utilities and transportation.[24]

The public ownership of corporations in all industries was also promoted by the man who became the public face of the antitrust movement in the late nineteenth century, Henry Demarest Lloyd. In 1894, building upon his earlier *Atlantic Monthly* article, Lloyd published the hugely successful *Wealth Against Commonwealth*, a treatise on the evils of the Standard Oil monopoly. Lloyd helped to articulate an emergent line of attack against large corporations that portrayed them as threats to the foundation of democratic accountability, as they represented entities that exercised "control without consent" and "rule without representation." Public ownership would thus extend the principle of democracy to the marketplace. The argument that large corporations represented an inherent violation of democratic principles was thus added to the antimonopoly indictment.[25]

The challenge to corporations found support in academia as well. The most prominent was a group of young economists who challenged the reigning paradigm of classical theory. These economists rejected the premise of laissez faire and argued instead that because large corporations had changed the fundamentals of capitalism, economic theory needed to change to match this new reality. They tended to accept large corporations and monopolies as inevitable products of capitalist development, but argued that the problem was that they served purely private ends. The logical solution to some within this new school was the creation of public monopolies, especially in industries like railroads that represented a natural monopoly. To organize their challenge to laissez faire and push their own ideas forward, they formed the American Economic Association in 1885.[26]

Though particularly influential, antimonopolism did not inspire all challenges to corporations. Socialism in America effectively began with the founding of domestic sections of the Marxian International Working Men's Association in 1867. Of course, socialism rejected not just the large corporation, but capitalism itself. From the beginning, a fault line existed between those who believed that trade union organization must precede political organization, and others who believed that victory in the political arena, based upon political organization, would form the basis of economic organization. Appeals for unity produced a merger of these factions in 1876, and the Workingmen's Party of the United States (WPUS) was formally established. Their platform, among other planks, called for the abolition of all monopolies, to be replaced by cooperative associations. Unity, however, did not prevail, as the political faction gained control of the party by the end of the following year. Changing the name to the Socialist Labor Party, the party was able to score some municipal and state electoral victories in the election of 1878.[27]

———

Ultimately, challengers' proposals fell into two camps, rejectionists and reformers. Rejectionists felt that the large corporation was irredeemable; any public purpose they might serve was trumped by the great harm that they did. As shown, the rallying cry of most antimonopolists was the elimination of large corporations. This would be accomplished through economic regulations aimed at controlling the size of corporations and limiting their market power. These included antitrust regulations and rules that proscribe anticompetitive practices (e.g., price-fixing, cartels) that could be enforced through regulatory commissions.

The camp of reformers accepted large corporations, but offered proposals that would mandate that they adhere to socially responsible practices. This would be accomplished through either social or economic regulations. The former included rules governing particular workplace practices, such as those that regulate hours and those that attempt to protect the health and safety of employees. The public ownership of corporations would qualify as an economic regulation that would ensure that the government had some influence over the economic decisions that corporations make.

In the last quarter of the nineteenth century, America found itself at a critical juncture. How would the large corporation be dealt with? Would rejectionists or reformers win out, and if the latter, which of the many and varied proposals would comprise the tethers of public purpose?

Social and Economic Regulations: The Paths Not Taken

Not all proposals are created equal. Societies do not simply choose among the logical possibilities. Instead, the odds of adoption are greatly affected by the preexisting constellation of political institutions that represent both opportunities and constraints, and which operate to either facilitate or obstruct challengers and their proposals. What follows, then, is a discussion first of the proposals that failed, since the political architecture that contributed to their defeat would continue to affect the fate of reform efforts throughout the twentieth century.

nationalization: In 1871, just as the large corporation began its rise to economic prominence, the federal government consisted of only 51,020 civilian employees for a nation of roughly forty-one million Americans. Of these federal workers, close to 37,000 were postal workers, leaving just 14,000 for all of the other functions of government. In short, America exhibited weak "administrative capacity," i.e., governmental departments and bureaucratic offices. As a result, America simply did not have the administrative experience or wherewithal to realistically explore the option of nationalization.[28]

This was in contrast to European countries where, because of their monarchical and feudal roots, a strong bureaucratic state preceded the rise of the large bureaucratic corporation. Very early on, France, Prussia, and Belgium successfully pursued the option of nationalizing their railroads. Instead of feudalism, America had experienced colonialism, and then a revolution where it forced England's colonial administration to leave. In the position to construct a new government upon a virgin base, the mostly land-owning drafters of the Constitution were driven by both antimonarchical sentiments and a fear of majority rule. As a result, they crafted a document meant to constrain centralized power, and in so doing hardwired government to be comparatively weak.

The most important guiding principle in this endeavor was the effort to diffuse power, which was accomplished in the architecture of abundant checks and balances. First, three, co-equal branches of government were established: executive, legislative, and judicial. Next, because the founders feared legislative power the most, they constricted it further by creating a bicameral legislature and giving the other two branches a legislative role: the presidential veto of legislation, and the doctrine of judicial review of legislation, which the Founders regarded as implied in the Constitution. They also adopted a federalist structure, so that most power would remain at the state level.

In this context, it is worth observing that the frequently cited anti-statism of America's political culture is more than a set of deep-seated sentiments; it is also a set of institutional rules. The cultural and the structural dimensions of antistatism are both real, and in many ways mutually reinforcing. However, it is also fair to say that given the redundancy of America's structure of checks and balances, very little is required in the form of antistate attitudes to activate a structure that is designed to slow down, if not obstruct, government action. The business community became expert in invoking an antistate ideology in their usually successful efforts to manipulate the obstructionist levers of government to prevent reformist action.

social regulations and welfare at the federal level: Still, even with the system of checks and balances, one might have expected the development of greater administrative capacity that could have supported some regulations at the federal level by the time of the rise of big business in the 1870s and 1880s. After all, it had been over a hundred years since the nation was founded. Beyond a predisposition for slow growth, the inability to develop greater administrative capacity can also be attributed to the role played by political parties in filling the organizational void during the early years of the republic.

Though the Constitution makes no mention of political parties, and though many Founders worried about the baneful effects of "factions," it was party organizations that began to provide operational coherence to government. The coherence that parties provided, however, was not based upon a consistent set of policies or an ideology. Instead of being programmatic, American parties of the nineteenth century were strictly patronage affairs. The seeds for this party variety were sown during the presidency of Andrew Jackson (1828–1836). His remedy for overcoming the "regime of notables" that he detested was to open up the political process to outsiders, like small farmers and master mechanics, and to limit the powers of government through practices such as the rotation of office and limited terms of appointment.[29] The resulting partisan control of the "spoils of office" ensured the loyalty of those who were appointed. Over time, these practices coalesced in the form of political machines that distributed thousands of offices. These, in turn, could be offered as rewards to precinct workers to mobilize voters and turn them out on election day.

Ultimately, the spoils system placed inherent limits upon the ability of government to build administrative capacity. Instead of cultivating a professional corps of administrators that could develop its own administrative expertise and interests, and which would have the protection of bureaucratic insulation, the combination of high turnover and a selection criterion of loyalty made politics and administration amateur enterprises. Of course, the expensive nature of patronage also accentuated the role that money played in politics. As business contributions fed political machines, both the elected officials and nonelected operatives of these machines were constrained to do the bidding of business, thus contributing to America's lopsided political economy.

The resulting mistrust of government also had a negative impact on efforts to build a welfare state, in which the government would assume greater social responsibilities, and thus relieve corporations of the same. Of course, as Theda Skocpol points out in *Protecting Soldiers and Mothers*, the federal government at the end of the nineteenth century did spend roughly one-quarter of its budget on pensions to Civil War veterans and their dependents.[30] So it is more accurate to say that efforts to expand welfare spending beyond this base were largely unsuccessful. Owners were unified in their opposition to welfare state programs. In the case of welfare spending, owners worried about any program that might give potential wage earners an alternative to the labor market. In addition, owners worried about any growth in government, not only because bigger government might be better able to impose mandates, but also because bigger government implied higher fees or taxes.[31]

social regulations at the state level: Federal efforts to mandate socially responsible workplace practices during the Gilded Age were mostly nonexistent. However, pushed by labor organizations and other reform advocates, state legislatures were quite active and passed dozens of laws that attempted, among other things, to regulate hours, working conditions, and wages. Owners, ever vigilant in protecting their prerogatives, were mostly united in their opposition to state mandates. While they were not always successful in preventing such laws from being passed, they were usually able to rely upon a second order of obstruction: courts frequently overturned state mandates on the basis that they represented an unconstitutional infringement upon the freedom of contract. In his study of the law and the American labor movement, William Forbath documented over sixty cases in which business-friendly state courts ruled such mandates null and void in the 1880s and '90s.[32]

To understand the impact of the court system upon government's ability to regulate corporations, one can look first at the types of lawyers that came to dominate it. In *The Market Revolution*, Charles Sellers views lawyers as having served as the early "shock troops of capitalism." Most lawyers in the early decades of the nineteenth century came from prosperous, market-oriented families and were naturally inculcated with a commercial perspective.[33] As businessmen involved in trade, land, and manufacturing became the main clients of law practices, these business-savvy lawyers developed doctrines to protect the rights of property, and then persuaded judges of the soundness of these principles.[34]

Judges, in turn, created a body of judge-made law that helped lay the groundwork for business expansion. For example, it was judicial decisions that were critical in establishing one of the primary advantages of the corporate form, "limited liability," in which a shareholder's liability for a corporation's debt is limited to the amount of that shareholder's investment in the corporation.[35] Of even greater consequence in helping to establish the corporate form was a series of Supreme Court decisions. Arguably the most important of these was the Santa Clara decision of 1886. In this case the Court held that corporate properties were subject to the "equal protection" provisions of the Fourteenth Amendment, an interpretive stretch since this amendment had been written to protect ex-slaves. In essence, the Court accepted the proposition that the term "person" in the amendment included corporations, thus extending to corporations the rights and privileges of personhood including, eventually, those of free speech. The results were ultimately far-reaching. While it is one thing to regulate an artificial creation of the state itself, it is something else entirely when the state attempts to regulate rights-bearing "persons."[36]

socialism and worker cooperatives: As noted above, the national political parties of the nineteenth century did not compete on the basis of coherent programs or philosophy, but instead represented coalitions of officials that competed for the right to distribute national spoils. This non-programmatic feature of early political parties contributed to a parochialism in politics that made it difficult to fashion policies that addressed the public interest. Parties were ill equipped, then, to develop a coherent program to deal with the emergence of large corporations, such as a program promoting socialism or worker cooperatives would entail.

There were two additional factors that militated against the advocacy of programs that challenged not only large corporations, but also the fundamentals of capitalism. First, mass suffrage was achieved early in the United States, when the nation was still largely preindustrial. American parties came of age before a class divide had developed, and therefore did not develop along class lines. This facilitated cross-class coalitions, as when skilled American craftsmen, small merchants, and farmers, who shared a producerist bond, together supported antimonopolist politicians. In Europe, by contrast, the expansion of the franchise was part of the broader political programs articulated by the working-class parties that formed after industrialization had taken root. This was conducive to the development of socialism, with its vision of an alternative economic system, which served to justify proposals that focused on abolishing or reforming capitalism itself, not just large corporations.

Second, by the time corporations were sinking roots, America had institutionalized a two-party system. The Apportionment Act of 1842 required that members of the House be selected from single-member districts. The single-member district, winner-take-all electoral rule that resulted provided the foundation for an enduring two-party system that favored parties that made centrist appeals, given the need to build broad-based coalitions that would yield a majority of votes. This limited the viability of third parties, such as those promulgating a working-class agenda, that could serve as the carriers of ideas and programs that represented strong challenges to either large corporations or capitalism.

By the 1870s, the large corporation was poised to take off. Government, however, was poorly positioned to grow in a corresponding fashion to mandate social responsibility. While reforms such as nationalization were not viable as a result of weak administrative capacity, reforms such as socialism lacked effective carriers due to a two-party system. Patronage politics eroded the public's trust in government, which was needed for regulatory expansion, while the court system operated to nullify the regulations that did arise. Therefore, though large corporations were generating tremendous opposition as they began to make their presence felt, the choice of regulatory pathways was severely constricted by a political economy that was already lopsided in the favor of business. What, then, was successful?

Economic Regulations: The Paths Taken

The first efforts to regulate big business involved state efforts that targeted the railroads, America's first big business. The main issue of contention, not surprisingly, was the practice of rebates. As indicated earlier, the main advocates of railroad reform were farmers and small businesses. With the rise of large corporations came the first appearance of a persistent cleavage within the business community between the interests of small and large establishments. But it was also consequential that the first successful champions of government regulations were by nature pro-business, and therefore not supportive of the more radical measures being advanced by others. The antimonopolism that they advocated favored a restoration of competition and fairness in the marketplace. The tacit assumption was that it was not size per se, but the unfair practices that size afforded that constituted the main problem.

the independent regulatory commission: The demands of these farmers and small merchants, who still had considerable clout at the local and state levels, resulted in several states passing what came to be known as Granger laws that involved the establishment of regulatory commissions. In some cases, commissions were empowered to impose rules and set rates. More typically, however, these new bodies merely possessed a "sunshine" function. Here, the regulatory commission would investigate citizen complaints and shine the public's light on railroad practices in the hopes that the threat of bad publicity would yield fairer rates.[37]

As these commissions usually had no direct enforcement powers of their own, this regulatory approach on the part of states was not up to the task of regulation. Railroads and the chief beneficiary of rebates,

Standard Oil, assaulted the Granger laws. First, they supported sympathetic candidates to public office through campaign contributions and, in some cases, outright bribery in order to overturn or weaken the laws; Rockefeller spent so freely on bribes to politicians in Ohio that the state legislature was known as the "Coal-Oil Legislature."[38] They also challenged the laws in both state and federal court, arguing, among other points, that state authorities violated their Fourteenth Amendment rights of due process by depriving them of property (that is, profits) in regulating rates. Ultimately, the Supreme Court killed these early efforts by deciding in the Wabash case of 1886 that only Congress had the authority to regulate interstate commerce. Even without this decision, however, it was clear that, since they increasingly crossed state lines, railroads constituted a national issue.

Logically, then, it was the railroads that saw the federal government's first attempt to regulate large corporations. In fact, Washington had been the site of efforts to regulate railroads for years. In the years leading up to 1887, a total of 150 bills had been introduced in Congress that proposed various means of federal control. An 1876 bill surmounted a number of hurdles and actually passed the House. At the time, however, Senators were still elected by state legislatures, and because it was not unusual for the road to the upper chamber to be paved with graft and influence peddling by the business community, the bill died in the Senate.[39]

However, the issue of rebates would not go away, and momentum for passing some sort of bill continued to build during the 1880s. The broad coalition of groups seeking reform once again featured farmers, small businesses, and merchants. The antimonopolists among them favored a restoration of competition. Others, however, sought intervention in the form of rate regulation to allow all to compete on equal footing. Some railroads executives themselves sought federal regulation, but they argued for the legalization of pooling.

The Interstate Commerce Act (ICA) of 1887 represented a set of compromises among the contending advocates of reform, but the result was a bill with contradictory provisions. On the one hand, the act attempted to protect competition by prohibiting the controversial practice of rebates, and it declared pooling illegal. One the other hand, the act included a mechanism for regulating rates. But instead of relying upon Congress or a department of the Executive Branch, the idea that took hold was to take regulation out of politics. With civil service reform now in the air, Congress adopted the states' model of the single industry, independent regulatory commission, and established the

Interstate Commerce Commission (ICC). To be run by experts in the field, and presumably free of political influence and corruption, this new agency was charged with the distinctly nonmarket goal of ensuring that railroad rates were "just and reasonable."[40]

To carry out this ambitious mandate would require an agency with unambiguous authority to ensure compliance with expert staff that could collect the necessary data, conduct the necessary investigations, and devise and implement policy regarding what constituted "just and reasonable." Instead, the ICC consisted of five commissioners appointed by the president for staggered six-year terms; to ensure impartiality, no more than three commissioners could come from one political party. By its limited size alone, the ICC was no match for the railroads. Then, before it could establish its footing, the Commission's authority to require testimony and records was quickly challenged by the railroads in the courts. Many of these were successful, as a series of court decisions effectively emasculated the Commission during its first decade of operation. Furthermore, with the government's limited administrative capacity, there was no mechanism for ensuring an independent source of expertise, as there was no infrastructure for public administration that could produce a professional corps. Setting a precedent for regulatory commissions, and government bureaus generally, the ICC drew its experts from the private sector instead. As a result, railroad executives soon dominated the commission, and essentially used it to enforce private agreements—the beginnings of what came to be known as "industry capture."[41]

antitrust: The passage of the ICA did not quell protests against big business. Instead, the focus shifted to the question of trusts. During the election of 1888, the platforms of both political parties condemned the economic concentration that they produced. Not surprisingly, Rockefeller and Standard Oil were the targets of increasing scrutiny. Not only did a New York state senate committee investigate the company, but the House Committee on Manufactures of Congress also issued a damning report on trusts, dedicating 1,000 of its 1,500 pages to the activities of the oil trust. A similar coalition of farmers and small businessmen that had lobbied against rebates also lobbied for legislation that would destroy the trusts. But antitrust resonated across class lines, since it was seen as a means of protecting the republican ideal of the independent small farmer, merchant, and craftsman through the restoration of competition. Of course, it did not hurt that this antimonopolist proposal was also consistent with the dominant ideology of laissez faire.[42]

Given his heightened notoriety, Rockefeller's public opposition to antitrust legislation only hastened passage of the Sherman Antitrust Act in 1890.[43] The bill deemed as illegal "every contract, combination in the form of trust or otherwise, or conspiracy in restraint of trade or commerce among the several States, or with foreign nations." Thus, instead of directly confronting the new economic reality of outsized enterprises, the bill attempted to build upon the common law tradition that focused upon the nature of the agreement in question, such as a trust agreement. In order to restore or maintain competition within an industry, it empowered US district attorneys and the attorney general to bring action against violators, and it also allowed private parties to seek legal judgments for treble damages.

It was the enforcement mechanism that revealed the first weakness with the bill. Not only did it not create a new government department, it did not even set up a separate regulatory commission. Effective enforcement required the vigilance of the Justice Department. Unfortunately, the attorneys general during the decade of the 1890s showed very little inclination to aggressively prosecute offenders— from 1890 to 1904, an average of fewer than 1.5 cases were initiated per year.[44] One of them, Richard Olney, wrote privately that he had "taken the responsibility of not prosecuting under a law I believed to be no good."[45] Of course, Olney's views were likely shaped by his previous experience as a railroad attorney and lobbyist—yet another sign that the door between the business sector and government service was becoming a revolving one.[46] Also limiting the Act's effectiveness was the tendency for prosecutors to target loose cartels of small companies, since their price-fixing practices were usually easier to demonstrate.[47]

When the Supreme Court first weighed in on the law, it rendered the Act ineffective with its 1895 decision in United States v. E. C. Knight, a case involving the acquisition of four refineries by the American Sugar Refining Company. In rejecting the Justice Department's claim that the merger violated the Sherman Act, the court made a dubious distinction between commerce and manufacturing. It then narrowly interpreted the commerce clause of the Constitution to mean that Congress could regulate interstate commerce, not manufacturing, which, since it is a local activity, could only be regulated by the individual states. Over the next several years the Court also struggled with the meaning of terms like "restrain of trade" and "monopolization."[48]

———

By 1890, the nation had established two main pathways for controlling large corporations that involved the economic regulations. The first of these involved the use of an independent regulatory commission to regulate a single industry, railroads. Though its charge to ensure "just and reasonable" rail rates suggested a tinkering with market forces, the goal was to ensure a fair playing field for railroads and their customers. The second pathway, which applied across industries, was antitrust. This approach aimed at upholding common law prohibitions against unfair trade practices, including the new forms that these practices took, such as the trust agreement. Neither form of economic regulation directly addressed the problem of size, though both, in essence, rejected the large corporation. Instead, both attempted to protect an environment of competition. The underlying assumption was that competition, because it would naturally favor smaller establishments, would serve as a natural check against big business. Furthermore, since it was big enterprises that were responsible for the growth in troubling corporate practices, competition would indirectly protect against corporate irresponsibility, obviating social regulations.

In the first round of efforts to use government to control the large corporation, large corporations won. America's political economy took a decidedly lopsided turn. It would fall to unions to attempt to fill the void left by government in the nation's efforts to control big business. But as corporations grew more powerful, unions' ability to negotiate greater social responsibility in the form of contracts was far from guaranteed.

Negotiated Responsibility

Gompers and the Voluntarist Path for Unions

Overconstruction of railroads, together with questionable financing, contributed to the Depression of 1893, the worst in the nation's history to that point. The estimated unemployment rate reached 12 percent in 1893 and 18 percent the following year. As was true during earlier depressions, employers adopted the practice of not only laying workers off but also cutting the wages of those workers that they retained. The Pullman Palace Car Company was no exception. Wages were cut by 25 percent, and in some cases by as much as 50 percent. To understand the workers' reaction, it is important to note that the company was located in Pullman, Illinois, a company town in which the corporation owned all of the buildings and, as such, was the sole landlord. At the same time that he decided to cut wages, company president George Pullman decided to keep rents at the same rate. As he viewed his town strictly as a business proposition, he decided to continue to pay a 6 percent dividend to his stockholders as well. Predictably, the contradiction between slashed wages and stable rents did not sit well with the worker-lessees of Pullman, and it forced to the surface festering tensions concerning Pullman's suffocating paternalism.[49]

In March of 1894, workers at Pullman began to organize local branches of the American Railway Union (ARU). In May, workers presented demands, including the restoration wage rates that had been recently cut. Pullman responded by refusing to negotiate on these or any issues. As a result, on May 11 four thousand workers stopped working, bringing Pullman's operations to a halt. With no progress after six weeks, the ARU nationalized the strike by joining the Pullman workers and directing its 125,000 members to refuse to handle trains that included Pullman sleeping cars. This effectively tied up rail traffic moving in or out of Chicago, which importantly included the transportation of mail. As the strike spread across the entire nation, the great Pullman Strike of 1894 had commenced.

Pullman's refusal to negotiate was supported by the General Managers Association, a group representing the twenty-four railroads based in Chicago. Formed in 1886 in order to standardize equipment and procedures in the industry, the group was committed to stamping out unions within its membership. To entice federal intervention on their behalf, the heads of the railroads conspired to make sure that mail was loaded onto to all trains with Pullman cars, insuring that mail delivery, a federal responsibility, was fully disrupted. Not that the government needed much encouragement to act on the railroads' behalf. The attorney general of the United States was Richard Olney, the former railway attorney and member of the General Managers Association, who still had sizable investments in the railroads. At his behest, the government won an injunction on July 2 that prohibited the ARU from hindering the operation of the railroads. The union's young leader, Eugene Debs, was jailed as a result. To enforce the injunction, President Grover Cleveland ordered federal troops to Chicago. This provoked a riot, with ten thousand people attacking the rail yards and fires breaking out throughout the city. By July 19, with twelve people dead, order had been forcibly restored. On August 2 the strike was broken.

The Pullman strike capped two years of dramatic labor conflicts. In 1892 the nation witnessed one of the most dramatic conflicts in its labor history, the Homestead Strike. The battle between the Carnegie Company and the Amalgamated Association of Iron, Steel, and Tin Workers featured a shootout that killed a dozen men, and the attempted assassination of the mill's chief executive, Henry Frick. Though much of the public sided with the workers, the strike ended in defeat after the governor of Pennsylvania ordered the state militia to protect the nonunion replacement workers when the mill reopened. Three other prominent strikes also ended in defeat in the same year, including one by silver miners in Coeur d'Alene, Idaho, in which federal troops were sent in at the behest of the mine owners, one by railroad switchmen in Buffalo, and one by miners in Tennessee. Like Homestead, the latter two were quashed when state militias were deployed.[50]

The Labor Problem

The string of defeats proved to be a critical juncture for the American labor movement. But to understand the path labor relations would take, it is important to first understand the "labor problem." As reviewed above, the problem of economic competition resulted in governance structures that could contain it—and which helped produce the large corporation. Another solution to the problem of maximizing profit in an economic environment of intense competition was to be forever vigilant in holding down costs. The easiest cost to control was that of labor. While this led to technological innovation and improved productivity, it also produced the imperative of keeping wages as low as possible. As Polanyi argued in *The Great Transformation*, for this to happen, labor had to become a commodity, with wages left to the fate of the market. This meant that labor had to be stripped of any layers of social protection, whether they came in the form of a "fair" or "just" wage, custom, craft tradition, or statute.

One outcome of this transformation involved the low, and frequently unlivable, wages paid to the ample supply of individuals who could perform the growing number of both factory operative and common laborer jobs found throughout the emerging manufacturing economy. Furthermore, contrary to the more modern convention that wages should only go up, wages were frequently cut, whether they were high or low, especially when economic circumstances worsened. Swings in the business cycle also resulted in tremendous job instability. One study of unemployment in Massachusetts shows that in a typical year, close to one-third of the workforce experienced a substantial period of unemployment.[51]

Beyond pay and job instability, the treatment of labor as a commodity was dramatically reflected in the growing expanse of the workday. It was not uncommon for workers to labor for twelve or more hours a day, six days a week. An additional corollary of such callous treatment was the unsafe working conditions that workers were forced to endure. Between 1880 and 1890, an average of 35,000 workers were killed each year, while an additional 536,000 were injured.[52]

Together, these harsh conditions of work comprised the default, low road to greater productivity and profits. In the United States, this commodification of labor was facilitated by the increasing size of corporations: the larger the business, the greater impersonality of the employment relationship, along with the concomitant obliviousness to workers' collective plight. Not surprisingly, then, the first site of challenges to large enterprises was the workplace itself. With growing exploitation and alienation, a growing conflict of interest between owners and workers took shape. While owners increasingly sought to maximize profits through low wages and deskilled jobs, workers increasingly sought to preserve or create a living wage and autonomous work. This conflict might manifest itself in worker resentment and withdrawal of effort, or it might also manifest itself in collective organization and action.

This was certainly the case with the issue of wage cuts, which not only triggered the Pullman Strike but also frequently served as a source of contention. For example, in 1877, wage cuts, once again involving railroad workers, produced a series of strikes in several states. Like Pullman, these too were only quashed after state militias and federal troops intervened on behalf of owners. Unemployment was also at the heart of many protests and riots during this period, such as the Tompkins Square riot of 1874. The same can be said of long working hours, an issue that engendered its fair share of strikes and demonstrations, including those in support of the campaign for an eight-hour day—the most infamous of which was the Haymarket Square riot in Chicago in 1886.[53]

For many workers, especially those who were skilled, the main point of contention was the control of work itself. In the first decades of industrialization, skilled workers were able to retain significant control over the work process, which entailed continued adherence to the traditional ethical codes that governed much craftwork. These typically included a "stint," which was a trade's collective definition of what constituted a reasonable day's work.[54] In fact, in early factories, it was the skilled workers who served as the independent contractors, hiring their own crews.

More and more, however, owners and skilled workers struggled over work rules involving such issues as the pace of work, the introduction of new machinery, and more generally, whose rules—owners or workers—mattered. As owners concluded that the system of inside contracting was incompatible with their efforts to maximize profits, foremen replaced skilled workers as front-line supervisors. Under tremendous pressure to increase output, foremen, in turn, came to rely upon what was later labeled the "drive system." Simply put, this meant the use of coercion (yelling at, threatening, or even hitting workers) to get workers to work harder and faster. As a result, "control strikes," where workers resisted employer-imposed work rules and drive methods, were increasingly common.

Political vs. Business Unionism

At the opening of the 1890s, labor strategy and organization was an unsettled affair. During the previous generation, labor strategy had moved back and forth between political unionism, in which political reform was viewed as the best route for protecting workers' interests, and business unionism, where amelioration was sought through collective bargaining (and strikes) that resulted in individual contracts with employers. In practice, most unions drew upon both legislative and contractual orientations in their quest to promote greater social responsibility through a decommodification of labor.

In the 1880s, the Knights of Labor (KOL) was the country's dominant union, and political reform was its main focus. Founded in 1878, the Knights sought to create "one big union" of both skilled and unskilled workers committed to restoring the republican ideal of autonomous work by creating a system of cooperatives to replace the wage system. In line with the precepts of political unionism, the platform adopted at their founding convention endorsed a range of legislative reforms to safeguard the interests of workers, including health and safety initiatives and a prohibition of child labor. However, its greatest success occurred when it won a strike against Jay Gould's railroad lines in 1885.[55]

The following year, the American Federation of Labor (AFL) was founded, consisting of twelve national unions and about 140,000 members. Led by Samuel Gompers, it favored a craft-based unionism to protect the interests of skilled workers alone. Instead of embracing the unskilled in a gesture of class solidarity, many skilled workers viewed the growing ranks of their unskilled brethren as a symbol of work in factories, and thus a threat to their livelihood and independence. The social distance between these groups was made wider by the fact that the unskilled were frequently immigrants who spoke a different language and belonged to a different faith. In contrast to the KOL and socialists, the AFL leadership did not seek an overhaul of the entire economic system, but instead stressed the narrower goal of increasing the wages of employees through a system of collective bargaining and the use of the strike weapon, i.e., business unionism.

The defeats of the early 1890s divided labor into distinct camps. For one segment of the labor movement, the lesson of these defeats was that only political action would bring about real change. Remnants of the KOL, by now diminished as a result of a series of defeats that followed the Gould victory, openly supported the recently formed Populist Party.[56] These events also helped to radicalize Debs and pushed him firmly into the political camp, and in the long term led him to form the Socialist Party of America in 1901.

But if the events of the early 1890s radicalized one segment of the labor movement, they had the opposite effect upon the leadership of the AFL. Instead of political action, the defeats only reinforced the conviction of Samuel Gompers that unions needed to rely exclusively upon "pure and simple unionism." For generations of labor historians, Gompers has been credited as the man that placed an indelible stamp of conservatism on the US labor movement, because of his acceptance of capitalism and focus upon "wage consciousness." But as more recent analysts have argued, his conservatism did not reflect an inherent preference, but instead represented a pragmatic adjustment to the events of this period.[57]

A Marxist in his youth, Gompers shared with labor republicans a vision of alternative economic arrangements. He also did not shy away from political action. But several factors led him to abandon these initial stances. One concerned the fate of third parties. Whether it was the short-lived National Labor and Reform Party or the quadrennial failures of the Socialist Labor Party, Gompers came to realize that third parties formed around workers' interests were simply not viable as vehicles for redressing workers' problems.

His faith in the political process was also seriously eroded by the increasing tendency on the part of a very conservative judiciary to nullify state labor and welfare legislation as a consequence of judicial review. The turning point was the 1884 Jacobs decision of the New York

Court of Appeals, which invalidated a state law that prohibited the making of cigars in tenement dwellings. As noted above, by the end of the century, dozens of similar workplace regulations were nullified by courts citing principles like the "liberty of contract" and "property rights."[58]

Over time Gompers increasingly sought to give his pragmatism a philosophical foundation. Using the "rights" language of the courts, he argued that unions were needed to "maintain the rights and liberties of the people" and to protect wage earners "as equals before the law."[59] He also borrowed a page from the ideology of antistatism, and opposed state intervention on the grounds that unions and owners should be allowed to bargain and freely contract for these kinds of improvements previously, but unsuccessfully, sought through legislation. The antistatism of business was now joined by the antistatism of labor, and the philosophy of "voluntarism" was born.

By the end of the century, then, labor was in two distinct camps. But the momentum was with the camp of business unionists. On the one hand, political unionists' major foray into politics ended in defeat in the 1896 election, further weakening those advocating a greater reliance upon mandated responsibility. On the other hand, the AFL had not only weathered the Depression of 1893, but membership in its affiliated unions doubled between 1897 and 1900 to 548,321. Furthermore, the AFL total represented nearly two-thirds of all union members in the nation. Though data for contracts during this period are scarce, it is likely that, at least in terms of pay, the skilled workers of the AFL did better than their nonunion counterparts. The problem was that unions covered only 6 percent of the civilian, nonagricultural labor force.[60]

—

In sum, at the turn of the new century, big business had not only successfully defeated political unionism through strong, and sometimes violent resistance, they had also severely limited the ability of unions to organize workers and negotiate socially responsible practices on their behalf. Weak unions now joined weak regulations as characteristic features of America's emergent regulatory structure for controlling corporations. But the forces pushing for greater social regulations and stronger unions were not defeated. Instead, they represented ongoing threats to prerogatives that worried many owners. As a result, a few owners were pushed to explore the high road of corporate social responsibility.

Voluntary Responsibility (CSR)

By the end of the 1890s, Proctor & Gamble was offering its employees a full array of benefits: free medical care for those living within three miles of the factory, non-contributory accident insurance that would replace regular wages until a worker had recovered from a workplace injury, a pension plan in which both the company and employees contributed half, a home buyers association to help employees purchase homes, and a profit-sharing plan. The company was also heavily involved in supporting the public institutions of Ivorydale, Ohio.[61] But Proctor and Gamble's road to corporate social responsibility ran through the problem of labor unrest. In the late 1880s the company was experiencing labor difficulties, having experienced fourteen strikes in 1887 alone.[62] As a result of this experience, "the young son of the president persuaded his governing relatives to make Saturday a half-holiday, and to try to seek a new bond with their workmen in a profit-sharing plan."[63]

During this same period of time, National Cash Register (NCR) distributed suggestion boxes to get feedback from workers and awarded prizes for the most efficient departments, beautified its factory grounds, built housing for its employees, gave them a clubroom for the diverse array of clubs that it organized for its employees, supported a Relief Association for its sick and injured, and sponsored a tremendous array of community institutions and associations to benefit its workers. These included a kindergarten, a library, an industrial school for girls, a company orchestra, and a Sunday school.[64] It was also heavily involved in the surrounding community of Dayton, Ohio. In one of its most extensive undertakings, it transformed the rundown community of Slidertown into the model suburb of South Park. There, unpaved roads and tenements were replaced with paved streets and detached houses with yards.[65] Of course, like Proctor and Gamble, NCR joined the vanguard of corporations adopting socially responsible practices only after several strikes, lockouts, and efforts by disgruntled employees to set the factory ablaze took place during the early 1890s.[66]

At the end of the nineteenth century, several studies were published showcasing the efforts of a vanguard of large employers, such as Proctor & Gamble and NCR, who were experimenting with both voluntary programs to improve the work experience of their employees and philanthropic endeavors to improve the communities in which they were located. These included William Tolman's *Industrial Betterment*, Nicholas Paine Gilman's *A Dividend to Labor*, and Edwin L. Shuey's

Factory People and Their Employees.[67] The federal government also showed interest in the trend with the Department of Labor's report, "The Betterment of Industrial Conditions."[68] This growing interest reflected the hopes of many that such voluntary programs held the promise of solving both workplace and community problems.

At the time, the voluntary practices of CSR were known variously as industrial betterment, welfare work, charity, and philanthropy. Most of these activities dealt exclusively with a company's workers, while others were directed at the broader communities in which the companies resided. But it is important to note that what we now treat separately as welfare capitalism and corporate philanthropy were two facets of a broader effort.

Welfare Work

As the industrial landscape became grim with factory pollution and garbage, one of the first attempts at industrial betterment involved adorning the grounds of factories. This included decorating the main entrance to the GE plant in Schenectady with flowers and surrounding the Waltham Watch Works near Boston with well-kept lawns. This beautification project was carried inside the plant as well, and encompassed planting palms inside the Patterson Brothers Building in Dayton and creating large window openings with attractive views for workers inside the National Cash Register plant, also in Dayton.[69]

Other owners put hygiene or eating healthy meals at the center of their attempts at social responsibility. This included building a filtering plant for drinking water at the Sherman-Williams Company in Cleveland and providing bathtubs, towels, and soap within oak-finished bathing rooms for the four hundred women and girls at the Ferris Brothers plant in Newark. For sustenance, the Willimantic Thread Company provided low-cost dinners for their workers, while Sherwin-Williams served free, healthy meals in a factory restaurant.[70]

Creature comforts and recreation constituted another early example of CSR. The women workers at New York Telephone were entitled to two twenty-minute rest periods in either a well-stocked reading room or in a designated "retiring room," while companies like Gorham Manufacturing near Providence built "club-houses" for their employees. This led to broader efforts to encourage "proper" leisure activities. The National Transit Company of New Jersey provided recreation facilities for roller skating, baseball, bicycling, and track and field.[71]

Probably the oldest socially responsible practice entailed providing housing for employees. This extended back to 1825 when the Merrimac Textile Corporation of Lowell, Massachusetts, built boarding houses for its factory girls. By the end of the century, employers were more likely to construct single-family houses. For example, the Westinghouse Air Brake Company sold lots to employees at cost and assisted in construction of the first seventy-five houses by signing large contracts to reduce costs.[72]

The items that are now considered standard fare in a menu of fringe benefits also had their origins in the latter part of the nineteenth century. When accidental deaths for employees passed thirty thousand by the late 1870s, railroads became the first industry to provide benefits for sickness, accidents, and death, in the form of mutual-benefit societies. The Baltimore and Ohio Railroad established a compulsory association in 1880, where both the company and employees contributed to a fund that was used to assist disabled workers and provide death benefits to families. By 1890, there were 120 mutual-benefit associations in America.[73]

Pensions also got their start in the railroad industry. This was natural not only because railroads were America's first big business, but also because they were the first to have the experience employing a growing number of older workers. This posed a dilemma, since railroad work was both demanding and dangerous; older workers might become a drag on efficiency and at the same time pose a greater risk for themselves, others they worked with, and rail passengers themselves. But simply discarding older workers was not an option. Not only would it hurt labor relations, it would be a public-relations fiasco. So by 1908, seventy-two railroads, representing close to 70 percent of all railroad workers, had some form of pension plan.[74]

The benefit of medical care was usually provided on site and in connection with workplace injuries. The Siegel-Cooper Company employed a physician who was on call at all hours, and on site in the store two hours a day. By 1887, most of the large businesses of Pennsylvania provided medical care for their employees in one form or another.[75]

Also making its first appearance was profit sharing. On October 9, 1869, Brewster & Company, carriage makers of New York, announced: "From the beginning of our next fiscal year, we will offer to all persons in our employ . . . a certain share of our annual profits, in addition to the regular wages, which we propose shall be no less than the highest wages paid in other similar establishments."[76] By the end of the century, a number of prominent names in American business experimented with profit sharing, including Edison Electric, Proctor & Gamble, and Rand McNally & Company, though it should be noted that no program lasted very long during this phase in the evolution of CSR.[77]

The stated motives for these sundry attempts at socially responsible behavior were varied. In the case of beautification, the working assumption was that better aesthetics would produce happier workers. For the various stabs at providing fringe benefits, many believed that such selective incentives would not only allow firms to recruit better workers, but any worker receiving them would be motivated to be more productive. For profit sharing, the idea was to get workers to think like owners, so as to overcome the perceived opposition of interests.

The overarching rationale, then, was that CSR was good for business. In a communication with William H. Tolman concerning his company's welfare activities, Charles E. Adams, vice president and general manager of the Cleveland Hardware Co., wrote: "We believe that the manufacturing plant of the future will not be designed without arrangements being made for club rooms, dining rooms, bath rooms, and similar conveniences, . . . for we realize that the cooperation and good will of our employees is money in the company's pocket." Using the analogy of animal husbandry, John H. Patterson, president of NCR, wrote to Tolman, "We buy physical and mental labor. If it pays to take care of a good animal that only returns physical work, how much more important is it for the employer to take care of the employee returning both physical and mental labor." Such sentiments were more likely to be expressed by owners of large corporations in capital-intensive industries with a year-round labor force, where high labor turnover was inefficient.[78]

But there was frequently an unstated motive as well. For many owners, forays into CSR represented efforts to address a worsening labor problem. In particular, as the examples of Proctor & Gamble and NCR show, a major goal underlying CSR was to use the newly adopted workplace practices to engender feelings of loyalty and commitment, and thus prevent labor unions from organizing their workers. While some large employers would have, no doubt, adopted socially responsible programs anyway, it is clear that the threat of unions acted as a catalyst to push a larger, critical mass of employers from the low road of commodification—the default path to profitability—to explore the money-making potential of the higher road of CSR.

As a result, an important dynamic tension between union threat and CSR was introduced. Just as fear of leftist parties had pushed conservative governments in Europe to build a system of public welfare, fear of unions pushed a number of owners of large corporations to build a system of private welfare. This included not only workplace practices, but also socially responsible practices in the community.

Corporate Philanthropy

Corporate philanthropy developed along two tracks in the nineteenth century. The first involved the support that large businesses gave to local public and cultural facilities, including elementary schools, libraries, and churches. This type of giving had its origins in the institution of the company town. Many early manufacturers were located in towns created by the company itself, frequently in virgin terrain. The reasons behind a company's decision to build these new towns on remote, undeveloped land included the availability of cheap land, access to a river or lake, access to transportation, and the availability of raw materials and resources. But in order to attract workers and fill the void that existed in the absence of preexisting government, companies not only would provide for the basic needs of their employees, like housing, but also provide for the institutions of public life, like schools, libraries, and churches.[79] In short, much early philanthropy was born of necessity, since America was not a country of old towns and cities whose infrastructure could be converted to industrial use.

The second track of corporate philanthropy involved support given to voluntary associations dedicated to ameliorating social hardship, especially that found in cities in the aftermath of the Civil War. Two national private relief agencies founded during this period, the United States Sanitary Commission and the United States Christian Commission (sponsored by the YMCA), began to receive support from the business community, though they received the bulk of their donations from individuals. Particularly noteworthy among early corporate givers was the Baldwin Locomotive Company, which dedicated 10 percent of its annual earnings to the Christian Commission. Rail companies also distinguished themselves in their efforts with the YMCA to establish railroad branches of the "Y" to provide assistance for their workers. As national director of the YMCA, Cornelius Vanderbilt built a separate building in New York, which was equipped with baths and game rooms, among other comforts. Here, too, the growth of corporate philanthropy was connected to weak government capacity for dealing with social problems.[80]

Of course, giving had deep roots in American society, as it was consistent with the cultural ethos of voluntarism. For the wealthy of the nineteenth century, giving to charities was also consistent with the Judeo-Christian doctrine of stewardship, where the wealthy, who owed their worldly success to God, had a responsibility to use part of their wealth to help those less fortunate. This certainly included the successful owners of large corporations such as Rockefeller and Carnegie. But the harsh world of competitive capitalism had a habit of corroding ethical principle. For corporate philanthropy to be sustained, it had to be as good for business as it was for the conscience. As Charles E. Adams of Cleveland Hardware Co. wrote: "Although we believe that what we are doing is most practical and philanthropic, our company does not feel that it is a philanthropy, but a good business proposition."[81]

Corporate philanthropy could be good for business in a number of ways. Like workplace initiatives, it might be used to avoid labor problems, in the hope that workers would become more productive. For example, when the Pullman Palace Car Company was founded in Chicago in 1867, the city was in the thick of most of America's major labor battles of the nineteenth century. Extremely troubled, if not frightened, by what he witnessed, Pullman decided to leave the city's labor caldron behind. He would build his own town twelve miles south of Chicago, aptly named Pullman. In constructing the roads, public buildings, and housing, he spared no expense. By creating a new town in a beautiful setting, Pullman believed that he could produce a superior worker with a superior character—the human equivalent of his high-quality sleeping car.

But in the case of corporate philanthropy, "good for business" could also refer to efforts to repair a tarnished image. Five years after the infamy it attained during Homestead Strike, the Carnegie Steel Company opened the Carnegie Library. It was

> a magnificent fireproof building . . . in the French Renaissance style . . . the use of it is given for the commencements of the high schools of Homestead and Mifflin Township, and for meetings "held for the general good of the public." The library proper occupies the center of the structure—the use of which is free to residents of Homestead and vicinity.[82]

More generally, voluntary giving could be good for business if it was good public relations and helped maintain a business-friendly political environment. While corporate philanthropy was born of necessity, it matured in an environment where large corporations were actively resisting government efforts to both regulate the workplace and adopt welfare programs. Not only did this resistance result in leaving the underlying social problems unaddressed, it added fuel to the protests that challenged the legitimacy of large corporations. To help keep government at bay, corporations had to be perceived as part of the solution to social problems. Therefore, just as the threat of unions helped welfare work initiatives achieve critical mass, the threat of government intervention helped corporate philanthropy achieve the same.

—

Ultimately, owners and managers of corporations had varied, and usually multiple, motives for pursuing CSR. The most important, however, involved the need of corporations to manage the constituencies connected to the problems of political economy, legitimacy, and labor relations: 1) the desire to keep government at bay, but at the same time address the problems left by few workplace mandates and a weak welfare state; 2) the desire to demonstrate to the public that fundamental reforms were unnecessary given the good citizenship of corporations, both in terms of charity and relief work, and contributions to a community's social and cultural institutions; and 3) the desire to resist unions, while at the same time seeking greater productivity from workers.

Summary

The swirling economic and social changes of the last quarter of the nineteenth century accelerated growth in both large corporations and in social problems ranging from unemployment to labor unrest. Because many viewed corporations like Standard Oil as the root cause of these problems, the large corporation became a contested institution. As the target of mounting protests, corporations generated an array of concrete challenges ranging from calls for their elimination to public ownership to proposals to mandate responsible practices, such as a shorter workday. Early on, then, America found itself at a crossroads in how to deal with corporations. The regulatory path it would initially take would be consequential, since once cleared, institutional pathways tend to encourage further use.

If outcomes of political challenges were best predicted by the passion of those making demands, the smart money would be placed on the elimination of large corporations. This, of course, did not happen. Instead, it was from this environment of unrest that the trend eventually known as corporate social responsibility was born. Since none of the opponents of corporations called for the self-regulation that CSR represented, what can explain its early appearance?

Instead of passion, the odds for success for any reform proposal were heavily conditioned by the set of opportunities, and especially constraints, posed by America's political architecture. For example, while the advocacy of more radical proposals, like worker cooperatives, was hampered by an already institutionalized two-party system (which reduced the viability of third parties), the chances for passing either strong regulations or nationalizing industries was diminished by chronically weak administrative capacity at all levels of government. As these early efforts to control corporations proceeded, they revealed the basic lopsidedness in America's political economy. Whereas large corporations showed a capacity to grow and diffuse rapidly, the capacity of government to expand in a commensurate fashion to regulate them was severely constrained.

By 1890, however, the nation did clear two regulatory pathways that attempted to control corporations with economic regulations. The first involved the use of an independent regulatory commission to regulate railroads. The second was antitrust, which applied to all industries. The passage of both regulations, against the opposition of most large corporation owners, can be attributed to the resonating appeal of America's homegrown ideology of antimonopolism. Viewing corporations as a threat to the republican ideal of an independent citizenry, and condemning them as inherently corrupt, most antimonopolists sought to abolish corporations. But the strong ideology did not translate into strong measures. Significantly, neither track directly attempted to limit corporate size, nor did either challenge the principles of the market economy in which corporations grew. Instead, they embraced competition as the solution.

But the effectiveness of these new regulations was immediately stymied by the same set of institutional constraints that defeated other proposals, whether it was a lack of administrative capacity that enfeebled enforcement, or a conservative judiciary that had the same effect through the opinions it rendered. Consequently, large corporations continued to improvise with governance structures that contributed to their ability to grow and spread. As a result, America's political economy became increasingly lopsided in favor of the business community.

From this position of strength, large corporations were able to affect other efforts to control them. With increasing power and resources, large corporations were able to quash most of the nascent efforts at the state level to mandate socially responsible practices through a set of social regulations. This, in turn, undermined the effectiveness and appeal of political unionism, the strategy of improving the lot of workers through legislation.

Unions adapted with the orientation of business unionism, where the focus was placed upon negotiations with individual employers over compensation and working conditions. This involved the tacit acceptance of managerial prerogatives, as no corresponding effort was made to negotiate on issues involving the decision-making authority of the firm itself. Even so, large corporations used their growing power to resist, at times violently, the efforts of workers to form unions.

The stern face of resistance was thus the dominant countenance of large corporations. However, it was not the only one to make an appearance. Corporations such as Proctor & Gamble and NCR displayed a benevolent face. With the more certain profits that their larger size allowed, the "welfare work" and community philanthropy that comprised their CSR practices attracted some intellectual interest, if only because they looked so different—and because it seemed like a possible path away from current troubles. But while "voluntary," the effective prod for many, if not most, CSR practitioners was fear, specifically the fear that the ongoing challenges would result in regulations and unions that constricted their prerogatives. By the turn of the century, large corporations had been able to shape the broad contours of America's nascent regulatory structure for large corporations: weak mandated responsibility, weak negotiated responsibility, and rising CSR.

Notes

1. Ron Chernow, *Titan: The Life of John D. Rockefeller, Sr.* (New York: Random House, 1998), 130.
2. Ibid., 149.
3. William G. Roy, *Socializing Capital: The Rise of the Large Industrial Corporation in America* (Princeton, New Jersey: Princeton University Press, 1997), 183–192.
4. Thomas C. Cochran, *Basic History of American Business* (Princeton, New Jersey: Princeton University Press, 1959), 61; Chernow, *Titan*, 134–136.
5. Chernow, *Titan*, 134–136, 203.
6. Ibid., 160, 205.
7. Ibid., p. 253.

8. Alfred D. Chandler, Jr., *The Visible Hand: The Managerial Revolution in American Business* (Cambridge, Massachusetts: The Belknap Press of Harvard University Press, 1977), 325; C. Joseph Pusateri, *A History of American Business*, 2nd ed. (Wheeling, Illinois: Harlan Davidson, Inc., 1988), 217, 205.

9. Ibid.

10. Thomas K. McCraw, *Prophets of Regulation* (Cambridge, Massachusetts: The Belknap Press of Harvard University Press, 1984), 67; John L. Campbell, J. Rogers Hollingsworth, and Leon N. Lindberg, eds., *Governance of the American Economy* (New York: Cambridge University Press, 1991), 39; Industrial Commission, *Final Report of the Industrial Commission* (Washington, DC: Government Printing Office, 1902), 606.

11. Roy, *Socializing Capital*; Charles Perrow, *Organizing America: Wealth, Power, and the Origins of Corporate Capitalism* (Princeton, New Jersey: Princeton University Press, 2002).

12. John L. Campbell, J. Rogers Hollingsworth, and Leon N. Lindberg, eds., *Governance*, 5–6; Gabriel Kolko, *The Triumph of Conservatism: A Reinterpretation of American History, 1900–1916* (Chicago: Quadrangle Books, 1963), 3.

13. Polanyi, Karl, *The Great Transformation* (Boston: Beacon Press, 1956), 33.

14. Sean Dennis Cashman, *America in the Gilded Age: From the Death of Lincoln to the Rise of Theodore Roosevelt*, 3rd ed. (New York: New York University Press, 1993), 107.

15. Ibid., 8.

16. C. Joseph Pusateri, *A History of American Business*, 237; Samuel P. Hays, *The Response to Industrialism, 1885–1914* (Chicago: The University of Chicago Press, 1957), 24ff.

17. Gretchen Ritter, *Goldbugs and Greenbacks: the Antimonopoly Tradition and the Politics of American Finance, 1865–1896* (New York: Cambridge University Press, 1997), 48–49.

18. Henry Demarest Lloyd, "Story of a Great Monopoly," *The Atlantic Monthly*, March 1881.

19. C. Joseph Pusateri, *Big Business in America: Attack and Defense* (Itasca, Illinois: F. E. Peacock Publishers, Inc., 1975), 14; Sidney Fine, *Laissez Faire and the General Welfare State: A Study of Conflict in American Political Thought, 1865–1901* (Ann Arbor, Michigan: University of Michigan Press, 1964), 109.

20. Ritter, *Goldbugs and Greenbacks*, 4–5.

21. John R. Commons et al., *History of Labour in the United States, Volume II* (New York: The Macmillan Company, 1926), 302–303.

22. Fine, *Laissez Faire*, 357–358; Philip S. Foner, *History of the Labor Movement in the United States: Volume I* (New York: International Publishers, 1947), 367.

23. Fine, *Laissez Faire*, 317.

24. Edward Bellamy, *Looking Backward* (New York: Magnum Books, 1968—originally published in 1888); Fine, *Laissez Faire*, 339.

25. Henry Demarest Lloyd, *Wealth Against Commonwealth* (Westport, Connecticut: Greenwood Press, 1976—originally published in 1894); Fine, *Laissez Faire*, 343.

26. Fine, *Laissez Faire*, 212.

27. John R. Commons et al., *History of Labour in the United States, Volume II*, 204, 231, 278.

28. United States Department of Commerce, Bureau of the Census, *Historical Statistics of the United States, Part 2, Colonial Times to 1970* (Washington, DC: US Government Printing Office, 1975), 1103; Stephen Skowronek, *Building A New American State: The Expansion of National Administrative Capacities, 1877–1920* (New York: Cambridge University Press, 1982).

29. Theda Skocpol, *Protecting Soldiers and Mothers: The Political Origins of Social Policy in the United States* (Cambridge, Massachusetts: The Belknap Press of Harvard University Press, 1992), 72.

30. Ibid., 65.

31. Ibid., 65, 9; Daniel Nelson, *Managers & Workers: Origins of the Twentieth-Century Factory System in the United States 1880–1920*, 2nd ed. (Madison, Wisconsin: University of Wisconsin Press, 1995), 42.

32. William E. Forbath, *Law and the Shaping of the American Labor Movement* (Cambridge, Massachusetts: Harvard University Press, 1991), 42.

33. Charles Sellers, *The Market Revolution: Jacksonian America, 1815–1846* (New York: Oxford University Press, 1991), 47.

34. Thomas C Cochran, *Business in American Life: A History* (New York: McGraw-Hill Book Company, 1972), 194.

35. Charles Sellers, *The Market Revolution*, 47.

36. Scott R. Bowman, *The Modern Corporation and American Political Thought: Law, Power, and Ideology* (University Park Pennsylvania: The Pennsylvania State University Press, 1996), 56; Allen Kaufman, Lawrence Zacharias, and Marvin Karson, *Managers vs. Owners: The Struggle for Corporate Control in American Democracy* (New York: Oxford University Press, 1995), 19.

37. Pusateri, *A History of American Business*, 237; McCraw, *Prophets of Regulation*, 19.

38. Chernow, *Titan*, 290.

39. Marver H. Bernstein, *Regulating Business by Independent Commission* (Princeton, New Jersey, Princeton University Press, 1955), 22; Richard White, *Railroaded: The Transcontinentals and the Making of Modern America* (New York: W. W. Norton & Company, 2011), 355–359.

40. Bernstein, *Regulating Business*, chapter 1; James A. Morone, *The Democratic Wish: Popular Participation and the Limits of American Government* (New York: Basic Books, 1990), 120–122.

41. Bernstein, *Regulating Business*, chapter1.

42. Ibid., 21.

43. Chernow, *Titan*, 294, 297–298.

44. Weaver, Suzanne, "Antitrust Division of the Department of Justice," in *The Politics of Regulation*, ed. James Q. Wilson (New York: Basic Books, 1980).

45. Edward C. Kirkland, *Industry Comes of Age: Business, Labor, and Public Policy, 1860–1897* (New York: Holt, Rinehart and Winston, 1961), 320.

46. White, *Railroaded*, 417–418.

47. McCraw, *Prophets of Regulation*, 78–79.

48. Ibid., 79; Harold U. Faulkner, *The Decline of Laissez Faire, 1897–1917* (New York: Harper and Row, Publishers, 1951), 178.

49. The discussion of the Pullman strike is based upon: Almont Lindsey, *The Pullman Strike: The Story of a Unique Experiment and of a Great Labor Upheaval* (Chicago: Phoenix Books, University of Chicago Press, 1964); Stanley Buder, *Pullman: An Experiment in Industrial Order and Community Power, 1880–1930* (New York: Oxford University Press, 1967).

50. Jeremy Brecher, *Strike!* (Boston: South End Press, 1972), chapter 3.

51. Melvyn Dubofsky, *Industrialism and the American Worker: 1865–1920*, 3rd ed. (Wheeling, Illinois: Harlan Davidson, Inc., 1996), 25–27; Alexander Keyssar, *Out of Work: The First Century of Unemployment in Massachusetts* (Cambridge, England: Cambridge University Press, 1986).

52. Stuart Bruchey, *The Wealth of the Nation: An Economic History of the United States* (New York: Harper and Row, Publishers, 1988), 135.

53. Brecher, *Strike!*, chapter 2.

54. David Montgomery, *The Fall of the House of Labor: The Workplace, the State, and American Labor Activism, 1865–1925* (Cambridge: Cambridge University Press, 1987), 13, 17.

55. Foner, *History of the Labor Movement in the United States: Volume I*, 506–507; Kim Voss, *The Making of American Exceptionalism: The Knights of Labor and Class Formation in the Nineteenth Century* (Ithaca, New York: Cornell University Press, 1993).

56. Voss, *The Making of American Exceptionalism*, 179–180.

57. Forbath, *Law and the Shaping of the American Labor Movement*.

58. Ibid., 38–39.

59. Christopher L Tomlins, *The State and the Unions: Labor Relations, Law, and the Organized Labor Movement in America, 1880–1960* (Cambridge, England: Cambridge University Press, 1985), 63.

60. Commons et al., *History of Labour in the United States, Volume II*, 13; United States Department of Commerce, Bureau of the Census, *Historical Statistics of the United States, Part 1, Colonial Times to 1970* (Washington, DC: US Government Printing Office, 1975), 127.

61. Victor H. Olmsted, "The Betterment of Industrial Conditions," *Bulletin of the Department of Labor*, Vol. 5, No. 31 (November 1900); William Howe Tolman, *Industrial Betterment, Monographs on American Social Economics* (New York: Social Service Press, 1900), 63–64.

62. Stuart D. Brandes, *American Welfare Capitalism, 1880–1940* (Chicago: University of Chicago Press, 1970), 85, 19.

63. Herbert Feis, *Labor Relations: A Study Made in the Proctor and Gamble Company* (New York: Adelphi Company Publishers, 1928), 16.

64. Tolman, *Industrial Betterment*, 25.

65. Ibid., 43–44; Edwin L. Shuey, *Factory People and Their Employers: How Their Relations are Made Pleasant and Profitable* (New York: Lentilhon and Company, 1900), 141.

66. Brandes, *American Welfare Capitalism*, 85, 19.

67. Tolman, *Industrial Betterment*; Nicholas Paine Gilman, *A Dividend to Labor: A Study of Employers' Welfare Institutions* (Boston: Houghton, Mifflin and Company, 1899); Shuey, *Factory People*.

68. Olmstead, "The Betterment of Industrial Conditions."

69. Tolman, *Industrial Betterment*, 5; Budgett Meakin, *Model Factories and Villages: Ideal Conditions of Labour and Housing* (London: T. Fisher Unwin, 1905), 7, 75.

70. Tolman, *Industrial Betterment*, 17, 25–26; Gilman, *A Dividend to Labor*, 258.

71. Gilman, *A Dividend to Labor*, 269; Tolman, *Industrial Betterment*, 41; Brandes, *American Welfare Capitalism*, 76.

72. Tolman, *Industrial Betterment*, 56–57.

73. Gilman, *A Dividend to Labor*, 272; Brandes, *American Welfare Capitalism*, 96.

74. Don D. Lescohier and Elizabeth Brandeis, *History of Labor in the United States, 1896–1932: Working Conditions, Labor Legislation* (New York: The Macmillan Company, 1935), 387.

75. Tolman, *Industrial Betterment*, 17–18; Brandes, *American Welfare Capitalism*, 96.

76. William H. Tolman, *Social Engineering: A Record of Things Done by American Industrialists Employing Upwards of One and One-Half Million of People* (New York: McGraw-Hill Book Company, 1909), 201.

77. Gilman, *A Dividend to Labor*, 378–379.

78. Tolman, *Industrial Betterment*, 81; Tone, *The Business of Benevolence*, 55.

79. Morrell Heald, *The Social Responsibilities of Business: Company and Community, 1900–1960* (Cleveland: The Press of Case Western Reserve University, 1970), 6.

80. Ibid., 10–12.

81. Tolman, *Industrial Betterment*, 81.

82. Gilman, *A Dividend to Labor*, 217–218.

3

Progressives Attempt to Tame the Beast

The nineteenth century ended with the economic regulation of anti-trust as the country's main tool for containing the large corporation. Up through the early 1890s it might have seemed reasonable to hope that stronger controls were unnecessary. After all, large corporations were still by no means dominant in the nation's economy. For example, in 1893 the combined capital of the twelve largest corporations was less than $1 billion. In manufacturing industries, the average number of wage earners per factory was twenty-two.[1] This, however, was about to change. Despite the fact that government was now officially charged with preserving the conditions of competition, business owners continued to search for governance structures that would restrain, if not eliminate, competition. At the beginning of the new century, the outcome of this search revealed itself in the nation's first merger wave, which would put the nation's economic regulations to the test.

Mandated Responsibility

Growth of Large Corporations: The First Merger Wave

While it was John D. Rockefeller who took up the cause of containing ruinous competition in one industry in the 1870s, it was investment banker J. P. Morgan who brought a single-minded devotion to the task of rationalizing all industries a generation later. The most dramatic illustration of his success occurred in steel. Morgan first orchestrated the merger of Western steel mills to create the country's second-largest steel corporation, Federated Steel. At the same time, Morgan created trusts in the related lines of bridges, pipes, and hoop steel, which were then instructed to purchase their raw material from Federated instead of the reigning king of steel, Andrew Carnegie. At first, peace in the industry prevailed, because the economic boom of the Spanish-American War generated enough business for everyone. This did not last. When steel demand subsided, a confrontation was inevitable.

In his mid-sixties during this period, Carnegie was not averse to selling out to the new steel goliath, an outcome that would avert economic warfare. However, he would not be cowed into doing so; such a transaction would have to be on terms that he controlled and benefited from. Showing his willingness to engage in battle, Carnegie set in motion a series of actions to compete head to head with Federated, such as building the company's own finishing mills and building a railroad that would connect Pittsburgh and the Atlantic coast. Though this initiated a war for control of the steel industry, it turned out to be a short war. Seeking to avoid the effects of what would surely qualify as ruinous competition, Morgan told his men to "Go and find his price." This turned out to be $492 million, which Morgan accepted, stating that he had just "made Carnegie the richest man in the world."[2] After more wheeling and dealing, including the purchase of ore properties from Rockefeller, the nation's first billion-dollar corporation was born. In 1901 U.S. Steel was capitalized at $1.46 billion, the final product of what had once been 138 separate companies. It immediately accounted for close to two-thirds of the national market for steel.[3]

The merger of U.S. Steel, while the largest and most dramatic in US history to that point, was but one of many mergers that took place across the economy. Between 1898 and 1902 alone, some 2,600 firms disappeared as a result of mergers.[4] When the wave finally subsided in 1904, most of the nation's two hundred largest corporations had been formed, including General Electric, International Harvester, and the aforementioned U.S. Steel. With the top 4 percent of American industrial enterprises now producing 57 percent of all industrial output, the era of big business had truly commenced.[5]

The merger wave ultimately had multiple causes, ranging from the rise of finance capitalism to the heightened aversion to competition stemming from the price wars experienced during the Depression of 1893.[6] But one of the causes, though unintended, was the economic regulation of antitrust itself. As discussed in the last chapter, the Sherman Antitrust Act, though driven by the desire to limit big business, actually targeted the despised practices that circumvented fair competition, such as pools and gentleman's agreements. The act did not explicitly outlaw, or even restrict, bigness as such. Therefore, as the need for an effective governance structure increased in the 1890s, businesses could not resort to any that involved cooperative agreements among smaller, independent businesses. Instead, they were almost constrained to pursue the path of horizontal integration. Indeed, upward of three-quarters of all of the consolidations during this period involved mergers of enterprises in the same line of business.[7] Once there were a few successful combinations, and once these were well publicized, owners in many industries began to consider the possibility of duplicating the pattern of companies like Standard Oil and U.S. Steel for their own businesses.

By 1904 the merger wave had left much larger corporations in its wake. These new entities also tended to dominate their respective industries. In at least fifty industries, one firm now accounted for 60 percent or more of total output; in sixteen of these, one company controlled at least 85 percent of output, including DuPont in the chemical industry, American Tobacco in the tobacco industry, and Pullman in the train car industry.[8] What these data reveal is not so much the creation of oligopolies, where several firms dominate an industry, but partial monopolies, in which a single firm assumes a position of industry dominance.[9]

The merger movement had proven that the new regulatory structure featuring antitrust was not up to task of controlling big business. In fact, it had inadvertently contributed to business becoming even bigger. As a result, America's political economy became even more unbalanced. But the emergence of these new behemoths also managed to stoke another round of popular indignation.

Ideological and Political Challenges: Muckrakers and Progressives

Government was initially silent when it came to the mergers taking place, and much of this can be attributed to the growing political influence of big business. Most of the credit for President William McKinley's victory over William Jennings Bryan in 1896 can be given to his campaign manager, Mark Hanna, an Ohio businessman turned political consultant. Able to mobilize the fear felt by the heads of big business at the prospect of a Bryan presidency, and unhindered by campaign finance restrictions, Hanna and the Republican National Committee were able to raise at least $3.5 million (approximately $50 million in today's dollars), or ten times the amount raised by Democrats. Solidifying the Republican Party's credentials as the party of the business community, the McKinley administration was not inclined to vigorously enforce the Sherman Antitrust Act during the merger wave.[10]

But though government was quiet on the subject of mergers, the public was not. At the beginning of the new century, the harshest voices raised against large corporations were those of muckraking journalists. In mass-circulation magazines such as *McClure's* and *Collier's*, muckrakers shocked the nation with articles that exposed social problems, like slums, and corruption that permeated government and the economy. Particularly popular were articles that revealed and attacked business corruption, including those of Charles Russell on the beef trust and Thomas Lawson on Amalgamated Copper. The most influential of this group were Ida Tarbell's sixteen-part series on Standard Oil. In book form, the standout was Upton Sinclair's stomach-turning exposé of the meatpacking industry in *The Jungle*.[11]

The resulting public outcry helped fuel the Progressive Movement, by far the dominant reform movement of the early twentieth century. Like critics of the nineteenth century, Progressives believed that large corporations were directly responsible for many of the problems of the day, whether it was political corruption or tainted meat. However, most critics now believed that these new economic organizations were also responsible for unparalleled economic growth and had the potential for great economic efficiency that could be used to achieve social goals. Furthermore, in contrast to the agrarian movement of the previous generation, this movement comprised middle-class professionals and reformers who were based in cities. It brought together social efforts to solve the social problems that were festering in the nation's cities and political efforts that sought to rid politics of corruption.

Social reformers rejected both the laissez faire conception of government and the Social Darwinist acceptance of social problems, doctrines that were popular at the time. For the adherents of the Social Gospel movement, as well as workers in the settlement house movement like Jane Addams, society had a moral duty to address social problems, and they saw government as the key. One group of reformers, composed of a network of women's clubs and associations, advocated policies focused on helping women and children, such as aid to widowed mothers. A second group of reformers pushed social insurance proposals that could benefit all citizens. Particularly influential was the American Association for Labor Legislation (AALL), established in 1906 and committed to lobbying for social insurance policies. Closely following the progress of welfare-state developments in Europe, the AALL drafted model legislation concerning social insurance programs, including unemployment, old age, health and disability insurance.[12] Some of these proposals would enlist the large corporation as the delivery system for social-welfare goods.

For political reformers, the key to cleaning up government involved taking partisanship out of politics. There were two prongs of their attack. The first was to restore power directly to the public by weakening those intermediaries—whether political parties, private interests, or legislators—that stood between the public and its government. The success of the reforms that were advocated, such as direct primaries, secret ballots, the initiative, and the referendum, changed the face of American politics forever.

The second prong involved an effort to escape the inherent corruption of politics, especially that which was engendered by big business, and it ultimately yielded two approaches for dealing with large corporations. The first was a refined version of antitrust strain of antimonopolism, and Louis D. Brandeis gave its most forceful expression. Before becoming a Supreme Court justice in 1916, Brandeis gained national fame as "the peoples' lawyer" for his work on behalf of small businessmen and railings against the "curse of bigness." In 1914 he published *Other People's Money*, a collection of articles that had appeared in *Harper's* magazine a year earlier. Harkening back to early America, Brandeis argued that the great monopolies that had been created in the last generation were destroying individualism and freedom, the very characteristics that made America great. In the book, Brandeis also attempted to make a strong economic case against the large corporation. In contrast to the growing consensus concerning business size, Brandeis argued that the large corporations were economically inefficient; not only were they too large for managers to effectively control them, large corporations used their power to keep new firms from entering industries that they dominated, thus suppressing innovation. Most importantly, by constraining competition, large corporations curtailed the one mechanism that worked to guarantee efficiency.[13]

It was also in 1914 that Brandeis made one of his most forceful political cases against the large corporation. In testimony before the Commission on Industrial Relations, Brandeis argued that as corporations grew, employers became "so potent, so well organized, with such concentrated forces and with such extraordinary powers . . ." that the modern employment situation amounted to nothing less than "industrial absolutism." Strengthening the antimonopoly charge that large corporations were an affront to democracy, he held that "you have created within the State a state so powerful that the ordinary forces

61

existing are insufficient to meet it." For both economic and political reasons, then, Brandeis rejected the large corporation as an inevitable institution. The solution continued to feature breaking up large corporations and restoring competition.[14]

This Progressive approach to large corporations also featured the advocacy of the economic regulation of independent government agencies, where the regulation of large corporations would be scientifically administered by non-partisan experts. Of course, the notion that regulation was best left to a cadre of experts, steeped in the science germane to the industry being regulated, was but a more highly articulated rationale for the expanded use of regulatory agencies and commissions. Also consistent with past efforts was the assumption that merely shining a light upon heretofore hidden and deceptive practices (the "sunshine" function) would produce salutary results.[15]

While drawing upon the same antimonopoly, populist fear of large corporations, the second Progressive approach accepted the reality of large corporations and developed a stronger rationale for reform—a more highly articulated version of the reformist strain of antimonopolism. The most developed statement of this school of thought was found in Herbert Croly's *The Promise of American Life*, published in 1909.[16] Croly argued that the change from a competitive economy into a noncompetitive economy, where large corporations control production and markets, had created a separate sphere of economic power based on the control of economic resources. This was distinct from political power, which was based upon the control of political resources and institutions. Over time, however, the highly centralized and organized group of corporate oligarchs had come to exercise control over the highly decentralized system of American government, which by the late nineteenth century comprised party bosses and their machines. Croly, then, shared with Brandeis the antimonopolist conviction that large corporations posed a direct threat to democratic accountability.[17] But since there was no turning back the clock on how the economy had changed, the task was to reform government so that it could both regulate corporate power and direct it toward socially useful goals. For Croly this meant strengthening the Executive Branch so as to disrupt the alliance between party machines and large corporations. Government, through regulation, would then be in a position to balance the power of big business.

—

Given the success of Progressive efforts to clean up government, it was reasonable to expect that reformers might also succeed in rebalancing the nation's political economy and bring large corporations to heel, either with more effective attempts at enforcing antitrust law, or by finally clearing a new path for stronger social regulations.

Economic Regulations: Staying the Antitrust Course

Early in his presidency, Theodore Roosevelt provided some evidence that he might be up to the job of taming corporate power. In 1902, the administration filed suit under the Sherman Act against the Northern Securities Corporation, the new holding company put together by J. P. Morgan that now controlled the major railroads of the Northwestern states. As this action withstood legal challenge and led to the breakup of the company, Roosevelt was given the moniker of "trust-buster."

But T.R. was not fully in the antitrust camp, as he saw the economic advantages of large corporations. In his first address to Congress: "The captains of industry who have driven the railway systems across this continent, who have built up our commerce, who have developed our manufactures, have on the whole done great good to our people."[18] Not only did Roosevelt view ongoing economic concentration as mostly beneficial, he concluded that bigness was the inevitable culmination of industrial development. While he also conceded that big business posed dangers, he did not view these as inevitable. Instead, the challenge was to cull the "bad trusts" from the group of mostly "good trusts," since he viewed the problem as one of character (bad people doing bad things), not structure. As a result, Roosevelt preferred regulatory oversight to antitrust action as the best method for dealing with the problem of trusts.

His tool in this endeavor was the Bureau of Corporations, established within the Department of Commerce in 1903. The Bureau's charge was to investigate trusts and combinations. With no real power beyond its "sunshine" function of exposing wrongdoing, the assumption was that the bad publicity generated by the Bureau's reports would be enough to curtail bad corporate behavior—an extension of Roosevelt's faith in the "bully pulpit." In practice, Roosevelt was also able to use the threat of a public report in order to gain access to relevant company information, as long as it was kept private. Good trusts, like U.S. Steel and International Harvester, were those that cooperated and formed gentlemen's agreements with the administration. As long as the data revealed no egregious examples of anticompetitive behavior, these corporations were thus able to avoid antitrust action.[19] Bad trusts, like Standard Oil, were those that did not fully cooperate. For these trusts, antitrust action was more likely, as when the administration filed suit against Standard Oil in 1907. But with no real power and a meager annual budget of only $100,000, the Bureau of Corporations was not equipped to have a substantial impact upon large corporations.[20]

As it turned out, however, this strategy of distinguishing good from bad trusts depended upon the discriminating powers and commitment of Roosevelt himself. His anointed successor, William Howard Taft, favored stricter antitrust enforcement. While the Roosevelt administration initiated just forty-four cases in seven years, Taft's Justice Department initiated sixty-five cases in just four years, from 1908–1912.[21]

Problems for antitrust enforcement remained. In the twenty years since it had passed, there was still no clear standard of what constituted a violation of the Sherman Act. In 1911 the Supreme Court attempted to clarify the issue of antitrust enforcement in its decision upholding a lower court's verdict against Standard Oil. As a result, the company was forced to divest itself of thirty-seven companies. At first, this was seen as a blow against big business, since Standard Oil had at one time been the nation's largest corporation. The blow was softened, however, in the court's written opinion that articulated the "rule of reason." The court argued that only those combinations that arose from the intent to restrain competition ("unreasonable") were in violation of the law. Companies that merged by normal, reasonable methods were viewed as legal. In other words, the court stuck to the common law tradition where what mattered were the motives of economic activity. Neither size nor market share by themselves were problems for the court.

the election of 1912: Differences over antitrust enforcement exposed a fissure between Roosevelt and Taft. Not only did Roosevelt feel that excessive enforcement threatened economic progress, he was personally irked by the case brought against U.S. Steel, which had been a party to one of Roosevelt's gentlemen's agreements. But differences over antitrust turned out to represent the beginnings of a growing rift between the two men. By the end of Taft's term, Roosevelt, who felt that his progressive legacy had been squandered by Taft, decided to run for the presidency again.

After losing the Republican nomination, Roosevelt embarked upon his third-party "bull-moose" campaign, as the candidate of the newly christened Progressive Party. Having read and admired Croly's *The*

Promise of American Life, Roosevelt adopted what was dubbed its "new nationalism" as the basis of his campaign. The Progressives' ambitious platform contained an array of social regulations, including calls for an eight-hour day, the prohibition of child labor, legislation to deal with involuntary unemployment, and the recognition of unions.

Turning to the purpose of corporations, the platform stated that "the test of corporate efficiency shall be the ability to better serve the public; that those who profit by control of business affairs shall justify that profit and that control by sharing with the public the fruits thereof." While recognizing large corporations as inevitable, it borrowed from the antimonopolist critique, contending that "the existing concentration of vast wealth under a corporate system, unguarded and uncontrolled by the Nation, has placed in the hands of a few men enormous, secret, irresponsible power over the daily life of the citizen—a power insufferable in a free Government and certain of abuse." The platform on business reform concluded, "We therefore demand a strong National regulation of inter-State corporations."[22] Ultimately, then, the Progressive Party presented the nation not only with a coherent rationale for the reform of corporations, but also a clearly articulated statement that it was the proper role of government to ensure greater corporate social responsibility.

The Democratic candidate Woodrow Wilson, a Southern conservative by constitution, became a remade Progressive. Given his Southern roots, however, Wilson was careful to avoid advocacy of programs that would create bigger government. While the federal government could be shown to be helpful in controlling big business, it could not be seen as becoming too powerful, since Southerners worried that an empowered central government would pose a threat to the region's Jim Crow practices. Instead of "new nationalism," the theme adopted by the Wilson campaign was "new freedom." He turned to Louis Brandeis to shape his stance on the issue of trusts, thus guaranteeing that it would be built upon the base of the antitrust strain of antimonopolism and its traditional rejection of large corporations. Since these behemoths were unnatural, not inevitable, what was needed was not more regulation, but instead the restoration of competition. The Democratic platform thus held:

> A private monopoly is indefensible and intolerable. We therefore favor the vigorous enforcement of the criminal as well as the civil law against trusts and trust officials, and demand the enactment of such additional legislation as may be necessary to make it impossible for a private monopoly to exist in the United States.[23]

The 1912 election represented a choice between the two poles of Progressive thought concerning large corporations, and therefore the two strains of antimonopolism: the dominant strain of "reject and abolish" vs. the growing strain of "accept but regulate." The candidacy of Wilson represented a strengthening of the antitrust track of economic regulation. By protecting a competitive economic environment, socially responsible behavior would be achieved indirectly by preventing big businesses from taking root—and the minimalist, negative role of government simply enforcing rules would be retained. The proposed alternative path offered by the Progressive Party represented a direct approach, in which the government would set standards for socially responsible behavior on the part of large corporations—and a positive role for government would be created.[24]

At this critical juncture for the nation's political economy, voters chose to stay on the path of antitrust, digging deeper institutional ruts as a result. Of course, Wilson won with only 42 percent of the vote, in part, because Taft and Roosevelt split the Republican vote—one of the dangers of third-party candidacies in a two-party system. But because he was reelected in 1916, it was Wilson's two terms as president and his approach to large corporations that would leave a lasting legacy in the form of two pieces of legislation.

the Clayton Act and the FTC: Wilson's antimonopoly agenda received an assist during his first year in office from the Pujo Committee of the House. Established in 1912 to investigate the "money trust" of Wall Street bankers and financiers, the committee's report issued in 1913 was hard hitting. It concluded that a small group of Wall Street bankers exerted significant control over the US economy through a sophisticated network of 341 interlocking directorships in 112 corporations worth more that $22 billion. At the center of the network were representatives of the banking empire of J. P. Morgan.[25]

With all of the negative attention focused on large corporations, Wilson moved quickly to mobilize political support for his approach to dealing with large corporations. By 1914 he was able to sign two pieces of legislation that fulfilled his promise to reinvigorate antitrust enforcement. The Clayton Act attempted to clarify the Sherman Act by specifying a number of practices that would be held to violate antitrust law. These included a prohibition on predatory price-cutting, price-fixing, ownership of stock in competing companies, and interlocking directorships of companies within the same industry. The act also required that companies contemplating mergers notify the Justice

Department's Antitrust Division if the resulting combination met certain thresholds concerning market power.

The president also signed the Federal Trade Commission Act. The act created the Federal Trade Commission (FTC), which was charged with preventing unfair methods of competition. To fulfill its charge, the FTC was given powers to investigate, hold hearings, and issue cease and desist orders. By specifying concrete anticompetitive practices (especially those identified by the Clayton Act), and by giving the new FTC more substantial power than the Bureau of Corporations that it replaced, many advocates, such as Brandeis, hoped that small companies would rebound as competition was restored.

The new law also stipulated that the commission would be composed of five presidential appointees serving seven-year terms. To ensure that the FTC would not become a tool of partisan politics, the law also mandated that the commission be bipartisan, with no more than three commissioners from one political party. The FTC was thus modeled after the Interstate Commerce Commission (ICC), the nation's first independent regulatory commission (IRC), created a generation earlier. Reflecting both their mistrust of politics and faith in scientific expertise, Progressives believed that a group of non-partisan experts, removed from the political process, could perform their regulatory function in accordance with the principles of scientific administration to find the best practice or rule. In addition to the FTC, the first term of the Wilson administration witnessed the creation of two other IRCs: the Federal Reserve Board (1913) and the Federal Farm Loan Board (1916).[26]

Political Economy at the End of the Progressive Era

Thirty years after the passage of the Interstate Commerce Act and the Sherman Antitrust Act, the federal government's approach to dealing with large corporations continued to center on the use of antitrust and regulatory commissions to strengthen competition in the hopes of creating conditions that would restore the dominance of smaller businesses. But such hopes also continued to be misplaced. By the end of his presidency, Wilson's antimonopolist efforts to restore an economy dominated by smaller concerns proved ineffective. Of the over 290,000 manufacturing enterprises that existed in 1919, no more than 10,000 or so produced goods totaling more than $1 million. But this fewer than 4 percent of establishments not only produced nearly 68 percent of manufactured goods, they also employed close to 57 percent of all wage earners.[27]

What, then, can explain the continued dominance of large corporations in the face of government's efforts to contain them? One reason is that with an ever more lopsided political economy, big business was better able to resist efforts to control them, whether through court challenge or intense lobbying. In other words, business's ability to restrict competition was greater than government's ability to maintain it. This was particularly true of the increasingly institutionalized independent regulatory commission, which proved to be no match for large corporations. A common weakness of both the ICC and the FTC was that these agencies were typically understaffed and underfunded.

But beyond the issue of resources, this regulatory strategy was built upon a dubious premise that regulation could be removed from politics. This premise was no doubt a reaction against the corruption endemic to American politics, and it reflected as well a fear on the part of many middle-class Progressive reformers that the masses in a democracy could not be trusted.[28] In the end, however, there is no scientifically discoverable "best way" to regulate, but instead, a set of policy alternatives that need to be decided politically. By taking regulation out of the political arena, commissioners lacked political direction and popular support, and as a result, they were subject to intense lobbying by those they were regulating. The success of such lobbying was almost assured by yet another design flaw. "Independence" meant independence from partisan politics. The architects of IRCs, however, seemed oblivious to the need for independence from the private firms being regulated. With no infrastructure for producing a supply of public experts, IRCs came to rely upon the expertise provided by the private sector. As a result, not only did these agencies represent yet another set of entry points for business to influence government, business was frequently the source of the knowledge and personnel necessary for agencies to perform their functions—the beginnings of the "revolving door" connecting business and government.

More importantly, the government's regulatory efforts, whether antitrust or independent regulatory commissions, were based upon the flawed assumption that competition was a condition that invariably favored small enterprises. Indeed, the antimonopolist vision of a restored economy dominated by small firms proved quixotic. As Alfred Chandler argued in an oeuvre dedicated to understanding the rise of American business, by the first decades of the twentieth century, large corporations in many industries had proven to be more efficient than their smaller brethren. To be sure, the actual reasons that led corporations to combine horizontally or vertically frequently involved the desire to control, if not eliminate, competition.[29] But once they were larger, many corporations were able to achieve "economies of scale," in which increased size leads to a reduction in the unit cost of production. In addition, as corporations grew larger, with more departments, locations, and employees, the dilemmas of coordination grew larger as well. Owners typically solved these by employing an increasingly professional cadre of full-time managers that were increasingly insulated from myopic investors, since the increased size of corporations translated into a more fragmented group of owners. Finally, with the greater number and complexity of transactions that resulted, the "visible hand" of managers in a hierarchy, where market functions are internalized, frequently proved more efficient than the invisible hand of the market.

Of course, Chandler also showed that bigness was not suited for all industries. Large corporations were more likely to emerge in technologically advanced industries requiring huge capital investments that could link mass production with mass distribution, like autos and steel—and which had very high "entry costs" that kept potential competitors from entering the field. In industries characterized by labor-intensive production and low entry costs, like textile and furniture manufacturing, consolidation did not work as a governance structure.

—

For the first two generations in which large corporations spread, the federal government was focused primarily on using economic regulations to contain them. These proved to be ineffective. Therefore, if the public was going to be protected from the harmful practices of large corporations, stronger social regulations would be necessary. The problem was that efforts to improve economic regulations sapped most of the energy for reforming corporations. The failure of economic regulations also resulted in an even more lopsided political economy, making it that much harder to pass social regulations.

Social Regulations and Welfare: Progressive Reforms Stall

In response to the Progressive Era's numerous efforts to pass social regulations, the business community adopted a two-pronged strategy of opposition, the first involving the courts and the second the legislative process. Overall, big business continued to receive favorable treatment in the judiciary when it challenged mandates affecting working conditions. In the landmark case Lochner v. New York, the Supreme Court in 1905 overturned a New York state statute that restricted the hours of bakery workers. In keeping with nineteenth-century precedents, the court ruled that the law denied the owner (Lockner) of property (i.e., potential profits from his employees) without due process. The court also held that the law interfered with his "freedom of contract," which it argued was protected by the Constitution.[30] Adhering to the prevailing economic philosophy of laissez faire, the court continued to treat workers and owners as if they were equal parties to a contract, turning a blind eye to the tremendous asymmetries of power ushered in by large businesses. Owners also continued to successfully invoke the Fourteenth Amendment's equal protection clause to nullify efforts to regulate corporations. Indeed, though the amendment was intended to protect civil rights, twenty of the twenty-six Supreme Court cases involving the amendment from 1891 to 1910 involved corporations as the principal party.[31]

To thwart legislative proposals before they became laws, corporations and business associations became increasingly sophisticated in their lobbying efforts. At the national level, the National Association of Manufacturers (NAM) assumed the lead in opposing labor legislation at the beginning of the new century. In the campaign against the eight-hour day, the NAM and other business associations ultimately turned over all lobbying to professionals—the beginning of a new era of resistance to big government.[32] Much of this increasing sophistication was a reflection of the increasing growth and dominance of large corporations. The huge sums of discretionary resources that they were able to amass further tilted America's political economy in the direction of the business community.

The effectiveness of this opposition can be seen in the case of the nation's efforts to create a rudimentary welfare state along the lines of Europe. For example, by 1911 both Great Britain and Germany had programs for health care, old-age pensions, and workmen's compensation, thus taking these practices from the purview of employer voluntarism in the form of CSR. In the United States, national health care was put on the public's agenda when the Progressive Party included it in its 1912 platform. Though the party lost, the AALL took up the issue in 1914, when it began to push for compulsory health insurance. But when a model bill was introduced in fourteen states by 1914, only two legislatures considered it, and it lost in both. A powerful alliance of employers, commercial insurers, and local medical societies effectively stymied the legislative proposals in every state. The reasons, both stated and unstated, for all of this resistance included worries about taxation, concerns that social and labor legislation would undermine work incentives and character, and the generalized fear that such legislation would represent the loss of managerial prerogatives and professional independence.[33]

The strength of business opposition to both social regulations and welfare proposals was amplified by weaknesses in the coalition of groups calling for social reform. Most importantly, the coalition typically did not include organized labor. As will be discussed further below, the Gompers-led AFL was firmly committed to the voluntarist principle that such regulations were best left for the negotiating table. Though many state labor federations did support individual measures, the public display of division within labor's ranks tended to undermine that support.[34]

Weaknesses in the reform coalition were also revealed in their general approach to social regulations, as illustrated in the failure of minimum wage proposals. True to the spirit of the Progressives' mistrust of politics, and wary of proposals that might feed patronage and corruption, reformers pushed for the creation of independent commissions. Therefore, instead of expanding an existing government bureau, the AALL minimum wage proposal for Massachusetts called for the creation of an independent Minimum Wage Commission that would be charged with investigating individual industries and making recommendations. The bill was passed in 1912, but only after compliance to recommended standards was made non-mandatory. Ultimately, the effectiveness of the new law was fully compromised when a textile manufacturer who had opposed the bill was appointed chairman several years later, thus "capturing" the Commission for business.[35]

Another weakness in reformers' push for welfare programs can be seen in the issue of old-age pensions. With the persistence of weak administrative capacity at the federal level, most reforms targeted the state level. The business community, once again, led the opposition. Not only did businessmen object to the potential cost of such a program, they also argued that any state that mandated pensions would put its businesses at a competitive disadvantage with companies in neighboring states that had no such mandate. Given the reality of "competitive federalism," in which states compete for businesses to locate within their borders, this objection rang true for many legislators.[36]

Paradoxically, even where social regulations were passed, the support of big business was sometimes the key. One example involved workmen's compensation. At the turn of the century, there were alarmingly high rates of industrial accidents and deaths. By this time, judges had begun to restrict the common law defense made by employers that employees accepted risk when they entered an employment contract. As juries began to hand out large plaintiff awards, business groups, including the NAM, began to lobby for workmen's compensation laws, since the standardized awards granted by commissions would be less costly; in this unique case, the business community perceived a social regulation as more cost-efficient. In contrast, because workers were beginning to benefit more from empowered juries, unions opposed the new legislative proposals. Ultimately, forty-two states passed laws between 1911 and 1920.[37]

Business support was also important in the passage in 1906 of both the Pure Food and Drug Act and the Meat Inspection Act. The new laws mandated that the US Department of Agriculture (first in the Bureau of Chemistry and then in the Food and Drug Administration) inspect food and drugs to insure against "adulteration" and "misbranding." While muckraking exposés were fairly credited in helping to secure the bills' passage by raising the public's ire and demands for new regulations, a vanguard of large corporations lobbied for the new laws as well. According to the tradition of "corporate liberalism," the support of these large corporations was the result of their desire to curb competition. Since industry leaders realized that their own experts would likely help craft inspection rules, the economic burden that compliance would impose would be too great for many small businesses to bear.[38]

—

Though reform was certainly in the air, the record of both economic and social regulations during the Progressive Era was mixed at best. If corporations were going to be constrained, and if the lives of workers were going to improve, the next best bet would be if unions grew stronger and were able to negotiate with owners to ensure greater social responsibility.

Negotiated Responsibility

The Trade Agreement

At the beginning of the century, the union movement seemed poised to deliver agreements that stipulated socially responsible practices. In January 1900, District 8 of the International Association of Machinists

(IAM) in Chicago proposed a trade agreement that included a minimum wage of twenty-eight cents an hour, a nine-hour day, a seniority rule to govern layoffs, and a closed shop, in which hiring would be restricted to union members. When machine shop owners in the city balked, five thousand workers went on strike. As the strike dragged on and spread to other cities, the leaders of the IAM and the National Metal Trades Association (NMTA), a newly formed trade association representing machine shop employers, realized that a national agreement was needed. As a result, both sides met in May at the Murray Hill Hotel in New York City to hash out an agreement. On May 18, the Murray Hill agreement was signed that reduced the workweek, provided for overtime work, regulated apprenticeship, and while owners held out against a closed shop, also stipulated that union members would not be discriminated against.[39] With the Murray Hill agreement freshly signed, Samuel Gompers toured New England with the head of the IAM to recruit new members. The president of the AFL felt vindicated. After all of the labor turmoil of the 1890s, Gompers entered the new century firmly committed to the philosophy of voluntarism. Not only had unions held their own in the years immediately following the failed strikes of 1892–94 and the Depression of 1893, but between 1897 and 1900 union membership nearly doubled, to 868,500, most of it within AFL-affiliated unions.[40] In contrast, the Knights of Labor were all but a past chapter in labor history.

His aversion to political unionism stronger than ever, Gompers not only saw no point in pursuing social regulations, which would likely be overturned by courts, he rejected appeals of antimonopolists to join new antitrust efforts to rein in the mega-corporations created by the merger movement. Gompers viewed trusts as the inevitable byproduct of economic development. But so too, he insisted, were unions, which he argued were the only way to deal with large corporations. What he now envisioned was a system of industrial democracy, where unions and associations of owners would jointly govern industrial affairs. Again though, this system would be built upon the foundation of voluntarism. This meant that labor's vision provided no ideological support for a positive role for government in guaranteeing a set of social rights, like fair wages and job security.[41]

The primary goal for Gompers and other union leaders was the attainment of trade agreements arrived at through collective bargaining. The most fundamental issue to negotiate was wages. By establishing wage scales and thresholds below which wages could not fall, unions sought to shelter wages from the full impact of the market. Some union leaders, in fact, believed that, because labor costs were "always one of the first points on which the economizing policy was applied" when business competition intensified, workers shared the basic goal of owners: protection from ruinous competition.[42]

Beyond wages, unions also sought negotiated outcomes that would, among other things, limit the hours of work, eliminate piecework, restrict the number of apprentices, and regulate the use of machinery. Since bargaining over such issues relied upon the strength of union numbers to counterbalance the power advantages of businesses, the recognition of unions as the legitimate representatives of an establishment's employees was of paramount importance. One way of effectively ensuring this was to attempt to limit hiring to union workers, the usual meaning of a "closed shop."[43] Upon closer examination, then, business unionism is better understood as "business and job control unionism." While not contesting the ownership of businesses, union leaders were seeking to establish "rights" in the job. In short, though business unionism eschewed political action or legislative remedies, it was distinctly political in the sense that it sought to constrain managerial prerogatives at the level of the job. In this way, trade agreements represented private legislation governing the behavior of employers and employees, which would, it was hoped, result in more socially responsible practices.

The Rise and Rapid Demise of Corporatism

By the turn of the century, some owners came to the same conclusion as Gompers, accepting that unions were inevitable and labor peace imperative if the economy were to be further rationalized and profits ensured. To bring this peace about, the heads of many of America's new corporate giants formed the National Civic Federation (NCF) in 1900. This group included Andrew Carnegie, utilities magnate Samuel Insull, and several partners of J. P. Morgan and Company. These leaders also reached out to "responsible" (i.e., "conservative") leaders of organized labor, with Gompers, not surprisingly, serving as the group's first vice president.

The initial charge of the NCF's was to explore the terms by which unions and owners could work together. This led to the formation of the group's Conciliation Department, set up to facilitate trade agreements between employer associations and unions affiliated with the NCF.[44] At the first conference on industrial arbitration and conciliation convened by the group in December 1900, the featured guests were the officers of the IAM and the NMTA who had negotiated the Murray Hill agreement.[45] In a statement adopted by the delegates, it was stipulated "We duly recognize that unless labor is regularly employed and has reason to be satisfied with its wages and conditions in life we cannot have permanent peace nor substantial prosperity." The document recommended "That employers and wage-earners should enter into annual or semiannual agreements or contracts."[46]

The high expectations of the group's early leaders were soon frustrated. Some NCF members, like Elbert Gary of U.S. Steel and Cyrus McCormick of International Harvester, were willing to accept unions in the abstract, and maybe for other employers, but they continued to resist them in their own shops. Then, in an early test of the group's effectiveness in promoting labor peace, the group was unable to avert what became a bitter strike between coal industry owners and the United Mine Workers in 1902.[47]

The NCF thus struggled in its efforts to lead the business community, a task made harder still by the fact that most businesses did not belong to the NCF, and most reacted to the labor upheavals of the nineties with renewed hostility toward unions. Small and medium-size manufacturers in particular continued to reject unions in both practice and in principle. In 1903, alarmed by the further growth of union membership that was approaching two million, the National Association of Manufacturers (NAM), which had previously shown little interest in labor matters, took up a "crusade against unionism," initiating an "open shop" campaign, where a company's employees would not be required to belong to a union.[48]

The campaign featured the use of "yellow dog" contracts, which made employment contingent upon a signed agreement from job applicants that they would not join unions, as well as the use of labor spies to help compile blacklists of workers with pro-union views. The success of such tactics was facilitated by the growing tendency of owners in various industries to form employer associations, often as a bulwark against unions. For example, beginning in 1904, the National Founders Association refused to deal with the Iron Moulders Union, while in 1905 the National Erectors Association broke off its relations with the Bridge and Structural Iron Workers Unions. Association members would also share blacklists and provide mutual aid in the case of strikes.[49]

Employers also continued to call upon the courts to help them curb unions. This led to a growing trend in which judges issued injunctions against unions when they called for sympathy strikes and boycotts, tactics that had proved effective for unions. Ironically, given the AFL's rejection of antitrust efforts, the Supreme Court ruled in the Danbury Hatters case of 1908 that the Hatters Union had violated the Sherman Antitrust Act. The Court held that by calling for a nationwide boycott of the Lowe Company, the union had engaged in a conspiracy to restrain trade.[50]

As a result, at the same time that the NCF model of labor-management conciliation was failing, the open-shop campaign gained momentum. Once again, labor suffered a series of major strike losses. Especially crippling was the defeat of steelworkers at U.S. Steel in 1909, which left the steel industry unorganized for the next thirty years. The best indicator of the effectiveness of employer resistance showed up in the membership rolls of unions. After almost doubling in number between 1901 and 1904 to a record high of 2,067,000, membership stagnated over the next several years and by 1909 actually declined, to 1,965,000.[51] Likewise, though the NCF's Conciliation Department was able to claim a number of successes in the early years of its operation, by 1914 it had, for all intents and purposes, ceased to exist.[52]

Ultimately, the NCF's failed effort to seek labor peace was probably inevitable. In many ways, its approach constituted the nation's first effort at a "corporatist" system of labor relations. These exist where peak associations (i.e., "an organization which purports, and is taken, to speak for a particular sector of society") of owners and workers negotiate labor agreements that are then applied to an entire industry or industries.[53] Such arrangements later become common in Western Europe, where they not only help to moderate class conflict by strengthening negotiated responsibility, but also operate as a governance structure, restricting economic competition. In the United States, however, they never took root.

As Robert Salisbury has argued, the problem is that American peak associations are congenitally weak. This is primarily due to institutional fragmentation of both business associations and labor organizations, which ultimately reflect America's basic federalist structure. Instead of peak associations, there are usually different groups representing owners or workers at the local, state, and federal levels of government, making coordination difficult at best. As a result, most trade agreements of this period covered only a single establishment, and at most, a single city.[54]

The dilemma of fragmentation was illustrated by the demise of the Murray Hill agreement, discussed above. Less than a year after the agreement was signed, it failed when the national leadership of the NMTA refused to arbitrate when the local members in one city refused to increase wages to compensate for the reduction in hours.[55] Furthermore, where corporatist regimes work, it is usually because government acts to both encourage peak associations and enforce the agreements that business and labor groups devise. In the United States, the weak administrative capacity of the federal government, together with an aversion to any form of compulsory arbitration on the part of labor and business, precluded this role.[56]

But while the NCF's failure aptly illustrated the difficulty in creating peak associations, it was labor that was particularly handicapped as a result. That is because an individual large corporation had greater resources to prevail in fights with individual unions. The strength of numbers, unions' main asset, was diminished further by the fact that its chief association, the AFL, was built as a federation of craft unions. Not only was this increasingly out of step with the development of the economy that was increasingly built along industrial lines and dominated by large corporations, but it drove a wedge between the skilled, native workers, who dominated the trades, and the unskilled, immigrant workers, who worked in the new, lower skilled factory jobs. Finally, the AFL's founding commitment to the "strict recognition of the autonomy of each trade" translated into an executive council with no power to interfere with the affairs of local member unions—yet another indicator of how any corporatist regime was doomed.[57]

Through it all, however, the AFL stuck to its voluntarist guns. Furthermore, it could continue to point to evidence that seemed to support the strategy. The trade agreements produced during the first generation of the new century typically yielded higher pay and better working conditions, especially in the form of a shorter workweek for union workers (union workers were much more likely than nonunion workers to work an eight-hour day).[58] Of course, given the AFL practice of only organizing craft workers, most of these gains were experienced by skilled owners alone; there was still no significant union presence in the major industries of autos, meat packing, agricultural machinery, or electrical manufacturing—or in other words, where workers most subject to corporate irresponsibility resided.

However, the experience of the semiskilled, mostly immigrant women of the International Ladies' Garment Workers Union (ILGWU) suggested that organizing these more vulnerable workers could produce more socially responsible practices. When Louis Brandeis was asked to mediate the strike between the union's workers and garment manufacturers in

1910, he was able to hammer out the "Protocol of Peace," which awarded these ILGWU workers higher wages, shorter hours, and a grievance-arbitration procedure to avoid future strikes.[59] It was left to a competing labor federation, however, to push for the rights of less skilled.

The Wobblies and Labor Radicalism

The renewed intransigence of owners in the early years of the new century, together with the conservatism of the AFL, led to formation of the International Workers of the World (IWW). At its founding convention in 1905, delegates representing miners and loggers from the Western states, migratory farm workers, unorganized industrial workers, as well as the two factions of American socialism, came together to form what was a radical counterpoint to the AFL. Where the AFL represented skilled, craft workers, and championed the interests of native-born white males alone, the IWW called for an all-inclusive union that would embrace both the skilled and unskilled, craft and mass production, native born and immigrant, white and black, and male and female. Their stance on being ethnically inclusive was particularly significant, since 75 percent of all industrial workers were either foreign born or children of a foreign-born father. Also, in contrast to the AFL's acceptance of capitalism and its large corporations, the IWW called for the elimination of the wage system.[60]

By 1908, however, the "Wobblies," as they were known, did come to share with the AFL an antistatist rejection of the path of political reform. But theirs was a radical voluntarism. Instead of peaceful relations with owners via collectively bargained contracts, IWW leaders like Big Bill Haywood advanced the goal of syndicalism, in which workers would directly and cooperatively control their places of work. The ultimate weapon of working-class power was the general strike.

In the short term, however, the IWW was not averse to everyday struggles over wages and working conditions. Without much organization, the group looked for opportunities to lead spontaneous revolts. Its greatest victory occurred in the Lawrence Strike of 1912, when it assumed the leadership of mostly unorganized textile workers who had gone out on strike to protest wage reductions. After two months, textile owners, unable to break the strike, relented and gave in to worker demands. Overnight, the IWW's membership jumped by over eighteen thousand among textile workers.[61] But the weakness of the strategy became apparent when the union was unable to protect these gains against employer tactics aimed at reversing them.

By 1915–1916, however, the union began to address its weaknesses. At its 1916 convention, the IWW recognized the need to move beyond shock troop tactics and propaganda to permanent organization. This would require tightened leadership and more dues paying members. With Haywood at the controls, membership finally surpassed the fifty-thousand mark that had been the high point in its first ten years.[62]

The Commission on Industrial Relations

The appearance of a radical wing in the labor movement helped to trigger a wave of industrial violence, especially the dynamiting of the Los Angeles Times building in 1910 by two union leaders. In response, Congress in 1912 established the Commission on Industrial Relations to examine the "general condition of labor." After 154 days of hearings conducted over the course of two years, during which 740 witnesses gave testimony, the Commission published its final report in 1915. It was remarkably strong in its conclusions, citing four major sources of labor unrest, none of which pointed a finger of blame at unions: 1) unjust distribution of wealth and income; 2) unemployment and denial of an opportunity to earn a living; 3) denial of justice in the creation, in the adjudication, and in the administration of law; and 4) denial of right and opportunity to form effective organizations.

The common denominator for all of these was the corporation, since "it is under this form that the great problems of industrial relations have developed." The commissioners reasoned that as the owners of large corporations became absentee stockholders, they had "no guiding interest in the permanent efficiency of the corporation. . . ." As investors, whose only concern was receiving the maximum return on their investments, this new class of owners was typically oblivious to the conditions of work in the corporations that they owned. Instead, boards of directors typically "insist that managers shall buy labor, as they buy material, in the cheapest market."[63]

In support of its conclusions, the Commission noted that even as the economy grew, the conditions of work for many remained harsh. It reported that roughly one-third of the families of wage earners in manufacturing and mining lived in abject poverty, and up to one-half lived in less than a "decent condition." Contributing to hardship was the lack of steady work, as the average worker was unemployed for 10 to 20 percent of the year—turnover rates in large firms frequently exceeded 100 percent. Work continued to be dangerous as well, with roughly 35,000 work fatalities per year and an additional 700,000 injuries that disabled a worker for four weeks or more. The report also detailed continued abuses in the employment of women and children.[64]

The Commission also investigated firms that had recently restructured their workplaces in accordance with scientific management, an increasingly popular management strategy, especially as promulgated by Frederick Winslow Taylor. This approach usually involved the use of "efficiency experts" to conduct time and motion studies so as to discover the "one best way" of performing work. Where applied, their studies generally produced a stultifying division of labor, in which individual jobs were deskilled; a loss of craft knowledge, which was transferred to management; and the tendency "to weaken the power of the individual worker as against the employer. . . ." Commissioners heard testimony in which an "almost unqualified opposition of labor to scientific management was manifested."[65] In separate Congressional investigations it was found that in a number of cases Taylorism (especially as symbolized by the stopwatch of time and motion studies) had replaced the tyranny of the foreman as the target of worker animus, and its introduction precipitated a number of strikes.[66]

Holding that the only hope for improving industrial relations was to extend the principle of democracy to industry, the Commission's Final Report contained a number of recommendations for new laws that would achieve this purpose, including the right to form associations to protect both individual and collective interests and the protection against the discharge of members of labor unions. Among its many other conclusions and recommendations, the report also held that collective bargaining was the best method for attaining just standards for wages, that the workday should not exceed eight hours, that women should receive the same pay as men for performing the same work, that a bureau of industrial safety should be created, and that the use of private security guards (typically employed as strikebreakers) by employers should be strictly regulated.[67]

Union leaders were understandably encouraged by the decidedly pro-union conclusions of the report. Indeed, they already had reason to be optimistic about the political prospects of the Commission's recommendations. First, after many years of campaigning for a "voice in the cabinet," the Department of Labor was created in 1913. Second, the Clayton Act of 1914 included a provision that was intended to curtail the use of court injunctions against unions. When Wilson signed the act into law, Samuel Gompers declared the act the "Magna Carta" of labor.[68] The optimism of labor leaders was reinforced by the trajectory of unionization during the 1910s. Having stagnated in the years immediately following the open-shop campaign, but with persistent low pay and alienating working conditions continuing to make unions attractive, and with intense competition between the AFL and IWW to organize new workers, unions were able to increase their numbers by nearly 50 percent between 1910 and 1917, from 2.1 million to 3 million. Of course, this still represented a scant 11 percent of the civilian non-farm labor force in 1917.[69] But as important as the unionization rate was the trend in that rate, which was up.

—

In sum, the large corporation remained a contested institution during the entire Progressive period. In page-turning exposés, muckrakers revealed pervasive corruption and unfair influence, sharpening the antimonopolist critique. Politicians and reformers continued to offer up both stronger economic and social regulations to contain their impact. The union movement showed an upward trajectory in membership at both the beginning and end of the period, grew a radical wing, and gained a voice in the cabinet.

Voluntary Responsibility (CSR)

As shown, large corporations pushed back on all of these fronts and, in retrospect, their resistance was quite successful. At the time, however, the leaders of these institutions no doubt felt under siege and worried that their sometimes heavy-handed tactics might engender further challenge. In an effort to demonstrate that neither regulations nor unions were needed, a critical mass of large employers were compelled to explore the high road of labor relations in the form of what came to be known at the time as "welfare work." Once again, U.S. Steel provides an illustrative case.

Welfare Work

When U.S. Steel was created in 1901, some of its constituent mills were unionized, while others were not. Executives of the new steel colossal had an important decision to make regarding labor relations. On the one hand, the company could allow unionism to expand to cover all of its workers. This would be consistent with the avowed commitment of the National Civic Federation and its members, who included the new company's chief executive, Elbert Gary, to create the conditions of labor peace. But given the bitter labor history of the steel industry, which featured the Homestead Strike several years earlier, this proved to be too great a step to take. On the other hand, the company could attempt to consolidate its new position of unprecedented power and quash unions altogether. But already wary of a political backlash to the merger itself, the company wanted to avoid instigating what would certainly be an ugly struggle.

Instead of the polar options, the company decided to steer the middle course of maintaining the status quo of having both unionized and nonunionized plants. This posed a dilemma for the Amalgamated Association of Iron, Steel, and Tin Workers. With no industry-wide trade agreement, the union was concerned that, over time, the company would move operations from its union to nonunion plants. Since the company refused to extend union contracts to all of its plants, the union initiated a strike. After several rounds of negotiations that involved the NCF acting as an intermediary, the strike failed. Further damage was done within the ranks of labor when Samuel Gompers and the leadership of the AFL refused to heed the call of the steelworkers for a general strike to force steel company concessions.[70]

In the aftermath of its victory, but still concerned that it was vulnerable, the company attempted to win over both the public and its workers with a stock purchase plan that favored its lower paid employees. More than 47,000 shares were sold in 1903 alone, and with the sale, the company's welfare program was born. Executives followed this move with an employee safety program in 1906 that placed the company in the forefront of efforts to improve industrial safety. By 1909, the company decided to rid itself of its remaining union workers by declaring that all plants would now be operated as "open shops." After the predictable strike of the remaining union workers failed, U.S. Steel continued to expand its welfare activities, which came to include improved sanitation, company recreational teams, in-house restaurants, children's playgrounds, and a visiting nurse service.[71]

U.S. Steel was part of a vanguard of employers that expanded welfare work at the beginning of the twentieth century. In many ways, this trend was also a byproduct of failed corporatism. When the National Association of Manufacturers initiated its open-shop campaign, the NCF realized that while its main mission was to mediate the class conflict between owners and unions, it now had to contend with an intra-class conflict as well. In order to counter the appeal of the NAM, the NCF needed a program with which it could reach out to antiunion employers. It turned to welfare work. Though the importance of welfare activities had been recognized at its inception, it was not until January 1904 that the Federation established its Welfare Department. Unlike the group's Trade Agreement Department, the Welfare Department excluded union leaders. Its charge was to educate the public as to the meaning and value of welfare work, and "to interest employers not engaged in welfare work by emphasizing their moral obligation to give consideration to the general welfare of their employees."[72]

The campaign against unions was thus Janus-faced. While the NAM wore the stern, traditional expression of intolerance, the NCF's welfare work program represented the positive profile of business. To fulfill this charge, the Welfare Department served as a clearinghouse of welfare work information. The new department held conferences for employers, sponsored lectures, and at its headquarters in New York, it set up a "practical working welfare exhibit."[73] The dissemination of welfare news was also facilitated by the publication of articles and pamphlets, and the quarterly journal, the *Review*.[74] To further encourage the exchange of ideas and innovations, and to nurture a common identity and network of connections, the Welfare Department recommended that participating employers establish the position of welfare secretary within their firms.

Over time, the Welfare Department took its mission on the road. In cooperation with local Chambers of Commerce, and with a directorship that included prominent intellectuals and reformers like Nicholas Murray Butler and Jane Addams, the Traveling Exhibit of Welfare Work visited over twenty cities in 1917. In order to participate and showcase their practices, employers paid hefty fees for rental space. The forty-four companies that signed up included General Electric, H. J. Heinz, and National Cash Register.[75]

Beyond appeals to the moral obligation of employers, advocates attempted to sell welfare work on the premise that it was good for business. And no doubt it was, as there was evidence that treating workers well represented the high road to greater profitability. The problem was that, even with its inherent inefficiencies, the low road of the low pay and harsh treatment had proven to yield higher profits as well; indeed, because it was easier to implement, it had become the default option. Merely enlightening employers to the benefits of welfare work was not enough to diffuse it. Instead, the threat of unions operated as the unstated motive that pushed some to the alternative high road.

This can be illustrated with Henry Ford's famous decision to pay his workers a premium wage of $5 day in 1914. It was certainly true that the combination of low pay and alienating working conditions stemming from assembly line production contributed to the tremendously inefficient labor turnover rate of 370 percent of Ford workers. But it is also true that these same conditions made Ford Motor Company one of the most profitable corporations in the country. It is probably no coincidence, then, that the rabidly antiunion Ford made his decision to pay his workers better shortly after the IWW had launched a major campaign to organize auto workers in Detroit.[76]

Of course, whether it was the Traveling Exhibit or the public announcements of programs like those of Ford, the intended audience was not restricted to potential employers or union members. The fact that the former was open to the public who could attend for free, and the latter was widely publicized reflected a growing number of efforts on the part of employers to advertise a more benevolent style of capitalism. These included the publication of pamphlets promoting welfare work efforts that were distributed to employees. The fact that these materials were also distributed to critics, social science journals, and politicians suggests that another audience was the public at large.

As before, an additional incentive for adopting welfare work was to preempt legislative efforts. With Progressive initiatives seeking to break the bonds of laissez faire restraints in order to pass social regulations, employer efforts to keep government at bay increased as well. Another of the merger movement's prominent progeny provides a good illustration. When it was created in 1902, International Harvester controlled 85 percent of the nation's grain-harvesting machinery. By 1907 it had no effective competition, a situation that stoked the resentment of farmers, who worried about the impact of this new monopoly; the same worries of monopoly precipitated an investigation by the US Bureau of Corporations. Writing to J. P. Morgan, George W. Perkins, the company's most influential director, observed with alarm that "We have been having one continuous battle all Spring with the various State Legislatures that have been attacking the Harvester Company right and left, and with the national Government that has threatened several times to bring the company before the Grand Jury in Chicago. . . ."[77] With the heat turned up, Perkins, also a prominent Republican fund-raiser, began to institute a comprehensive welfare program that included profit sharing, pensions, and "sick and accidental insurance." He was then able to convince his friend, Teddy Roosevelt, that instead of a monopoly, International Harvester more properly fell into his category of a "good trust."

International Harvester was not alone. As proposals were floated in various state legislatures to provide public pensions or health care, U.S. Steel made a well-publicized $5 million investment in the company's own pension and health programs. In other cases, companies attempted to show the superiority of voluntary programs by doing better than public programs. Just as states were passing minimum safety standards and protective legislation for women, NCR instituted "rejuvenating" callisthenic breaks, while Curtis Publishing Company created a well-appointed rest area. In both cases, the companies were not shy about sharing news of their new programs with the public.[78]

Increasingly, consumers also comprised an audience for companies' efforts to publicize their enlightened practices. As the American economy was increasingly built upon a mass-production, mass-consumption foundation, consumers began to organize around the issue of how certain workplace hazards, such as those associated with food production, posed a danger to the consuming public. Groups such as the National Consumers League sought to mobilize the purchasing power of consumers to promote cleaner and safer working conditions. Realizing there was a growing market segment of educated consumers, employers found a material incentive in advertising their socially responsible practices. But while consumerism might be enough to justify a larger advertising budget, there is not much evidence to suggest that it was enough, by itself, to inspire the investment in actual CSR practices. While attracting consumers was certainly a reinforcing motive, it was the incentive to avoid unions and government mandates that did the heavy lifting of putting employers on the path of CSR.[79]

The overall success of welfare plans during this period can be seen first in the growth in the membership of the NCF's Welfare Department. When it was established in 1904, roughly 100 members participated, but only 50 employers of importance included welfare programs in their establishments. By 1906 the department had 250 members, and by 1911 this figure had doubled to 500.[80] Welfare practices also spread beyond NCF member employers. A NCF survey conducted in 1914 found that over 2,500 employers reported having such practices.[81]

As welfare work spread, the Bureau of Labor Statistics (BLS) decided to conduct its own review, which, published in 1916, defined welfare work as "anything for the comfort and improvement, intellectual or social, of the employees, over and above wages paid, which is not a necessity of the industry nor required by law."[82] These practices can be grouped into three categories: paternalism and loyalty (clubs, education, training), direct incentives (e.g., profit sharing, stock ownership), and private welfare (e.g., pensions and medical care).

paternalism and loyalty: As corporations grew, so did the social distance between owner and worker, resulting in the loss of the personal ties that frequently bound the two when establishments were smaller. The employers in the CSR vanguard came to believe that the key to solving the labor problem was to nurture feelings of loyalty, team spirit, and goodwill, which would thus rebuild personal ties between employer and employee. These included company teams and leagues, company picnics and company clubhouses, where socializing could take place. The BLS survey revealed that 137 firms had clubhouses or clubrooms, of which 52 had gymnasiums and 41 had swimming pools; 152 firms had baseball fields, many of which sponsored company teams and leagues; 188 companies sponsored social gatherings, like dances or parties; and 140 had company "outings," like picnics.[83]

Many of the efforts aimed at instilling loyalty were further grounded in the paternalistic desire to mold the character of workers, many of whom were immigrants. These included worker-training programs, instruction in cooking and home decorating, on-site libraries, reading rooms, the benefit of music and theatre, and the sponsorship of lectures on both work and non-work-related topics. The most ambitious, and notorious, paternalistic intervention was the new wage system introduced by the Ford Motor Company in 1914. To be eligible for the "$5 a day" premium, workers had to pledge that they would comply with certain rules of conduct at work and at home. To ensure that the rules regarding thrift, cleanliness, and sobriety, among others, were being followed, the company dispersed several hundred investigators from its Sociology Department to interview workers and observe how they managed their households.[84] More generally, the BLS survey showed that 72 companies provided classroom instruction, 155 had either their own library or a branch of the local public library, and 94 provided lectures on various topics.[85]

direct incentives: In their drive to keep their plants union free, U.S. Steel refined the basic profit sharing idea by offering a stock-ownership plan, which, it was felt, would better place the capitalist and the worker on the same level. Board Chairman Elbert Gary believed that it was the actual ownership of stock that "makes the wage earner an actual partner . . . a real capitalist. . . ." Others who joined in the practice, like

Cyrus McCormick felt that stock ownership was a "very practical step toward removing any possible danger of Bolshevism," and the American Mining Congress Journal declared that the ownership of a company's stock by workers would act as "a prophylactic against government ownership." By the end of the Progressive period, growth was only moderate, with the number of companies with profit sharing, stock ownership, or both reaching 250. Of these, only 60 included a stock ownership plan.[86]

pensions: As the BLS suggested in a report on pensions, "Undoubtedly, one purpose was, if possible, to lessen the attractiveness of the labor unions and to make the men loyal to their employer rather than to one another or to any brotherhood" of railroad workers.[87] The use of pensions as a weapon in the war against unions became increasingly prevalent in manufacturing industries at the turn of the century. In 1901, the Carnegie Steel Company instituted a pension plan; Standard Oil followed in 1903.[88] Between 1900 and 1919 a total of 302 pension plans were initiated among US firms.[89] The BLS survey found that 75 of the 431 firms that it surveyed had pension plans, covering over 1.1 million workers.[90]

medical care: The most prominent approach to providing health care for workers was the "mutual-benefit association," in which corporations disbursed funds to their employees, who could then pay for medical services. This was usually a fixed sum that would cover only part of the cost of medical care. Early on, some employers extended such coverage selectively, sometimes excluding women, blacks, union members, or non-citizens. Eventually, however, most had no restrictions, and some—10 to 15 percent—made membership compulsory. Though workmen's compensation laws were passed in most states after 1911, the growth of employer-provided health care did not slow, in part because such laws only covered accidents. By 1916, the US Commissioner of Labor reported 425 funds in existence, covering 749,000 workers. After 1911, however, group insurance policies began to supplant the mutual-benefit association. Given the hazardous conditions of manufacturing and mining, many companies also had on-site doctors (45 percent) or nurses (50 percent).[91]

As this brief survey of practices reveals, CSR, though covering a broad array of practices, covered only a small minority of workers. William H. Tolman estimated that of the eighteen million wageworkers in the United States in 1908, about 1.5 million worked for establishments that had some form of welfare program.[92] Furthermore, while hundreds of firms experimented with some form of welfare work, fewer adopted extensive programs. In his review of the surveys of welfare firms conducted by both government and promoters of welfare work, Daniel Nelson identified only forty firms that had comprehensive welfare plans in place by 1915. These included General Electric, U.S. Steel, International Harvester, National Cash Register, Proctor and Gamble, H. J. Heinz, Goodyear Tire, and Dan River Mills.[93]

Businesses adopting welfare programs shared a number of common features. In her study of welfare work during the Progressive Era, *The Business of Benevolence*, Andrea Tone shows that most were large corporations, with over 80 percent having more than one thousand employees. Not only were large firms more likely to be able to afford welfare plans, they were more likely to exhibit the impersonal, exploitative labor relations that put them at greater risk of unionization. Large firms were also much more likely than their smaller counterparts to suffer the scorn of the public. Tone also shows that welfare firms were more likely to have a skilled labor force and to be located in cities. As both skill and the availability of multiple employers would give workers some greater leverage and mobility, employers in such firms would have been more likely to experiment with the positive incentives comprising welfare plans in order to attract and keep good employees. Finally, Tone shows that few welfare firms were located in the South. As Southern states experienced fewer legislative initiatives to regulate business and the workplace, employers there would have had a weaker need to keep the government at bay.[94]

Ultimately, though affecting only a small minority of workers, welfare work had a demonstration effect that magnified its impact. In other words, the trend of welfare work was large enough to impress some of the era's leading reformers, and just enough to smooth some of the rough edges of the critique of the large corporation. It was also just enough to keep some workers out of unions, and just enough to quiet some legislative demands for mandates.

—

In short, the trend of welfare work seemed large enough to hold out the promise that there was now a vanguard of employers that would lead the rest to the higher ground of corporate social responsibility at the workplace. The same could be said of corporations engaged in good works in their communities.

Corporate Philanthropy

Without a government infrastructure that could cope with mounting social problems, Chicago became one of the first cities to produce a leadership group within the business community to work for civic betterment. In 1893, with civic pride running high as a result of the Columbian Exposition that took place in the city, but worried by the fallout of the Panic of 1893, business luminaries including Cyrus McCormick, Marshall Field, and Franklin MacVeagh joined with leaders in the city's civic and reform communities to form the Chicago Civic Federation (CCF).[95] Its mission was "to focus the new ideals of civic cooperation and social efficiency on the task of renovating society."[96] With former journalist and teacher Ralph Easley as its secretary and guiding spirit, the CCF mobilized a relief effort for Chicago's unemployed, and it organized and financed the Bureau of Associated Charities, which raised and distributed aid to the poor in Chicago for years to come. The CCF also encouraged business leaders to engage in philanthropic activities of civic improvement, beautification, and cultural enrichment.

Chicago was not alone, as businessmen in other cities mobilized in campaigns for civic improvement. For example, the Cleveland Chamber of Commerce became involved in these efforts after 1900 and helped form the Committee on Benevolent Association, which was set up to examine, and then endorse, appropriate charities. Soon afterward, committees were formed to investigate housing conditions and education in the city. After 1905, service clubs such as Rotary and Kiwanis, whose purpose was to enlist business aid for hospitals and other social purposes, began to spread among American cities.[97]

The turn of the century also witnessed the growth of philanthropic foundations established by some of the leading business owners of the era. These included the Carnegie Corporation of New York, the Carnegie Foundation for the Advancement of Teaching, the Rockefeller Foundation, the Rockefeller Institute for Medical Research, the Milbank Memorial Fund, and the Russell Sage Foundation. As Bremner argues in his history of American philanthropy, what was noteworthy about these foundations was not necessarily the size of their assets but the boldness of their vision. Instead of a narrowly defined purpose, these funds were frequently dedicated to research that would advance the knowledge that was needed to improve human welfare.[98]

Though the motives behind the establishment of these foundations were no doubt complex, one certainly stemmed from the need to counteract the many challenges to both corporations and their found-ers. After all, these early foundations arose in the era of journalistic muckraking and trust busting, when the need to curry public favor was running particularly high. Standard Oil is a case in point. By the early years of the twentieth century, and after years of negative journalistic attention, Standard Oil had a huge public image problem. Under con-stant threat of being dissolved as an illegal monopoly, Rockefeller and his top executives needed to show the nation that the company stood for more than the ruthless suppression of competition and corrup-tion of public officials. A fortuitous opportunity arose with the 1906 earthquake in San Francisco. The company quickly provided the city generously with fuel, money, and other resources. And not only did the company turn over tankers from its fleet to help shelter the city's refugees, it also established "Camp Rockefeller," a thirty-acre relief camp for the city's homeless.[99]

It was also in the spring of 1906 that the company hired Joseph I. C. Clarke to run a publicity bureau in which he led the company to abandon its traditional aversion to publicity and opened his office to reporters, so as to give the company's response to stories in which it was involved. It was Clarke who also sought to gain much greater publicity for all of Rockefeller's philanthropic pursuits. Other corporations fol-lowed suit and began to open their own publicity staffs and offices. Thus was born the field of public relations, as companies increasingly sought to advertise both their philanthropic and welfare plan activities.[100]

Summary

When the new century opened, the nation was in the midst of its first merger wave, which, when it subsided, left the large corporation in the dominant position in the American economy. Industries that had once featured dozens of competitors were being reshaped as oligopolies as a result. Owners and investors in search of governance structures to contain competition had wholly overwhelmed a nascent regime of antitrust that had been set up a decade earlier to contain the further spread of large corporations.

But greater size did not translate into greater acceptance. The large corporation remained a fervently contested institution. Part of this was the result of the country transforming at breakneck speed into an industrialized dynamo dominated by large corporations, which were leaving a huge footprint for all to see. Consequently, these newly cre-ated giants became the favorite targets of a new breed of muckraking journalists, whose investigative reports frequently featured lurid tales of corruption in the conduct of business and in the effort to exert political influence. These muckrakers helped to fuel the Progressive Movement that cut across party lines and that sought to both cure social ills and scour both business and politics of corruption.

As the strongest period of reform to date, the Progressive Era produced lasting changes to the nation's politics. The same, however, cannot be said of the contest over the large corporation. While it certainly appeared as though big business would be more strongly tethered, by the end of the period the strongest constraints binding corporations to responsible practices remained the weak ties of self-regulation, i.e., CSR.

Of course, things may have been different had Americans chosen differently at the period's main critical juncture. The presidential election of 1912 provided the nation with a clear choice between the two poles of Progressive options for dealing with large corporations, each derived from the antimonopolist tradition. The Democratic Party platform of Woodrow Wilson offered to bolster antitrust in an effort to restore the reign of competition among smaller firms. The Progressive Party platform of Theodore Roosevelt called for a robust set of social regulations that would be enforced by the federal government. But because Roosevelt's was a third-party candidacy, he could do no better than to split the Republican vote. At this critical juncture, then, America chose to remain on the antitrust path, which was where most reform energy was then spent.

However, just as economic regulations failed to slow the growth of large corporations in the 1890s, they continued to fail through the 1910s. As a result, the political economy continued to tilt in the direction of the business community, which then used enhanced economic power to continue to shape the dimensions of America's regulatory structure for large corporations. In an era where cries for all varieties of reform reverberated, including calls for an eight-hour day, unemployment insurance, and national health care, large corporations were largely able to stave off substantial social regulations and welfare programs at the federal level. With unions showing staying power, battles against them became more organized, and conservative owners were able to defeat the efforts of their more liberal brethren to construct a broad-based corporatist accord that might legitimize unions and strengthen negotiated responsibility.

Now, however, it was not enough to just say no. With demands for reform so widespread, a more organized vanguard of CSR leaders convinced a growing number of employers that they needed to demonstrate that large corporations could take care of the problems on their own. So even though CSR remained a minority movement, it drew outsized attention because it seemed so promising. It appeared as if this vanguard of owners might lead corporations to a new, more enlightened path to making money. As a result, CSR as a form of positive resistance contributed to the success corporations had in fending off both government and unions. The relationships among government regulations, unions, and CSR—whereby the threats of the former yielded growth in the latter—became stronger. As a result, the relative durability of the individual pillars that comprised America's regulatory structure remained: weak mandated responsibility, weak negotiated responsibility, and CSR growing in strength.

Notes

1. Francis G. Walett, *Economic History of the United States* (New York: Barnes and Noble, Inc., 1954), 156; Anthony Patrick O'Brien, "Factory Size, Economies of Scale, and the Great Merger Wave of 1898–1902," *Journal of Economic History*, Vol. 48, No. 3 (1988).

2. Matthew Josephson, *The Robber Barons* (San Diego: A Harvest Book, Harcourt, Inc., 1934), 420–426.

3. H. W. Brands, *The Reckless Decade: America in the 1890s* (Chicago: University of Chicago Press, 1995), 85–89; Gabriel Kolko, *The Triumph of Conservatism: A Reinterpretation of American History, 1900–1916* (Chicago: Quadrangle Books, 1963), 33.

4. C. Joseph Pusateri, *Big Business in America: Attack and Defense* (Itasca, Illinois: F. E. Peacock Publishers, Inc., 1975), 224.

5. James Weinstein, *The Corporate Ideal in the Liberal State: 1900–1918* (Boston: Beacon Press, 1968), 63; Stuart Bruchey, *The Wealth of the Nation: An Economic History of the United States* (New York: Harper and Row, Publishers, 1988), 126–130.

6. Naomi R. Lamoreaux, *The Great Merger Movement in American Business, 1895–1904* (Cambridge: Cambridge University Press, 1985).

7. Ibid., 1.

8. Bruchey, *The Wealth of the Nation*, 128.

9. J. Fred Weston, *The Role of Mergers in the Growth of Large Firms* (Berkeley, California: University of California Press, 1953), 32.

10. Michael Kazin, *A Godly Hero: The Life of William Jennings Bryan* (New York: Anchor Books, 2006), 66–67.

11. Harold U. Faulkner, *The Decline of Laissez Faire, 1897–1917* (New York: Harper and Row, Publishers, 1951), 370–371; Upton Sinclair, *The Jungle* (New York: Penguin Classics, 2006—originally published in 1906).

12. John Mack Faragher, et al., *Out of Many: A History of the American People, Volume Two*, 2nd ed. (Upper Saddle River, New Jersey: Prentice Hall, 1997), 654–655; Charles Noble, *Welfare as We Knew It: A Political History of the American Welfare State* (New York: Oxford University Press, 1997), 38–39.

13. Louis D. Brandeis, *Other People's Money and How the Bankers Use It*, ed. Richard M. Abrams (New York: Harper Torchbooks, 1967—originally published in 1914).

14. Commission on Industrial Relations, *Final Report of the Commission on Industrial Relations* (Washington, DC: Barnard & Miller Print, 1915), 82–83.

15. James A. Morone, *The Democratic Wish: Popular Participation and the Limits of American Government* (New York: Basic Books, 1990), chapter 3; Marver H. Bernstein, *Regulating Business by Independent Commission* (Princeton, New Jersey, Princeton University Press, 1955), 36.

16. Herber Croly, *The Promise of American Life* (Indianapolis: Bobbs-Merrill, Company, Inc., 1965—originally published in 1909).

17. This worry was expressed satirically in 1902 in W. J. Ghent's *Our Benevolent Feudalism*, where he envisioned corporate power creating a system of lords and servants. (New York: The Macmillan Company, 1902).

18. Kolko, *The Triumph of Conservatism*, 66.

19. Robert H. Wiebe, *Businessmen and Reform: A Study of the Progressive Movement* (Cambridge, Massachusetts: Harvard University Press, 1962), 46–47.

20. Faulkner, *The Decline of Laissez Faire*, 178, 185.

21. Kolko, *The Triumph of Conservatism*, 167.

22. Minor/Third Party Platforms, "Progressive Party Platform of 1912," November 5, 1912, online by Gerhard Peters and John T. Woolley, The American Presidency Project, http://www.presidency.ucsb.edu/ws/?pid=29617.

23. Democratic Party Platforms, "Democratic Party Platform of 1912," June 25, 1912, online by Gerhard Peters and John T. Woolley, The American Presidency Project. http://www.presidency.ucsb.edu/ws/?pid=29590.

24. It should be noted that the platform of the Socialist Party, which took 6 percent of the vote, supported collective ownership of many types of business: railroads, telephone, telegraphs, all large scale industries, mines, forests, water power, land, and the banking system.

25. Kolko, *The Triumph of Conservatism*, 220.

26. Morone, *The Democratic Wish*, 117.

27. Faulkner, *The Decline of Laissez Faire*, 155.

28. Bernstein, *Regulating Business by Independent Commission*, 36–45.

29. Alfred D. Chandler, Jr., *Scale and Scope: The Dynamics of Industrial Capitalism* (Cambridge, Massachusetts: The Belknap Press of Harvard University Press, 1990), 17.

30. Christine B. Harrington and Lief H. Carter, *Administrative Law and Politics: Cases and Comments* (Washington, DC: CQ Press, 2009), 61.

31. Industrial Commission, *Final Report of the Industrial Commission*, 55–56.

32. Wiebe, *Businessmen and Reform*, 170–171.

33. Jill Quadagno, *One Nation Uninsured: Why the U.S. Has No National Health Insurance* (New York: Oxford University Press, 2005, 18–21; Jacob S. Hacker, *The Divided Welfare State* (Cambridge, England: Cambridge University Press, 2002), 195.

34. Theda Skocpol, *Protecting Soldiers and Mothers: The Political Origins of Social Policy in the United States* (Cambridge, Massachusetts: The Belknap Press of Harvard University Press, 1992), chapter 4.

35. Edward D Berkowitz and Kim McQuaid, *Creating the Welfare State: the Political Economy of the 20th Century Reform*, rev. ed. (Lawrence, Kansas: University Press of Kansas, 1992), 40–41.

36. Jill Quadagno, *The Transformation of Old Age Security: Class and Politics in the American Welfare State* (Chicago: The University of Chicago Press, 1988), 100–101.

37. Skocpol, *Protecting Soldiers and Mothers*, 9.

38. Kolko, *The Triumph of Conservatism*; Morton Keller, *Regulating a New Economy: Public Policy and Economic Change in America, 1900–1933* (Cambridge, Massachusetts: Harvard University Press, 1990) 23–24.

39. David Montgomery, *The Fall of the House of Labor: The Workplace, the State, and American Labor Activism, 1865–1925* (Cambridge, England: Cambridge University Press, 1987), 259–269.

40. John R. Commons et al., *History of Labour in the United States, Volume II* (New York: The Macmillan Company, 1926), 501; Selig Perlman and Philip Taft, *History of Labor in the United States, 1896–1932, Volume IV* (New York: the Macmillan Company, 1935), 13.

41. David Montgomery, "Industrial Democracy or Democracy in Industry?: The Theory and Practice of the Labor Movement," in *Industrial Democracy in America: The Ambiguous Promise*, eds. Nelson Lichtenstein and Howell John Harris (Cambridge, England: Cambridge University Press, 1993), 28; Perlman and Philip Taft, *History of Labor in the United States, Volume IV*, 10.

42. Industrial Commission, *Final Report of the Industrial Commission*, 155

43. Perlman and Taft, *History of Labor in the United States, Volume IV*, 83.

44. Weinstein, *The Corporate Ideal in the Liberal State*, 8, 14.

45. Montgomery, *The Fall of the House of Labor*, 262.

46. National Civic Federation, *Industrial Conciliation: Report of the Proceedings of the Conference* (New York: G. P. Putnam's Sons, 1902), 269–271.

47. Perlman and Taft, *History of Labor in the United States, Vol. IV*, 38–47.

48. Weinstein, *The Corporate Ideal in the Liberal State*, 14–15; Marguerite Green, *The National Civic Federation and the American Labor Movement 1900–1925* (Westport, Connecticut: Greenwood Press Publishers, 1973—originally published in 1956), chapter 3.

49. Harry A. Millis and Royal E. Montgomery, *Organized Labor*, (New York: McGraw-Hill Book Company, Inc., 1945), 96; Robert Franklin Hoxie, *Trade Unionism in the United States* (New York: D. Appleton and Company, 1923), 191–206; Louis Galambos, *Competition & Cooperation: The Emergence of a National Trade Association* (Baltimore: The Johns Hopkins Press, 1966), 52–54.

50. Melvyn Dubofsky and Foster Rhea Dulles, *Labor in America: A History*, 7th ed. (Wheeling, Illinois: Harlan Davidson, Inc., 2004), 180–181; David Brody, *Workers in Industrial America: Essays on the 20th Century Struggle* (New York: Oxford University Press, 1979), 25.

51. United States Department of Commerce, Bureau of the Census, *Historical Statistics of the United States, Part 1, Colonial Times to 1970* (Washington, DC: US Government Printing Office, 1975), 177.

52. Green, *The National Civic Federation*, 69.

53. Robert H. Salisbury, *Interests and Institutions: Substance and Structure in American Politics* (Pittsburgh: University of Pittsburgh Press, 1992), 271.

54. National Civic Federation, *Industrial Conciliation*, 146.

55. Montgomery, *The Fall of the House of Labor*, 265.
56. Salisbury, *Interests and Institutions*, 274.
57. Foster Rhea Dulles and Melvyn Dubofsky, *Labor in America: A History*, 5th ed. (Arlington Heights, Illinois: Harlan Davidson, Inc., 1993), 153.
58. W. Jett Lauck and Edgar Sydenstricker, *Conditions of Labor in American Industries: A Summarization of the Results of Recent Investigations* (New York: Funk and Wagnalls Company, 1917), 180, 183; Harry A. Millis and Royal E. Montgomery, *Labor's Progress and Some Basic Labor Problems* (New York: McGraw-Hill Book Company, Inc., 1938), 213.
59. Dubofsky and Dulles, *Labor in America*, 192–194.
60. Ibid., chapter 12; Lauck and Sydenstricker, *Conditions of Labor in American Industries*, 1–2; Brody, *Workers in Industrial America*, 35–39.
61. Dubofsky and Dulles, *Labor in America*, 205.
62. Ibid., 201–205; Brody, *Workers in Industrial America*, 38.
63. Commission on Industrial Relations, *Final Report of the Commission on Industrial Relations*, 23, 16–17, 20.
64. Ibid., 10, 95.
65. Ibid., 221, 209.
66. Montgomery, *The Fall of the House of Labor*, chapter 5; Robert Kanigel, *The One Best Way: Frederick Winslow Taylor and the Enigma of Efficiency* (New York: Viking, 1997), 459–484.
67. Commission on Industrial Relations, *Final Report of the Commission on Industrial Relations*, 1, 90–102.
68. Dubofsky and Dulles, *Labor in America*, 190.
69. United States Department of Commerce, Bureau of the Census, *Historical Statistics of the United States, Part 1*, 126.
70. Perlman and Taft, *History of Labor in the United States, Volume IV*, chapter 9.
71. Ibid., chapter 14; Lauck and Sydenstricker, *Conditions of Labor in American Industries*, 230.
72. Green, *The National Civic Federation*, 268.
73. Ibid., 269
74. Andrea Tone, *The Business of Benevolence: Industrial Paternalism in Progressive America* (Ithaca, New York: Cornell University Press, 1997), 47.
75. Ibid., 100.
76. Stephen Meyer, III, *The Five Dollar Day: Labor Management and Social Control in the Ford Motor Company 1908–1921* (Albany, New York: State University of New York Press, 1981), 83, 91–93.
77. Robert Ozanne, *A Century of Labor-Management Relations at McCormick and International Harvester* (Madison, Wisconsin: The University of Wisconsin Press, 1967), 72.
78. Tone, *The Business of Benevolence*, 33.
79. Ibid., chapter 3.
80. Daniel Nelson, *Managers & Workers: Origins of the Twentieth-Century Factory System in the United States 1880–1920*, 2nd ed. (Madison, Wisconsin: University of Wisconsin Press, 1995), 108.
81. Weinstein, *The Corporate Ideal in the Liberal State*, 19.
82. United States Department of Labor, Bureau of Labor Statistics, *Welfare Work for Employees in Industrial Establishments in the United States, Bulletin No. 250* (Washington, DC, Government Printing Office, 1919), 8.

83. Ibid., chapters 5–6.

84. Meyer, *The Five Dollar Day*, chapter 5.

85. United States Department of Labor, Bureau of Labor Statistics, *Welfare Work*, 84, 94, 96.

86. Stuart D. Brandes, *American Welfare Capitalism, 1880–1940* (Chicago: University of Chicago Press, 1970), 86, 87, 83.

87. Jill Quadagno, *The Transformation of Old Age Security*, 81.

88. Don D. Lescohier and Elizabeth Brandeis, *History of Labor in the United States, 1896–1932: Working Conditions, Labor Legislation* (New York: The Macmillan Company, 1935), 388.

89. Quadagno, *The Transformation of Old Age Security*, 81.

90. United States Department of Labor, Bureau of Labor Statistics, *Welfare Work*, 107.

91. Brandes, *American Welfare Capitalism*, chapter 10; Lescohier and Brandeis, *History of Labor in the United States*, 364.

92. William H. Tolman, *Social Engineering: A Record of Things Done by American Industrialists Employing Upwards of One and One-Half Million of People* (New York: McGraw-Hill Book Company, 1909), 355.

93. Nelson, *Managers & Workers*, 113.

94. Tone, *The Business of Benevolence*, 52–61.

95. Morrell Heald, *The Social Responsibilities of Business: Company and Community, 1900–1960* (Cleveland: The Press of Case Western Reserve University, 1970), 21–22.

96. Christopher Cyphers, *The National Civic Federation and the Making of a New Liberalism, 1900–1915* (Westport, Connecticut: Greenwood Publishing Group, 2002), 20.

97. Heald, *The Social Responsibilities of Business*, 25–26.

98. Robert H. Bremner, *American Philanthropy*, 2nd ed. (Chicago: University of Chicago Press, 1968), 110–111.

99. Heald, *The Social Responsibilities of Business*, 44.

100. Alan R. Raucher, *Public Relations and Business, 1900–1929* (Baltimore: Johns Hopkins Press, 1968), 22–23; Tone, *The Business of Benevolence*, chapter 3.

4

The 1920s: Cooperation is Key

At the beginning of 1917, reform was still in the air. Progressive reformers were pushing hard at the state level to pass social regulations and welfare policies, and the hope existed that such efforts might eventually congeal at the federal level. With the recently passed Clayton Act and the newly constituted Federal Trade Commission, the government also seemed poised to assume a greater role as a countervailing power to large corporations. Furthermore, with the AFL and IWW competing to organize more workers, unions seemed ready to break through the threshold of low unionization. Should these efforts succeed, the momentum of growing CSR might be slowed if stronger government and unions curtailed the discretion of owners to choose whether or not to act in a socially responsible manner. But the nation's attention was about to become focused exclusively upon foreign affairs, as the country was about to enter the First World War.

Mandated Responsibility

War and the Political Economy of the United States

Though three years had lapsed between the outbreak of World War I and America's decision to join the conflict in April 1917, America was ill prepared for the large-scale mobilization of manpower and materiel that would be required. With little administrative capacity to tap, Congress had authorized the creation of the Council of National Defense in 1916 to devise plans for placing the economy on a war footing. An advisory commission performed the council's main work, and was largely composed of private industry executives like Daniel Willard of the B&O Railroad and Julius Rosenwald of Sears Roebuck. But as late as six weeks before America's entrance, the army still did not have a plan for organizing or equipping the large force that it would need to fight.[1]

Noting its failure, as well as the failure of other advisory commissions, the Council established the War Industries Board (WIB) in July of 1917 to coordinate government purchases. Its first chairman was broken by the strain, and his successor resigned because the position lacked real power to act. In the spring of 1918, however, President Wilson appointed Wall Street speculator Bernard Baruch as chairman and issued an executive mandate giving the Board real authority to coordinate the war effort. The WIB was now empowered to set production and distribution priorities, convert industries to new uses, coordinate government purchases and award no-bid contracts, build new plants, and fix prices for raw materials. Much of the work of the Board was achieved via meetings with corporation boards, where members were persuaded to cooperate. Since the price structure of a WIB contract usually guaranteed a healthy profit margin, most willingly complied. Of course, some executives railed against what they considered the government's abuse of power, and for them cooperation depended upon coercion. When Elbert Gary of U.S. Steel, along with other steel executives, refused to go along with WIB directive, Baruch issued an ultimatum: cooperate or their steel plants would be taken over by the government.[2]

While the WIB was the most powerful of the lot, other agencies were created for the war effort as well, including the Food Administration, Fuel Administration, and Emergency Fleet Corporation. Like the WIB, many staff positions were filled by "businesscrats"—personnel temporarily recruited from the business community.[3] Since America had failed to develop an insulated, professional corps of public administrators and civil servants, this reliance upon private-sector expertise reinforced the use of the revolving door between public and private spheres. But, in short order, this instant bureaucracy mobilized the US economy for war. By mid-1918 the War Department had entered into over thirty thousand contracts with builders and producers, and war expenditures represented 25 percent of the nation's GNP.[4]

Just as this nascent command economy was humming, the war ended with the armistice of November 11, 1918. In less than two weeks, President Wilson ordered the WIB and the other agencies dismantled. The business executives on loan to the government left their Washington offices and returned to their peacetime jobs. Consistent with his "new freedom" program of restoring competitive markets, Wilson wanted to reestablish the prewar status quo as quickly as possible. Fearful of permanent governmental bureaucracy, businessmen were in strong agreement.

Ideological and Political Challenges: War and the End of Dissent

While both government and business sought a restoration of prewar arrangements, a return to normalcy was not in the cards. The war had shaken the status quo, changed people's expectations, and helped to bring a number of underlying tensions to the surface. As a result, 1919 was a turbulent year. The migration of Southern blacks to Northern cities, and the ensuing competition that it triggered, led to more than two dozen race riots during the summer, including one in Chicago in which thirty-eight people were killed. Changes in gender relations culminated in the passage of the Nineteenth Amendment, which gave women the right to vote. The long-fought moral crusade against alcohol finally reached fruition with the ratification of the Eighteenth Amendment, which ushered in the era of Prohibition. The heightened aspirations of union members produced a series of labor strikes across the nation that put upwards of four million men and women on the picket line—a topic for later in the chapter.

Events from afar also inspired hopes for change at home. Emboldened by the success of the Russian Revolution of 1917, the left wing of the Socialist Party (SP) believed that the time was ripe for a revolutionary insurrection in the United States. Stymied in their efforts to capture the party, they formed their own party, the Communist Party USA (CPUSA); another faction, also thwarted in their efforts to control the SP, was thrown out and formed the Communist Labor Party. Born of division, factional strife continued to plague both Communists and socialists for much of the 1920s. But even when they were not caught up in internecine combat, American Communists largely abandoned efforts to reform or regulate corporations. Instead, regardless of faction, they adopted the orthodox Marxism of their Soviet counterpart that held that economic crises would soon bring about the collapse of capitalism. Consequently, the CPUSA shunned calls for immediate reforms, as well as participation in reform movements, since the practice of democracy within capitalism was considered a sham. Instead of involvement in the political arena, the party sought to both radicalize American workers and assume control of American unions through a "boring from within" strategy.[5]

But if such positions largely consigned Communists to irrelevance in the long run, their sheer radicalism contributed to a climate of fear among elites, both business and government, who felt that the entire system of capitalism was under siege. This fear was reinforced by a series of anarchist attacks. In April 1919, the New York City Post

Office discovered a package containing a bomb that was addressed to J. P. Morgan; it was just one of thirty such bombs that were sent to prominent businessmen. On June 2, bombs exploded in seven cities, including one that tore off the front of the house of Attorney General A. Mitchell Palmer. In turn, Palmer concluded that Communists planned to overthrow the American government, since they spoke of revolution and included a large contingent of immigrants from societies touched by the Russian Revolution. Beginning in November, and possibly to enhance his presidential ambitions, Palmer authorized the Justice Department to conduct raids of union offices and the headquarters of Communist and socialist organizations. In the end, over ten thousand individuals were arrested without warrants, and many were deported. While controversial, the patriotic fervor created by the war, together with a legal crackdown on dissent in the form of the Espionage and Sedition Acts, created an environment where many viewed such actions as necessary. As a result, not only did the Palmer Raids help to drive the CPUSA and CLP miles underground for years to come, the subsequent Red Scare had a more general chilling effect upon challenges to the economic system and corporate America.[6]

—

It is hard to say what direction the country would have headed at this critical juncture had the war lasted longer than it did. It will never be known whether, with time, a professional corps of government administrators would have been nurtured out of necessity, or whether government intervention in the economy would have been legitimized, thus rebalancing the nation's political economy. It is also unclear whether a prolonged period between the Russian Revolution and end of the war would have averted a Red Scare and kept the spirit of Progressivism alive to the point where it finally produced a stronger regulatory structure for large corporations. What is clear is that in the aftermath of America's short war, and in the reaction to the domestic turbulence that followed, the political pendulum swung to the right as the nation sought some semblance of stability. The Progressive Era was effectively over, putting the previous generation's efforts to control corporations in jeopardy.

Economic Regulations: The Associative State

Even though the new government agencies built for war were quickly dismantled, there were some in government who thought that the cooperation exhibited during the war between businesses, and between business and government, set an example that should be explored. One such individual was Herbert Hoover, the director of the Food Administration during the war. Hoover believed that the largely voluntary cooperation of the war effort had yielded many benefits for the economy, including the containment of waste and the standardization of production methods. Most importantly, war had brought a temporary end to volatile competition. This perspective was only strengthened during the postwar depression of 1921, which served as a reminder of the destructive possibilities inherent in the economy.

With the election of 1920, Republicans regained control of the White House. In the new Harding administration, Herbert Hoover ascended to the post of secretary of commerce in 1921, a position he held until 1928. He brought to the Executive Branch of government the same diagnosis of economic trouble long promulgated by leaders of large corporations: too much competition had ruinous results. Consequently, the government's chief tool for combating large corporations for thirty years, i.e., the restoration of competition via antitrust enforcement, would have to be abandoned. In its place, he sought to create an "associative state" where economic cooperation would thrive.

Secretary Hoover's tool for achieving greater inter-firm cooperation was the trade association, which he felt could help all firms in any given industry. Collectively, these associations could operate to rationalize the economy as a whole. Their functions, among others, would be to collect and share statistics, standardize accounting practices, develop programs of research and development, and promote an industry's products through advertising. Instead of tight government regulations and bureaucratic control, trade associations would conduct internal self-policing to root out bad practices. Instead of government mandates, voluntary cooperation and enlightened self-interest would serve as the governing principles.[7]

Hoover's vision fit neatly within the political culture parameters of small government and voluntarism. The actual role of government in this plan would be to encourage and facilitate the formation of trade associations through what has been labeled "adhocracy," while broadly monitoring their activities. In essence, government's role was to create a governance structure for private industry in which government-sanctioned cooperation would function to contain competition. By 1926, there were more than one thousand associations, including the American Institute of Baking, the Portland Cement Association, and the National Association of Baby Vehicle Manufacturers.[8]

The associative state can also be seen as yet another attempt to erect a corporatist regime in the United States. Unlike the effort of the National Civic Federation of the previous era, where business took the lead, government initiated this one. Also in contrast to the NCF plan, the role of unions was never articulated, though Hoover was not hostile to this type of association. Like this earlier effort, the associative state was a weak, soft corporatism of voluntary compliance without an enforcement mechanism. The level of effectiveness varied greatly by industry and was generally contingent upon the strong economy of the 1920s. The effort to create an associative state did, however, have an impact upon economic regulations.

antitrust: Trade associations raised the specter of the sort of price-fixing undertaken by cartels and trusts at the end of the nineteenth century. With this image in mind when he entered office in 1921, Attorney General Harry Dougherty initiated a program to aggressively prosecute any associational activity that even hinted at price-fixing. But while Hoover agreed that such flagrant activity should not be tolerated, he knew that if his plans for an associative state were to proceed, it would require an environment of relaxed antitrust enforcement. Consequently, through a combination of energetic advocacy and lobbying, Hoover got Dougherty to back off. Over the course of the next eight years, though many trade associations skated close to edge of the law, and some no doubt broke it in their efforts to stabilize prices and markets, the antitrust efforts of the Justice Department were anemic for the rest of the decade. With a small budget and only twenty-five lawyers, the Antitrust Division focused on easy targets, which were typically price-fixing arrangements among smaller firms in industries that were not heavily concentrated to begin with, such as lumber, apparel, and furniture. It initiated few cases against large corporations located in oligopolistic industries. Of the hundreds of mergers that occurred during America's second merger wave of the 1920s, the government challenged only sixty, and only one was blocked.[9]

Part of this reluctance to prosecute was also shaped by recent Supreme Court decisions. In 1920 the Court finally delivered a decision in the U.S. Steel case that was begun in 1911. Writing for the majority, Justice McKenna wrote that, even though U.S. Steel was huge and the result of the combination of scores of formerly independent companies, "The law does not make size . . . or the existence of unexerted power an offense." In other words, mere size and even near monopolistic power were not necessarily problems, as long as these characteristics were not used in a predatory or illegal fashion. The presumption was that corporations achieved their size and industry position through the "normal methods of industrial development."[10]

regulatory agencies: If the antitrust track of economic regulation of business was weakened in the 1920s, so was the track of regulatory commissions. As shown in the last chapter, the Federal Trade Commission was established in 1914 to investigate and if necessary "issue an order requiring persons using unfair methods of competition to cease and desist."[11] During the war, the FTC actually saw its mission and budget greatly expanded, as it was asked to conduct special investigations of the costs of production to help in the regulation of prices. But, like the rest of the war bureaucracy, both mission and budget were quickly restored to their prewar levels as soon as the war was over. With a budget of only a little over $1 million by 1929, the Commission was not up to the task of fulfilling its mission.[12] More importantly, as the decade of the 1920s progressed, a major flaw with the FTC became increasingly apparent. While it possessed wide powers to investigate and issue decrees, the Commission's effective exercise of these powers depended upon the cooperation of the courts. This it did not receive. In 1920, the Supreme Court held that "it is for the courts, not the commission, ultimately to determine as a matter of law what they include."[13]

But even without the court's ruling, the business-friendly leanings of the incoming Harding administration would have demanded that the FTC drop any pretension of being an "independent" regulatory commission. In 1925, Harding's successor as president, Calvin Coolidge, appointed William E. Humphrey as the Commission's new chairman. A former lobbyist for the lumber industry, Humphrey reflected the belief of many in the business community when he said that the Commission had been "an instrument of oppression and disturbance and injury." Its new role would be to assist business.[14] Consistent with the principles of the "associative state," the dominant activity of the FTC came to be its sponsorship of "trade-practice conferences," in which executives from a single industry would attempt to standardize rules of conduct for their constituent businesses.

The growing cooperation of business and government during the decade also reinforced the tendencies of corruption at the federal level. Earlier in the decade, the "Teapot Dome" scandal helped to earn Harding his reputation as the nation's worst president and the 1920s as an era marked by much political corruption. At its core, Teapot Dome was a case of bribery, pure and simple. After a two-year

Senate investigation, Secretary of the Interior Albert Hall was found to have accepted $400,000 in cash and gifts from oil company executives in exchange for leases for oil fields located on government land. Democrats attempted to make corruption the chief issue during the presidential campaign of 1924, charging that "There is scarcely a department of the government under this administration that is not discredited by its record, and many bureaus not already scandalized are under suspicion."[15] Unfortunately for the Democrats, their frontrunner, William G. McAdoo, ended up being tainted during the same investigation.

—

In the lax regulatory environment of the 1920s, the owners of large corporations were largely liberated of the worries about government constraints that had accumulated during the Progressive Era. They could once again feel that government was on their side, and they largely approved of its efforts to create an associative state. But they were not about to wait around to see if it would work. Instead, these business leaders continued their search for governance structures that would contain competition and rationalize their economic environments. An important step toward this end was taken in the automobile industry and featured the rise of General Motors.

Growth of Large Corporations: The General Motors Model

In 1921 Henry Ford stood atop the automotive world. His inexpensive Model T accounted for 56 percent of all cars sold in the United States, while his nearest competition, General Motors, controlled only 13 percent. But Ford, the quintessential entrepreneur, was not content to be the owner of one of America's largest corporations or the nation's wealthiest man. Instead, he embarked upon a campaign to build upon his success and rededicated himself to the principle of producing an even cheaper, higher quality version of his one product. Plowing his profits back into the business, he began building an enormous manufacturing plant at River Rouge during the depression of 1921. To keep this expensive investment running at full capacity, Ford enthusiastically embraced vertical integration, buying parts suppliers and writing strict franchising agreements with those who would sell his Model T. To maintain absolute control, he bought back all outstanding shares of the company in 1919 and took it private.[16]

Unfortunately, things did not go as planned. By 1929 Ford's share of the domestic market had slipped to 31 percent. It had been surpassed by GM, which, with 32 percent, was now well on its way to becoming the nation's largest corporation. This reversal of fortunes is even more remarkable when one considers that as late as 1920, GM was losing money and considered an administrative disaster. But in that year, new CEO Pierre DuPont appointed Alfred P. Sloan his chief assistant, giving him full reign to reorganize the corporation. A master administrator, Sloan recognized the rise of the American consumer with different tastes and with a growing desire to use consumption to reflect social standing. He therefore developed a full line of different cars to respond to this opportunity. Instead of one car, there would be Chevrolets, Pontiacs, Oldsmobiles, Buicks, and Cadillacs—"a car for every purse and purpose."[17]

Both business historians and organizational theorists have presented this story as signifying an important change that was taking place in the evolution of large corporations during the decade of the 1920s. Ford Motor Co., along with most large corporations at the time, was a highly centralized, multiunit enterprise, organized along functional lines, with separate departments for functions like sales and manufacturing. But Ford had pushed this form to its natural limit. As complexity grew with size, the quality of decision making suffered, especially since Ford insisted on maximum control and minimum delegation. Sloan's, and GM's organizational innovation was to have each of the company's cars produced by a separate division, each with its own managerial hierarchy. By injecting a dose of decentralization into the structure, this multidivision design is generally credited with improving decision making and accountability.

More importantly, the multidivisional design facilitated the growth of even larger corporations by replacing functional departments with product divisions as the building blocks of organizational structure. Companies began to discover that they could take greater advantage of their manufacturing assets and experience to introduce related product lines, in the process achieving "economies of scope." For example, the Du Pont Corporation's production of, and research into improving explosives, gave it the infrastructure and expertise to develop chemical, dyestuff, and paint product lines.[18]

The resulting product diversification represented a new and different mode of rationalizing one's economic environment: with different divisions producing different products, a company might decide to spread its risks instead of focusing exclusively on containing competition.

As Ford came to find out when interest waned in the Model T, relying solely upon a single product makes one vulnerable to the vagaries of the marketplace, especially the fickleness of consumer preference. Indeed, as his market share dwindled, Ford, who could not rely on the sales of other products as he retooled for the Model A, chose to shut down his River Rouge plant for close to a year.

With its new organizational blueprint, the American corporation continued to grow larger during the 1920s. The top two hundred nonfinancial corporations saw their assets grow 85 percent during the decade to a total of over $81 billion.[19] Most of this growth was accomplished through internal expansion, and much of this was achieved through profits reinvested into product diversification.[20] The rest of this growth was brought about via consolidation, as the nation experienced its second merger wave. Between 1919 and 1928 there were almost 1,300 mergers that eliminated roughly 7,000 firms.[21] Much of this activity involved vertical integration, as constituent members of manufacturing oligopolies absorbed firms that supplied them with raw material or distributed their products. Ford, for example, acquired steel mills, railroads, and iron mines.

As corporations continued to grow, economic power continued to become increasingly concentrated. For the economy as a whole, the largest two hundred nonfinancial corporations controlled almost 50 percent of all corporate wealth, while the other three hundred thousand plus nonfinancial corporations divided the rest.[22] The process of concentration continued at the level of individual industries as well. While near or partial monopolies continued to exist in some industries (e.g., Alcoa in the aluminum industry), America's major industries continued to evolve into oligopolies, including petroleum, automobile, meat packing, tobacco, many food industries (e.g., breakfast cereals, crackers), and almost all raw materials (e.g., copper).[23] Particularly prone to oligopolistic development were industries where expensive new production technology created barriers to entry sufficiently high to stave off most potential competitors.

In some cases, bigness and the tendency toward oligopoly were facilitated by yet another unintended byproduct of legislation. With the small entrepreneur in mind, patent law was created to encourage innovation through the granting of a temporary monopoly. Over time, however, companies became expert at manipulating patent law to gain legal protection while they built large enterprises impregnable to competition. Corporations such as Singer Sewing Machine and the United Shoe Machinery Company were able to secure control of all of the patents on the manufacture of the machinery that they utilized.[24] Patent law thus came to function as a governance structure.

But as corporations grew in size, the costs of whatever competition remained grew as well. With so much to lose, many business leaders believed more fervently than ever in the need to contain competition. Fortunately for them, increased size not only increased financial risk, it also gave corporations the power, and oligopolies gave them the arrangement, to employ new or improved governance structures to contain competition that helped ensure that profits were dependable over time. These included price leadership, where members of an industry adopt the prices of the dominant firm; price discrimination, where the same product is sold at different prices to maximize profits; and trade associations—predictably, all of these devices tended to discriminate against smaller firms.[25]

Of course, since each governance device depended upon voluntary compliance, none was totally effective in controlling domestic competition. But at least corporate leaders did not need to worry much about competition from abroad. A set of protective tariffs passed in the nationalistic aftermath of the war helped to limit foreign competition, especially for domestic manufacturers—and therefore functioned as a governance structure. As long as the economy grew, so that all could benefit, and as long as foreign imports of an oligopoly's products were minimal, so as to contain competition, the firms comprising an oligopoly competed for market share, not survival.[26]

The growth of corporations also changed the nature of ownership. As securities markets continued to mature, issuing new stock became a dominant means of funding corporate expansion. But this meant that, while corporate assets became progressively concentrated, stock ownership became progressively dispersed. The stock of the largest industrial corporation in 1929, U.S. Steel, was dispersed among 182,585 owners; the twenty largest stockholders owned but 5.1 percent of its stock. The aggregate number of those holding stock in 144 of the 200 largest corporations, for which complete information was available, reached nearly six million. For Adolf Berle and Gardiner Means, in their classic, *The Modern Corporation and Private Property* (1932), this heralded a critical transformation: the separation of ownership of a corporation from control of a corporation. With control referring to the actual power to direct the affairs of the corporation, they found that 44 percent of the two hundred largest corporations were under the effective control of management ("management control") by the end of the 1920s.[27]

Chandler characterizes this change as the rise of "managerial capitalism," in which the typical large corporation came to be administered by a group of experienced and salaried managers with little or no ownership stakes.[28] This development had important implications for the prospects of corporate social responsibility. The vanguard of CSR had comprised corporations run by their original owners (or their offspring), who acted in terms of the long-term interests of their creations, as they frequently hoped to pass them along to their heirs. These interests included investments in CSR. As corporations gained multiple owners, however, the danger existed that these new owners would think more like speculators, hoping to maximize short-term profits. But as the number of stockholders continued to grow, ownership stakes became smaller, thus diluting the power of owner-investors. With additional insulation provided by complicated proxy rules, the cadre of professional managers, too, was in the position to act in the long-term interests of the companies they ran.

—

Overall, as corporations continued to grow and more effectively wield political influence during the 1920s, the government's main approaches to economic regulation (regulatory commissions and antitrust) were compromised even further. Though the nation's political economy was now more lopsided than ever, and though the country's mood was more conservative, voices, or at least echoes, from the Progressive Era could still be heard, and they were still demanding social regulations to tether large corporations.

Social Regulations and Welfare: The Business Template

Dismayed by the rightward shift in the country, a coalition of union, farmer-labor parties, and the Socialist Party formed the Conference for Progressive Political Action (CPPA) in 1922. By 1924 the group passed a platform that included the antimonopolist commitment to "the use of the power of the federal government to crush private monopoly, not to foster it." But the CPPA also drew from the Progressive period's reform tradition, and the platform included calls for the creation of a government agency to protect consumers, stronger child labor laws, and the end of legal discrimination against women. Senator Robert "Fighting Bob" La Follette, one of the most revered reformers of the Progressive Era, accepted the offer to run as the group's presidential candidate under its newly adopted name of the Progressive Party.[29]

With his progressive credentials re-burnished as the chair of the Senate committee that investigated the Teapot Dome scandal, La Follette declared that the primary issue of the 1924 campaign was to break the "combined power of the private monopoly system over the political and economic life of the American people."[30] Though he lost, "Fighting Bob" demonstrated the continued resonance of populist appeals by polling 17 percent of the vote, the best third-party showing since the Republican Party of 1856.

Though a number of states also continued attempt to pass reform legislation, the hurdles only got higher as businesses got bigger and more powerful. This can also be seen in the resistance to passing social welfare legislation. For example, in Illinois, the Employers' Association of Chicago and the Illinois Manufacturers' Association lobbied hard to make sure that neither state nor national legislators were tempted by the types social regulations and welfare state systems that were being erected by a number of European countries. These were typically dismissed as examples of "European parasitism," and wholly inappropriate for America. These groups were so successful that, with only one exception, no reform legislation that they actively opposed passed in Springfield between 1911 and 1929.[31] Of course, the business community continued to have a strange bedfellow in the person of Samuel Gompers, still the head of the AFL, and still committed to the antistate philosophy of voluntarism.

Even where social regulations and welfare state programs could not be quashed, the features of America's political economy and culture constrained the options available and ensured a meager effort. This is evident in the federal initiatives to provide vocational education and rehabilitate disabled workers. In the absence of a strong non-market ideology, whether socialist or social democratic, that could frame the expansion of welfare in terms of justice, equity, or citizen rights, these programs were justified as profitable investments that would increase the productivity of workers. Instead of creating new bureaucratic entities, which would then have the potential to grow, the independent Federal Board of Vocational Education had two full-time employees in 1918. The Federal Board for Vocational Rehabilitation, on the other hand, remained small because its work largely consisted of promoting the creation of rehabilitation councils at the state level—largely headed, of course, by local and state business leaders. These efforts were further limited by the nation's federalist bias for local and state control, which encouraged federal grants-in-aid. While this did keep control local, the requirement that federal funds be matched by local and state dollars worked to keep the programs underfunded. Finally, given that these programs were justified as investments, success was measured, not in terms of achieving lofty goals like justice, but in terms of achieving economic returns (i.e., more productive workers), however small, that could be demonstrated from a cost-benefit analysis.[32]

Social regulations at the federal level remained a path not taken during the 1920s; mandates, in whatever form, were not to be. Furthermore, government was not about to pick up the slack with stronger welfare state policies. Greater social responsibility on the part of businesses would depend upon strengthening unions. As there had been a surge in union membership during the war, labor relations were at a critical juncture at the end of the war, and greater negotiated responsibility appeared to be a distinct possibility.

Negotiated Responsibility

The Great Steel Strike of 1919

While it is an amoral logic that proves that war is good for business, it is often true that war is also good for labor. This relationship certainly held for labor during World War I. With increased economic demand, millions called to service, and a decline in immigration, the tight labor market that resulted gave workers greater leverage than usual with employers. More importantly, since there was an urgent need for labor peace during the period of war mobilization, the Wilson administration implemented a number of policies long sought by unions. Most of these were associated with the National War Labor Board (NWLB), which was constituted in April of 1918 to serve as the tribunal for settling the most intractable labor disputes. Comprising an equal number of business and labor representatives, it operated on the principle that workers had the right to organize and bargain collectively.[33] The cochair of the NWLB, Frank Walsh, who had been chair of the Commission on Industrial Relations before the war, went so far as to link the board's mission with the fight against autocracy abroad: "Political Democracy is an illusion unless builded (sic) upon and guaranteed by a free and virile Industrial Democracy."[34]

The results of this combination of favorable labor market conditions and governmental benevolence produced positive results: increased wages, a shorter workweek, and growth in union membership. Between 1917 and 1919, membership in AFL unions increased by almost 40 percent, from 2.3 million to 3.2 million. In addition, though the pre-war, open-shop status of an employer was honored, the NWLB helped promote shop representation committees in these firms, where employees elected their own representatives. War seemed to place America labor at a crossroads where an alternative path became visible.[35]

It was with high hopes, then, that the leadership of the AFL decided in the summer of 1918 that the time was ripe for organizing workers in the steel industry. Working conditions in most steel firms were deplorable. Like most manufacturing industries, the drive system continued to operate as the default option for labor relations. As many as half of the steel labor force worked twelve-hour days, six days a week, and wages lagged increasingly behind rising living costs. If unions could gain a foothold in this strategically important sector of the economy, so the thinking went, other industries might succumb as well.

Though the war produced a more favorable environment for unions, organizing steelworkers would be no easy feat. Since the suppression of strikes at U.S. Steel in 1909, labor had largely given up efforts at organizing workers in this rabidly antiunion industry. Furthermore, the newly formed National Committee for Organizing Iron and Steel Workers (NCOISW) would be taking on the nation's largest employer, which could draw upon deep pockets to resist unionization. Then there were America's perennial barriers to successful organizing, two of which stood particularly high in the steel industry. First, the campaign would require the cooperation and coordination of the twenty-four separate craft unions that claimed jurisdiction over some aspect of steel industry work. Second, and complicating matters even further, workers were divided along ethnic lines, with as many as thirty different nationalities represented in the mills.[36]

To spearhead the drive, the NCOISW chose William Z. Foster, who had honed an impressive set of organizing skills with the IWW, and who would eventually utilize these skills to become general secretary of the Communist Party USA. The campaign, which began in September 1918, was an immediate success, and by May of 1919 the union had signed up close to one hundred thousand workers eager for representation. Emboldened, Samuel Gompers, still head of the AFL, formally requested a meeting between union representatives and the head of U.S. Steel, Judge Gary. When the letter received no response, the membership voted to strike unless the steel companies agreed to a meeting with the unions. With still no response except the discharge of union organizers, a strike began on September 22. By the end of the month 350,000 steelworkers had left their jobs.[37]

Predictably, the steel industry pushed back with great force. Thousands of strikebreakers, including a large contingent of blacks, were brought in, and labor spies were hired to stir up ethnic and racial animosity. Local authorities aided steel owners by forbidding outdoor meetings and marches, and deputized guards smashed picket lines— violence took the lives of eighteen strikers. Owners also launched a propaganda offensive, taking out advertisements that linked strikers with the Russian Revolution of 1917, and suggesting that the strike was a plot devised in Moscow to spark a revolution to overthrow American capitalism. Most ominously, the federal government resumed its role as labor's adversary. The war had ended just after the campaign to organize steelworkers had begun, and with the NWLB disbanded, there was no longer the exigency of war, nor a mechanism in place that might force owners to compromise. Instead, Attorney General Palmer declared that the steel strike represented a Bolshevist threat on American soil, and the Justice Department conducted "red raids" of steelworkers, and locked up or deported many immigrant workers. Discouraged, many workers, or at least those who were not blacklisted, drifted back to work. On January 5, 1920, the NCOISW declared the strike to be at an end.[38]

the American Plan: Though elated by labor's defeat in the steel strike, many in the business community felt that the larger surge in unionism demanded a more systematic response. In a manner reminiscent of the actions taken by their predecessors at the turn of the century, business leaders forged two very different approaches. The first came from businessmen who felt that the time was again ripe for an antiunion campaign. Launched at a convention of Midwestern employers in Chicago in 1921, and spearheaded by employer groups like the National Association of Manufacturers and the National Metal Trades Association, the "American Plan" was presented as an effort to uphold the institution of the open shop. Building upon the heightened nationalism of the war, the campaign was also framed as an effort to restore the American values of individualism and equal opportunity. In contrast, the collectivism of unions and the practice of the closed shop were painted as un-American. The fight against unions was thus linked to the fight against Bolshevism. In short order, employers formed dozens of open shop associations around the country.[39]

The Plan itself was composed of the standard, though much improved upon, set of antiunion practices. The most effective practice was to discriminate against and discharge union members, especially union organizers, and then place them on a blacklist of workers that members of employers' associations would refuse to hire. Like the open-shop campaign of the Progressive Era, the Plan also featured the writing of "yellow-dog contracts," in which employment was contingent upon a pledge not to belong to unions. The use of industrial spies proliferated to the point that those attending a union meeting could be fairly certain that someone across the table or in the audience was an employed agent of the employer. The practice of employing strikebreakers also grew more sophisticated, with strikebreaking agencies becoming a minor industry during the period of the American Plan.[40]

In their antiunion campaign, employers received a significant assist from the courts. The Clayton Act of 1914 had specified that labor unions were not conspiracies in the restraint of trade, and subsequently labor leaders assumed that this had given them immunity from court injunctions that had plagued them since the 1890s. However, in the *Duplex Printing Press* case of 1921, the Supreme Court decided that the act did not permit labor unions to engage in activities that departed from "normal and legitimate objects," and that resulted in the restraint of trade. Of course, it would be up to the courts to determine what constituted "normal and legitimate." In another decision handed down the same year, the high court struck down an Arizona law that sought to do away with injunctions in labor disputes. Lower courts thus resumed the custom of issuing injunctions during strikes, and by 1928 the AFL was able to list 389 that had been issued during the decade.[41]

Judging by the numbers, the Plan was an unqualified success. While overall union membership reached a peak of 5,047,800 in 1920, it fell to 3,622,000 by 1923. At the end of the decade, membership fell even further and stood at 3,442,600, which meant that barely 10 percent of the workforce was unionized. Of course, the Plan itself cannot take full credit; unions' response to the Plan contributed to declining unionization as well. In the face of this serious challenge to their very existence, unions typically responded with complicity, inertia, and acquiescence. Instead of challenging employers in their red-baiting efforts to link union activity to Communism, labor leaders piled on. The charters of many small locals that were dominated by Communists were revoked, and hundreds of members, including many in positions of importance, were expelled. Inertia manifested itself in the AFL's continued adherence to craft-based organization, which was increasingly incompatible with industrial-based work comprising many semiskilled and unskilled workers. Instead of organizing the mass of semi- and unskilled workers in the emerging industries of autos, rubber, and chemicals, unions frequently devoted their energies to protecting antiquated jurisdictional territories and attacking "dual unionism." The AFL's mode of organizing also continued to allow ethnic and racial diversity to pose a barrier to working-class solidarity, as employers grew increasingly sophisticated in their ability to use these divisions to divide and conquer.[42]

Acquiescence was a byproduct of the AFL leadership's continued commitment to "voluntarism," the philosophy that relied upon the self-organization of workers, and not the state or politics, as the most effective route to counterbalancing the power of employers. With the passing of the torch to William Green upon the death of Samuel Gompers in 1924, the tepid adversarial stance toward owners that characterized Gompers's voluntarism turned into "union-management cooperation" under Green. Where this was practiced, it meant that labor would commit itself to assisting owners in making the workplace more efficient, whether that meant tolerating "scientific management" reorganization schemes or plans whereby employers divided their workforce into permanent and temporary groups. And because cooperation was also incompatible with conflict, the strike weapon came to be used sparingly. By 1930, strike activity was so low that less than two hundred thousand workers were involved in work stoppages nationwide.[43]

the benefits of business unionism: Of course, even with all of the setbacks that organized labor experienced during the 1920s, union workers tended to experience greater social responsibility at the workplace than their nonunion brethren in the form of better pay and working conditions. In its review of the trade agreements reached in 1927, the Bureau of Labor Statistics showed that though the nation as a whole had no minimum-wage law, most agreements had provisions that not only established wage scales but also included a minimum below which wages could not fall. Likewise, though there was still no federal legislation that regulated the hours of work, most agreements stipulated an eight-hour day; heralding the future, several agreements even stipulated a forty-hour, five-day workweek. Working conditions for many union workers were also improved with agreement provisions that established safety and sanitation codes. In order to circumscribe the power of supervisors and foremen, many agreements set out rules for the use of grievance and arbitration committees—which included employee representatives—for settling disputes.[44] Many trade agreements of the period also included work rules intended, in part, to constrain the drive system that still governed much work. For example, in reaction against the time and motion studies of scientific management, and in order to limit speed-ups at the workplace, some agreements limited the use of stopwatches.[45]

Even in the face of the open shop plank of the American Plan, unions made some progress in establishing closed shops in trade agreements, so as to prevent employers from undermining unions via the hiring of nonunion workers. Of the 250 trade agreements negotiated between 1923 and 1929 that were examined by Sumner Slichter in his *Union Policies and Industrial Management,* 168 had some form of closed shop provision, usually the stipulation that union members be hired if available. In the more traditional crafts that had apprenticeship programs, union agreements frequently attempted to control the number of apprentices that a company could hire, so as to protect the wage rates of journeymen.[46]

The main problem with negotiated responsibility during the twenties was that it continued to cover relatively few workers. As noted above, just 10 percent of the workforce was unionized at the end of the decade. Furthermore, continuing to reflect the organizational bias of the AFL, most trade agreements covered the more skilled craft workers. Those most vulnerable to corporate irresponsibility, especially the unskilled and semiskilled workers who filled the factories of mass-production industries, continued to be underserved by union organizers.

As alarming, it was not unusual for the benefits of greater social responsibility that unions won to be short-lived. For example, by 1920, carpet and upholstery weavers in Philadelphia had successfully unionized most of the city's shops. As a result, these union workers won trade agreements in which they typically made 10 to 20 percent more than their nonunion counterparts, controlled hiring through the union office, and had the right to name foremen from a seniority list. By 1926, however, the number of union members had been cut in half, as lower cost nonunion mills successfully competed against their union counterparts. At the end of the decade, the remaining union workers were making contract concessions, including the reduction in wages. A similar story of unionized firms losing out to nonunion competitors, leading to concessions in pay and socially responsible practices, was told in a number of industries during the decade, including those of full-fashioned hosiery, bituminous coal, men's shoes, and pottery. While some of these losses reflected the antiunion climate of the 1920s, in which nonunion employers felt empowered to resist further unionization within an industry, most of this shift reflected the inability of unions to fashion agreements that covered an entire industry—once again, a failure of corporatism. In short, in the absence of industry-wide agreements, economic competition between union and nonunion firms tended to have the effect of undermining union agreements.[47]

—

During the 1920s, the "sticks" wielded by the employers of the American Plan were mostly successful in staving off unions, at least in the short run. But there was a second group of employers who realized that such tactics did nothing to resolve the underlying labor problem. Not only would the drive system continue to make unions attractive, the high turnover rates that the system continued to produce (at least 100 percent per year for most large companies as late as 1919) was increasingly viewed as undermining optimal productivity.[48] Like the business leaders of the National Civic Federation a generation earlier, this vanguard of employers felt that a better alternative involved the path of corporate social responsibility, using a set of "carrots" in the hopes of resolving the labor problem for the long term. The centerpiece of these 1920s initiatives, now referred to as "welfare capitalism," was the employee representation plan, the roots of which stretched back to the Ludlow Massacre of 1914.

Voluntary Responsibility (CSR)

Welfare Capitalism

The violence began on the morning of April 20, 1914, when members of Colorado's National Guard fired into the Ludlow camp with machine guns. Striking miners in the tent colony fired back, and for the next fourteen hours the battle raged. During the fighting, women dug pits under some of the tents in order to protect themselves and their children from the crossfire. Under the cover of darkness that evening, guardsmen entered the camp and set fire to the tents. The next day a survey of the ruined camp found that ten men and one child had died by gunfire. Even greater horror struck when the charred remains of two women and eleven children were discovered in one of the protective pits.

What came to be infamously known as the Ludlow Massacre was a public-relations disaster for the absentee owner of the Colorado Fuel and Iron Company (CF&I) where the strike occurred, John D. Rockefeller, Jr. As the national media picked up on the story, readers learned of the horrible working conditions of the miners and the deplorable living conditions that they and their families had to endure in the company owned shantytowns. The public also learned of the seeming indifference on the part of Rockefeller during the fourteen months the strike had lasted, as well as his rejection of the plea from the secretary of labor, William Wilson, to engage in arbitration. With letters to the editors assailing his conduct and picketers marching outside the company's headquarters in New York, and in the context of years in which the family had served as a prime target of muckraking journalism, Rockefeller felt strongly that something had to be done to clear the family's name.[49]

The first thing that he did was to assume direct control of CF&I's labor policies. Rockefeller next hired W. L. Mackenzie King, who had organized the Canadian Ministry of Labor and served as its minister, to come up with a plan to solve the company's labor problem. King developed a blueprint for a company union. Variously known as the "Colorado Industrial Plan" or the "Rockefeller Plan," the plan had two parts. The first part, "The Industrial Constitution," called for employees to elect their own representatives (one for each 150 workers) at annual meetings. These representatives would then meet with management in joint committees to deal with industrial cooperation and conciliation, sanitation, safety, and education. The company also agreed to observe mining laws and publicly post wage scales and safety rules. Though the company reserved the right to hire, fire, and direct the workforce, the agreement included a grievance procedure in which workers could appeal orders of mine superintendents, and it stipulated that the company would not discriminate against union members. The second part, a "Memorandum of Agreement," covered working conditions and wage scales. First introduced in September of 1915, workers approved the plan by an overwhelming margin in October.[50]

As the intended audience of the plan was the public as much as it was the workers, Rockefeller assigned PR expert Ivy Lee the task of advertising the initiative. The plan was thus launched in a blaze of publicity, marking the beginning of a new phase in corporations' use of public relations.[51] To show that he was now in charge and accountable, Rockefeller began a two-week inspection tour of CF&I facilities and spoke with miners and their families. In early 1916, Lee began to distribute half a million copies of *The Colorado Industrial Plan*—padded with over sixty pages of Rockefeller speeches and articles highlighting his philanthropy—to newspapers, government officials, clergy, and other business executives. The strategy was a success, as formerly critical commentators came to express support.[52]

The Rockefeller Plan may have been no more than a footnote in American labor history, except that it was introduced shortly before America's entrance into WWI. As described above, the war period witnessed a dramatic growth in union membership. Employers were further troubled by the fact that the NWLB had not only legitimized unions, but it had granted legitimacy to the idea of industrial democracy, whether in the form of unions or shop committees. Therefore, to preempt a cry for greater democracy in the workplace after the war and forestall the progress of unions, a number of business leaders, like Judge Gary of U.S. Steel, came to the conclusion that better treatment of workers would leave "no just ground for criticism on the part of those who are connected with the movement of unrest."[53]

As a result, many large employers began to adopt Employee Representation Plans (ERP), and many were modeled on the Rockefeller Plan. Pushing this trend was the Special Conference Committee (SCC), founded in 1919 by executives from ten large corporations to coordinate labor relations and personnel policies. The group had close ties to the various Rockefeller interests, as well as to the newly formed American Management Association. The trend became so pervasive that between 1919 and 1922 alone, 317 company unions were formed, which was twenty-six times the number created in the preceding twenty years. Among companies adopting such plans were the marquee names of Standard Oil, Goodyear Tire and Rubber, International Harvester, and General Electric. By 1928, 399 companies had plans covering a total of 1.5 million workers.[54]

While ERPs constituted the centerpiece of the SCC program, the program also called for a set of pecuniary measures. These were derived from the view taking hold among a growing number of welfare capitalists that lower than optimal productivity and the threat of unions represented two sides of the same labor-problem coin. The poor pay and working conditions of the drive system were not only "counterproductive," since they led to high turnover rates and burnout, they also engendered hostility to employers and nurtured loyalty to co-ethnics at the workplace, or worse, unions. The emerging vision was that employers could deal with both problems by adopting practices that individualized the relationship between employer and employees and thus developed a bond of loyalty between the two. At least implicit in this position was the same belief in the power of cooperation that underlay the associative state: the greater cooperation between employer and employee secured by welfare practices would have the same profitable impact as that produced by the greater cooperation among businesses.[55]

As the twenties were about to begin, therefore, the executives of many large corporations were once again pushed by the threat of unions to navigate a course toward the high road of labor relations. And again, the main justification that was offered was that the socially responsible policies that they were adopting were good for business. Simply stated, by making workers more productive, welfare practices would make companies more profitable. There was a growing recognition that the inefficient drive system had to give way to the more scientific approach represented by personnel administration. As viewed by the National Industrial Conference Board (NICB), "the individual employee represents a definite investment, and that sound business principles require that the investment be capably handled in order that it may yield a fair return." As a result, personnel administration should not be seen "as frill or as a vehicle for the fulfillment of philanthropic impulses, but as a natural and business-like method of dealing with the . . . work force to secure results."[56]

In addition to the uptick in unionization, many employers continued to worry about the possibility of social regulations. After all, the glow of the Progressive Era, though growing dimmer, still illuminated politics. Many states continued to adopt reforms, and many reformers, taking note of the growth of welfare programs in Europe, argued that the federal government should follow suit. As stated by the NICB later in the decade, it was not enough for employers to simply oppose such initiatives; instead, they needed "to offer adequate alternative proposals for meeting the need. . . ."[57]

As the 1920s progressed, welfare capitalism continued to add to its array of voluntary practices. They included instituting new incentive plans that would individualize earnings: instead of piecework pay, workers would earn a base pay and then be offered incentives or bonuses for greater performance. Larger, hierarchical corporations would also take greater advantage of their organizational structure to develop job ladders where workers, as individuals, could seek to improve their lot via promotions. And, of course, these new practices featured an array of fringe benefits.[58]

stock ownership: If ERPs were viewed as a way of forging a bond of loyalty between worker and capitalist, stock ownership was viewed as a tool that "makes the worker a capitalist in viewpoint and this renders him a conservative and immune from radical ideas."[59] Their introduction was frequently accompanied by advertisements that touted the plans as rewards for faithful service and that would encourage the character-building traits of savings and thrift. Implementation usually involved allowing workers to purchase their company's stock, usually through an installment plan at below-market prices. Largely supplanting the profit-sharing schemes of the earlier era, stock-purchasing plans received their first boost during the war years and then proliferated during the 1920s. By the end of the decade 315 companies had plans, with eight hundred thousand employees owning shares that had a market value of over $1 billion. However, this represented only about 30 percent of the total workforce of these generally large corporations, and only 2 percent of all non-farm employees.[60]

pensions: Though the estimates vary, the most generous of these puts the number of firms with pension plans at 364 in 1929. Most of these were large corporations in the railroad, steel, petroleum, public utility, and electrical industries, and most plans had been established before 1920. Approximately 3.7 million workers were covered under these plans, most of which were non-contributory, in which the entire cost of the plan was borne by the employer.[61] This feature was no doubt preferred because it allowed employers to retain full control over their administration. Not only did this permit employers to terminate a plan whenever they pleased, it also gave employers the greatest flexibility in determining eligibility. As a result, most of these plans were fairly restrictive, and only a small percentage of employees usually qualified. For example, continuous service for as long as thirty years might be required for pension entitlement. Most also contained clauses that clearly stated the voluntary, if not arbitrary nature of this benefit, such as "It is expressly understood that every pension hereunder will be granted only in its pleasure, and may be revoked by it at any time."[62] According to one estimate, only 5 to 10 percent of the workforce of a company with a pension plan would ever qualify, and by 1930 only 150,000 individuals received one.[63]

medical care: As the decade of the 1920s began, most of the companies that provided a health care benefit to employees continued to do so via mutual-benefit societies. These involved workers (and sometimes employers as well) contributing to a company-administered fund from which they could draw a pre-set sum to pay for private doctors in cases of sickness and for a prescribed sum for a set of weeks in cases of injury. By 1931, 825,000 workers were covered by 398 associations. Beginning in 1911, a related delivery system appeared in the form of group insurance policies, where commercial insurance providers, such as Traveler's Insurance Company, assumed the administrative costs of providing a medical benefit. By 1926, 404,000 workers were covered by group insurance.[64]

In was the institution of the company doctor (and nurse), however, that saw the greatest growth during this period. Again, this involved an employer contracting with an independent doctor or putting one on the payroll, which had the advantage of providing more immediate, and in the case of the latter, on-site care. A NICB study of these practices at ninety firms in New England found 37 had full-time physicians, 63 part-time physicians, 29 doctors on call, and 204 nurses—showing that the company doctor was more often than not the company nurse. Of course, many workers viewed the company doctor as a "company man," more interested in identifying malingering than treating sickness. Because of their higher costs, company doctors were generally only found in large corporations, which could afford them. In 1926 over four hundred companies with at least three hundred employees provided this form of health care for close to two million American workers. This, however, represented only 6 percent of all non-farm employees.[65]

personnel departments: Many of the company benefits were administered by a new institution: personnel departments. Reacting to the tight labor market of the war years, which helped unionization campaigns, and in an effort to deal more systematically with the labor problem that still yielded high turnover and absenteeism, some employers attempted to professionalize the management of labor. If mechanical engineers had improved the efficiency of machines, what were needed, according to GE's CEO Owen Young, were "human nature engineers to keep its human machinery frictionless."[66] This meant taking functions, like hiring, discipline, and firing, away from the frequent lightening rod of labor discontent, the foreman, and placing them in the hands of college-educated personnel managers. Some early advocates went so far as to argue that these professionals practice an ethos of impartiality. But the combination of the unfavorable labor market conditions of the postwar depression, and the resurgence of traditional notions of managerial prerogatives, helped to place personnel departments in the position that they ultimately came to occupy—subservient to the cause of profit.[67]

—

As in the earlier era, some welfare capitalists chose these practices à la carte, while others enacted an entire package. A standout in this later group was Standard Oil of New Jersey, the biggest of the Rockefeller companies. In the year following the Ludlow Massacre, the company experienced a bitter strike at its Bayonne refinery. Clarence Hicks, who had worked with Mackenzie King at CL&P, was brought in from Colorado to design a new labor policy. Implemented in 1918, the Hicks program, not surprisingly, had a company union as its centerpiece. But it had much more than that. Over the next few years the program came to include a company-financed pension plan, an on-site medical staff, a stock-purchase plan, and benefits for the sick, the injured, and survivors. In a virtually unprecedented move, the company offered paid vacations to salaried workers in 1918 and hourly workers in 1922. In another noteworthy move, the workweek was reduced in stages from fifty-four hours per week in 1918 to forty hours per week by 1930. In addition to Jersey Standard, the "vanguard firms" in the era of welfare capitalism offering a full package of benefits included Procter & Gamble, General Electric, Sears Roebuck, and Du Pont.[68]

Similar to the "welfare work" firms, welfare-capitalist firms shared a common set of traits. Size still mattered, with most of these firms being large corporations. A survey published by the National Industrial Conference Board in 1929 revealed that whereas 16 percent of large firms (over 250 employees) provided group health and accident insurance, only 4 percent of small firms (fewer than 50 employees) did so; the comparable figures for companies providing pensions was 26 percent vs. 1 percent.[69] While the labor problem was typically more pronounced in large firms, it was usually only large corporations that could afford the price tag of the new or expanded practices. Of course, only those large corporations that enjoyed large, stable profits had the resources to foot the bill. These firms were more likely to be found in industries that had relatively effective governance structures, especially those in capital-intensive industries with steady demand, such as soap making and oil refining. Interestingly, as was true in the previous era when it was the visionary (and paternalistic) founders who typically blazed the CSR trail, ownership continued to make a difference. One study of large firms found that corporations controlled by their original owners (or their heirs) were more likely to have welfare programs. "Laggard firms" were more likely to be situated in industries that produced durable goods subject to fluctuating demand, such as that due to seasonal or cyclical factors (e.g., autos, steel, rubber).[70]

Overall, while welfare capitalism continued to receive a fair amount of attention, the brief survey above shows that it was still not particularly extensive. But did welfare capitalism achieve its goals of avoiding unions and fostering loyalty between employee and employer? As reviewed earlier, unionization declined over the course of the decade, and it is improbable that this was solely the outcome of the American Plan. The indirect evidence of the success of ERPs in thwarting unions is that union leaders invariably hated them. In part, this was because workers tended to like and take advantage of the benefits offered by their employers, thus reducing the incentives to join unions. For example, workers lined up for the free medical care offered at a clinic run by Wisconsin Steel, while close to a quarter of the employees of Swift & Company took the company up on the opportunity it offered to employees to purchase the company's stock.[71]

In regards to loyalty, the evidence suggests that employers achieved some success here as well. A survey of 361 firms with ERPs conducted in 1922 found that 356 reported beneficial effects in labor relations.[72] In his case study of Endicott Johnson, Gerald Zahavi suggests that the company achieved at least a contingent, "negotiated loyalty."[73] Of course, this came at the cost of any hope for power, bargaining or otherwise. Without true bargaining power, and without the ability to authorize strikes, there is little evidence that these company unions obtained significant wage improvements for the workers they represented. An exhaustive study of the original Rockefeller Plan itself published by the Russell Sage Foundation in 1924 found that employee representatives, fearing discharge, typically failed to press worker grievances.[74]

Corporate Philanthropy

As with both America's political economy and labor relations, World War I helped to spur its development of corporate philanthropy. At the outset of America's participation, President Wilson organized a conference of businessmen to discuss ways of expanding the Red Cross for the war effort. This resulted in the naming of a War Council, which, with Henry P. Davison of J. P. Morgan as chair and with corporate executives filling the top positions of the agency, mobilized business and community leaders and raised more than $175 million by the end of 1918.[75]

As business aggressively resumed its antigovernment stance after the war, including opposition to welfare state initiatives, some company leaders felt that business would need to step up its philanthropic efforts. P. W. Willard, manager of Western Electric, argued that if businessmen were going to work to keep industry free of government regulation, it was then the job of corporations to provide for "the aged, the defective, and the indigent."[76] While some executives resisted such appeals, many embraced charity as a means of showcasing their corporation's socially responsibly practices, and thus keeping government at bay.

An example of this dynamic took place in Alabama. At the beginning of the 1920s, newspapers in the state regularly editorialized against the Alabama Power Company and wrote in support of a proposal where the government would develop Muscle Shoals for power generation. To counter the growing support for this public alternative, the company initiated a number of programs that were intended to highlight the company's efforts to promote economic development in the state, many of which were philanthropic in nature. It donated to the Alabama Polytechnic Institute, threw its support behind scientific farming, and helped to make rural electrification easier. By 1924, *Forbes* noted that over 90 percent of the state's newspapers ran favorable editorials about the company, which the magazine attributed to the company's new policies—and an effective public-relations campaign of advertising and press relations. Of course, later investigations revealed that the PR campaign also included secretly paying newspaper service agencies that supplied many town newspapers with editorials. But in 1925, *Forbes* magazine awarded a silver cup to the Alabama Power Company for its public-relations work during the previous year.[77]

In addition to serving as an example of the growing trend of corporate philanthropy, Alabama Power also illustrates the rising use of public relations to burnish a corporation's image. As suggested in the last chapter, in an increasingly consumer-driven economy, owners found it increasingly imperative to cultivate loyal customers using the various tools of this new trade. So not only did good corporate citizenship help fend off challenges from workers, the public, and the state, it made for good copy for current and potential customers. Press releases and advertising might highlight some new philanthropic or workplace initiative. Or they might highlight the philosophical commitment of the owners and managers of the business.

The overall increase in corporate giving during and after the war did not go unnoticed, as many social welfare agencies, as well as educational and medical institutions, began to move beyond their traditional appeals to wealthy individuals and directly approach corporations for support. As a result, businessmen soon found themselves overwhelmed by the sheer number of causes, and many were unsure which were worthy of their largess. This gave rise to efforts to both organize and screen the various appeals. The most successful of these was the community chest movement, which spread to 350 cities by 1929 from a base of 40 cities at the beginning of the decade. Like the doctrine of cooperation that inspired the associative state, the community-chest idea reflected the notion that reducing competition could produce better results, in this case a more rational distribution of charitable funds.[78]

In 1928, businesses gave five hundred gifts of $1 million or more, showing that corporate giving had caught on. However, there were two factors that served to dampen even greater growth. The first was the 1916 Michigan Supreme Court decision in Dodge v. Ford, in which the Court held in favor of the Dodge brothers, who, as investors in Ford Motor Company, had complained that Ford had no right to halt dividend payments so as to use profits to make huge investments in new plants and pay workers a wage premium in the form of his $5 a day plan. The purpose of the corporation was to make money for their stockholders, and they could not be run "for merely incidental benefit of shareholders and for the primary purpose of benefiting others."[79] Though some states, such as New York and Ohio, had passed legislation permitting corporate giving to the Red Cross, the legal status of corporate philanthropy remained ambiguous. The second factor holding potential giving down was the desire of the corporate executives to receive the same sort of tax break afforded to individuals as a result of the 1917 change to the tax law that allowed a deduction of charitable contribution up to 15 percent of taxable income.[80]

A Philosophy of Corporate Social Responsibility

As the twenties began, the main justification for CSR continued to be that it was good for business. Simply stated, by making workers more productive, welfare practices would make companies more profitable. As the decade progressed, however, CSR was cast in loftier terms, elevating the mission of business above the bottom line. This was best expressed in the idea of trusteeship. In a speech delivered to the Park

Avenue Baptist Church in New York City, Owen Young, reflected upon the changing justification of big business:

> Then came the new idea in management. It is not yet fully grown but it is showing signs of rapid development and the greatest promise. I must say I think that the new idea sprang largely from the fact that lawyers were advanced to high managerial positions. . . . If there is one thing that a lawyer is taught, it is knowledge of trusteeship and the sacredness of that position. Very soon we saw rising a notion that managers were no longer attorneys for holders of stock; they were becoming trustees of an institution.[81]

This was echoed by Charles Schwab, the longtime steel executive, who told the American Iron and Steel Institute in 1929 that "the responsibilities that repose upon us in the steel industry . . . a real trusteeship . . . for hundreds and thousands of families. We seek to prosper ourselves but above all seek the welfare, progress and happiness of our people."[82]

As the philosophy of CSR began to embrace stakeholders beyond a firm's shareholders, it ultimately encompassed the communities in which corporations were located, especially as socially responsible practices increasingly comprised both philanthropy and welfare work. Such an inclusive notion was expressed clearly by International Harvester's Cyrus McCormick:

> I believe that every company or organization of men doing business in any community, no matter where or how removed from the central office, is, in duty bound to do something to help build that community, aside from the things required by law or the things beneficial to itself. The Harvester Company is a citizen of every community in which it sells a machine, and it is not a good citizen if it does not perform some service in that community, the same as any citizen who lives there would be expected to perform.[83]

Summary

At the end of the 1910s, many business leaders were worried that stronger mandates were imminent. Not only were there continued efforts at the state level to enact labor and welfare legislation, but the growth of government during WWI threatened to set a precedent for government intervention. These leaders were also anxious about the significant surge in unionization that was taking place, which together with social unrest and challenges to capitalism itself threatened to curtail managerial prerogatives.

But at these critical junctures for both the political economy and labor relations, the business community, led by the owners of large corporations, fought back. Aided by the more conservative political climate that took hold after the war, one in which the large corporation was less likely to be challenged, corporate leaders pushed for the dismantling of wartime government bureaus, lobbied against state mandates, and sought court reversals of state laws that did pass.

They also helped elect and then support the business-friendly Republican administrations that reigned in the twenties. As government pursued an "associative state," where its role was to facilitate success for businesses, antitrust and regulatory enforcement were curtailed. In such a lax environment, business continued to successfully pursue governance structures to contain competition, which contributed to big business getting bigger. And, of course, as they got bigger, and the political economy became more lopsided, large corporations were able to do an even better job keeping government at bay.

Against unions, business adopted a two-prong strategy of sticks and carrots. The first featured the American Plan, an aggressive set of antiunion tactics, against which the AFL's voluntarism was no match. This contributed greatly to the level of unionization that stalled and then declined by the end of the decade. The path of negotiated responsibility suffered from erosion as a result.

The second prong was CSR, beginning with a refined set of "welfare capitalist" practices, including improvements in pensions and medical care. Instead of industrial democracy, owners offered the Employee Representative Plan, a form of company union that rapidly spread. This strategy, too, helped to fend off unions. Together with the growth in corporate philanthropy, corporate social responsibility matured to the level where some now espoused a philosophy or "trusteeship," in which owners recognized that large corporations had important public obligations, especially for its primary stakeholders, i.e., employees and local communities.

By the end of the 1920s, the contours of America's regulatory structure continued to take its distinctive shape: weak regulations, weak unions, and growing CSR. But this pattern was built upon a foundation in which the corporation was contested. In particular, voluntary initiatives at the workplace and in the community tended to grow in response to threats to managerial prerogatives in the form of government regulations and unions. But what if the threats were to diminish, as they did by the end of the decade?

After showing dramatic growth at the beginning of the decade, the number of firms adopting welfare programs slowed by the end of the decade. Some firms even dropped programs during the second half of the decade, though these were more likely to involve amenities such as in-house cafeterias and employee magazines, and not core programs such as health insurance and pensions. Furthermore, investment in these programs, as a proportion of total payroll, did not increase over the course of the decade, even though the economy was growing at a healthy pace at decade's end.[84] In short, there was at least some evidence that the waning of threats led to a waning of interest in CSR.

Notes

1. Robert Sobel, *The Age of Giant Corporations: A Microeconomic History of American Business, 1914–1970* (Westport, Connecticut: Greenwood Press, Inc., 1972), chapter 1.
2. Ibid., 11–12.
3. Louis Galambos, *Competition & Cooperation: The Emergence of a National Trade Association* (Baltimore: The Johns Hopkins Press, 1966), 205.
4. Sobel, *The Age of Giant Corporations*, 21–22; George Soule, *Prosperity Decade: From War to Depression, 1917–1929* (New York: Holt, Rinehart and Winston, 1947), 81; Jonathan Hughes, *American Economic History* (Glenview, Illinois: Scott, Foresman and Company, 1983), 453.
5. Bittelman, Alexander, "Outline for a History of the Communist Party in America. [circa 1923]," published as "Hynes Exhibit No. 4" in *Report of the Special Committee to Investigate Communist Activities* (Washington, DC: Government Printing Office, 1930), 435–448; James Weinstein, *Ambiguous Legacy: The Left in American Politics* (New York: New Viewpoints, 1975), chapter 2.
6. Beverly Gage, *The Day Wall Street Exploded: A Story of America in its First Age of Terror* (New York: Oxford University Press, 2009), 27.
7. Ellis W. Hawley, "Herbert Hoover, the Commerce Secretariat, and the Vision of an 'Associative State,' 1921–1928," *Journal of American History* 61 (June 1974).
8. Morton Keller, *Regulating a New Economy: Public Policy and Economic Change in America, 1900–1933* (Cambridge, Massachusetts: Harvard University Press, 1990), 37.
9. Ibid., 36; Thomas K. McCraw, *Prophets of Regulation* (Cambridge, Mass.: The Belknap Press of Harvard University Press, 1984), 145–147.
10. Scott R. Bowman, *The Modern Corporation and American Political Thought: Law, Power, and Ideology* (University Park, Pennsylvania: The Pennsylvania State University Press, 1996), 172.
11. Carroll H. Woody, *The Growth of the Federal Government, 1915–1932* (New York: McGraw-Hill Book Company, Inc., 1934), 181.
12. Ibid., 183.
13. Keller, *Regulating a New Economy*, 40.
14. McCraw, *Prophets of Regulation*, 151; David Kennedy, *Freedom From Fear: The American People in Depression and War, 1929–1945* (New York: Oxford University Press, 1999), 33.

15. J. Leonard Bates, "The Teapot Dome Scandal and the Election of 1924," *American Historical Review* 60, no. 2 (January 1955): 305.

16. Thomas K. McCraw, *American Business, 1920–2000: How It Worked* (Wheeling, Illinois: Harlan Davidson, Inc., 2000), chapter 1.

17. Sobel, *The Age of Giant Corporations*, 34; McCraw, *American Business*, 19.

18. C. Joseph Pusateri, *A History of American Business*, 2nd ed. (Wheeling, Illinois: Harlan Davidson, Inc., 1988), 300; Alfred D. Chandler, Jr., *Scale and Scope: The Dynamics of Industrial Capitalism* (Cambridge, Massachusetts: The Belknap Press of Harvard University Press, 1990), 161–165.

19. Adolf A. Berle and Gardiner Means, *The Modern Corporation and Private Property* (New York: Macmillan, 1932), 33.

20. J. Fred Weston, *The Role of Mergers in the Growth of Large Firms* (Berkeley, California: University of California Press, 1953), chapter 2.

21. Keller, *Regulating a New Economy*, 36.

22. Berle and Means, *The Modern Corporation and Private Property*, 32.

23. Sobel, *The Age of Giant Corporations*, chapters 2–3.

24. Arthur Robert Burns, *The Decline of Competition: A Study of the Evolution of American Industry* (New York: McGraw-Hill Book Company, Inc., 1936, 11.

25. Ibid.

26. Hughes, *American Economic History*, 471; Soule, *Prosperity Decade*, 264–265.

27. Berle and Means, *The Modern Corporation and Private Property*.

28. Chandler, *Scale and Scope*.

29. Dulles, Foster Rhea and Melvyn Dubofsky, *Labor in America: A History*, 5th ed. (Arlington Heights, Illinois: Harlan Davidson, Inc., 1993), 246.

30. Solon DeLeon and Nathan Fine, eds., *The American Labor Year Book 1925, Volume VI* (New York: Labor Research Department of the Rand School of Social Science, 1926), 120–121, http://www.marxists.org/history/usa/eam/other/cppa/cppa.html.

31. Lizabeth Cohen, *Making a New Deal: Industrial Workers in Chicago, 1919–1939* (Cambridge, England: Cambridge University Press, 1990), 182.

32. Edward D. Berkowitz and Kim McQuaid, *Creating the Welfare State: the Political Economy of the 20th Century Reform*, rev. ed. (Lawrence, Kansas: University Press of Kansas, 1992), chapter 4.

33. Dulles and Dubofsky, *Labor in America: A History*, 218.

34. Joseph A. McCartin, "'An American Feeling': Workers, Managers, and the Struggle Over Industrial Democracy in the World War I Era,'" in *Industrial Democracy in America: The Ambiguous Promise*, eds. Nelson Lichtenstein and Howell John Harris (Cambridge, England: Cambridge University Press, 1993), 71.

35. Selig Perlman and Philip Taft, *History of Labor in the United States, 1896–1932, Volume IV* (New York: the Macmillan Company, 1935), 410; John G. Rayback, *A History of American Labor* (New York: The Free Press, 1966), 274.

36. Jeremy Brecher, *Strike!* (Boston: South End Press, 1972), 120; Rayback, *A History of American Labor*, 286.

37. Perlman and Taft, *History of Labor in the United States, Vol. IV*, 463–465.

38. Dulles and Dubofsky, Labor in America: A History, 226–227; Perlman and Taft, *History of Labor in the United States, Vol. IV*, 467; Brecher, *Strike!*, 123–124.

39. Dulles and Dubofsky, *Labor in America: A History*, 237–238; Rayback, *A History of American Labor*, 291.

40. Irving Bernstein, *The Lean Years: A History of the American Worker, 1920–1933* (Baltimore: Penguin Books, 1960), 149–152.

41. Dulles and Dubofsky, *Labor in America: A History*, 240–241; Rayback, *A History of American Labor*, 294.

42. Bernstein, *The Lean Years*, 84, 88–92; Rayback, *A History of American Labor*, 302.

43. Rayback, *A History of American Labor*, 306–307; Dulles and Dubofsky, *Labor in America*, 251.

44. United States Department of Labor, Bureau of Labor Statistics, *Trade Agreements, 1927, Bulletin No. 468* (Washington, DC, Government Printing Office, 1927), 3–4, 7.

45. Sumner H. Slichter, *Union Policies and Industrial Management* (Washington, DC: The Brookings Institution, 1941), 58–59, 10, 175.

46. Ibid., 57–58.

47. Ibid., chapter 12.

48. Michael Katz, *In the Shadow of the Poorhouse: A Social History of Welfare in America* (New York: Basic Books, 1986), 186–187; Slichter, *Union Policies and Industrial Management*, 100, 102.

49. Andrea Tone, *The Business of Benevolence: Industrial Paternalism in Progressive America* (Ithaca, New York: Cornell University Press, 1997), 117.

50. Bernstein, *The Lean Years*, 161.

51. Alan R. Raucher, *Public Relations and Business, 1900–1929* (Baltimore: Johns Hopkins Press, 1968), chapter 2.

52. Bernstein, *The Lean Years*, 160; Tone, *The Business of Benevolence*, 120–122.

53. David Brody, *Workers in Industrial America: Essays on the 20th Century Struggle* (New York: Oxford University Press, 1979), 57.

54. Berkowitz and McQuaid, *Creating the Welfare State*, 65; Sanford M. Jacoby, *Modern Manors: Welfare Capitalism Since the New Deal* (Princeton, New Jersey: Princeton University Press, 1997), 21; Greg Patmore, "Employee Representation Plans in North America and Australia, 1915–1935: An Employer Response to Workplace Democracy," (paper presented at the Workplace Democracy Conference, Labour Council of NSW/Work and Organisational Studies, School of Business, University of Sydney, June 2001), 4, http:/worksite.econ.usyd.edu.au/employer.html.

55. E. K. Hall, "The Spirit of Cooperation Between Employer and Employee," in *Industrial America in the Twentieth Century*, ed. David Brody (New York: Thomas Y. Crowell Company, 1967), 87, 90.

56. National Industrial Conference Board, *Industrial Relations: Administration of Policies and Programs* (New York: National Industrial Conference Board, 1931), 104.

57. Ibid., 20–21.

58. Sanford M. Jacoby, *Employing Bureaucracy: Managers, Unions, and the Transformation of Work in American Industry, 1900–1945* (New York: Columbia University Press, 1985), 181.

59. Bernstein, *The Lean Years*, 183.

60. Ibid.; Don D. Lescohier and Elizabeth Brandeis, *History of Labor in the United States, 1896–1932: Working Conditions, Labor Legislation* (New York:

The Macmillan Company, 1935), 382; United States Department of Commerce, Bureau of the Census, *Historical Statistics of the United States, Part 1, Colonial Times to 1970* (Washington, DC: US Government Printing Office, 1975), 126.

61. Bernstein, *The Lean Years*, 181.
62. Stuart D. Brandes, *American Welfare Capitalism, 1880–1940* (Chicago: University of Chicago Press, 1970), 107.
63. Jacoby, *Employing Bureaucracy*, 199; Lescohier and Brandeis, *History of Labor in the United States*, 385.
64. Brandes, *American Welfare Capitalism*, 96–97.
65. Ibid., 93–99; Lescohier and Brandeis, *History of Labor in the United States*, 365; United States Department of Commerce, Bureau of the Census, *Historical Statistics of the United States, Part 1*, 126.
66. Jacoby, *Employing Bureaucracy*, 137.
67. Ibid., 159, 180.
68. Bernstein, *The Lean Years*, 166–167; Jacoby, *Modern Manors*, 26–27.
69. National Industrial Conference Board, *Industrial Relations Programs in Small Plants* (New York: National Industrial Conference Board, 1929), 16.
70. Jacoby, *Modern Manors*, 26–29.
71. Cohen, *Making a New Deal*, 183.
72. Brandes, *American Welfare Capitalism*, 128.
73. Gerald Zahavi, "Negotiated Loyalty: Welfare Capitalism and the Shoemakers of Endicott Johnson, 1920–1940," *Journal of American History* 71, no. 3 (December 1983).
74. Bernstein, *The Lean Years*, 163.
75. Robert H. Bremner, *American Philanthropy*, 2nd ed. (Chicago: University of Chicago Press, 1968), 123–124.
76. Cohen, *Making a New Deal*, 182.
77. Raucher, *Public Relations and Business*, 85–86.
78. Bremner, *American Philanthropy*, 133–134.
79. Joel Bakan, *The Corporation: The Pathological Pursuit of Profit and Power* (New York: The Free Press, 2005), 36.
80. Bremner, *American Philanthropy*, 127.
81. David Brody, ed., *Industrial America in the Twentieth Century* (New York: Thomas Y. Crowell Company, 1967), 85.
82. Brody, *Workers in Industrial America: Essays on the 20th Century Struggle*, 61.
83. Morrell Heald, *The Social Responsibilities of Business: Company and Community, 1900–1960* (Cleveland, Ohio: The Press of Case Western Reserve University, 1970), 53.
84. National Industrial Conference Board, *Industrial Relations: Administration of Policies and Programs*, 84–86; Jacoby, *Employing Bureaucracy*, 199.

5

The Great Depression: Everything Changes, But Remains the Same

By the end of the twenties, challenges to the large corporation, the main catalyst for corporate social responsibility had withered. Of course, the voluntary programs of social responsibility also depended upon effective governance structures that yielded the healthy profits, which then allowed corporations to fund their socially responsible initiatives. During the 1920s the American economy was mostly healthy. Though there were ups and downs, GNP grew by 45 percent during the decade and profits were up in most industries. Maybe CSR could be sustained by a healthy economy alone. This possibility, however, would not be tested. As the country was about to be reminded as it entered the decade of the 1930s, no one had discovered a way to suspend the economic laws of gravity.[1]

Mandated Responsibility

The Failure of the Minimalist State

On November 19, 1929, less than a month after the Great Crash on Wall Street, President Hoover held the first of what would be nearly two weeks of meetings with the nation's leading business leaders. Rejecting the precedent of letting economic downturns run their course, he hoped to use the office of the president to forge a consensus on what actions should be taken to forestall further economic calamity. Of course, this meant voluntary actions, and not direct government intervention or spending programs. Attempting to build upon his vision of an associative state, President Hoover attempted to use his office as a clearinghouse of ideas and information concerning private efforts to reduce misery. Committed to individualism and the primacy of the private sector, and worried that public relief would nurture a crippling dependency, Hoover's view of the role of government remained constrained, even in the face of the crisis: "It is not the function of the Government to relieve individuals of their responsibilities to their neighbors, or to relieve private institutions of their responsibilities to the public. . . ."[2]

Prominent in the group of businessmen that was convened were Owen Young and Gerald Swope of General Electric, Walter Teagle of Standard Oil of New Jersey, and Julius Rosenwald of Sears Roebuck, all of whom were leaders in CSR. At Hoover's urging, and in contrast to the standard practice of simply slashing labor costs during an economic downturn, the nation's leading employers agreed to maintain wage rates, so as to protect both people and purchasing power.[3] Large corporations honored this commitment for most of 1930.

As early as the spring, however, smaller companies began to cut wages, and by the middle of 1931 the National Association of Manufacturers, as the representative of small firms, openly supported wage reductions as a way of coping with dire circumstances. As the year wore on, larger companies also found it increasingly difficult to hold rates steady, and some found that the only way to do so was to cut the number of hours worked or, even worse, cut the number of workers. In September of the following year, U.S. Steel became the first major employer to break the 1929 agreement by cutting wages by 10 percent. It was enough to burst the dam, as General Motors quickly followed suit, as did many other firms in the textile, rubber tire, and automobile industries. Most conspicuous was Ford Motor Company, which having promised many times not to cut wages, announced reductions of up to 40 percent in October.[4]

This effort at what came to be called "wage rigidity" was one of several failed efforts that relied upon private industry, with government encouragement, to act responsibly toward its employees during this crisis. Another was "employment stabilization." This program was aimed at controlling unemployment, and consisted of measures that attempted to counteract cyclical or seasonal fluctuations. It received the enthusiastic endorsement from the President's Emergency Committee for Employment (PECE), constituted by Hoover in 1930 to facilitate efforts on the part of state and local government agencies and private organizations to stimulate employment. But this, too, was ineffective, as one estimate at the time put the number of workers affected by such plans at less than 1 percent of all workers.[5]

Another strategy to combat unemployment was work sharing. This involved efforts to spread work around by shortening daily or weekly work hours and rotating shifts. Some argued that this would help maintain consumer demand, since a smaller paycheck was better than none, and because some workers earned more than they needed. Like employment stabilization, work sharing was endorsed by PECE, and in 1932, President Hoover initiated a "Share-the-Work-Movement," headed by Standard Oil's Walter Teagle. Because the large firms comprising the Special Conference Committee began to worry that Congress might adopt "radical legislation" in the face of mounting pressure over unemployment, the business community publicly endorsed the Hoover initiative. Data does indicate that average weekly hours for workers in manufacturing did indeed drop. Of course, this may or may not have entailed work sharing, since many employees not only laid-off workers, but cut the hours of their remaining workforce as well. Indeed, the record unemployment rate of 25 percent of 1933 suggests that many employers did just that.[6]

In short, government-initiated private programs were not up to the task of coping with the problems of the Depression. As will be shown below, neither was CSR, with many large corporations abandoning their socially responsible practices in order to cut costs. The shortcomings of both sets of programs and practices grew starker as the economic situation worsened. Bankruptcies soared, setting a record of 26,355 in 1930. The economy continued upon its descent, reaching its nadir in 1933, when over four thousand banks failed, and at which point the GNP had contracted nearly 50 percent since 1929. As a result, in addition to the roughly 25 percent of the labor force without work, another 25 percent had taken wage cuts or were now working part time. With no federal welfare state and only weak programs as the state level, most of those in distress received no help. Though private charities expanded their efforts, they were not nearly enough to meet the growing needs of American families. Consequently, Hoovervilles (homeless encampments) began to appear across the nation, and as many as 50 percent of children lacked adequate shelter, food, or medical care.[7]

———

As America was now fully industrialized, with most of its population now subject to the swings of the business cycle, the Depression represented the worst economic crisis in the nation's history. The combination of minimal government and CSR was a clear failure in the face of crisis. Business leaders quickly went from being heroes responsible for the "roaring twenties" to villains whose actions were wreaking havoc in the lives of millions of Americans. Indeed, the viability of capitalism was now being questioned, as was its leading institution, the large corporation. With demands that something be done growing louder and louder, the status quo of minimalist government was no longer an option, and the promises of CSR rang hollow. Instead, the country found itself at a critical juncture. It appeared as though government was finally in a position to contain large corporations and substitute social regulations and social welfare for CSR's self-regulation and private welfare.

Ideological and Political Challenges: Big Business Comes Under Assault Once Again

The Depression triggered a number of movements and events that kept the business community worried for much of the decade. Beginning in 1930, unrest among the unemployed manifested itself first in looting for food, and then in marches and demonstrations in cities across the nation, which sometimes led to clashes with local police. The demonstration that gained the greatest attention was the Bonus Army, a group of unemployed World War I veterans who sought early payment of war service bonuses. Descending upon Washington in 1932, this group of veterans established a shantytown, took over some unoccupied government buildings on Pennsylvania Avenue, and eventually numbered twenty thousand before being forcibly removed by the army. The despair of the unemployed also manifested itself in rent riots, in which families resisted an alarming wave of evictions, and disruptions in local relief offices—the growing unrest within the ranks of labor will be covered later in the chapter.[8]

The Communist Party of the United States of America organized many of the demonstrations of the unemployed. While the CPUSA experienced an all-time high of 102,000 votes in the presidential election of 1932, the party focused most of its efforts in the 1930s on orchestrating demonstrations and organizing industrial workers into unions. In intellectual circles, the Depression led a number of observers to look favorably upon the "Soviet experiment." In 1931–32 alone, several pro-Soviet books appeared, including Joseph Freeman's *The Soviet Worker*, Waldo Frank's *Dawn in Russia*, and William Z. Foster's *Toward Soviet America.*[9] Most menacing from the perspective of business was the foundation upon which these analyses—as well as the

CPUSA's agitation—was built: the Depression represented capitalism in its death throes.

Socialism also received a renewed lease on life. Upton Sinclair, who had initially gained notoriety in 1906 as the muckraking chronicler of *The Jungle*, had rejected capitalism and become a lifelong member of the Socialist Party. Given his politics and his prolific and popular writing, Sinclair was a perennial thorn in the side of the business community by the time of the Depression. In 1934 he struck fear into the heart of this community when he won the Democratic primary for governor of the state of California, running on a platform entitled End Poverty in California (EPIC). With millions out of work, Sinclair proposed that the state rent idle factories and farms where the unemployed could establish cooperatives, producing goods and food for use. To get the money to create this cooperative system, he called for a tax on property valued above $250,000, which he argued would "fall almost entirely upon our great corporations. . . ."[10] Clearly worried, the business owners led the strong opposition that formed in reaction to the EPIC movement, and in the end it was effective; Sinclair was decisively defeated, though he did garner over 880,000 votes, or 37 percent of those cast in a three-way race.[11]

American-style populism also blossomed during the decade. One of its most colorful offshoots was Huey Pierce Long of Louisiana. As the state's railroad commissioner in the 1920s, Long gained a reputation as the peoples' champion by taking on big corporations like Standard Oil, a reputation he enhanced as governor when he raised taxes on oil and gas producers. In 1934 he founded the Share Our Wealth Society to advance the proposal that all large fortunes above a certain amount be confiscated and redistributed to American families. Another populist threat to business was the radio priest, Edward Coughlin. While Father Coughlin is now remembered most for his anti-Semitic rants in the latter years of the thirties, he first gained national attention with sermons that drew upon Catholic social-justice doctrine to criticize capitalism. Reaching millions of listeners and receiving more mail than any other person in the United States, Coughlin launched the National Union for Social Justice in 1934. Included in its sixteen-point platform was a call for the nationalization of banking, oil, natural gas, and lighting corporations.[12]

Probably the greatest threat to managerial prerogatives was centralized economic planning. Of course, some corporate leaders helped to legitimize this idea, when many concluded that only planning could contain the kind of ruinous competition that had brought about the Depression. But proposals from the business community left businessmen firmly in control of any planning process. It was the alternative proposals, which had government in the seat of control that had the business community worried. The critics of big business who authored these alternatives usually started from the "new nationalist" premises of their Progressive Era forebears. Large corporations, which had voided the laws of economic competition, and hence a precondition for laissez faire, were an economic fact of life; but the concentrated power of these behemoths demanded government regulation to overcome the harmful effects that this power wrought. Indeed, the experience of the Depression had only strengthened the evidence of these harmful effects and therefore the need for government intervention.

The range of opinion calling for government planning was wide. From the academic world, economists like Stuart Chase advocated "A Ten Year Plan for America," while George Soule published *A Planned Society*. In 1932 the noted historian, Charles Beard published "A Five Year Plan for America." From the ranks of religious leaders, theologian Reinhold Niebuhr wrote a critique of capitalism that included a call for planning and government controls. The Federal Council of Churches of Christ in America prepared a document that condemned the system of economic competition and declared that the Christian ideal demanded "hearty support of a planned economic system." A number of these voices found an outlet in the periodical, *Common Sense*, which became an unofficial journal of planning perspectives.[13]

In contrast to the advocates of centralized planning, a new generation of antimonopolists used the increasing concentration of economic power as evidence to revive calls for aggressive antitrust prosecution. The apostle of New Freedom himself, and now Supreme Court justice, Louis D. Brandeis, published a collection of papers in 1934 entitled *The Curse of Bigness*.[14] The book's central theme was that the concentration of economic power was undermining the ability of communities to be self-sufficient. Furthermore, bigness in business engendered bigness in government, labor, and agriculture, developments that together threatened the health of the nation's democracy. Brandeis's prescribed solution remained what it had been a generation earlier: the breakup of large corporations and decentralization—in other words, a restoration of American to its roots.[15]

—

With crisis comes opportunity. The Depression simultaneously weakened the political position of business and created a fertile ground for new thinking about the role of government. The large corporation was once again a contested institution, with many calling for reforms to control it. With the election of Franklin Delano Roosevelt in 1932, America was once again at a critical juncture, seemingly poised to rebalance its political economy.

Economic Regulations: The Failure of the NRA

When Franklin Roosevelt was sworn in as president on March 4, 1933, he carried the hopes of the nation on his shoulders. Not only had the country been mired in a depression for over three years, but in the weeks leading up to Inauguration Day, there was also a run on banks, leading to government proclamations closing all banks in thirty-two states and most banks in six others. Immediate and bold action was demanded to revive the economy. Fortunately, there were already hundreds of proposals for what to do. Most were derived from a much smaller set of diagnoses of what constituted the basic problem. For some, the problem was under-consumption caused by the failure of business to pass along the productivity gains of the 1920s to workers in the form of higher wages, or to consumers in the form of lower prices. One cure for this imbalance was to shorten the workweek, which would increase the number of jobs and the purchasing power of consumers. For others, the problem was simply one of mass unemployment. The solution here, and probably the most popular of all of the proposals, involved expanding public works projects.[16]

If these two solutions were particularly popular with labor, the executives of some large businesses were particularly attracted to proposals that would forge cooperative relationships among businesses. Echoing the concerns of John D. Rockefeller in the 1870s, J. P. Morgan at the turn of the century, and Herbert Hoover in the 1920s, the problem with the economy for these executives was one of excessive competition; this, in turn, resulted in overproduction, price deflation, and the collapse of investment. However, the mixed results of the associative state of the 1920s, in tandem with the magnitude of the current crisis, convinced many business leaders that a stronger role for government was now needed in order to help business contain competition by enforcing cooperation—of course, even these progressive businessmen worried about allowing government to become more powerful.[17]

In many ways Franklin Roosevelt was ideally suited for the challenge. From his privileged upbringing in Hyde Park he gained a preternatural self-confidence, and from his education at the Groton School, where he came under the spell of headmaster Reverend Endicott Peabody, he acquired a strong sense of Christian duty and commitment to public service. Like his cousin Teddy, he effused optimism and was eager to take bold action. He was not, however, a deep thinker, nor did he hold a coherent philosophy, or even a consistent set of beliefs. He was, instead, a preeminent politician, deft at the pragmatic arts of compromise and coalition building. With the nation desperate for deliverance from its economic tumult, he saw a unique opportunity in an unsettled political environment to achieve not only economic recovery and social reform, but also a political realignment that would solidify Democrats' current position of electoral supremacy. His New Deal proposals would be bold and pragmatic, but they would grow from ideological justifications with shallow roots at best.[18]

All of these traits and desires were on display in the centerpiece of the Hundred Days legislation, the National Industrial Recovery Act (NIRA) of 1933, which Roosevelt declared as perhaps "the most important and far reaching legislation ever enacted by the American Congress." For the advocates of public works, $3.3 billion of the act was dedicated to the new Public Works Administration (PWA). For the under-consumptionists, there was section 7(a) of the act, which gave the president the authority to approve or prescribe maximum hours and minimum wages in certain industries—this section also famously recognized the right of workers to form unions, a subject that will be explored later. For those in the business community who saw the problem as one of overproduction, the bill created the National Recovery Administration (NRA), a mechanism that would allow industry to restrict output and plant capacity, and thus operate as a governance structure to control competition.[19]

The act was certainly bold, and Roosevelt was able to get it through Congress within one month of its introduction as a bill. But not only did the act not represent a coherent plan, its ill-fitting parts were arguably at cross purposes, at least with respect to the problem of unemployment: while public works projects would create new jobs, restrictions on hours and production would likely reduce them. It did, however, strongly reflect his desire to keep the business community on board, which followed from his overall commitment to capitalism and his sense he would need the cooperation of the leaders of large corporations if real change was to be implemented and not resisted. Always the politician, it was also his hope that he could graft at least part of this community onto a new Democratic electoral coalition.

Through the NRA, the government sanctioned each industry to create a "code of fair competition," usually through its trade association. Such codes could include standardizing wages and hours, setting minimum prices, and establishing maximum quotas for the industry as a whole, as well as for individual firms within the industry. Those that were approved would then be exempt from antitrust laws and administered by Code Authorities.

Since the law mandated the participation of labor and consumer groups in the construction of the codes, the NRA represented a full-blown effort to both rationalize the economy and provide a mechanism for achieving greater social responsibility on the part of corporations. Some latter-day "new nationalists" within the administration, like Rexford Tugwell, even had hopes that the NRA would evolve into a tool of centralized economic planning by the government. Neither vision came to fruition. Instead, businesses, and especially large corporations, came to dominate both code creation and enforcement. This was fairly predictable, and followed precedent. Instead of being placed within a preexisting government bureau, like the Department of Commerce, the NRA was started from scratch. However, since the federal government still suffered from weak administrative capacity, and thus without the governmental expertise to draw upon, but with a mandate to move quickly, many personnel were once again "businesscrats." Not only were codes usually drafted by trade associations, the experts on the code authorities were also mostly selected and staffed by the relevant trade groups. Business dominance then manifested itself in opposition to the participation of government, consumer groups, and unions.[20]

With the business community as the strong, if not sole, partner in these new arrangements, the NRA, like the "associative state" project of the previous decade, represented an attempt at a business-dominated corporatism, in which the business community would attempt to regulate itself. This was not going to be easy. While over five hundred codes were written, many conflicts arose, including those between new and old industries, chain stores and independents, and manufacturers and distributors. Small businesses were especially exercised over what they perceived as large businesses benefiting at their expense, and they mounted a legal challenge. The only issue uniting businesses of all shapes and sizes was mounting concern regarding section 7(a), the section that legalized unions. But with the set of controversies growing, the NRA, like its corporatist predecessors, was probably doomed to failure. The Supreme Court ensured this outcome in May of 1935, when it declared NIRA unconstitutional. The unanimous decision held that Congress had illegitimately delegated its inalienable lawmaking authority to the NRA.[21]

regulatory agencies: With the dissolution of the NRA, so went much of the enthusiasm for developing a broader regulatory capacity, as well as the desire to experiment further with central planning. What it did was reinforce the New Deal's more targeted efforts to deal with economic and social problems. By 1935, sixty new agencies had been created: Agricultural Adjustment Administration (AAA), Tennessee Valley Authority (TVA), National Bituminous Coal Commission (NBCC), Federal Power Commission (FPC), Securities and Exchange Commission (SEC), among others. This proliferation of "alphabet agencies" blossomed from the unique political environment that allowed FDR to take bold action. They were also the result of the notion, held by many New Dealers, that many current problems had been caused by the lack of balance between different sectors and groups in the economy; in particular, the power of business was disproportionate in relation to agriculture. The government, acting as a broker, could create greater balance by providing an arena where groups would have a voice and where they could seek assistance: farmers had the AAA, coal operators the NBCC, and by 1936, workers would have the National Labor Relations Board (NLRB).[22]

In practice, most of the alphabet agencies were modeled after the independent regulatory commissions (IRC) that had been created in the previous forty years. Also following precedent was the problem that in practice, the best-organized interests, and those groups with the greatest resources, received the greatest attention—a profile that frequently matched that of large corporations. Like their Progressive Era forebears, New Deal agencies subscribed to the idea that specialization and expertise could tackle any problem. But once again, given that these agencies were typically created from scratch and without administrative personnel to draw upon from within government, experts frequently came from the industries within the agency's purview. Instead of adopting an adversarial or even neutral stance, these public agencies often became advocates for private enterprise. Predictably, it was a short distance between advocacy and capture, and the New Deal's creation of narrow government agencies ultimately pushed the nation further down the path of "interest group liberalism," where private interests use public authority to their own advantage.[23]

In the short run, even the architect of the New Deal himself became concerned about the operation of IRCs. From Roosevelt's perspective, the problem with these agencies was their independence from the Executive Branch. Hoping to exert greater influence, he appointed a committee to study their strengths and weaknesses. The 1937 report of the President's Committee on Administrative Management delivered the following year found that these regulatory bodies acted as a "fourth branch" of government and recommended integrating them within existing cabinet departments. The timing of the report, however, delivered at roughly the same time as the administration's "court packing" proposal, led to its defeat, as an emerging conservative coalition in Congress became convinced that FDR intended to expand the power of the president at the expense of the other branches of government.[24]

the return of antitrust: The NRA's demise in the late spring of 1935 marked the turning point in Roosevelt's relationship with big business. Though most New Deal programs were either business friendly or designed to benefit the business community, many businessmen became increasingly wary of the growth of government, as was their well-honed reflex. By August, these concerns crystallized into active opposition to the New Deal when a group of businessmen organized the American Liberty League to "combat radicalism," "preserve property rights," and "preserve the Constitution." While it included businesses of all sizes, and while it attracted a bipartisan collection of conservative politicians, the League was dominated by big business, especially executives from Du Pont and General Motors.[25]

As business opposition mounted, Roosevelt grew increasingly resentful and began to have serious doubts about the viability of a cross-class alignment. He came to rely more heavily upon advice of those in his administration who believed that big business was the problem to begin with. Prominent in this group were a coterie of disciples of Louis Brandeis, especially Felix Frankfurter. They held to the old antimonopoly position that the solution to economic and social problems was to break up the concentrated power of large businesses and restore competition. Revealing a broader populist orientation as well, the administration's Second Hundred Days featured the Revenue Act of 1935, also known as the Wealth Tax Act, which included an excess profits tax, and also raised capital gains, estate, and gift taxes. This period also witnessed Roosevelt's signing of the National Labor

Relations Act, an anathema to the business community. At his acceptance speech at the 1936 Democratic National Convention, Roosevelt railed against "economic royalists."[26]

By 1937, the economy had slid back into a recession, and antimonopoly voices grew louder. Robert Jackson, the head of the Antitrust Division of the Justice Department, declared in a couple of speeches that the economic collapse was the result of a "capital strike" of business owners who were withholding investment so as to sabotage the New Deal. Secretary of the Interior Harold Ickes blamed the recession on the domination of America's richest families and spoke of the danger of a "big-business Fascist America—an enslaved America."[27] This was one of the strongest statements ever by a member of the Executive Branch of government against the inherent structural power of large corporations in which their control over investment not only determines the fate of workers, but that of the broader economy.

Consistent with his approach in 1933, Roosevelt entertained other proposals for dealing with the recession. The business leaders who had supported the NRA, such as Owen Young of General Electric, remained convinced that the culprit was excessive competition, which now stood in the way of restoring the "business confidence" needed for investment. They pushed for a new effort at devising a system of corporatist cooperation. Yet another group within the administration advocated for greater public investment, their position recently strengthened by the growing influence of economist John Maynard Keynes and his advocacy of deficit spending to encourage consumption.[28]

The position of the antimonopolists ultimately won out. This was due to the fact that there was no clear path for corporatists past the Supreme Court's earlier decision nullifying the NIRA, while the Democrat's huge losses in the election of 1938 reduced the chances of public investment legislation to near zero. As the field of alternative proposals was thus cleared, the winning approach developed two prongs. The first involved an effort to strengthen antitrust enforcement—America's default strategy for controlling big business. Leading the charge was the new head of the Antitrust Division of the Justice Department, Thurman Arnold, a Yale law professor and author of a devastating critique of antitrust enforcement, *The Folklore of Capitalism*.[29] But Arnold was not cut from the Brandeisian "curse of bigness" cloth. Instead of a moral crusader, Arnold was more a technocrat who believed that antitrust enforcement was needed in order to create the conditions of economic competition. Contrary to the traditional antimonopolist position, he did not believe that a competitive economy was a natural state. He thus decoupled antitrust enforcement from the philosophy of antimonopolism.[30]

Arnold did, however, aggressively seek to fulfill his charge. Between 1938 and 1943 the Justice Department hired scores of new antitrust lawyers who initiated more antitrust cases than any previous administration; in fact, the division's caseload during this period represented 44 percent of all cases undertaken since the Sherman Antitrust Act was first passed in 1890. But given the track record of antitrust enforcement, the ultimate effectiveness of this approach to regulating big business was dubious. Soon, the question was moot. After five years the antitrust push was abandoned, since the mobilization for World War II once again required business cooperation, if not collusion.[31]

For the second prong of the antimonopoly approach to dealing with the recession, the president proposed and Congress authorized the Temporary National Economic Committee (TNEC) to investigate monopolies and the concentration of economic power. In calling for the investigation, Roosevelt declared "The power of a few to manage the economic life of the Nation must be diffused among the many or be transferred to the public and its democratically responsible government."[32] Antimonopolists were therefore encouraged that a "great investigation" would produce a definitive report on how to regulate and break up monopolies.

After three years of exhaustive hearings and dozens of volumes of testimony, monographs, and reports concerning every major American industry, the Committee did issue a monumental report, at least in terms of size: a 783-page final report, 20,000 pages of direct testimony of over five hundred leaders of American industry, and thirteen monographs on particular economic problems. It was harshly critical of big business, noting that as the country was about to enter the war, it was conceivable that the country could secure democracy abroad only to find that it was "under the domination of economic authority far more concentrated and influential than that which existed prior to the war." However, given the rise of fascism and Communism, the authors of the report were also fearful of the scenario where, in an effort to balance the concentration of economic power, government power becomes overly centralized. As such, the report reads like a manifesto of the classical strain of antimonopolism: "On the broad scale, therefore, the committee recommends the maintenance of free, competitive enterprise by the effective suppression of the restrictive practices which have always been recognized as evil."[33]

The report displays both the strengths and weaknesses of these aging ideological underpinnings: a strong condemnation of big business coupled with an enthusiastic embrace of the free market system, nearly to the point of being indistinguishable from laissez faire. Not surprisingly, then, the main recommendations of the committee involved the strengthening of antitrust law and enforcement, so as to restore competition among smaller businesses. In addition, however, the committee also proposed that large corporations be chartered by the federal government, an idea that was recommended a generation earlier by the previous President Roosevelt. The major problem concerning the report was the timing of its release in 1941, just as the country's attention was becoming focused on the impending war. As a result, class resentment and concern over corporate power were displaced by patriotic fervor.[34]

reforms of the financial sector: It is important to note that in addition to IRCs and antitrust, the Roosevelt administration and the Democratic Congress also moved against the powerful corporations within the financial industry. In a 1933 investigation of the Wall Street Crash and subsequent financial collapse, the Pecorra Commission uncovered a variety of abusive practices and conflicts of interest in both the banking and securities industries. The group's findings rallied public support for greater regulation and helped ease passage of both the Glass-Steagall Banking Act of 1933 and the Securities Exchange Act of 1934. The former piece of legislation included the bold provision to break up the concentration of power in the banking industry by separating commercial and investment banking. The latter established the Securities and Exchange Commission to regulate the stock exchanges.[35]

—

With the NIRA, the nation came close to creating a wholly different path for the economic regulation of corporations. When the Supreme Court ruled against the bill, however, it became yet another example of failed corporatism. As a result, the New Deal dug more deeply into the preexisting pathways, both with the expansion of independent regulatory commissions and reinvigorated antitrust enforcement. Still, if one were to add up the various blows that landed against big business during the 1930s, including a more robust regulatory capacity and serious challenges to the legitimacy of the economic system, it would be reasonable to expect that large corporations took a beating during the Depression. If nothing else, the devastating economic downturn might have been expected to rebalance the nation's political economy naturally, through a reduction in corporate size.

Growth of Large Corporations: Impact of Economic Disaster and Big Government

Most businesses suffered during the Depression, especially the early years. But with greater assets to draw upon, larger corporations were in a much better position to ride out the storm of price cuts necessitated by the contraction of consumer demand. They could cut staff, or cut back on "non-essential" expenditures, such as CSR programs. Small companies, by contrast, had slim resources to cut and were more highly exposed to the threat of bankruptcy. Hundreds of thousands of small businesses failed during the Depression decade, and though many small establishments emerged to take their place, most of these quickly perished as well.[36]

Of course, some large corporations were better positioned than others. Those in the consumer-goods sector of the economy did better than those that were situated in heavy industry. The reason for this is that, whereas consumers could defer the purchase of cars, which then led to steep declines for car and steel manufacturers, they still needed to purchase daily items, like food and soap. Also helping companies survive, as well as contributing to larger size, was the practice of "product differentiation." For example, Proctor and Gamble (P&G) developed multiple brands of its products, like soap and laundry detergent, and then aggressively marketed these different brands, frequently to different consumer markets. By spreading risk around, product differentiation was well adapted to an increasingly consumer-driven economy. At the end of the decade, the company was marketing 140 different brands of soap worldwide and controlled 50 percent of the market. Procter and Gamble's "brand management" of its products also included heavy investments in market research and advertising, and in the new media of radio. In the end, firms like P&G learned that nurturing long-term consumer loyalty was an effective way of maintaining consistent sales. Such loyalty, in turn, helped construct higher entry barriers for prospective, usually smaller competitors.[37]

The combination these two trends—that larger corporations fared better than small companies, and consumer-goods establishments fared better than those in heavy industry—also helps to explain the particular success of retail chain stores. Large food chains, including Albertson's

Supermarkets and Publix Super Markets, as well as pharmacy chains, like Long's Drug Stores and Payless Cashways, all had their start during the 1930s. Interestingly, while chain outlets increased their share of total retail sales by 8 percent during the decade, the number of chain stores actually decreased to 123,000 in 1939 from a peak of 160,000 in 1929—the 1920s representing the decade when chain stores took off. This means that the average size of a chain outlet increased. Part of the reason for this was that, much like today, chain stores engendered opposition from local businesses, and many communities responded with tax laws that discriminated against chain outlets—typically a graduated tax based upon the number of outlets. The unintended effect of yet another government policy was a larger chain outlet: as chain stores reduced their number of outlets, they increased the size of those that they kept.[38]

Paradoxically, the expansion of the federal government also strengthened the position of large corporations. While the proliferation of New Deal programs signified that the federal government had finally grown beyond its congenital small size, the new government agencies that administered the programs frequently contracted with the private sector for goods and services. More often than not, it was large businesses that benefited from this spending. For example, IBM grew tremendously when it won the contract to maintain the employment records for twenty-six million people as a result of the Social Security Act of 1935.[39] This new symbiosis in America's political economy was mightily reinforced with the growth of military spending during World War II, discussed later in the chapter. In other words, instead of having its power curbed by the proliferation of New Deal programs, big business was arguably the greatest beneficiary of government expansion.

By the end of the Depression decade, it was clear that the large corporation had more than weathered the storm. In fact, its place in the US economy had actually improved, as measured by the concentration of corporate assets. In 1927, two years before the Wall Street crash, the one hundred largest corporations controlled 36 percent of all corporate assets. In 1939, this figure had increased to 43.5 percent.[40] During the Depression, then, large corporations not only survived, some actually thrived. But because social problems persisted, the political clout of the heads of big business was sufficiently weakened that neither they, nor the business community generally, could hold back demands for social regulations and social welfare programs. However, business leaders were still strong enough to shape the form that these programs would eventually take.

Social Regulations and Welfare: Big Government Finally Arrives

The Depression opened a window of opportunity to overcome the usual obstacles confronting the expansion of government. With mounting social problems and growing unrest, FDR would need to break the mold of minimalist government. But though the New Deal welfare programs did just that, they still revealed the influence of business.

social security: The signature piece of New Deal welfare legislation, which came to form the foundation of America's modern welfare state, was the Social Security Act of 1935. This was the end product of FDR's decision in 1934 to seize the welfare initiative and create what he envisioned as an expansive, cradle-to-grave social insurance system that included unemployment insurance, old-age pensions, assistance to the poor and needy, and health care. To study the problems and formulate legislative proposals he constituted the Committee on Economic Security (CES), headed by his secretary of labor, Francis Perkins.[41]

In 1934 the administration was still in the mode of seeking business support for its New Deal proposals, and the one involving old-age pensions was no exception. The staff of the CES therefore needed the support of the five business members of its Advisory Council on Economic Security for any proposal that it wanted to put forward. These five were all leaders in the area of welfare capitalism, including Gerald Swope of General Electric, Walter C. Teagle of Standard Oil, and Marion B. Folsom of Kodak. While they recognized the need for a public system of social security, they were only interested in one that would not displace their private initiatives. According to Folsom, government should only provide "basic minimum protection and it should not be intended to cover all needs of everyone." In other words, public welfare should only represent a minimal foundation upon which the structure of private welfare, or CSR, would now be built.[42]

The proposal that was put forward was not framed as a new social right, derived from a social democratic, egalitarian philosophy, to which all citizens were entitled. Nor would it draw from the government's general budget. Instead, the old-age pension program was modeled after private insurance. It would be funded by a contributory, and regressive, payroll tax. Furthermore, instead of an egalitarian benefit, pensions would be tied to work, so as not to undermine work incentives, and they would become an unequal property right based upon an inegalitarian system of previous earnings. To placate Southern politicians needed to maintain the Democratic voting majority, the program left out agricultural workers and domestic servants, or in other words, most blacks living in the South. These workers would be relegated to the social assistance programs of the Act, such as Aid to Dependent Children, where state and local officials would determine eligibility for the meager benefit levels that were usually set.[43]

The unemployment proposal that was drawn up by the CES was also a pale reflection of the more generous vision that originally prompted the group's efforts. In fact, the proposal did not constitute much of a federal system at all. Instead, in deference to the tenet of states-rights federalism, unemployment insurance became a federal-state program with forty-eight disparate state plans and only minimal national standards. With respect to a proposal for national health care, the president decided to drop it. This was the result of the calculation that the overwhelming opposition from employers and the American Medical Association, which such a proposal would surely engender, would jeopardize the entire Social Security bill.[44]

the Fair Labor Standards Act: The New Deal also witnessed the first substantial federal legislation that mandated socially responsible employment practices—but only after FDR was able to surmount tremendous obstacles. When the Supreme Court ruled against the NIRA in 1935, it effectively ended the president's efforts to get employers to sign a "blanket code" that set maximum hours and minimum wages; those that did could display the Blue Eagle poster, which patriotically declared, "we do our part." The following year, the Court also voided a New York State minimum wage law as unconstitutional.

Wage and hour legislation thus became a campaign issue during the 1936 election. The Democratic Party platform called for higher labor standards, and Roosevelt promised legislation that would protect workers. In June, as a preview of a bigger bill that would follow, the president signed the hotly contested Public Contracts Act. Building upon the Davis-Bacon Act of 1931, which required those bidding for the construction of public buildings to pay the "prevailing wage," the provisions of the Public Contracts bill required that all government contractors abide by an eight-hour day, forty-hour work week and pay a "prevailing minimum wage" to be determined by the secretary of labor. As the federal government was in a growth mode, this was a significant achievement for the employees of government contractors.

FDR's landslide victory, and his threat to "pack" the Supreme Court to overcome the obstruction of the "nine old men" of the bench, provided the environment, and possibly the incentive, for the Court's reversal in 1937, when it upheld a Washington State minimum wage law. Emboldened, the administration pushed for the passage of the Fair Labor Standards Act. Though ultimately watered down in order to overcome the opposition of Republicans and conservative Southern Democrats, the act was signed into law in June 1938. Its basic provisions were a minimum wage (twenty-five cents an hour), a maximum workweek (forty-four hours per week) and the banning of most child labor. Though the bill covered only about one-fifth of the labor force at first, it was a watershed moment in the history of workplace mandates.[45]

—

With the crisis of the Depression, America was finally able to clear away the perennial obstacles in order to lay the foundation for its modern welfare state. But instead of a universalistic system that would relieve corporations of key social responsibilities, like those of pensions and health care, the welfare state was built upon a minimalist foundation. Instead of being derived from social democratic principles that enumerate a set of social rights, these programs were drawn in accordance with market principles and viewed by their business supporters as supplementary to the structure of private welfare. This, then, ensured that CSR would remain an integral feature of the nation's regulatory structure for large corporations. Still, an important step had finally been taken. The same can be said for social regulations. During the New Deal, the federal government finally opened the regulatory pathway of workplace mandates that required socially responsible practices. With mandated responsibility experiencing fundamental change, it seemed reasonable to expect that the changed political environment would also represent an occasion to fortify the system whereby greater social responsibility was the result of contract negotiations with unions.

Negotiated Responsibility

The Great Sit-Down Strike of 1937

In an effort to stop the decline of membership of its affiliated unions that represented autoworkers, the AFL merged them to form the United Auto Workers Union (UAW) in August 1935. At that point membership stood at twenty thousand. But in the spring of the following year, the UAW switched its affiliation from the AFL to the newly formed Committee of Industrial Organizations (CIO), which was committed to organizing workers along industrial lines. By way of comparison, General Motors was, by most measures, the world's largest manufacturing corporation, with 110 plants in 14 states and 18 countries, employing 150,000 workers. It sat at the center of an industry that had been virulently antiunion since its inception. Therefore, before one of the most important battles in labor history, the UAW was David to GM's Goliath.[46]

The odds seemed to be in the auto industry's favor, when the UAW decided to wage an all-out campaign to win a union contract with one of the auto manufacturers. The odds seemed longer still when the UAW chose GM as its target, instead of the much smaller Chrysler, as the CIO recommended. But though GM was big and powerful, it was not without vulnerabilities. The company had only two plants that contained the body dies for all of the 1937 new model cars (the Fisher body plants in Flint, Michigan, and Cleveland); a successful strike, then, could slow production to a trickle. Furthermore, this would be a different kind of strike. During 1936 there had been dozens of sit-down strikes, in which striking workers occupied a plant. These were frequently spontaneous and short-lived affairs, but they proved very effective, since they nullified the tactics of hiring replacement workers and using violence.

By the evening of December 30, the Great Sit-Down Strike had commenced. For the next six weeks, high-drama ensued.[47] The main goal of the union was to be recognized as the bargaining agent for GM's workers. When the company charged that the strike constituted an unlawful invasion of property rights, the union's president escalated the rhetoric and countered, "What more sacred property right is there in the world today than the right of a man to his job?"[48] When in the dead of winter the company turned off the heat, the men stayed. When the police rushed the plant, the workers greeted them with a hail of iron bolts, hinges, coffee mugs, and bottles. When the police attacked a second time with tear gas, the workers turned the plant's fire hoses on them—the retreat of the police that followed became known as the "Battle of the Running Bulls."

A settlement was finally reached on February 11. Though it did not win exclusive representation rights, at least at first, the union did achieve victory in getting the company to officially recognize the UAW as the bargaining agent for its members. The full significance of this victory can only be understood within the context of the several years leading up to the strike. The good economic times of the 1920s, together with the promise of welfare capitalism, had raised workers' expectations for economic improvement and security. While the abandonment by many of welfare capitalism had been experienced as a betrayal, the Depression undermined faith in the economic system itself. Furthermore, large-scale layoffs led to greater exploitation of the workforce that remained. Together, these factors unleashed a new militancy among workers, who now turned to unions to realize their hopes.

But in 1933 union workers still comprised just 10 percent of the nonagricultural workforce—unchanged in thirty years. Hopes rose when the NIRA was passed, which included section 7(a) that gave workers the "right to organize and bargain collectively through representatives of their own choosing." These hopes were dashed when the NIRA was declared unconstitutional.[49] In 1935, hopes were raised once again when FDR signed the National Labor Relations Act (NLRA). Not only did this legislation legalize workers rights to form unions, it set up the administrative apparatus (National Labor Relations Board) to hold elections so that workers could exercise these rights.[50] Convinced that the NLRA would suffer the same fate as the NIRA, employers mostly ignored it as well, with many winning court injunctions that delayed enforcement while the constitutionality of the act was challenged in court.

Resistance went well beyond simply ignoring the law. Between 1936 and 1937 Congress held hearings on the methods used by employers to combat unions. The report of the La Follette Civil Liberties Committee revealed, among other things, that 2,500 corporations had employed 3,871 labor spies whose main job was to disclose the names of union organizers so they could be fired. The investigation also revealed that many corporations had built arsenals for industrial warfare, including Youngstown Steel, which had in its possession eight machine guns, 369 rifles, and 109 gas guns.[51]

In the context of the concerted resistance to unions, the victory at Flint in 1937 was monumental. Workers had not only overcome tremendous resistance, but for the first time a union had won an agreement from one of the nation's premier, open-shop industries; indeed, the auto workers had defeated the world's largest corporation. Its impact quickly reverberated throughout the economy. Within a few weeks of UAW-GM agreement, the Steel Workers Organizing Committee

(SWOC) signed a contract with U.S. Steel, while the UAW scored yet another victory when, after a short sit-down strike, Chrysler came to terms with the union.[52]

The resistance of employers withered further still when the Supreme Court, in the NLRB v. Jones & Laughlin Steel Corporation, declared the National Labor Relations Act constitutional on April 12. By the end of 1937, successful organizing campaigns in the textile and rubber industries yielded a 50 percent unionization rate in the former and 60 percent in the latter. Ultimately, no mass-production industry was ignored, and unions made progress across the board.[53]

While these events represented a victory for unions in general, they also represented a triumph for the CIO and industrial unionism in particular. After decades of dominance by the AFL and its antiquated craft structure that privileged skilled workers, the CIO was organizing and giving voice to millions of semi-skilled and unskilled workers in the nation's main industries. It also opened its membership doors to blacks and immigrants. By the end of 1937, after only two years of activity, the CIO had a total membership of over 3.7 million workers, more than the older AFL.[54]

The Benefits of Business Unionism

As unionization increased, so did studies that examined the wage effect of unions. In an analysis of earnings of 8.5 million production workers in manufacturing and extraction industries between 1933 and 1945, Arthur M. Ross found that the greater unionization rate of an industry was related to greater wage increases. There was growing evidence, then, that unions were making progress toward the goal of negotiating a "fair day's pay for a fair day's work," and thus decommodifying labor. This can also be seen in the growing resistance of unions to bonus systems of pay that tied greater pay to extra output, since these were seen as devices for speeding up work. In the case of the hours of work, unions continued to chip away at the average workday and workweek, even before passage of the Fair Labor Standards Act.[55]

However, employers continued to resist bargaining over welfare benefits like health insurance or pensions. These were still seen as falling strictly within the purview of managerial prerogatives: benefits offered or withheld at the complete discretion of managers. As a result, a minority of unions continued to offer benefits to their members. By 1937, seventy unions offered death benefits, twenty-nine offered sick benefits, twelve offered old-age benefits, and eleven offered unemployment benefits.[56]

Job Control

Beyond pay, as union contracts began to proliferate, the other features of negotiated responsibility began to take a more discernable shape. In an atmosphere still thick with Depression memories, unions' traditional stress upon job security was only strengthened. Most important in this regard, seniority was increasingly pushed as a criterion in layoff, rehiring, and promotion decisions. Not only did older, long-tenured workers find the seniority principle appealing for obvious reasons, all workers were attracted to the fact that seniority lessoned the power of foremen. In the case of layoffs, the use of seniority spread so rapidly that by 1938, close to 95 percent of union firms used it in some form when employees were let go.[57]

The job instability experienced during the Depression also compounded the problems experienced by workers in industries that only offered seasonal employment. As a result, several of the new CIO unions began to push the idea of wage or employment guarantee plans to compensate for the income that these workers lost as a result of the seasonal nature of their jobs. Though not widely diffused, the vast majority of the 138 firms reported by the National Industrial Conference Board (NICB) to have such plans in 1939 were unionized.[58]

Yet another route to greater job security involved the regulation of employee discipline and dismissal, which became one of first issues that new unions typically broached with management. For example, as unions finally succeeded in unionizing auto and steelworkers at the end of the thirties, the major contracts signed in these industries had provisions for a multistep grievance system that included arbitration as the final step. Once again, the popularity and importance of such procedures can only be understood in the context of decades of experience with the frequently arbitrary decisions of foremen.[59]

Work rules also proliferated in the union contracts signed during this period, thus reinforcing the job control dimension of business unionism. Such rules served several purposes. In the absence of unemployment insurance, some work rules, like those regulating crew size, helped to stabilize employment, while others served to soften the impact of technological unemployment, such as rules governing the use of machines. For other rules, like those regulating the speed of work, the target was labor exploitation, especially as practiced by foremen.

Some rules, like those that controlled output, aimed at both protecting jobs and constraining bosses.[60]

It might have seemed to some that the conditions for a more permanent labor peace were in place. Comparatively speaking, the goals of business unionism were conservative: collective bargaining over wages and working conditions. There were no demands, at least none made by senior leadership, for a share in corporate decision making or participation on boards of directors. But even if not radical by European standards, bargaining with workers over items such as hiring, firing, wages, hours, and work rules was certainly seen by employers as radical, and as a direct threat to traditional managerial prerogatives. Therefore, though employers had suffered a setback when the Supreme Court upheld the constitutionality of the NLRA, they did not all of a sudden throw in the towel and embrace unions.

Instead, some employers continued to rely upon intimidation and violence to resist unions, and some continued to hone the arts of discriminatory hiring and firing, surveillance, and antiunion propaganda. Where companies were forced to recognize unions, they used their superior resources to negotiate contracts that protected managerial prerogatives. At the same time, the National Association of Manufacturers, together with many industry associations attacked the NLRB as unfairly pro-union and lobbied hard for amendments to the NLRA. By 1940 several states had passed antiunion laws, and by the end of 1941, thirty antiunion bills were introduced in Congress.[61]

But many employers conceded that the ability to use harsh methods of union avoidance was increasingly difficult. With unions growing dramatically, CSR became a more important option for those large corporations hoping to keep unions out.

Voluntary Responsibility (CSR)

Welfare Capitalism

No firm exemplified the words and deeds of CSR in the twenties better than General Electric. Fleshing out its commitment to a philosophy of managerial trusteeship, in which "the duty of management is no longer solely to the investor," the company initiated a full array of progressive workplace practices. A bond of loyalty between employer and employee was nurtured with programs that offered workers security in the form of life insurance, pensions, and disability insurance. In 1930 the company broke new ground in the field of employee benefits when it adopted an unemployment plan for its employees.

But within sixteen months the fund was bankrupt. It was simply no match for the devastation that rained upon the company during the early years of the Depression. With its net income falling precipitously from $60.5 million in 1930 to $14.7 million in 1932, the company reduced its payroll by thirty thousand workers. After abandoning efforts to fix the program, company President Gerald Swope declared, "This was too ambitious a plan for any one company to undertake."[62]

The unemployment plan was not the only casualty. By the end of 1932 the company had rescinded the majority of the welfare benefits it had extended to its workers. But the plight of GE was in no way unique among CSR firms. Many of the signature practices of welfare capitalism were upended as the crisis worsened. Employee Representation Plans were also early victims, as approximately 20 percent of these company unions were eliminated between 1929 and 1932. Noncontributory health and pension plans fell, as employers increasingly required employees to foot part of the bill. Due to under-funding, many pension plans turned out to be actuarially unsound, and by 1932 less than half were in a position to guarantee payment to retirees. Also, in the afterglow of the Great Crash, employee stock ownership lost its allure, and with profits nonexistent, profit sharing lost its appeal as well. Particularly vulnerable to cuts were recreational and education programs.[63]

The case of GE supports the conventional wisdom that welfare capitalism was significantly weakened by the Depression. But if one traces developments in welfare capitalism beyond the first few years of this economic calamity, a different conclusion is warranted. In a survey conducted in 1935, the NICB found that not only had welfare capitalism rebounded, but it actually surpassed levels found in a survey conducted in 1927, at the height of trend in the 1920s. For example, while 14 percent of companies reported offering pensions in 1927, 37 percent did so in 1935. Other examples include group health and accident insurance, which rose from 14 percent to 30 percent, and group life insurance, which increased from 40 percent to 59 percent.[64]

Given the argument that CSR was a form of resistance to threats to business autonomy, this is not surprising. The business community was particularly worried about the threat of unionization. After all, section 7(a) of the NIRA had mandated what employers had actively resisted for decades, the right of employees to organize. Welfare capitalist and department store magnate, Edward A. Filene conducted his own study of the NRA in early 1934 and concluded that employers, especially big ones, "do not intend to allow labor to successfully organize A.F. of L. unions in their plants."[65]

Predictably, company unions roared back into existence as many employers, especially in the automobile and steel industries, interpreted compliance to include unions established by employers. Concentrated in large firms, nearly two-thirds of the six hundred to seven hundred company unions in existence in 1935 were established after the NIRA was passed in 1933.[66]

Events in the second half of the decade only heightened business worries. With the passage of the NLRA in 1935, employers launched an all-out legal and propaganda offensive, claiming that the act was unconstitutional and potentially ruinous to harmonious relations between management and labor—distinctly the wrong prescription for an economy still recovering from a depression. At the same time, they continued to restore benefits and restructure employee relations. Management of General Motors held a meeting to discuss a "program to reduce employee grievances," while the National Association of Manufacturers recommended that its members adopt reforms to avoid "labor difficulties." With the formation of the CIO in 1936 and with the Supreme Court decision of 1937 upholding the constitutionality of the NIRA, the strength of union threat as a stimulus to CSR was only reinforced. For example, in the face of CIO drives to organize its workers, International Harvester twice improved their profit-sharing plan, once before the Jones & Laughlin decision, and once after.[67]

The resurgence of welfare capitalism also occurred as many in the business community grew increasingly worried about the push for social welfare legislation. As usual, these worries centered on the impact such legislation would have upon labor costs, in particular, and taxes, in general. Business leaders also worried that new laws might undermine work incentives or lead to an erosion of managerial prerogatives. Lastly, employers in the vanguard of welfare capitalist practices worried that public welfare would undermine their preference for private welfare. As a result, most employers objected to the Social Security Act as it began to take shape.[68]

But as Congress did indeed pass social welfare and labor polices, and as unions won recognition, the nature of the impact of government and unions upon CSR changed. With new laws like Social Security and the Fair Labor Standards Act on the books, employers now needed to heed federal regulations as they developed their new labor policies. More importantly, as unions began to win recognition and negotiate contracts, employers in the nonunion sector began to monitor and imitate the practices of their union peers.[69] The clearest example involved pay. Studies, such as the one by Arthur M. Ross reported earlier, found that over time, the wage differential between union and nonunion firms narrowed. In a period of rapid unionization, one of the most important factors explaining this trend was found to be "sympathetic pressure." As defined by Harold M. Levinson in his 1951 analysis of the union pay effect between 1914 and 1947, this occurs when nonunion employers feel that there is a chance that their firms would be unionized, and therefore raise wage rates in the hopes of appeasing their own employees. Of course, this is just another way of saying union threat.[70]

Another area of influence involved the practice of using seniority in layoff and promotion decisions. Historically, nonunion firms had resisted using seniority, since it was seen as limiting managerial discretion. These employers stressed the importance of merit instead. By 1938, however, as seniority diffused rapidly in union firms, 50 percent of nonunion firms reported using seniority as a criterion in layoff decisions, though it was typically more narrowly and flexibly applied in comparison to unionized firms.[71] As time went on, not only would this percentage continue to grow, seniority was increasingly used a criterion in promotion decisions as well.

More generally, the greater contractualism resulting from the growth of collective bargaining was matched by a growing formalization of personnel practices in nonunion companies. This can be seen in the proliferation of company handbooks and policy statements that detailed the rules and regulations of a company's employment practices. While initially perceived as placing limits upon managerial discretion, and thus resisted, employers ultimately embraced formalization. Of course, both seniority and formalization also reflected the ongoing bureaucratization of large corporations.[72]

The change of heart for nonunion employers also involved the growing realization that rationalized rules reduced the kinds of arbitrary decisions that might nurture pro-union sentiment. As a result, one effect of this formalization trend was to finally end the reign of foremen, since it had frequently been the abuse of their considerable powers that lay at the center of workplace controversies, work stoppages and unionization campaigns. But their fall from power also marked the continued rise of personnel departments, which had experienced their initial popularity in the 1920s. By 1936, they were already standard features of large corporations, with over 80 percent of firms with at least five thousand employees reporting their presence.[73] In nonunion firms, while personnel management both claimed and sometimes assumed a more neutral position, their de facto mission was to thwart unionization. In practice this sometimes meant preempting unions by initiating the practices that unions sought.

Overall, nonunion firms like National Cash Register and Proctor and Gamble remained in the vanguard of welfare capitalism at the end of the 1930s. Dynamic newcomers, such as IBM and Delta Airlines, who enthusiastically embraced welfare practices, joined them. As was true earlier, the likelihood that welfare practices would sink roots in a corporation's culture seemed contingent still upon a company's founder or top manager taking an active interest in personnel matters. Not coincidentally, these leaders frequently had a special loathing of unions and were willing to spend what it would take on welfare programs to keep unions from impinging upon their managerial prerogatives.

Also consistent with the past were the economic conditions conducive to the growth of welfare practices. As always, size mattered. For example, the 1935 NICB survey showed that while 45 percent of corporations with at least ten thousand employees offered health and accident insurance, only 18 percent of firms with less than one hundred employees did the same; the comparable figures for pensions showed 53 percent for large firms and only 3 percent for small firms.[74] But again, not all large corporations were positioned well to be socially responsible. Such behavior was more likely to be found in industries that produced products with a steady demand (e.g., food products), industries with effective governance structures, especially those that were oligopolies (e.g., automobiles and parts, rubber, public utilities), and industries offering newer, dynamic products (e.g., electrical manufacturing). The practices of welfare capitalism were less likely to be found in industries marked by intensive competition (e.g., clothing, textiles).[75]

Corporate Philanthropy

Not wavering from his views that relief for the poor and destitute was the responsibility of private charities and local government, President Hoover saw his role during the Depression as a facilitator and cheerleader for these efforts. As he did with his program to stimulate jobs in the private sector, Hoover appointed a corporate executive—this time

Walter S. Gifford of American Telephone and Telegraph Company—
to head the Organization for Unemployment Relief. To aid the
Organization in its mission to distribute model relief plans to cities and
towns nationwide and raise millions of dollars, Hoover also enlisted
the help of dozens of other business leaders. Of course, the effort lost a
bit of credibility early on when many of these same leaders announced
wage cuts of 10 percent or more just as the campaign began.[76]

At the same time, the Association of Community Chests and
Councils (ACCC) ramped up its efforts as well. It quickly recognized
that corporations, as opposed to individual donors, seemed the best
bet to meet the unprecedented sums required to address the magnitude
of the problems. Consequently, the ACCC formed the Committee on
Business Corporations and made the solicitation of corporate donations an integral part of its annual fundraising drives, known as the
Mobilization for Human Needs. Ironically, it was with greater business
participation that the philanthropic community was able to overcome
its historic bias against simple relief and almsgiving, as opposed to the
community's preference for character-building charity work.

The motives behind corporate philanthropy during the Depression
were no doubt multi-faceted, but they certainly included the pragmatic.
The ACCC explicitly encouraged executives to give as a way of defend-
ing against current and potential criticism of the business community
during this economic crisis. Chain stores and other multi-location
corporations were particularly sensitive to charges of culpability for
economic distress at the local level, as they were increasingly portrayed
as socially irresponsible, absentee owners. Staving off government was
also a motive, as fund-raisers raised the specter of expanding federal
intervention as a way of opening corporate coffers wider. This was
reinforced in campaigns launched by the Chamber of Commerce and
an organization known as the Sentinels of the Republic warning against
the "menace of paternalism" of government programs.

Though data are lacking to fully assess business community response,
a number of cities reported increases in corporate giving; for example,
corporate donations in Pittsburgh rose from $147,000 in 1929 to
$600,000 in 1935. By the mid-thirties, the ACCC reported that corpo-
rate donations to community chests in four hundred cities were roughly
$20 million annually. Another study showed that six chain stores and
ten large manufacturing firms increased their level of donations. But if
most evidence suggests that corporate contributions went up, the total
receipts of community chests decreased during the worst years of the

Depression and the chests' efforts did not come close meeting overall need. The executive director of the ACCC estimated that chest funds represented, at best, only 30 percent of the total needed for relief in cities with community chests.[77]

While the trend of corporate philanthropy was encouraging, a large barrier stood in the way of even greater corporate generosity: its questionable legality. By the early 1930s, it was still unclear whether managers of publicly owned corporations could legally spend shareholders money for non-business-related purposes. Their legal mandate, after all, was to maximize shareholder value. In this unsettled environment, corporations wanting to give frequently resorted to creative accounting devices when reporting charitable gifts. Some included them under miscellaneous expenses, while others would pay an executive extra with the understanding that he would then make a charitable contribution with his bonus. Many took the position that charitable gifts represented payment to the communities in which they resided to compensate them for the benefits they received from these communities.

To clear these muddy legal waters, and to provide a material incentive to encourage greater corporate giving, business leaders pushed for a change in the tax law that would make a corporation's contributions tax deductible, which was the case for individual contributions. Ironically, the Revenue Act of 1935, discussed earlier as a reflection of FDR's turn against big business, included an amendment that allowed corporations to deduct charitable contributions for up to 5 percent of taxable income. Given the continued impact of the Depression, the immediate effect of the amendment was nil. It was not until economic conditions improved in the 1940s that corporate philanthropy showed a substantial increase.

By the end of the 1930s, corporate giving was not only up compared to the beginning of the Depression, it constituted a greater share of all philanthropy. A study by NICB showed that corporate contributions to community chests in 1941 constituted 27 percent of the total, compared with the 22 percent annual average for the years 1920–1929.[78] Like welfare capitalism, corporate philanthropy rebounded after the initial shock of the Depression.

—

The end of the 1930s represented an uncertain time in America. On the one hand, government was still pushing beyond its minimalist bounds, and a renewed antitrust regimen and ongoing Congressional investigations of the monopoly question threatened the dominance of the large corporation. On the other hand, a growing conservative coalition in Congress was applying the brakes on the New Deal, as public works programs were ended. In the case of labor relations, while unions were enjoying their greatest acceptance in growth in the nation's history, big business did not abandon their efforts to resist them. But these uncertainties were about to be suspended as the country once again entered a world war.

World War II

The Military Industrial Complex Is Born

As America's eventual entrance into the war became clear, FDR chose to follow the precedent established during the First World War and rely heavily upon the business community for war mobilization planning and personnel. From 1939 to 1943, one special governmental agency after another was established to coordinate the nation's war effort, and following the precedent set in WWI, business executives on loan from the private sector headed most. By 1942, with executives such as Edward Stettinius of U.S. Steel at the helm (War Resources Board), dozens of "dollar-a-year" men staffed the array of agencies charged with the mammoth tasks of converting existing industrial facilities to war production, securing new facilities where needed, and procuring and allocating all of the raw materials necessary for production.[79]

With the military contracting with the private sector, many businesses prospered. By the end of the war, corporations had produced two million army trucks, twelve thousand warships, forty-one billion rounds of ammunition, and three hundred thousand planes. While it was spending for the war that finally pulled the nation out of the Depression, and while thousands of businesses benefited from government spending, it was big companies that benefited the most. Already in 1942 a Senate committee reported that, though the country had 184,000 manufacturing establishments, three-quarters of all military contracts had been awarded to fifty-six corporations. The largest firms, those employing over ten thousand workers, saw their share of total manufacturing employment rise from 13 percent in 1939 to 30 percent by 1945. In contrast, tens of thousands of small businesses with no connection to the war effort, such as service stations and appliance dealers, were forced to close their doors.[80]

A symbiotic relationship thus developed between the business community and the military. For the military, each branch had an interest in a bigger budget, with more men in uniform and more weapons to fight with. Because they had no intrinsic interest in actually making the uniforms or weapons, they were happy to align themselves with the business community, since this increased the probability that their interests would be satisfied. From the vantage point of business, the military distinguished itself as the branch of government whose growth did not threaten managerial prerogatives. Furthermore, in order that the military got what it needed in a timely fashion, companies were granted incentives, such as subsidies and low-interest loans. To insure that profits were not sacrificed even in war, companies also received cost-plus contracts.[81] These practices, together with multiyear (and sometimes no-bid) contracts that reduced competition among the very largest corporations, functioned as a new type of governance structure. With war preparation and mobilization, America's military-industrial complex was born.

A Forced Peace Benefits Unions

As was true with World War I, labor benefited from America's entrance into World War II. Most immediately, it was the mobilization for war that brought an end to the Depression by putting people back to work. While nonagricultural employment stood at twenty-seven million in 1938, it grew to thirty-eight million by war's end; an additional eleven million men and women donned uniforms. To ensure the cooperation between labor and management, FDR called a conference of union and business leaders who agreed to a program of no strikes or lockouts for the duration of the war. While they committed themselves to peacefully resolve all disputes, they also agreed upon the creation of a National War Labor Board (NWLB) that would handle those disputes that required mediation. Constituted by the president in 1942, the Board included appointees representing business, labor, and the public.

By the end of the war, the NWLB had involved itself heavily in labor-management relations. It ultimately imposed settlements in 17,650 disputed cases, affecting over twelve million workers, and it approved over 415,000 wage agreements that applied to roughly twenty million workers.[82] The Board also encouraged the development of grievance procedures and their formalization in contracts. But while Board actions frequently benefited workers, they sometimes also supported management, as when it sided with the latter's efforts to limit the scope of grievances, so as to protect traditional managerial prerogatives. Instead of allowing grievances over issues of investment strategy or plant closures, the Board only allowed grievances on issues such as work schedules and the number of workers required for a particular operation, or, in other words, the job control dimension of business unionism.

Welfare Capitalism and Fringe Benefits

In 1942 Congress gave the NWLB responsibility of holding all wage increases below 15 percent. The problem was that by 1943 inflation reached 124 percent. The resulting erosion in workers' purchasing power precipitated a wave of strikes, though most of short duration. Under intense pressure, and the target of growing criticism, the NWLB found a creative solution that both helped quiet workers protests and assisted employers in their efforts to retain workers during a period of full employment. It ruled that employer contributions to medical insurance and pensions would not be counted as wages, and therefore not subject to the 15 percent limit.

The Revenue Act of 1942 served to reinforce the subsequent surge in employer-based benefits. Designed to raise funds for the war effort, one of its provisions amended a 1926 law that gave corporations a tax deduction for contributions to pension trust funds. Since, in practice, it was frequently used to avoid taxes, the new rule required that pension plans cover at least 70 percent of employees to receive the tax benefit. It also required that the formulas used to determine both eligibility and the size of the pension benefit not discriminate in favor of highly paid employees. The second provision was an "excess profits tax" on corporate earnings such that profits made during the war that exceeded prewar levels would now be taxed as high as 90 percent. This led employers to place more of their earnings in exempt pension trusts so as to reduce their pretax profits. As a result of both the new law and the NWLB policy, employer contributions to pension funds increased by over 500 percent between 1941 and 1945, from $171 million to $857 million.[83]

Summary

The scope and duration of the Great Depression shook the foundations of America's political economy. Reliance upon self-correcting mechanisms and government sponsored voluntary measures proved wholly inadequate with the economy mired in a cyclical trough. Early on, the voluntarism of corporate social responsibility was also put to the test and failed, as previously exemplary corporations such as GE drastically cut employees and socially responsible practices.

In the ideological climate that featured questions about the viability of the free-market system itself, the large corporation once again became a contested institution. In response, the New Deal government engaged in programmatic experimentation to a degree never before seen in the nation's history. The exploration of new institutional pathways prominently included a government led effort to forge a corporatist accord in the form of the National Recovery Administration.

At this critical juncture, America's political economy both changed and remained the same. On the one hand, the dominance of the large corporation in the economy paradoxically grew. On the other hand, the federal government grew as well. But the ways in which government grew did not fundamentally alter the lopsided nature of the relationship between business and government. Those forms of government intervention that might have had that effect, such as the NRA and public works projects, were ultimately terminated. Instead of new regulatory pathways, deeper ruts were dug for antitrust and independent regulatory commissions. Given their track records, this did not bode well for truly controlling corporations or growth in corporate size and domination. Furthermore, greater government spending, whether for depression-related programs or for the war effort, served to benefit the large corporation through the practice of private contracting, which functioned as a governance structure.

Even so, the days of minimalist government were over. For example, the government laid the cornerstones for both a welfare state and workplace mandates. Of course, the influence of business was felt even here. For example, Social Security was constructed from the business template of private insurance and meant to serve as a minimalist foundation for the expansion of private welfare in the form of CSR. In the case of the Fair Labor Standards Act, various stipulations, lobbied for by the business community, restricted coverage at the outset to a minority of workers. Still, given the long history of business resistance to any form of social welfare or any regulations mandating social responsibility, these were significant and substantial accomplishments. Furthermore, they were important precedents that held the promise of further growth in government mandates.

Just as government grew beyond its inveterate small size, so did the union movement. This was due, in part, to the appearance of the

Congress of Industrial Organizations, a more militant labor federation dedicated to organizing workers of all skill levels along industrial, as opposed to craft lines. Even more important, Congress passed the National Labor Relations Act that finally created an institutional means for seeking collective representation, and which granted legitimacy to unions. As a result, membership rolls soared, as did union contracts and contract provisions dealing with remuneration and control of the job site. By the end of the war, unions were at their strongest ever, with over fourteen million members, a four-fold increase since 1930; the unionization rate stood at 35.5 percent, up from 11.6 percent at the beginning of the Depression. The future of unions and negotiated responsibility looked particularly bright.[84]

In sum, the crisis of the Depression weakened, if only temporarily, the political clout of the business community, and in this environment of opportunity both regulations and unions grew stronger. But this did not spell the end of CSR, as the leaders of America's large corporations did not resign themselves to either unions as partners or interventionist government. In the face of union threat, nonunion employers not only mimicked union establishment practices, such as the use of seniority, they also greatly expanded their offering of fringe benefits. In the face of greater social regulations and welfare, nonunion employers expanded their philanthropic giving. The result, then, was that CSR showed substantial growth during both the Depression and the war.

By 1945 the country had spent over fifteen years coping with two of the greatest crises in the nation's history. Though not fundamentally transformed, the regulatory structure had changed, as each of its three pillars had experienced growth. The question was whether these trajectories would continue and lead to more fundamental change. As with most facets of American society at the end of the war, uncertainty was the only constant, and this included the environment for large corporations and the efforts to control them.

Notes

1. United States Department of Commerce, Bureau of the Census, *Historical Statistics of the United States, Part 1, Colonial Times to 1970* (Washington, DC: US Government Printing Office, 1975), 226.
2. Broadus Mitchell, *Depression Decade: From New Era through New Deal 1929–1941, Volume IX, The Economic History of the United States* (New York: Harper Torchbooks, 1947), 87.
3. Ibid., 82–83.
4. David Kennedy, *Freedom From Fear: The American People in Depression and War, 1929–1945* (New York: Oxford University Press, 1999), 87; Sanford

M. Jacoby, *Employing Bureaucracy: Managers, Unions, and the Transformation of Work in American Industry, 1900–1945* (New York: Columbia University Press, 1985), 216–217.

5. Jacoby, *Employing Bureaucracy*, 207–209.

6. Ibid., 212–213.

7. Kennedy, *Freedom From Fear*, 58; Louis Galambos and Joseph Pratt, *The Rise and Fall of the Corporate Commonwealth: United States Business and Public Policy in the 20th Century* (New York: Basic Books, 1988), 101.

8. Frances Fox Piven and Richard A. Cloward, *Poor People's Movements: Why they Succeed, How They Fail* (New York: Vintage Books, 1979), 49–60.

9. Joseph Freeman, *The Soviet Worker: An Account of the Economic, Social, and Cultural Statue of Labor in the USSR* (New York: International Publishers, 1932); Waldo Frank, *Dawn in Russia* (New York: Charles Scribner's Sons, 1931); William Z. Foster, *Toward Soviet America* (New York: Coward-McCann, Inc., 1932).

10. Upton Sinclair, "Outstanding Issues of the Forthcoming Campaign and the Fundamental Problems Confronting by Country Today," *Literary Digest*, October 13, 1934, http://www.sfmuseum.org/hist/sinclair.html.

11. William E. Leuchtenburg, *Franklin D. Roosevelt and the New Deal, 1932–1940* (New York: Harper Torchbooks, 1963), 114–115.

12. Alan Brinkley, *Voices of Protest: Huey Long, Father Coughlin, and the Great Depression* (New York: Vintage Books, 1983).

13. Stuart Chase, "A Ten Year Plan for America," *Harper's Magazine*, 163, June 1933; George Soule, *A Planned Society* (New York: The Macmillan Company, 1932); Charles A. Beard, "A Five Year Plan for America," *Forum* 86, July 1931; Reinhold Niebuhr, *Moral Man and Immoral Society* (New York: Charles Scribner's Sons, 1932); Arthur M. Schlesinger, Jr., *The Crisis of the Old Order: 1919–1933, The Age of Roosevelt, Volume 1* (New York: Houghton Mifflin Harcourt, 2003), 212.

14. Louis D. Brandeis, *The Curse of Bigness: Miscellaneous Papers of Louis C. Brandeis*, ed. Osmond K. Fraenkel (New York: Viking Press, 1934).

15. Ellis W. Hawley, *The New Deal and the Problem of Monopoly* (Princeton, New Jersey: Princeton University Press, 1966), chapter 15.

16. Kennedy, *Freedom From Fear*, 132–133; Alan Brinkley, *The End of Reform: New Deal Liberalism in Recession and War* (New York: Alfred A. Knopf, 1995), chapter 4.

17. Irving Bernstein, *Turbulent Years: A History of the American Worker, 1933–1941* (Boston: Houghton Mifflin Company, 1970), 19–25.

18. Kennedy, *Freedom From Fear*, 114–115.

19. Theda Skocpol and Kenneth Finegold, "State Capacity and Economic Intervention in the Early New Deal," *Political Science Quarterly* 97, no. 2 (Summer 1982).

20. Ibid.; Hawley, *The New Deal*, chapters 3–7; Leuchtenburg, *Franklin D. Roosevelt and the New Deal*, chapter 4.

21. Skocpol and Finegold, "State Capacity and Economic Intervention," 265–266; Kennedy, *Freedom From Fear*, 328.

22. James A. Morone, *The Democratic Wish: Popular Participation and the Limits of American Government* (New York: Basic Books, 1990), 130–134.

23. Ibid., 131–133, 179; Leuchtenburg, *Franklin D. Roosevelt and the New Deal*, 87–89; Theodore J. Lowi, *The End of Liberalism: The Second Republic of the United States*, 2nd ed. (New York: W. W. Norton & Company, 1979), 51.

24. Marver H. Bernstein, "Independent Regulatory Agencies: A Perspective on Their Reform," *The Annals of the American Academy of Political and Social Science* 400 (March 1972); Brinkley, *The End of Reform*, 21–22.

25. Leuchtenburg, *Franklin D. Roosevelt and the New Deal*, 91–92; Hawley, *The New Deal*, 152; Kim Phillips-Fein, *Invisible Hands: The Businessmen's Crusade Against the New Deal* (New York: W. W. Norton, 2009), chapter 1.

26. Leuchtenburg, *Franklin D. Roosevelt and the New Deal*, chapter 7.

27. Brinkley, *The End of Reform*, 57.

28. Ibid., 89.

29. Thurman W. Arnold, *The Folklore of Capitalism* (New Haven, Connecticut: Yale University Press, 1937).

30. Brinkley, *The End of Reform*, chapter 6.

31. Ibid., 111–116; Leuchtenburg, *Franklin D. Roosevelt and the New Deal*, 147–158; Richard Hofstadter, "What Happened to the Antitrust Movement," in *The Making of Competition Policy*, eds. Daniel A. Crane and Herbert Hovenkamp (New York, Oxford University Press, 2013), revised version of article originally published in 1964.

32. Temporary National Economic Committee, *Final Report and Recommendations of the Temporary National Economic Committee: Investigation of Concentration of Economic Power* (Washington, DC: United States Government Printing Office, 1941), 15.

33. Ibid., 1, 9.

34. Brinkley, *The End of Reform*, 122–127.

35. Leuchtenburg, *Franklin D. Roosevelt and the New Deal*, 59–60.

36. Galambos and Pratt, *The Rise and Fall of the Corporate Commonwealth*, 125; Thomas K. McCraw, *American Business, 1920–2000: How it Worked* (Wheeling, Illinois: Harlan Davidson, Inc., 2000), 39.

37. McCraw, *American Business*.

38. Ibid., 40–41; Mitchell, *Depression Decade*, 261–264.

39. Ibid., 40.

40. Phillip I. Blumberg, *The Megacorporation in American Society: The Scope of Corporate Power* (Englewood, New Jersey: Prentice-Hall, Inc., 1975), 27.

41. Kennedy, *Freedom From Fear*, 262.

42. Sanford M. Jacoby, *Modern Manors: Welfare Capitalism Since the New Deal* (Princeton, New Jersey: Princeton University Press, 1997), 209, 207.

43. Jill Quadagno, *The Color of Welfare: How Racism Undermined the War on Poverty* (New York: Oxford University Press, 1994), 20–22.

44. Kennedy, *Freedom From Fear*, chapter 9.

45. Ira Katznelson, *Fear Itself: The New Deal and the Origins of Our Time* (New York: Liveright Publishing Corporation, 2013), 267–272.

46. John G. Rayback, *A History of American Labor* (New York: The Free Press, 1966), 353; Bernstein, *Turbulent Years*, 516–517.

47. Ibid., chapter 11.

48. Foster Rhea Dulles and Melvyn Dubofsky, *Labor in America: A History*, 5th ed. (Arlington Heights, Illinois: Harlan Davidson, Inc., 1993), 292.

49. Ibid., 259.

50. Sanford Cohen, *Labor in the United States*, 3rd ed. (Columbus, Ohio: Charles E. Merrill Publishing Company, 1970), 469–470.

51. Dulles and Dubofsky, *Labor in America*, 268; Jerold S. Auerbach, *Labor and Liberty: The La Follette Committee and the New Deal* (Indianapolis: The Bobbs-Merrill Company, Inc., 1966).

52. Dulles and Dubofsky, *Labor in America*, 294.

53. Rayback, *A History of American Labor*, 355.

54. Ibid., 288–289.

55. Arthur D. Butler, *Labor Economics and Institutions* (New York: The Macmillan Company, 1961), 370; Harry A. Millis and Royal E. Montgomery, *Organized Labor* (New York: McGraw-Hill Book Company, Inc., 1945), 407, 422.

56. Jacoby, *Employing Bureaucracy*, 245; Millis and Montgomery, *Organized Labor*, 334.

57. Jacoby, *Employing Bureaucracy*, 245; Sumner H. Slichter, *Union Policies and Industrial Management* (Washington, DC: The Brookings Institution, 1941), chapter 4.

58. Jacoby, *Employing Bureaucracy*, 248.

59. Ibid., 268.

60. Slichter, *Union Policies and Industrial Management*, 166, 206.

61. Rayback, *A History of American Labor*, 365–373.

62. Ronald W. Schatz, *The Electrical Workers: A Story of Labor at General Electric and Westinghouse* (Urbana, Illinois: University of Illinois Press, 1983), 58–59, 60–61.

63. National Industrial Conference Board, *Effect of the Depression on Industrial Relations Programs* (New York: National Industrial Conference Board, 1934); Jacoby, Employing Bureaucracy, 219–221.

64. National Industrial Conference Board, *What Employers are Doing for Employees* (New York: National Industrial Conference Board, 1936), 26. This data must be read with some caution. They come from two surveys published by the National Industrial Conference Board. It is not clear how representative the sample of companies in either year (1927 and 1935) is, and in all likelihood, the samples are not strictly comparable.

65. Bernstein, *Turbulent Years*, 804.

66. Kennedy, *Freedom From Fear*, 187; Jacoby, *Employing Bureaucracy*, 226–227.

67. Robert Ozanne, *A Century of Labor-Management Relations at McCormick and International Harvester* (Madison, Wisconsin: The University of Wisconsin Press, 1967), 94.

68. Charles Noble, *Welfare as We Knew It: A Political History of the American Welfare State* (New York: Oxford University Press, 1997), 59.

69. Jacoby, *Employing Bureaucracy*, 254.

70. Butler, *Labor Economics and Institutions*, 374.

71. Jacoby, *Employing Bureaucracy*, 245.

72. Ibid., 250–253.

73. National Industrial Conference Board, *What Employers are Doing for Employees*, 61.

74. Ibid., 34–35.

75. Ibid., Tables 21, 36, 39, 45, 54.

76. This section draws primarily from Robert H. Bremmer, *American Philanthropy*, 2nd ed. (Chicago: University of Chicago Press, 1968).

77. Morrell Heald, *The Social Responsibilities of Business: Company and Community, 1900–1960* (Cleveland: The Press of Case Western Reserve University, 1970), 151, 168.

78. Ibid., 203.

79. McCraw, *American Business*, 78.

80. Ibid., chapter 5.

81. Edward D. Berkowitz and Kim McQuaid, *Creating the Welfare State: the Political Economy of the 20th Century Reform*, rev. ed. (Lawrence, Kansas: University of Kansas Press, 1992), 150.

82. Dulles and Dubofsky, *Labor in America*, 331.

83. Stevens, Beth, "Blurring the Boundaries: How the Federal Government Has Influenced Welfare Benefits in the Private Sector," in *The Politics of Social Policy in the United States*, eds. Margaret Weir, Ann Shola Orloff, and Theda Skocpol (Princeton, New Jersey: Princeton University Press, 1988), 130–131; Sumner H. Slichter, James J. Healy, and E. Robert Livernash, *The Impact of Collective Bargaining on Management, Washington* (DC: The Brookings Institution, 1960), 373.

84. United States Bureau of the Census, *Historical Statistics of the United States, Part 1, Colonial Times to 1970* (Washington, DC: US Government Printing Office, 1975), 178.

6

The Postwar Triumph of America's Peculiar Regulatory Structure

As America entered the post-Depression, postwar period, mounting uncertainty left the country at a set of critical junctures for both its political economy and labor relations, which created real possibilities for fundamental change in the overall approach to controlling large corporations. Worries about unemployment in the postwar economy led many to argue for a stronger interventionist role for government, one that would constrain traditional managerial prerogatives, and thus rebalance the political economy. Others hoped to build a much sturdier welfare state, one that would make government, not corporations, responsible for welfare goods such as health care. An emerging vanguard of labor leaders was crafting proposals that would give workers a say in the decision-making process of corporations. Should these alternative paths be explored, America's regulatory structure could undergo substantial change, with the reliance upon CSR significantly reduced.

Mandated Responsibility

Rebalancing the Political Economy: The Fight for Full Employment

As had occurred a generation earlier, the mobilization for war fundamentally altered America's political economy, at least temporarily. Through an array of agencies, the federal government now intervened in the most important sectors of the economy, with a direct hand in investment, price, and wage decisions. In contrast to World War I, however, there was considerable sentiment in favor of maintaining a substantial economic role for government as the end of the war came into view. Many economists encouraged strong governmental action in order to forestall the possibility that an economic depression would follow on the heels of cancelled defense contracts and returning soldiers in search of work. Such views were buttressed in both theory and practice. While the analyses of British economist John Maynard Keynes argued that market economies required government intervention, the huge sums spent by government during the war were increasingly credited with actually ending the Depression of the thirties. The remaining New Dealers in the administration, fearful of a return to a laissez-faire past, also sought to institutionalize an interventionist role for the government in the economy. Accordingly, by 1944 there were thirty-three federal agencies actively engaged in postwar planning, or what was called "reconversion."[1]

The support for a permanent economic role for government coalesced around the issue of whether government should assume an active role in guaranteeing work. With memories of the Depression still vivid, many in the country thought that it should. A survey conducted in 1944 found that 67 percent of the public supported the proposition that the government should, if necessary, assure everyone a job. This, then, was the environment in January 1945 when the Full Employment Bill was introduced in the Senate. The major provisions of the bill provided that "All Americans able to work and seeking work have the right to useful, remunerative, regular, and full-time employment . . ." and that "it is the policy of the United States to assure the existence at all times of sufficient employment opportunities. . . ." At the outset, the bill's prospects seemed good, as Democrats enjoyed a 56-38 majority. Senator James Murray, a liberal from Montana, introduced the bill, which was then referred to the Banking and Currency Committee, chaired by the champion of liberal causes, Senator Robert Wagner of New York. The Committee heard testimony from sixty-seven witnesses who overwhelmingly spoke in favor of the bill, including twelve of fifteen business representatives. With the active support of organized labor and liberal groups like the Union for Democratic Action, the Full Employment Act of 1945 passed by a lopsided 71-10 vote on September 28, 1945.[2]

Because the implications of this bill were far-reaching, the nation found itself at a critical juncture. Giving the federal government the mandate to guarantee full employment would go a long way toward creating a more balanced political economy, one where the government would be better able to control large corporations. Building upon the New Deal's project of legitimizing government, it would likely lead to stronger social regulations and welfare measures, thus obviating the expansion of CSR.

But while both the Senate reconversion debate and vote in favor of full employment displayed a strong consensus in favor of government intervention, there was a stubborn, dissenting voice: the majority of the business community. Realizing that fundamental managerial prerogatives were at stake as the war came to an end, business leaders launched a public-relations campaign to resell the American public on the virtues of the free-enterprise system, which had been tarnished during the Depression and obscured by the war. In the forefront of this campaign was the National Association of Manufacturers (NAM), which produced articles, pamphlets, editorials, and ultimately a two-volume study entitled *The American Individual Enterprise System*.[3] Within the context of this broader campaign, business leaders took direct aim at the Full Employment Bill. Claiming philosophically that a free society could not make such a guarantee, these spokesmen also charged that the bill would, among other results, kill initiative, undermine business confidence, and produce rampant inflation.[4] But after the bill was passed in the Senate, the NAM also realized that it would have to go beyond its public-relations efforts to shape the climate of opinion and ramp up its lobbying efforts in the other chamber of Congress.

The ultimate fate of the Full Employment Act represents yet another case study of the difficulties of passing substantial legislation in the American system of multiple checks and balances. While Democrats in the House also enjoyed a healthy majority (242–190), it was decidedly more conservative than the Senate. In practice, a coalition of the chamber's Republicans and the contingent of Southern Democrats was in a position to block most progressive social legislation. Its power was magnified by the tendency of Southerners to be committee chairmen, the result of the South's one-party domination and House rules that assigned chairmanships according to seniority. This included Carter Manasco of Alabama, the chairman of the committee to which the House version of the bill was referred, the Committee on Expenditures in the Executive Departments.

Compared to Senate's Banking and Currency Committee, Manasco's committee was much more sensitive to the concerns of the business community, so much so, in fact, that it was NAM lobbyists who helped Manasco devise a strategy to defeat the bill. This included coming up with the witnesses that would testify before the committee. Of the fourteen business representatives on the witness list, only one

175

registered support for the bill, thus reversing the lopsidedness of the Senate witness list. The highly contentious hearings lasted twenty-one days, almost twice the amount of time taken by the Senate. In the end, the campaign against the bill was successful, as the Committee easily defeated the bill in November.[5]

Had this been the pre-Depression era, the question concerning government's economic role would have been resolved right there. But the political culture had in fact changed as a result of government's strong performance during the crises of depression and war. Just saying no was no longer enough in an environment that demanded some solution. The House would need to offer a substitute bill. Lending a hand in redrafting employment legislation was the newly formed Committee for Economic Development (CED), composed of corporate liberals like Paul G. Hoffman of Studebaker and Marion B. Folsom of Eastman Kodak. Unlike the NAM, the CED realized that restoring the minimalist government of the 1920s was not a viable option. Instead, it sought to create a positive role for government in maintaining overall economic stability. So while the substitute bill that passed eliminated the declaration of full-time employment as a right, and though much weaker than the Senate version, the House bill did articulate a role for government, which was to "to promote maximum employment, production, and purchasing power." The bill also established the Council of Economic Advisors that was charged with submitting recommendations for action whenever inflation or unemployment threatened.[6]

The compromise version of the bill that ultimately passed both chambers, now entitled the Employment Act of 1946, closely resembled the House version.[7] This marked an important turning point for the nation's political economy. The government did not disengage completely from the economy. Instead, it began to travel down a Keynesian path of adopting broad-based monetary, fiscal, and tax policies aimed at managing the economy. But this would be done without managing the key institution of the economy, the large corporation. In other words, New Deal challenges to big business were effectively dead. Gone were calls for centralized planning, government-led efforts to build corporatist structures of cooperation, or even limited nationalization. In short, the power of large corporations to make investments as they pleased was left intact, and the public purpose of corporations was left to chance. The business community, with the help of conservatives in Congress, had thus resisted any form of government intervention after the war that would impinge upon managerial prerogatives. Instead, growth in government would continue to benefit large corporations.

Growth of Large Corporations: The Cold War and Defense Spending

Before the Employment Act passed, demobilization did at first look like it might restore the old political economy. Indeed, President Truman issued an executive order that instructed federal agencies "to move as rapidly as possible . . . toward the removal of price, wage, production, and other controls. . . ."[8] This process included the rapid divestment of facilities built by the government during the war. Not surprisingly, large corporations fared particularly well in this reconversion process. Having operated 79 percent of government-financed plants, the 250 largest manufacturing firms acquired 70 percent of divested assets at what were frequently fire-sale prices.[9]

But in addition to the macroeconomic role established by the Employment Act, foreign policy intruded to keep government from shrinking to its minimalist form. Early on in his administration, Truman adopted a hardline stance against the Soviet Union, and his administration fashioned a set of military, economic, and diplomatic strategies designed to prevent Communism from spreading beyond its current borders. He justified his policy of containment, which came to be known as the Truman Doctrine, as necessary to preserve the freedom of all Americans. With the intervention on the side of the monarchy during the civil war in Greece in 1947, in order to prevent a Communist victory, the Cold War had commenced.[10]

By the end of the decade, Congress had authorized $1.3 billion to deploy American troops in newly created army bases around the world. But this would just be the beginning. Instead of contracting to its prewar level, as had been true after previous wars, defense spending, though reduced, continued to represent a large share of the federal budget. As the Cold War escalated, including the outbreak of the Korean War in 1950 and the beginnings of a nuclear arms race, pressures to increase defense spending continued throughout the decade of the fifties. By 1960, defense spending was $45.9 billion, or nearly half of the entire federal budget; by themselves, defense outlays represented over 9 percent of GNP.[11]

Consistent with the pattern set during WWII, roughly half, or $23 billion, of all defense spending went to private contractors. Also consistent with precedent, large corporations received the lion's share of this spending: the top one hundred contractors received

73 percent. One of these beneficiaries was Boeing Airplane. In 1939 this midsized company of two thousand employees was on the verge of bankruptcy. As a result of Pentagon orders, especially the contract to produce thirteen thousand B-17 bombers, the company grew to 45,000 employees by the war's end. Though briefly threatened with the need to downsize when the government cancelled an order for B-29s in 1945, Boeing won a series of contracts to build aircraft that met the needs of the Cold War. Included in this group was an order for the B-52 Stratofortress, a plane outfitted to carry nuclear weapons that became the mainstay of the nation's Strategic Air Command. Taking advantage of the fact that much of the government underwritten new technology was transferable to the civilian market, Boeing became the largest producer of commercial aircraft after introducing the hugely successful 707-passenger jet in 1954.[12]

Beyond the security of winning a government contract, the form that defense contracting often took minimized the risks of competition, and thus functioned as a type of governance structure. For example, over two-thirds of the total amount awarded was the result of negotiations between the Pentagon and one contractor, and only 14 percent was the result of true competitive bidding.[13] Even where bidding was involved, the losers, which were typically other large corporations, were frequently used as subcontractors.[14] Risk was also minimized with "cost-plus" contracts, where businesses received a negotiated rate of profit in addition to the amount needed to cover their costs. Given the lucrative nature of defense contracts, firms like General Dynamics operated in "monopsonies," in which there was only one buyer (the Pentagon) for most of a company's business.

Concern over national security was also a major impetus of the largest domestic initiative during the Eisenhower administration. At the height of the Cold War, the need for a modern and efficient highway to transport men and munitions in case of war helped to justify the Federal-Aid Highway Act of 1956. The bill authorized $25 billion for the years 1957 to 1969 to build 41,000 miles of the Interstate Highway System. Almost all of this money was awarded to private contractors.[15]

But even where there was no connection to national security, the pattern of government using private contractors to achieve public goals could be found at all levels of government and in all manner of government spending, whether it was the building of schools, office buildings, low-income housing, libraries, hospitals, or airports. The significance of this pattern grew as government grew. From 1950 until 1960, the federal budget alone more than doubled, from almost $40 billion to over $92 billion, and by the mid-1960s, local, state, and federal spending accounted for 21 percent of the gross national product. Predictably, the main beneficiaries of governments' contracting with the private sector were, more often than not, larger corporations.[16]

Government spending was not the only way in which government contributed to the continued growth and dominance of big business in the postwar period. By fostering foreign trade, the federal government assisted in the rise of the multinational corporation. Up until the postwar period, American businesses overwhelmingly served an expanding domestic market. Of the minority of companies that had developed overseas operations earlier in the century, many were forced to retrench as a result of the Depression and the Second World War. But after the war, most European economies and their major corporations were reeling from the war's devastation. As the United States was not a theater of war, American corporations were unscathed, and thus in an optimal position to take advantage of the lack of international competition to push into foreign markets. They were encouraged to do so by the European Recovery Program of 1947. Passed for both humanitarian reasons and to contain the spread of Communism, the Marshall Plan, as it was known, spent billions to help Europeans buy American goods.[17]

Between 1950 and 1960, American exports nearly doubled, to $20.6 billion. To facilitate further growth, and to avoid tariff and trade barriers, many American corporations established divisions in the foreign markets they served. In the decade of the fifties alone, foreign direct investment by American corporations nearly tripled, from $11.8 billion in 1950 to $31.8 billion in 1960. General Motors is a case in point. Though the company already assembled cars abroad before the war, it invested heavily in new plants and greatly expanded its international production from 1946 to 1960. While its Vauxhall (British) subsidiary boosted production from 19,713 to 145,742 cars, its Opel subsidiary (German) saw production soar from 839 to 370,073 cars. In addition, GM was making cars in Australia (Holden), trucks in Great Britain (Bedford), and by 1959 it had pushed into South America, with its GM do Brasil division.[18]

With the aid of government policy and spending, America's leading corporations grew larger and more dominant after the war. But a favorable response from the public to the restoration of big business could not, at least at first, be taken for granted. NAM's propaganda campaign during the debate over full employment revealed that big business was worried about public opinion. After all, memories of the Depression, and business's culpability, were still vivid. In addition, just before the war the Roosevelt administration had launched a two-prong attack against big business, featuring a reinvigoration of antitrust enforcement and an examination of big business practices and dominance conducted by the Temporary National Economic Committee that threatened to recommend dramatic reforms to curtail the power of big business.

Ideological and Political Challenges: The Cold War Inoculates Large Corporations

The prewar campaign to reign in large corporations had been fueled by a revival of antimonopolism. At the war's end, this tradition proved to be alive and well in the person of Estes Kefauver. A New Dealer from Tennessee, Kefauver won a special election to the House in 1939. Though the war had quieted criticism of large corporations, Kefauver attempted to shine the spotlight again on big business as soon as the hostilities ended. In 1946 he chaired the Monopoly Subcommittee of the House Small Business Committee as it investigated the problems associated with economic concentration.

In a talk given at the meetings of the American Economic Association in 1948, Kefauver articulated several concerns with the dominance of big business: the lack of competition led to higher prices; standards of human welfare were lower in communities dominated by large, absentee owners; and the extraordinary power of big business threatened democratic liberties and political rights. Adhering to the tenets of the antimonopoly tradition, Kefauver viewed an economy dominated by small businesses as the best guarantor of freedom and democracy. Refining the tradition to reflect prevailing Cold War sentiments, he also argued that getting tough on big business was also the best defense against Communism. What was needed, then, was a strengthening of antitrust law, which would restore competition, and thus favor smaller enterprises. After being elected to the Senate, Kefauver followed through by being one of the architects of the Cellar-Kefauver Act of 1950, a successful effort to amend the Clayton Act—discussed below.

Involved in other legislative causes in the early fifties, Kefauver was able to resume his crusade against big business in 1957 as chair of the Senate's Antitrust and Monopoly Subcommittee. Until his death in 1963, Kefauver's subcommittee investigated economic concentration in American industry, ultimately producing twenty-nine volumes that included discussions of practices like administrative pricing in the steel, automotive, and pharmaceutical industries. In the case of the auto industry, where he found no real price competition, he even recommended breaking up General Motors.[19]

In the end, however, Kefauver was mostly a lone warrior in his antitrust battle against large corporations. Antimonopolism no longer resonated with large segments of the American public. Instead of the return of big-business antipathy, and in light of their contributions to the war effort, large corporations rebounded in public opinion. In a survey conducted in 1950, 76 percent of respondents believed that the good effects of big business (higher wages and job security) outweighed the bad effects (too much power). The softening of anti-business sentiment was also shown in the result that less than half of respondents (47 percent) understood the term "monopoly," while only 23 percent understood the term "antitrust suit," and just 10 percent recognized the "Sherman Act."[20]

Big business also benefited from the ideological environment created by the domestic front of the Cold War. In 1947, President Truman established the Federal Employees Loyalty and Security Program, which barred members of the Communist Party from working for the federal government. To aid this effort, Attorney General Tom C. Clark published a list of subversive organizations to screen against the employment of Communists. With a vague criterion for what constituted "subversive," the list grew to include hundreds of organizations, thus stigmatizing many thousands engaged in lawful activities. Following suit, many state and local governments passed laws that required loyalty oaths of their public employees. As all levels of government were attempting to weed out Communists, the House Un-American Activities Committee began its highly sensationalized hearings into the Communist subversion of the American way of life via Hollywood movies.

Following the precedent set after WWI, the post-WWII milieu nurtured another Red Scare. By 1949, Attorney General J. Howard McGrath warned in 1949 that "Communists . . . are everywhere—in factories, offices, butcher shops, on street corners, in private business. . . ."

In 1950 Congress passed the Internal Security Act, which required Communist organizations to register with a government board. It was also in that year that the culminating manifestation of what was now anticommunist hysteria made its appearance. After gaining national attention with inflammatory speeches in which he branded government officials as Communists, Senator Joseph McCarthy in 1953 began to use his perch as chairman of the Senate Permanent Subcommittee on Investigations to expose and root out Communists wherever they exited, especially those he charged were currently working for the Executive Branch.[21]

In effect, the crusade against Communism lopped off the left tail of the American ideological spectrum, as the climate of opinion created by anticommunism was wholly hostile to dissent. With America's freedoms and entire way of life presumably at stake, the critique of any American institution was automatically suspect. Since the contrast between Communism and capitalism started with the contrast in economies, the level of intolerance was particularly high for ideas that challenged the "free enterprise system," or its leading institution, the large corporation.

Of course, large corporations were not wholly immune from criticism during this period, but most of this did not expand beyond the walls of academia. Unlike Kefauver, however, most of these critics had abandoned the antimonopoly position that the reign of small businesses could be restored. Instead, critics accepted that large corporations were here to stay. The challenge, then, was to keep the power of these entities in check. According to liberal economist John Kenneth Galbraith, such a system was, in fact, already emerging. Reflecting the dominance of a pluralist paradigm in the social sciences during this period, in which groups competing for power balance one another's interests, Galbraith argued in his 1952 book *American Capitalism* that the previous generation had not only witnessed the growth of big business, but also the growth of big labor unions, big retailers, and big government.[22] These later institutions were becoming "countervailing powers," balancing the power of large corporations and supplanting competition as the main check against the abuse of economic power.

Others did not hold out much hope in achieving a pluralistic ideal, but instead took aim at what was seen as an emerging elite. The tradition that critically examined the corrosive effects of large corporations upon public government was updated to examine the corrosive impact of big business upon big government. Most prominent here was the appearance of C. Wright Mills's *Power Elite* in 1956.[23] The Columbia sociologist argued that instead of a democratically accountable government, an elite comprising the leaders of three sectors of society made decisions that were increasingly national in scale. These leadership positions consisted of the executives of the nation's largest corporations, members of the Executive Branch of the federal government, and high-ranking military officials, especially the Joint Chiefs of Staff. A shared background and education nurtured a common worldview, which included a strong commitment to the free-enterprise system, as well as the belief that one of the primary responsibilities of government was to maintain a favorable business climate. Given the increasing interconnections among these three sectors, elite roles were becoming more and more interchangeable.

By the end of the fifties, concerns about these institutional intersections found expression in the belief that America was increasingly dominated by a "military-industrial complex" (MIC). Defense contractors, especially those that operated in monopsonies, became increasingly dependent upon the defense budget and gained an interest in, and actively sought, its continued growth. The various branches of the military also gained an interest in the continued growth of the defense budget; as they competed with one another for appropriations for new weapons systems, they sought the support of defense contractors with whom they could establish stable relations and tight cooperation. This confluence of interests further manifested itself in the sharing of personnel. In contrast to the standard trajectory where businessmen enter government, the flow of expertise in the MIC was from the military to private industry. In 1959, one study showed that 768 former military officers had jobs in ninety-seven of the top one hundred defense contractors.[24] Concern over the MIC was sufficiently high that it spread beyond academic circles. Indeed, in his farewell address to the nation in 1960, President Eisenhower's warned of the "unwarranted influence, whether sought or unsought, by the military-industrial complex."[25]

In addition to the economic and political impact of large corporations, some opened a cultural line of criticism by exploring how the structure of work in large, and increasingly bureaucratic corporations was shaping individual character. In *The Lonely Crowd*, Harvard sociologist David Riesman detected a new personality type among white-collar workers. Instead of being guided by an internalized set of standards acquired in childhood (inner-directed), these workers appeared to be other-directed, in the sense they were guided more by what others thought and by the desire to gain approval. C. Wright Mills echoed this in *White Collar*, where he contrasted the greater independence of the old middle class of entrepreneurs, artisans, and professionals with the typical white-collar worker who is "no longer free to plan." By 1956, *Fortune* magazine writer William H. Whyte gave this type of worker the label of "organization man"—someone who subordinates his personal goals and wishes to the demands of the corporation for which he works.[26]

—

Overall, for the first generation after the war, there was no serious challenge to the large corporation as it resumed its position of dominance in the peacetime economy. This was the result, in part, of the prestige that the business community recovered due to its performance during the war, as well as the fact that the anticommunism after the war made any form of dissent more difficult. But as important, the performance of the economy during this period continued to inoculate large corporations from attack. With productivity growing by an average of 3.4 percent annually between 1948 and 1966, GNP grew two and a half times in real dollars from the end of the war to the end of the 1960s. With literally millions of Americans ascending into the middle class as a result, business was able to fully reclaim its standing among the public that had been so damaged by the Depression.[27]

In short, there was no strong push for more robust regulation. Even so, an important change was made to antitrust law.

Economic Regulations: The Persistence of Old Pathways

antitrust: Though Senator Kefauver was unable to jump-start the antimonopoly movement, his efforts in the late 1940s to strengthen antitrust enforcement did bear some fruit. The moribund Federal Trade Commission, hoping to revive its prospects, sought to strengthen the Clayton Act, so that mergers that tended to lessen competition would be outlawed, even where there was no evidence of intent on the part of the acquiring company to produce such a result. Heeding calls for reform, Congress passed the Celler-Kefauver Act of 1950. The bill amended the Clayton Act by empowering the Justice Department to pursue antitrust action in cases of economic concentration, even where there was no evidence of a conspiracy among owners to restrain competition. By this time, however, big business was not an easy target. Not only had the business community recaptured the trust of most Americans and the Cold War dampened dissent, but the Korean War and the concomitant need for business cooperation also hobbled stricter enforcement.[28]

The early years of the 1950s therefore witnessed relatively few cases brought against firms listed on the New York Stock Exchange. However, in 1953 Herbert Bromwell, Jr., the incoming attorney general of the new Eisenhower administration, established the National Committee to Study the Antitrust Laws. In 1955, the committee issued a report that called for more aggressive enforcement of antitrust laws already on the books. Two court decisions aided supporters of this recommendation within the Justice Department. The first, rendered by the Supreme Court in 1957, held that the Clayton Act applied to vertical as well as horizontal mergers.

Arguably, Federal Judge Edward Weinfeld delivered the more consequential decision in 1958, when he blocked the merger of Bethlehem Steel and Youngstown Sheet and Tube, which would have been one of the largest mergers in the nation's history. The suit represented the Justice Department's first court test of the Celler-Kefauver Act. Consistent with the law's intent, Judge Weinfeld argued that steel was "an industry already highly concentrated," and he reasoned that the proposed merger would most likely set off a chain reaction of further mergers, yielding even greater concentration and "heading in the direction of triopoly."[29]

In essence, the decision reversed over fifty years worth of court decisions that had found that business size, by itself, did not matter. Because the companies did not appeal, the decision stood. As a result of favorable court decisions and Justice Department resolve, antitrust cases against NYSE firms increased to thirty-four in 1959 and sixty-one in 1960. But as historian Richard Hofstadter later noted, this marked the first time in the history of the antitrust movement that greater enforcement was not the result of underlying popular support for actions against big business. Instead, antitrust had become institutionalized. As Hofstadter ironically observed, "once the United States had an antitrust movement without antitrust prosecutions; in our time there have been antitrust prosecutions without an antitrust movement." But in the absence of a mobilized public or agitated Congress, it remained doubtful that an uptick in antitrust enforcement alone could reverse the long-term growth and dominance of large corporations.[30]

regulatory agencies: As discussed in the last chapter, regulatory agencies proliferated during the decade of the 1930s. While some of these did not survive beyond the Depression years, others rose to prominence. One of these was the Civil Aeronautics Board (CAB). Created in 1938, the CAB was charged with a number of tasks, including developing safety programs, maintaining navigational facilities, and investigating accidents. Its main function, however, was to foster the growth of the fledgling industry of commercial aviation. The importance of this charge grew as commercial air travel expanded after the war. The main tools at the board's disposal to execute its charge were the regulation of both routes and fares.[31]

In effect, the CAB operated as a government sponsored cartel, and thus as a governance structure. While new carriers were prevented from entering the field, existing airlines were guaranteed a profit. The same benefits accrued to telecommunications companies, and especially AT&T, that came to be regulated by the Federal Communications Commission, established in 1934. In the case of ground transportation, it was trucking companies that prospered from the Transportation Act of 1940, which gave the progenitor of independent regulatory commission, the Interstate Commerce Commission (ICC), the mandate of extending its regulation of railroads to other forms of ground transport.[32]

The fact that the ICC, or any independent regulatory commission for that matter, had come to operate as a cartel might seem odd in light of the mandate of the first independent regulatory commissions. Whether it was the early charge of the ICC or the fundamental purpose of the Federal Trade Commission, the point of economic regulation had been to curtail the anticompetitive practices of large corporations, so as to allow smaller establishments to compete. The change of orientation came about as a result of the Depression. In the environment of economic catastrophe, one of the guiding assumptions was that economic competition, or at least too much competition, led to ruinous results. It was this assumption that led to the National Industrial Recovery Act, the government-led effort to create a corporatist regime that would produce conditions of economic stability. But though the legislation was declared unconstitutional in 1935, similar thinking helped to shape the new regulatory commissions. In essence, the new IRCs represented quasi-corporatist structures that aimed at producing economic stability for select industries.

Of course, this was a stripped-down corporatism in which neither workers nor consumers had a role. Therefore, the ability of these newly fashioned commissions to regulate in the public interest was presumably ensured by the defining features of IRCs: expert personnel and independence. However, during the 1950s, IRCs were the subject of a number of studies that showed that these features were no more secure than they were in the early days of the ICC. Expertise was found to be undermined by the frequent use of partisanship as a criterion for appointment, as well as by the pattern of short tenure for most commissioners. According to a report written by the Bureau of the Budget in 1950, the exalted and uniquely American asset of regulatory independence (i.e., being located outside, or at least insulated from, an existing department of the Executive Branch) was found instead to be a liability. Without the active direction provided by either Executive or Legislative Branches, and without the organized support of the public, decisions by "independent" commissioners in controversial policy areas were more likely to be driven by the "the ability of the commissions to live with the industries and trades subject to regulation." In other words, after sixty years of experience, IRCs were still vulnerable to industry capture.[33]

The most damning critique was delivered by James M. Landis, the architect and second chairman of one of the most prominent IRCs of the New Deal, the Security and Exchange Commission, as well as a former chairman of the CAB. In a report written in 1960 at the request of the newly elected president, John F. Kennedy, Landis found that regulatory commissions had come to display a common set of problems. For one, they were typically slow to act. For example, the average age of dockets requiring formal proceedings for the CAB was thirty-two months, while thirty "cease and desist" orders facing the FTC had been pending for over three years. Most of these delays were due to inadequate budgets—in short, things had not changed much since the first paltry budget was set for the Interstate Commerce Commission back in 1887. Furthermore, while flagrant cases of bribery had been uncovered, even more serious were the "subtle but pervasive methods pursued by regulated industries to influence regulatory agencies by social favors, promises of later employment in the industry itself, and other similar means."[34]

Other studies showed that whereas the flow of personnel was still usually from industry through the doors of government, over time, a reverse flow was witnessed as well, creating a revolving door. For example, of the 813 scientific, medical and technical staff that left the Food and Drug Administration between 1960 and 1963, at least eighty-three ended up working for companies that the FDA regulated.[35] In effect, the ability to build administrative capacity and nurture the public-sector expertise required to carry out the mandates of IRCs was increasingly undermined by the practice of cashing in accrued experience for more lucrative positions in the private sector.

The Political Economy of the Early 1960s

By the early 1960s, America had a new political economy. An emergent peacetime big government joined a restored big business. But the increasing size of government did not create a counterweight to business. Instead, with much government spending benefiting large private contractors, and with regulatory agencies now functioning as cartels, substantial segments of the federal government now helped large corporations rationalize their economic environment. The new political economy thus remained lopsided in its pro-business orientation, if not in the size of its constituent parts.

The growth of large corporations and their increased dominance of the US economy in the first generation after the war can be illustrated with just a few numbers. In 1946 there were roughly 526,400 active corporations. Of these, 531 had assets over $100 million, which accounted for 49 percent of all corporate assets. In 1965 there were nearly 1.5 million active corporations, of which 1,901 had assets of over $100 million, and these accounted for 60 percent of all corporation assets.[36] If one focuses only on the largest 200 manufacturing corporations, the picture is even starker: while controlling 45 percent of all manufacturing assets in 1947, this elite group controlled 56 percent of all manufacturing assets by 1965.[37] Furthermore, while corporations continued to get bigger, key industries (e.g., automobiles, aluminum, cereal foods, cigarettes, rubber tires, and soap-detergents) continued to operate as oligopolies in which constituent companies administered prices with practices such as price leadership and long-term contracts.[38] Many grew larger still by becoming multinational corporations, and because Europe and Asia were rebuilding, they could engage in foreign trade and not worry about foreign competition.

—

Still, government had permanently broken free of its minimalist bonds. Furthermore, the proper economic course for government represented only one of the critical junctures concerning the proper role of government that arose after the war. Many in government, including the president himself, hoped to build upon the New Deal momentum regarding social regulations and welfare.

Social Regulations and Welfare: An Attempt at Universal Health Care

The postwar period witnessed the expansion of welfare states across Europe, including the establishment of a national health service in England that provided free medical care for all. Efforts to expand America's welfare state began in earnest less than a week after the war, when Harry Truman let the country know that he was a New Dealer. The new president presented a domestic program to Congress that featured a proposal that would establish a program of government health insurance, modeled after Social Security. This was the first time a sitting American president had endorsed a specific plan for national health care. With surveys conducted in previous years showing strong majority support for such a plan, the time seemed ripe for change.[39] The success of this effort would have tremendous repercussions. Not only would the plan establish health care as a basic right, it would greatly diminish the need for CSR as a form of private welfare and remove what was becoming CSR's workplace centerpiece.[40]

Organized labor threw its full support behind the proposal. But such support was no match for the resources of the opponents of the proposal. The American Medical Association once again led the campaign and over the next several years spent millions of dollars to secure the defeat of national health care. In addition to doctors and commercial insurers, all of the major business groups lined up against the proposal. Furthermore, the political center of gravity after the war shifted decidedly to the right. Not only did the growing Cold War increase the resonance of suggestions that national health care would place the country on the path to Communism, but the election results of 1946 gave control of Congress to Republicans. The slim chances that the proposal initially had for passage were now effectively squashed. While the election of 1948 returned Congress to the control of Democrats, the conservative coalition of Southern Democrats and Republicans continued to obstruct domestic initiatives. As important, the proliferation of private health plans in both union and nonunion establishments seemed to suggest a private health care alternative—see discussion below.[41]

Following a pattern established decades earlier, business ideology and organization served as a template for other welfare programs. Taking office in 1953, President Dwight Eisenhower promised efficient management of the federal bureaucracy. In what has become a staple of Republican administrations ever since, efficiency translated into reduced spending for social welfare programs, since the working assumption was that prior mismanagement had produced bloated budgets. For program administrators, the focus shifted from the elimination of a social problem to the elimination of waste. In his one welfare initiative, Eisenhower successfully pushed legislation to expand vocational rehabilitation programs, which had begun during the previous Republican administrations of Coolidge and Hoover. Instead of issuing cash grants, rehabilitation promised to help the disabled "to return to employment and lives of usefulness, independence, and self-respect."[42] Not only did this approach protect work norms, it assumed that the problem was with people and their inadequate training, and not with an economic structure that yielded an insufficient number of jobs.

What was true of welfare-state legislation was also true of social regulations during this period. The progress that had been achieved during the Depression stalled after the war. For example, instead of creating wholly new workplace mandates, Congress mostly tinkered with the Fair Labor Standards Act (FLSA) of 1938, adding amendments that broadened coverage and increased the minimum wage. The most substantial of these, however, did foreshadow greater regulations of employment that would follow. In 1963 Congress passed the Equal Pay Act as an amendment to the FLSA that was intended to prohibit wage discrimination against women.[43]

—

Just as the defeat of the original Full Employment Act in 1946 marked the end of New Deal efforts to expand government's capacity to regulate large corporations, the defeat of President Truman's initiative to create universal health care represented the end of New Deal efforts to build a more robust welfare state. Once again, this placed the onus upon unions to strengthen the negotiated form of responsibility if the efforts, born of the Depression, to regulate the large corporation were to survive. Given the tremendous momentum achieved by unions as a result of the Wagner Act, this seemed to be an eminently plausible path.

Negotiated Responsibility

The GM Strike

As the war drew to a close, union leaders had every reason to feel hopeful. In the decade since National Labor Relations Act was passed, not only had unions experienced a fourfold increase, to over fourteen million members, but because of the war production regime and the tight labor market that prevailed during the war, workers had also been able to gain some control over the production process in a number of factories. Many CIO progressives thought that it was time that workers gained a stronger foothold in decision making, from the shop floor to the boardroom. With a labor-friendly administration, and with unions flexing their growing political muscle in the form of the newly established Political Action Committee of the CIO, anything seemed possible. The resolve of these leaders was further reinforced by the desire to prevent a repeat of the precedent of World War I, when gains made by unions during the war quickly eroded after hostilities ceased.[44]

What union progressives had in mind was a pro-labor version of a corporatist accord. The centerpiece of the plan, as advanced by CIO President Phillip Murray was the industry council. The basic idea was that for each major industry, representatives of labor, management, and government would negotiate agreements that would apply to all establishments within the industry. While the first order of business would be to bargain over wages, hours, and working conditions,

> Eventually, the council would pass upon all matters having to do with the operation of the business, specifically, planning and improvement of product; pricing; trade practices; division of the proceeds in rent, interests, profits, and wages; correlation of business operation to the rest of the economy.[45]

The idea of industry councils had been circulating in labor circles both domestically and internationally for a number of years. In fact, at the outset of the war, the CIO had floated the idea of industry councils, while Walter Reuther, the head of the United Auto Workers union, offered a concrete plan based upon the idea as part of a proposal to convert the auto industry to wartime production. While business leaders rejected the Reuther Plan, employer associations and unions in Sweden reached a basic agreement in 1938. After the war, England established such councils on a permanent basis in 1947, while West Germany's codetermination law of 1951 mandated that labor have representatives on the boards of directors of individual establishments.[46]

The hopes that these union leaders had for instituting industry councils in the United States were matched by business fears. From the perspective of business leaders, traditional managerial prerogatives were already under assault. This began on the shop floor, where management's ability to restore what they saw as a breakdown in workplace discipline was being eroded by collective bargaining agreements in which workers were gaining some influence over personnel issues. The greatest fear was that unions' collective bargaining success in the area of personnel could easily expand into collective-bargaining demands concerning production and investment decisions, a fear that was compounded by the perception that the NLRB was biased in favor of unions. As General Motors President Charles E. Wilson stated to Congress, collective bargaining had to be restricted to "its proper sphere." Otherwise, "the border area of collective bargaining will be a constant battleground . . . as the unions continuously attempt to press the boundary farther into the area of managerial functions."[47] It was clear, then, that business had no interest in pursuing a union-led corporatist accord.

With unions hoping to solidify the gains they had made and broaden the scope of their power, and with the business community prepared to reassert their "right to manage," the stage was set for battle. The first battleground would be General Motors. In the company's home turf of the Detroit area, workers' hopes mixed with anger. The no-strike pledge of the war years had produced pent-up frustration among many union militants concerning grievances that were not addressed. Not yet ready to propose a full-blown corporatist accord, Reuther devised a plan that would tap into this vein of discontent. On August 16, 1945, he unveiled his proposal for a new contract with General Motors that called for wages to be raised by 30 percent *and,* with a touch of audacity, without an increase in the price of its cars. To show that this was feasible, Reuther suggested that the company open its books for inspection. But instead of framing his proposal in terms of equity and justice, Reuther used the new language of Keynesian economics. He argued that a substantial wage increase, without a concurrent price increase, would increase the purchasing power of consumers, raise aggregate demand, and thus keep the economy humming at full capacity, as had been experienced during the war. To clearly convey the message that failure to accept this proposal could lead to a strike, the union rescinded its no-strike pledge on August 25.[48]

Predictably, the UAW proposal did not fall upon receptive ears in the boardroom of General Motors. Wilson formally rejected the proposal on October 3, arguing that the company's prices and their relationship to wages and profits fell within the purview of the prerogatives of management. He also flatly refused to open the corporation's books, since this too would infringe upon the rights of private property. If both sides seemed more in the mood to fight than to reconcile, this mood was shared broadly in the labor and business communities.

Shortly after negotiations between GM and the UAW began, the National Labor-Management Conference convened in Washington, DC. In the context of trying to smooth the path to the postwar economy, President Truman had earlier called for a conference of business and labor representatives to try to formulate "a broad and permanent foundation for industrial peace and progress."[49] But in the charged atmosphere of an impending showdown between labor and management, very little was accomplished. In the case of the committee responsible with finding consensus on "Management's Right to Manage," a stalemate was declared after labor leaders refused to agree to a list of specific functions that exclusively belonged to management. After conducting meetings for most of November, the conferees finally left town, having failed yet again to fashion the ever-elusive corporatist accord.

If the prospects for the conference were dim at the outset, they were probably doomed on November 21, when 180,000 workers at GM across the nation went on strike. Soon after, meatpackers and electrical workers walked off their jobs, followed by 750,000 steelworkers. By the beginning of 1946, close to two million industrial workers were on strike. By the end of first anniversary of the end of the war, this strike wave spread to include 4,630 separate work stoppages involving five million strikers, who were off their jobs for a collective 120 million days.[50]

The postwar strike wave turned out to be a critical juncture in US labor relations. In contrast to the past, this high-stakes confrontation did not end with violence. In fact, there was little violence at all during the strikes, and plants remained closed, without replacements workers, for the duration of the strikes: the union movement was now too big to destroy. However, following the lead of General Motors, owners in all industries held the line on broader union demands. In none of the strike settlements of 1946 did unions make inroads onto the turf of managerial prerogatives, at least with respect to the big-ticket decisions that owners make. But while no progress was made in achieving the goal of a corporatist accord, workers did not come away empty handed. Instead, workers generally won higher wages in the contracts that were signed. But this step forward in labor relations was coupled with a step backward in labor law.

Taft–Hartley

Though the foundation of labor peace had been laid in the contract settlements, the strike wave created tremendous disruptions in the economy and in the lives of millions of Americans. Led by the NAM, the business community exploited this environment to initiate a public-relations campaign against unions, in which the latter were portrayed as selfish, special interests that were threatening the nation's economic well-being. The campaign seemed to resonate with the public, as opinion polls showed a majority of the public expressing displeasure with union militancy, as well as a fear of "irresponsible" union leaders.[51] In contrast to previous antiunion campaigns, however, the goal was not to destroy unions, but to weaken their ability to grow further. With their conservative allies in Congress strengthened by the results of the 1946 election, business leaders achieved this goal through a series of amendments to the National Labor Relations Act. Among the many provisions of Taft-Hartley Act of 1947,[52] the bill banned secondary boycotts and jurisdictional strikes, and it authorized the use of injunctions to prevent obstructive picketing. In addition, employers were given the right to fully express their views of unions to employees before an election. Of even greater consequence, the act also banned the closed shop and permitted states to bypass federal legislation that allowed union shops. This led to a proliferation of "right-to-work" laws in a number of Southern states—laws that still make the South harder to organize.

This omnibus bill of antiunion items also included a provision that required that union leaders sign anticommunist affidavits before using the NLRB. In the midst of the Cold War, and with union leaders fully backing the foreign policies of the Truman administration, unions set out to purge their ranks of Communists. Not only did this turn unions in on themselves, the anticommunism within the labor movement, like its effect upon society generally, quieted radical voices, thus contributing to the narrow focus of business unionism. Together with the strike settlements of 1946, the wave of anticommunism within unions effectively killed challenges to managerial prerogatives in the form of corporatist proposals.

Fringe Benefits: The Fight Over Pensions

In the same unsettled waters produced by the 1946 strike wave, unions were forced to rethink their traditional opposition to employer-provided fringe benefits. To begin with, the prospects for passing national health care had grown dimmer. In addition, the antiunion campaign leading up to Taft-Hartley had led to erosion in the public's support for unions. In such an environment, demanding higher wages alone might serve to confirm the business community's claim that unions were selfish, especially in a period of high inflation. Demands for benefits, however, might seem reasonable. Labor's new position became official in 1946, when both the AFL and CIO announced drives to win benefits at their annual conventions. Of course, union leaders like Walter Reuther, now president of the UAW, did not give up on the goal that government would become the main provider of welfare benefits. His hope was that by forcing them to finance expensive fringe benefits through collective bargaining, employers would see the light and join the effort to expand the welfare state.[53]

Pensions became the first battleground in the struggle over benefits. For employees with memories of the Depression still fresh, an early focus on economic security was certainly understandable. Furthermore, while Social Security was now provided to retirees, it not only paid a meager benefit, the relative value of the benefit had shrunk due to inflation; while the average Social Security benefit replaced 30 percent of the average wage in 1940, it replaced only 19 percent of this wage by 1950.[54] For employers, pensions were also increasingly viewed in a favorable light, and not simply because of the tax-shelter feature that they had acquired in the Revenue Act of 1942. Most importantly, they were a means of inducing loyal service. Of course, employers continued to view pensions as falling squarely within the purview of managerial prerogatives, and thus not a legitimate item to be placed on the bargaining table.

The resulting conflict over benefits came to a head in 1948 when the NLRB ruled that the Inland Steel Company was required to bargain with the steelworkers union over pensions. Most employers continued to resist offering pensions during negotiations, even after the Supreme Court upheld the Board's decision in 1949, in part because the ruling did not require employers to offer pensions, only that they discuss them at the bargaining table. Tensions boiled over into a series of strikes where benefits were the main issue of contention. These were so numerous that strikes over benefits comprised 55 percent of all strikes in 1949 and 70 percent of all strikes in the first half of 1950. Employer resistance finally broke when the Steel Industry Board, appointed by President Truman to investigate and recommend settlement terms during a steel strike in 1949, recommended raising pensions and other benefits as a solution. Soon afterward Ford signed a contract with the UAW that contained a pension plan. Plans were soon won in a number of other key industries as well, making 1949 the year of the pension.[55]

After winning the fight over pensions, unions quickly pressed for negotiations over health insurance as well. Labor leaders had an even keener interest in pressing for this benefit, since unlike pensions, which were viewed as a supplement to the public system of Social Security, private health insurance became the only game in town after the defeat of the Truman public health care initiative. But before 1949, union employers viewed health benefits as they did pensions, as a voluntary personnel practice determined by managerial prerogative. After the Supreme Court decision regarding pensions, employers relented fairly quickly, since, compared to pensions, health insurance did not have the same long-term cost implication.

The Treaty of Detroit

The next major breakthrough in collective bargaining occurred with the GM-UAW contract of 1950. Hailed as the Treaty of Detroit, the agreement between the nation's largest employer and one of the labor movement's biggest unions would become the template for many of the negotiations between large corporations and their unions that would follow. In terms of the two major benefit items, the contract not only called for a monthly pension, it also helped establish a precedent for health care by agreeing to pay half the cost of a new health insurance plan. But the central features of the unprecedented five-year contract between GM and the UAW dealt with income, reflecting the reality that the fight over managerial prerogatives was effectively over.

The Treaty was the culmination of trend established in the 1946 strike settlements. A grand compromise between union and owners, now known as the "capital-labor accord," had emerged. As a tacit set of understandings, instead of a formal agreement, the accord meant that in exchange for higher wages and union security, workers would respect the traditional rights of management. At this juncture, an older dream of worker empowerment, this time in the form of a corporatist accord, once again slowly faded away. The business unionism of Samuel Gompers was finally institutionalized and showed improvements in both wages and benefits:

wages: By the end of the GM-UAW contract in 1955, the real income of GM's autoworkers rose by 20 percent. This helped to lay a foundation for unions' growing emphasis on income, as opposed to employment security, especially as memories of the Depression faded. This can be seen in the next GM-UAW contract, which included a supplemental unemployment benefit (SUB), where workers who were laid off would receive a supplement to their unemployment check, thus helping to guarantee an annual wage. To deal with seasonal or cyclical variation in the need for workers, employers would lay off workers, using seniority as the criterion, and these workers would receive a combination of unemployment insurance and SUB. When demand picked up, these workers would be rehired. By the end of the 1960s, close to 40 percent of union contracts called for layoffs when hours were slack, up from just 5 percent in 1954. Overall, union workers continued to enjoy a wage premium when compared to their nonunion brethren.[56]

benefits: As negotiated plans proliferated, a union imprint became discernable. In particular, unions pushed hard for greater liberalization of benefits, so that more of a company's workers were covered and eligibility established after fewer years of service. With respect to pensions, unions bargained hard to make pensions non-contributory. They also worked to bring pension coverage to the employees of smaller enterprises, some of whom had only intermittent work in industries like construction and clothing. This was a function of unions' ability to negotiate multi-employer plans that entailed joint union-management trustee control. As a result, members of unions were more likely to have pensions than workers employed by nonunion establishments. By 1960, even though they comprised 31 percent of the labor force, union members constituted roughly 50 percent of workers who received a private pension.[57]

For health insurance, negotiated plans also had a particular look. For one, unions were more likely to bargain for uniform benefits rather than having the level of benefits graduated to match different wage levels. And like pensions, unions frequently bargained to make health insurance a non-contributory benefit. Unions also pushed for the expansion of medical benefits beyond hospitalization and surgery coverage to include routine home and office visits. Once in place, unions in future rounds of bargaining typically attempted to broaden the boundaries of coverage to include dependents and retired workers. As with pensions, union workers were more likely to receive health benefits. At the end of 1954, while union workers made up 35 percent of the labor force, they represented 40 percent of all workers who received some sort of health benefit (e.g., hospitalization, surgical, medical care).[58]

Unions thus took the lead in securing both pensions and health insurance as fringe benefits. This was particularly true during the decade of the 1950s, and it was a pattern that held for other benefits as well, such as vacations and paid holidays. Some of this was no doubt the result of success at the bargaining table, as early victories encouraged further demands. Unions' growing emphasis upon deferred compensation, especially pensions, also reflected the longer job tenure of union members resulting from long-term contracts and rules of seniority.[59]

Developments in Job Control

At the same time that wages and benefits improved for union workers, so did the job-control features of business unionism. For example, after gaining a strong foothold after the Wagner Act passed, seniority continued to grow as a criterion for layoffs and promotions. In the case of the layoffs, the principle of last hired, first to be laid off found its way into nearly every agreement in the manufacturing and transportation industries during the postwar period. Management was more resistant to the practice of using seniority for promotions, seeing it as seriously undermining its prerogatives regarding personnel decisions. Unions, however, pushed hard, since they viewed seniority as an objective substitute for promotion criteria that were frequently experienced as arbitrary and biased. They were ultimately successful, and as the practice of using seniority for promotion decisions proliferated, large corporations came to rely more heavily upon their internal labor market, promoting more from within. Seniority also expanded to other areas, including job transfers, shift preferences, and work assignments. It also came to be used to determine benefit privileges, as in the amount of vacation time earned. Overall, the growing importance of seniority reflected the growing importance of fairness as a principle governing workplace affairs: workers with longer service were entitled to greater job security and benefits.[60]

Yet another work norm that took shape in postwar contracts was that jobs should be regular, if not relatively permanent, and provide sufficient hours to make a livable wage. This manifested itself in contract provisions that attempted to control layoffs, including limits on subcontracting during periods of slack business. In some contracts, unions attempted to restrict the practice of subcontracting more generally, so as to protect union jobs and standards from the persistent temptation of employers to shift work to cheaper, nonunion workers. Unions also increasingly rejected work-sharing schemes, since these tended to produce insufficient hours, and in cases where layoffs were unavoidable, unemployment insurance was now available to tide workers over.[61]

With each new bargaining cycle, then, contracts got longer, as more and more rules were written to specify various policies. Rules were now needed to specify how seniority was to be measured and what constituted a promotion or a job transfer. Detailed rules were also needed to determine both bumping rights in cases of layoffs, and procedures for recalls of those who had been laid off. In fact, rules came to be written for most areas of the workplace, whether they dealt with work assignments, job descriptions, safety procedures, or break times. From the perspective of workers, such rules were needed to restrain supervisors' powers, thus increasing the scope of job rights. Of course, with more rules there was a greater need for more highly articulated grievance procedures to deal with growing instances of employees protesting management decisions on the grounds of rule infractions. Management reciprocated, pushing for rules that protected their shop-floor prerogatives; to maintain control of the workplace, management wrote rules that, if broken, would have disciplinary consequences, which, of course, demanded rules that regulated disciplinary procedures.

Therefore, whereas business unionism conceded the managerial prerogatives of boardroom decisions, it tended to circumscribe them on the shop floor with union contracts that established an intricate web of rules for the workplace. The adversarial grievance structure that accompanied this workplace contractualism helped to cement a culture of mutual distrust between management and labor. Even so, for the first generation after the war, the system seemed to work, if the robust rate of growth of GDP was any indication. In other words, in the union sector, the productivity gains that accrued from a more secure and contented workforce appeared to outweigh the inefficiencies emanating from the rigidity of rules. But business unionism, which focused upon job control instead of real power sharing in the boardrooms of corporations, was vulnerable.[62]

AFL-CIO

While the anticommunist purge of the late 1940s contributed to a more divided labor movement, the efforts of the early 1950s to merge the AFL and the CIO helped to unite the house of labor. These efforts surged in 1952 when George Meany became the new president of the AFL and Walter Reuther became the new president of the CIO. By 1955 an agreement was finalized that merged the former's eighty unions with the latter's thirty unions to create a new federation that included the vast majority of America's union members.

The prospects for unions were certainly promising. Not only had the competing labor federations merged, but the year before the American labor movement had also once again achieved its peak unionization rate, at 35 percent.[63] However, unions' achievements and prospects did not represent a tipping point where the business community finally accepted unions as partners, with negotiated responsibility becoming the dominant pillar of America's regulatory structure for large corporations. Instead, the increasing strength of the labor movement only represented a growing threat, which more and more nonunion employers met by adopting the growing practices comprising CSR.

Voluntary Responsibility (CSR)

Welfare Capitalism

Like many cities across the country, Rochester, New York, was a site of labor strife during the strike wave of 1946. While workers at American Brake Shoe and General Motors-Delco walked off their jobs, leaders of the local AFL and CIO labor federations, who had never previously cooperated with one another, got together to coordinate a one-day general strike. This was precipitated by the firing of several hundred municipal garbage men who had been engaged in an effort to form a union, and the city's decision to transfer trash collection to a private contractor. Encouraged by the solidarity exhibited by Rochester workers, the Electrical Workers (UE) launched an effort to organize employees of the Camera Works division of the Eastman Kodak Company.

A small upstart of six employees in 1881, Kodak grew to become Rochester's largest employer by the 1920s, employing one in five of the city's labor force. Kodak also distinguished itself by being an early member of the vanguard of welfare capitalists who voluntarily introduced socially responsible practices into the workplace, including a suggestions system, recreation programs, and profit sharing. In addition, the company's local philanthropic efforts made it a model of corporate citizenship. A number of factors motivated the company's founder, George Eastman, in his efforts to forge a bond with both his workers and the residents of Rochester. Being at the head of a large, integrated corporation with a near monopoly in the making of film, Eastman constantly worried about real and potential antitrust action; having the loyalty of so many local residents seemed a good hedge should a local jury be seated. A deeply conservative man, Eastman was also a staunch opponent of unions representing his employees. To keep them as bay, he consistently added to the company's private welfare efforts and created a system of highly secure employment. Kodak's orientation to its workforce outlived its founder's death in 1932, and as a result, his company remained nonunion.[64]

It was not surprising, then, that Kodak responded to the UE organizing drive by first reforming work standards and raising wage rates by 5 percent. Next, it opened a new cafeteria for its workers and paid a record wage dividend. By April of 1947, the UE suspended its organizing drive. The company, however, did not suspend its welfare efforts. In the decade of the fifties, the company continued to expand its benefit programs, offering Blue Shield coverage for its workers in 1951, company-paid retiree health insurance in 1954, and a survivor income plan in 1956.[65]

Kodak therefore remained in the CSR vanguard. But in the postwar period, Kodak was joined by many other employers who, in the face of growing unionization, began to offer fringe benefits in order to keep their establishments union free—this was on top of the increasing wages that nonunion workers achieved in establishments faced with the threat of unions. Summarizing their review of employee benefits in the 1960 Brookings Institution study, *The Impact of Collective Bargaining on Management*, the authors concluded that "Non-union companies with a strong desire to remain nonunion are likely to keep up in the procession and even to lead if financially able."[66]

Of course, the threat of unions was not the only worry that employers had after the war. Surveying the challenges that large corporations faced at the time, Ralph J. Cordiner, the president of General Electric, listed not only "growing, unchecked union power," but also "excessively high taxes" and "a fantastically growing federal government."[67] As discussed above, the business community was particularly agitated by President Truman's proposal to institute national health care, and they successfully mobilized to defeat it. However, with the growing legitimacy of government, it was no longer enough to simply oppose welfare legislation. The business community was now compelled to show why such legislation was not needed by voluntarily adopting socially responsible practices.

The impact of the combined threats of unionization and government expansion can be found in the growth of health care as a fringe benefit among nonunion employers. Once national health care was defeated, and as union contracts increasingly included health care, many nonunion employers followed suit. The Republican administration of Dwight Eisenhower then facilitated the institutionalization of this emergent system of employer-provided health care via the tax code. The Revenue Act of 1954 clarified the tax status of employer-sponsored health insurance by providing a blanket tax exemption for employer contributions and expanding the individual medical expense deduction. The encouragement of private health care provision was now public policy.[68]

Human Relations

By the early 1960s, benefits packages had largely converged for union and nonunion large corporations. The same cannot be said, however, for workplace practices. Instead, two distinct systems began to take shape. The growing workplace contractualism of union establishments reflected the underlying conflict over control of the shop floor. In contrast, a growing number of nonunion employers began to redesign workplace practices inspired by insights provided by the "human relations" school of management. The overriding purpose of these efforts was to harmonize the interests of management and workers in the hopes of increasing productivity, while keeping unions at bay.

The human relations movement had its roots in the studies conducted by Harvard psychologist Elton Mayo and his team of researchers at Hawthorne Works of Western Electric from the late 1920s to the early 1930s. These experiments involved changing various work conditions (length of the workday) and pay systems (group incentive pay) to determine which factors enhanced productivity. The researchers concluded that social factors such as group pressure and non-material incentives such as security had a greater impact upon output than the physical environment of work or material incentives. This led to a wave of studies in the 1940s and 1950s that examined the impact of factors ranging from informal group norms to different leadership styles. The common hypothesis that guided these studies was that the same social and psychological factors that are associated with higher-functioning social groups generally are also related to higher functioning (and productive) work groups. These job design studies were complemented with attitudinal surveys of workers that attempted to determine what factors produced greater satisfaction and morale. The common conclusion was that humanizing work was likely to yield better results than treating people as replaceable cogs in a machine.[69]

As was true of the original Hawthorne project, the companies being studied sponsored many of the workplace studies during this period. So while academic behavioral scientists, and especially psychologists, frequently conducted the research, it simultaneously represented a series of applied efforts on the part of employers to forge stronger bonds with their employees. In essence, the human relations movement added a workplace design component to the welfare capitalism's traditional focus upon material incentives and workplace amenities as a means of aligning the interests of owners and workers so as to resolve the labor problem—and thus keep unions out. Sears, for example, experimented with store size, leadership styles, and eliminating status distinctions in job titles in order to foster strong social bonds and loyalty. At the same time the company encouraged internal promotion and offered both a pension and profit-sharing plan to encourage an individual, as opposed to the collective orientation of unions to material betterment and long-term job security. If there was any doubt as to the impetus behind these efforts, the company's top personnel manager, Clarence Caldwell, reminded company managers in a memo to "continue to look at all our policies with the question: Are they likely to keep out unions?"[70]

The proliferation of human-relations practices in nonunion firms was facilitated by the increasing professionalization of personnel departments that were now standard features in most mid to large corporations, as well as by the commercialization of workplace consultancy. But the introduction of these same practices in union establishments was slowed by a couple of factors. First, the locus of power over personnel issues in unionized firms was more likely to reside in industrial relations departments that administered labor contracts and grievance procedures, and not personnel offices. Second, the suspicion that unions historically had concerning the ulterior motives behind welfare practices, like fringe benefits, was now transferred to workplace practices.[71] The fear that human relations amounted to a union avoidance strategy was supported not only by comments by nonunion corporate executives, like Caldwell's above, but also by those of the leaders of unionized companies. Roger M. Blough, Chairman of the unionized U.S. Steel Corporation, hoped that progressive work practices would create a "climate which all members of the group would so well understand and approve of, that they would feel no need for separate representation among themselves."[72]

—

In sum, in an effort to protect managerial prerogatives in the face of the surging strength of unions and an expanding government, an increasing number of large corporations were pushed to explore the high road of welfare capitalism. Similar worries contributed to greater corporate philanthropy as well.

Corporate Philanthropy

In 1947 the Commission on Higher Education, created by President Truman the year before, issued its report on the role of colleges and universities in postwar America. Noting the increasing importance of these institutions for economic opportunity and political freedom, the Commission called for the expansion of postsecondary education. As this would require a tremendous infusion of resources, the Commission examined ways of increasing individual giving, and it also stressed the importance of tapping into corporate giving. But projecting a gap between the costs of expansion and private giving of all forms, the Commission also strongly recommended an expansion of federal support of education.[73]

Many business leaders had already discovered the value of close relations with leaders of education and science during the war. It was therefore likely that corporate contributions to higher education would have grown even in the absence of the Commission's report. But at a time when the business community was concerned about the government pushing beyond its minimalist confines, its recommendations for greatly increased federal aid pushed business to act more quickly and with greater generosity as a way of tamping down yet another federal initiative. Heavyweights such as Frank W. Abrams of Standard Oil and Irving S. Olds of U. S. Steel published articles and gave speeches that strongly advocated corporate giving to colleges and universities. Alfred P. Sloan, Jr., of General Motors, explicitly argued that business support of higher education was infinitely preferable to federal aid.[74]

By 1951 the NAM and other business organizations joined the cause of encouraging corporate giving to education. However, due to lingering doubts about the legal propriety of contributions to education, some corporations hesitated. As a result, the NAM arranged a test case between a manufacturing company and one of its stockholders in the hopes of clarifying the issue. The verdict rendered by the New Jersey Supreme Court achieved the desired effect. The court wrote that not only were such contributions legal, but it was the "solemn duty" of corporate executives to support private education. The Smith decision of 1953, subsequently upheld by higher courts, thus removed a major obstacle and helped pave the way for the dramatic increase in corporate support for higher education. By the end of the fifties, such support comprised roughly 30 percent of all corporate philanthropy.[75]

The Smith decision also paved the way for corporations to burnish their images by making contributions to the arts. With the public resistant to providing greater subsidies for museums, opera companies and the like, fund-raisers for these cultural institutions began to look to the deep pockets of corporations for support. Symphony orchestras were particularly successful in this regard. By the middle of the fifties, the city orchestras in Detroit, Cleveland, Pittsburgh, and Minneapolis were on a growing list of cities whose orchestras were recipients of corporate donations. By the end of the decade, however, the arts remained a relatively small target for corporate philanthropy, comprising roughly 3 percent of total gifts.[76]

While expanding into new areas like education and the arts, most of this activity was focused on local communities. This was true for corporations' expanded support for community welfare activities. This manifested itself in both higher levels of giving and a growing number of corporations with community relations departments. But the limits of this traditional area of corporate citizenship were also more starkly revealed. Even greater generosity could not narrow the widening gap between the problems associated with urbanization and poverty and the capacity of corporations to make a difference. The closeness of the bond between company and local community also grew more distant as corporations sprouted branch locations and chain stores proliferated. This bond would diminish further still as corporations increasingly followed the middle class out to the suburbs. Furthermore, as the problems connected to urban race relations began to receive greater attention in the 1950s and early 1960s, "business executives were noticeable by their absence from public discussion and action."[77]

As corporate giving increased, some also sought to institutionalize their philanthropic activities in the form of company foundations, including many in the CSR vanguard, such as General Electric, U.S. Steel, and Proctor and Gamble. Between 1952 and 1960 alone, company foundations grew from 12,295 to 45,124, though this still represented only a small percentage of all corporations. Of course, beyond the organizational efficiency that they brought to corporate philanthropy, foundations held great tax advantages. As tax-exempt entities, foundations became convenient locations to place a company's profits without paying taxes. For example, the number of company foundations soared during the Korean War, when an excess profits tax was instituted. But by the early 1960s, the use of foundations as tax-avoidance schemes led to Congressional hearing that revealed many abuses involving expenses, investments, and contributions.[78]

Ultimately, the same antigovernment and antiunion motives that inspired corporate philanthropy in previous decades were even stronger in the postwar period. Also stronger were material incentives for corporate gift giving, which grew in a couple of ways. First, with the growth of consumerism that accompanied swelling ranks of the middle class, more and more companies were encouraged to burnish their images with CSR practices in the hopes of fostering brand loyalty. Second, the tax advantages to giving improved. In 1954 Congress modified the tax code to permit deductions of greater than the 5 percent limit for a given year as long as the excess was absorbed within the following two years. As a result, between 1945 and 1969 corporate giving more than tripled from $266 billion to $900 billion. But even with this increase in giving, total corporate giving never represented much more that 1 percent of the total net profits of American corporations for any given year.[79]

The Philosophy of Corporate Social Responsibility

As CSR proliferated during the 1950s, so did the justifications for adopting its practices. Summarizing dozens of interviews with businessmen, economist Howard Bowan found the commonly expressed worry "that if business fails demonstrably to serve the interests of consumers, workers, and the general public it will be inviting repudiation in the form of deteriorating public relations, increased public control, and even socialization."[80]

But the business community also aspired to loftier ideals. Chairman of Sears, Theodore V. Houser, captured the mood of many businessmen, writing "I would like to see business *for* things, rather than everlastingly *against*. I would like to see business more closely identified in the public mind as interested in and working for the common good."[81] This comes from Houser's book, *Big Business and Human Values*, which is representative of the outpouring of books and articles by corporate executives articulating how and why their businesses were socially responsible. As a result, the 1950s were in many ways the golden age of CSR philosophy. Public-relations efforts were ratcheted up in the form of company reports, publicity, pamphlets, and speeches. Institutional advertising was also increasingly used, especially as the Advertising

Council, originally formed to assist the war effort, came to be used more to showcase business philanthropy.[82]

The cornerstone of this emergent philosophy was the idea that corporate managers needed to act as the trustees, or stewards for not only the stockholders of the corporation, but also its workers, suppliers, customers, as well as their local communities and the public generally. While this notion was first introduced into CSR philosophy back in the 1920s, it received elaborate articulation in the 1950s. Reflecting, perhaps, the dominant paradigms of pluralism and equilibrium in the social sciences, many spokesmen discussed the importance of "balancing" the interests of the various stakeholders of corporations. For Cordiner of GE this meant, "A business must be managed in the balanced best interests of all the groups who contribute to its success. . . ."[83]

Given the tremendous proliferation of welfare capitalism during the first couple of decades after the war, it is not surprising that workers received so much attention in CSR philosophy. In addition to offering "fair wages" and "good working conditions" to workers, chairman of Standard Oil Frank W. Abrams believed that "modern business management might well measure its success or failure as a profession in large part by the satisfaction and opportunities it is able to produce for its employees."[84] According to U.S. Steel's Creed of Human Relations, "We believe in the dignity and importance of the individual employee and in his right to derive personal satisfaction from his employment."[85]

In the view of its architects, the socially responsible behavior of corporations was now possible because the management of corporations had acquired the characteristics of a profession. More and more managers were educated in the more than six hundred colleges and universities that by 1950 offered degrees in business—a more than 200 percent increase since 1925. As graduates in possession of an increasingly formalized body of knowledge, managers were now selected, in part, on the basis of whether, as symbols of the corporation, they would be seen as acceptable to, and able to work with, the various stakeholders of the corporation. But the "hallmark of a profession is its sense of duty. None of the great, recognized professions is without a strong sense of responsibility to the community." This commitment would presumably be reinforced by the codes of ethics that were increasingly being adopted by companies.[86]

As they articulated a philosophy, some businessmen pointed to the changed economic circumstances that facilitated the growth of CSR practices. For example, professionalization of management was a byproduct of the continued separation of management from ownership, which was in turn the result of the continued growth of large corporations with literally thousands of owners. Because the power of owners had become so diffuse, managers were increasingly liberated from the short-term time horizons of investors and in a position to look out after the long-term interests of mature, large corporations. Of course, the fundamental laws of capitalism had not been altered. Even professional managers had to make a profit. However, the managers of large corporations now typically had greater latitude to administer prices so that they could afford fair wages, philanthropic initiatives, and "a fair return, security, and a reasonable gain" for their shareholders.[87]

Summary

At the end of the war, America found itself at three critical junctures that could fundamentally change its political economy, labor relations, and thus the reliance upon CSR in the nation's regulatory structure. First, as a result of its performance in both depression and war, the government was poised to adopt a more interventionist role in the economy in a battle over legislation involving unemployment. Second, with his proposal for national health care, President Truman attempted to create a more robust welfare state, in which health care would become a social right, not a benefit contingent upon corporate social responsibility. Third, in a series of postwar strikes, unions attempted to breach the confines of business unionism with proposals seeking greater input into corporate decision making.

At each critical juncture, however, the business community, with large corporations in the lead, successfully defeated the proposed alternative. Instead of a government that intervened in the economy in ways that touched upon the affairs of particular businesses or industries, the Employment Act fashioned a hands-off, Keynesian macroeconomic role for government. Instead of national health care, the government ultimately facilitated the growing system of private welfare with tax breaks for companies offering fringe benefits. And instead of a labor-inspired corporatism, the strike settlements of the immediate postwar period further institutionalized business unionism in a capital-labor accord.

But though America's political economy remained lopsided, an interesting thing happened. Government grew permanently larger, even in the absence of crises. However, instead of becoming a counterweight to the power of large corporations, the growth of government paradoxically aided the growth of even larger corporations, whether in the form of private contracting or the fostering of foreign trade. For government to counterbalance business would therefore depend upon a change in the orientation of government, and not simply an increase in sheer size. But challenges to large corporations once again withered, just as they did during the 1920s. Consequently, the momentum of adopting social regulations stalled. Instead, the orientation of government remained that of assisting business, and with economic regulations maintaining their track record of ineffectiveness, large corporations became even more dominant in the first generation after the war.

Unlike the 1920s, however, unions thrived and worked to secure greater social responsibility at the workplace via the negotiated contract. Though they were kept out of boardroom decisions, unions continued to grow, with unionization rates reaching a high of 35 percent of the labor force by the middle of the fifties. With the increasing clout that comes from representing over a third of the labor force, unions successfully pushed for contracts that included health care and pensions. After decades of adversity, unions appeared to have finally won acceptance, and the pillar of negotiated responsibility grew considerably stronger.

For many large corporations, however, resisting unions was too deeply ingrained to abandon. But with the old toolbox of negative resistance no longer available, an increasing number of nonunion employers attempted to keep the surge of unions at bay by voluntarily adopting a broadening array of socially responsible practices. On the one hand these included following the lead of union firms on wages and benefits. On the other hand, these CSR firms began to experiment on the shop floor with a human relations alternative to the workplace contractualism of union firms.

By the early 1960s, America's regulatory structure not only seemed to have stabilized, its relatively unique contours seemed to be working to connect large corporations to broader social goals. In particular, the rapidly expanding system of private welfare that resulted from the competition between union and CSR employers gave every appearance of being a viable alternative to public welfare, as more and more Americans received health insurance and could retire with private pensions that supplemented Social Security. In data compiled by the Social Security Administration that compared overall coverage between 1950 and 1965, this expansion included increases in regular medical insurance (16 to 58 percent), hospitalization (48 to 69 percent), pensions (22 to 40 percent), and life insurance (39 to 64 percent).[88] Data collected by the National Industrial Conference Board from surveys in 1948 and 1964 shows large corporations leading the trend.[89] During this time, the number of large employers reporting that they offered group accident and sickness insurance increased from 69 to 80 percent, while the number offering pensions increased from 26 to 78 percent. In another generation, it appeared as if universal coverage with respect to health care and pensions could be achieved.

Notes

1. Stephen Kemp Bailey, *Congress Makes a Law: the Story Behind the Employment Act of 1946* (New York: Columbia University Press, 1950), 10.
2. Ibid., 179, 243, 125.
3. National Association of Manufactures, *Economic Principles Commission, The American Individual Enterprise System, Its Nature, Evolution, and Future* (New York: McGraw-Hill, 1946).
4. Bailey, *Congress Makes a Law*, 130–131.
5. Ibid., chapter 8.
6. Ibid.
7. Ibid.
8. Stuart Bruchey, *The Wealth of the Nation: An Economic History of the United States* (New York: Harper and Row, Publishers, 1988), 185.
9. Brian Waddell, *The War Against the New Deal: World War II and American Democracy* (DeKalb, Illinois: Northern Illinois University Press, 2001), 133.
10. John Mack Faragher, et al., *Out of Many: A History of the American People, Volume Two*, 2nd ed. (Upper Saddle River, New Jersey: Prentice Hall, 1997), 837–839.
11. United States Bureau of the Census, *Statistical Abstract of the United States 1972*, 93rd ed. (Washington, DC: US Government Printing Office, 1972), 386, 248.
12. Thomas K. McCraw, *American Business, 1920–2000: How it Worked* (Wheeling, Illinois: Harlan Davidson, Inc., 2000), 100–101.
13. Morris K. Udall, "Military Spending—Let's Stop the Waste," Congressman's Report, October 12, 1961, University of Arizona Library Manuscript Collection, Tucson, Arizona, http://library.arizona.edu/exhibits/udall/congrept/87th/611012.html.
14. Robert Sobel, *The Age of Giant Corporations: A Microeconomic History of American Business, 1914–1970* (Westport, Connecticut: Greenwood Press, Inc., 1972), 189.
15. Richard F. Weingroff, "Federal-Aid Highway Act of 1956: Creating the Intestate System," *Public Roads Magazine* 60, no. 1 (Summer 1996), http://www.fhwa.dot.gov/publications/publicroads/96summer/p96su10.cfm.
16. Louis Galambos and Joseph Pratt, *The Rise and Fall of the Corporate Commonwealth: United States Business and Public Policy in the 20th Century* (New York: Basic Books, 1988), 124; Sobel, *The Age of Giant Corporations*, 179.
17. Waddell, *The War Against the New Deal*, 147.

18. United States Bureau of the Census, *Historical Statistics of the United States, Part 2, Colonial Times to 1970*, Bicentennial Edition (Washington, DC: US Government Printing Office, 1975), 884, 870; Frederic G. Donner, *The World-Wide Industrial Enterprise: Its Challenges and Promise* (New York: McGraw-Hill Book Company, 1967), chapter 3; Editors of Automotive Quarterly Magazine, *General Motors: The First 75 Years of Transportation Products* (Detroit: General Motors Photographic, 1983), 218–219.

19. Joseph Bruce Gorman, *Kefauver: A Political Biography* (New York: Oxford University Press, 1971).

20. Burton R. Fisher and Stephen B. Withey, *Big Business as the People See It: A Study of a Socio-Economic Institution* (Ann Arbor, Michigan: The Survey Research Center, Institute for Social Research, University of Michigan, 1951), 20, 54.

21. Faragher, et al., *Out of Many*, 845–850.

22. John Kenneth Galbraith, *American Capitalism: the Concept of Countervailing Power* (Boston: Houghton, Mifflin Company, 1956).

23. C. Wright Mills, *The Power Elite* (New York: Oxford University Press, 1956).

24. Udall, "Military Spending."

25. Sobel, *The Age of Giant Corporation*, 186.

26. David Riesman, *The Lonely Crowd: A Study of the Changing American Character* (New Haven, Connecticut: Yale University Press, 1950); C. Wright Mills, *White Collar: The American Middle Classes* (New York: Oxford University Press, Inc., 1951); William H. Whyte, *The Organization Man* (New York: Simon and Schuster, 1956).

27. Arthur Link, *Technological Change and Productivity Growth* (New York: Taylor and Francis, 1987).

28. Neil Fligstein, *The Transformation of Corporate Control* (Cambridge, Massachusetts: Harvard University Press, 1990), 177–190.

29. Richard J. Barber, *The American Corporation: Its Power, Its Money, Its Politics* (New York: E. P. Sutton & Co., Inc. 1970), 175–176; Time Magazine, "Corporations: One Merger Stopped," *Time Magazine*, December 1, 1958.

30. George Bittlingmayer, "Regulatory Uncertainty and Investment: Evidence from Antitrust Enforcement," *Cato Journal* 20, no. 3 (Winter 2001); Richard Hofstadter, "What Happened to the Antitrust Movement," in *The Making of Competition Policy*, eds. Daniel A. Crane and Herbert Hovenkamp (New York, Oxford University Press, 2013—revised version of article originally published in 1964).

31. In 1958, the functions of safety and accident investigation were spun off to the newly created Federal Aviation Administration.

32. David Kennedy, *Freedom From Fear: The American People in Depression and War, 1929–1945* (New York: Oxford University Press, 1999), 371.

33. Marver H. Bernstein, *Regulating Business by Independent Commission* (Princeton, New Jersey: Princeton University Press, 1955), 144, 150.

34. James M. Landis, *Report on Regulatory Agencies to the President Elect, US Senate, Committee on the Judiciary, 86th Congress, 2nd session* (Washington, DC: Government Printing Office, 1960).

35. Martin Mintz and Jerry S. Cohen, *America, Inc.: Who Owns and Operates the United States* (New York: Dial Press, 1971), 247.

36. United States Bureau of the Census, *Historical Statistics of the United States, Part 2*, 914, 938, 924.

37. Phillip I. Blumberg, *The Megacorporation in American Society: The Scope of Corporate Power* (Englewood, New Jersey: Prentice-Hall, Inc., 1975), 27; United States Bureau of the Census, *Statistical Abstract of the United States 1972*, 481.

38. Sobel, *The Age of Giant Corporations*, 212; Barber, *The American Corporation*, 22–25; John Kenneth Galbraith, *The New Industrial State*, 2nd ed. (New York: A Mentor Book from New American Library, 1971), 47.

39. Social Security Administration, "Chapter 3: The Third Round 1943–1950," *Social Security History*, http://www.ssa.gov/history/corningchap3.html.

40. Ibid.

41. Ibid.

42. Edward D. Berkowitz and Kim McQuaid, *Creating the Welfare State: the Political Economy of the 20th Century Reform*, rev. ed. (Lawrence, Kansas: University Press of Kansas, 1992), 181.

43. Equal Employment Opportunity Commission, "The Equal Pay Act of 1963," Equal Employment Opportunity Commission, http://www.eeoc.gov/laws/statutes/epa.cfm.

44. United States Bureau of the Census, *Historical Statistics of the United States, Part 1, Colonial Times to 1970*, Bicentennial Edition (Washington, DC: US Government Printing Office, 1975), 178; David Brody, *Workers in Industrial America: Essays on the 20th Century Struggle* (New York: Oxford University Press, 1979), chapter 5; Nelson Lichtenstein, *Labor's War at Home: The CIO in World War II* (Cambridge, England: Cambridge University Press, 1982), 117–121.

45. Neil W. Chamberlain, *The Union Challenge to Management Control* (New York: Archon Books, 1967—originally published in 1948), 260.

46. Nelson Lichtenstein, "Labor in the Truman Era: Origins of the 'Private Welfare State,'" in *The Truman Presidency*, ed. Michael J. Lacey (Cambridge, England: Cambridge University Press, 1989), 132–133; Lichtenstein, *Labor's War at Home*, 84–85.

47. Brody, *Workers in Industrial America*, 178, 181.

48. Lichtenstein, *Labor's War at Home*, 221–228.

49. Foster Rhea Dulles and Melvyn Dubofsky, *Labor in America: A History*, 5th ed. (Arlington Heights, Illinois: Harlan Davidson, Inc., 1993), 336.

50. Ibid., 336, 340.

51. Ibid., 343.

52. President Truman vetoed the legislation, but Congress voted to override his veto.

53. Beth Stevens, "Labor Unions, Employee Benefits, and the Privatization of the American Welfare State," *Journal of Policy History* 2, no. 3 (1990): 246, 236; Beth Stevens, "Blurring the Boundaries: How the Federal Government Has Influenced Welfare Benefits in the Private Sector," in *The Politics of Social Policy in the United States, eds. Margaret Weir*, Ann Shola Orloff, and Theda Skocpol (Princeton, New Jersey: Princeton University Press, 1988), 137.

54. Steven A. Sass, *The Promise of Private Pensions: The First Hundred Years* (Cambridge, Massachusetts: Harvard University Press, 1997), 120.

55. Stevens, "Blurring the Boundaries," 141; Sass, *The Promise of Private Pensions*, 133; Nelson Lichtenstein, *The Most Dangerous Man in Detroit: Walter Reuther and the Fate of American Labor* (New York: Basic Books, 1995), 283; Sumner H. Slichter, James J. Healy, and E. Robert Livernash, *The Impact of Collective Bargaining on Management* (Washington, DC: The Brookings Institution, 1960), chapter 13.

56. Slichter, Healy, and Livernash, *The Impact of Collective Bargaining*; Sanford M. Jacoby, *Modern Manors: Welfare Capitalism Since the New Deal* (Princeton, New Jersey: Princeton University Press, 1997), 252–256; George Milkovich, "Union Role in Wage and Salary Administration," McGraw Hill Education Answers, 2013, http://www.answers.mhecucation.com/management/compensation/union-role-wage-and-salary-administration.

57. Alfred M. Skolnik, "Twenty-Five Years of Employee-Benefit Plans," *Social Security Bulletin* 39, no. 9 (September 1976); Slichter, Healy, and Livernash, *The Impact of Collective Bargaining*, 375; Sass, *The Promise of Private Pensions*, 139.

58. Slichter, Healy, and Livernash, *The Impact of Collective Bargaining*, 404–406; Monthly Labor Review, "Senate Investigation of Welfare and Pension Plans," *Monthly Labor Review* 79, no. 7 (July 1956): 812.

59. Slicher, Healy, and Livernash, *The Impact of Collective Bargaining*, 443; Richard B. Freeman, "The Effect of Trade Unionism on Fringe Benefits," *Industrial Labor Relations Review* 34, no. 4 (July 1981): 491; Richard B. Freeman and James L. Medoff, *What Do Unions Do?* (New York: Basic Books, Inc., 1984), 77.

60. Slichter, Healy, and Livernash, *The Impact of Collective Bargaining*, chapter 5.

61. Ibid., chapters 6, 10.

62. Ibid., chapter 25; Jacoby, *Modern Manors*, 239, 254.

63. United States Bureau of the Census, *Historical Statistics of the United States, Part 1*, 178.

64. Jacoby, *Modern Manors*, chapter 3.

65. Ibid.

66. Slichter, Healy, and Livernash, *The Impact of Collective Bargaining*, 444.

67. Ralph J. Cordiner, *New Frontiers for Professional Managers* (New York: McGraw-Hill Book Company, Inc., 1956), 37.

68. Jacob S. Hacker, *The Divided Welfare State* (Cambridge: Cambridge University Press, 2002), 239.

69. Jacoby, *Modern Manors*, 220–221.

70. Ibid., 123.

71. Ibid., 244.

72. Roger M. Blough, *Free Man and the Corporation* (New York: McGraw Hill Book Company, Inc., 1959), 60.

73. Morrell Heald, *The Social Responsibilities of Business: Company and Community, 1900–1960* (Cleveland: The Press of Case Western Reserve University, 1970), chapter 8.

74. Ibid.

75. Ibid., 234; Clarence C. Walton, *Corporate Social Responsibilities* (Belmont, California: Wadsworth Publishers Company, Inc., 1967), 49–50.

76. Heald, *The Social Responsibilities of Business*, 234.

77. Ibid., 227–228.
78. Heald, *The Social Responsibilities of Business*, 267; Robert H. Bremmer, *American Philanthropy*, 2nd ed. (Chicago: University of Chicago Press, 1968), 181.
79. Heald, *The Social Responsibilities of Business*, 265, 264, 260.
80. Howard R. Bowen, *Social Responsibilities of the Businessman* (New York: Harper and Row, 1953), 51.
81. Theodore V. Houser, *Big Business and Human Values* (New York: McGraw-Hill Book Company, Inc., 1957), 61.
82. Bowen, *Social Responsibilities of the Businessman*, 57.
83. Cordiner, *New Frontiers for Professional Managers*, 22–23.
84. Frank W. Abrams, "Management's Responsibilities in a Complex World," *Harvard Business Review* 29, no. 3 (May 1951): 31.
85. Blough, *Free Man and the Corporation*, 57.
86. Bowen, *Social Responsibilities of the Businessman*, 78; Abrams, "Management's Responsibilities in a Complex World," 29.
87. Abrams, "Management's Responsibilities in a Complex World," 30.
88. Alfred M. Skolnik, "Twenty-Five Years of Employee-Benefit Plans."
89. National Industrial Conference Board, *Personnel Practices in Factory and Office, revised, Studies in Personnel Studies, No. 88* (New York: National Industrial Conference Board, Inc., 1948); National Industrial Conference Board, *Personnel Practices in Factory and Office: Manufacturing, Studies in Personnel Policy, No. 194* (New York: National Industrial Conference Board, Inc., 1964). It should be noted that NICB data for 1948 include hourly workers only, while for 1964, they include both blue- and white-collar employees.

7

The 1970s: The Peak of America's Regulatory Structure

Though they exercised unprecedented power by the early 1960s, America's large corporations seemed to be delivering the goods. They dominated an economy that grew at such a healthy clip that millions of Americans were propelled into the middle class, able to enjoy a constantly improving standard of living that included private health insurance and pensions—due in part to the featured role played by CSR in America's regulatory structure. Instead of a contested institution, the large corporations appeared to have finally surmounted challenges to its legitimacy. But this apparent respectability and acceptance was about to be put to the test. As the nation left the 1950s, it entered a decade of swirling protests and new social movements that demanded changes in all of America's major institutions—including the large corporation.

Mandated Responsibility

Growth of Large Corporations: The Conglomerate

After World War II, International Telephone and Telegraph (ITT) found itself caught on the horns of an organizational dilemma. As an American based operator of foreign communication systems, many of its telephone companies had been expropriated during the war. Independence movements and nationalist fervor in Cuba and Latin America during the 1950s continued the trend. The impregnable monopoly of AT&T precluded the option of competing in the domestic telephone market. As a result, CEO Harold Geneen decided in the early 1960s to build the domestic side of the business, but outside the communication industry. This he did with a single-minded dedication. Between 1964 and 1970, ITT acquired over seventy-five companies in industries as diverse as rental cars (Avis), hotels (Sheraton), food (Continental Baking, the makers of Wonder Bread), insurance (The Hartford), and home construction (William Levitt & Sons).[1]

ITT was a pioneer of the conglomerate, defined as a company that has product lines in two or more unrelated industries. As one of the most significant organizational innovations in the second half of the twentieth century, the conglomerate represents an extreme form of product diversification. The original logic of diversification was that companies could grow and become more profitable by taking fuller advantage of their technological infrastructure and developing related product lines. As originally practiced by Du Pont in the 1920s, this meant that a firm in the explosives industry could expand to make products in the chemical and paint industries. By expanding into unrelated industries, the conglomerate took diversification to its logical conclusion.[2]

Corporations conglomerated to varying degrees. At one end of the spectrum were conglomerates like RCA that remained anchored in a primary industry, but with one or more subsidiaries in unrelated industries. At the other end of the spectrum were firms like ITT (and Textron, Litton Industries, and LTV) that were conglomerates par excellence, each merely a name associated with a diverse array of subsidiaries with no primary industry at its core. Since up through the 1950s it was the single industry giant, whether Standard Oil, U.S. Steel, or General Motors, that had reigned supreme, the rise of the conglomerate represented a rapid and radical change.

There were many reasons behind this transformation, but one of the most important was the changed environment of antitrust enforcement. By the late fifties and early sixties, the impact of the Celler-Kefauver Act of 1950, which aimed at reducing economic concentration within industries, began to be felt in the Justice Department's prosecutions and court decisions. In 1962 the Supreme Court upheld a lower court's decision to void the proposed merger of Brown Shoe and Kinney Shoe, since it would lead to greater concentration in an industry that had already experienced substantial horizontal and vertical integration. As the decision reverberated throughout the business community, many executives concluded that any merger that might increase economic concentration and lessen competition within an industry would be a likely target of antitrust prosecution. As a result, the growth strategies of horizontal and vertical integration were substantially curtailed. Instead, growth through the acquisition of firms producing related or unrelated products seemed to escape antitrust scrutiny.[3]

Like the Sherman Antitrust Act years earlier, the Celler-Kefauver Act had the unintended effect of producing even larger corporations. While antitrust policy now had the effect of favoring diversification (into both related and unrelated product lines) as a vehicle of corporate growth, mergers soon became the preferred route. For firms deciding to conglomerate, mergers were almost mandatory, since this involved diversifying into unrelated industries in which a corporation had no preexisting infrastructure to build upon. But even where firms had the option of internal investment to develop related products, mergers became an expedient way of avoiding being left at a competitive disadvantage once this strategy was shown to be profitable. For these and other reasons, the country experienced the longest merger wave in its history from 1954 to 1969, with 15,944 total mergers. Early in this period (1956–1960) nearly half of all large mergers (over $10 million) continued to involve horizontal or vertical integration. As evidence of the Celler-Kefauver effect, by the end of the merger wave (1966–1970), only 20 percent were of the horizontal or vertical variety. In contrast, mergers of companies with related products increased from 38 to 51 percent, while conglomerate mergers increased from 16 to 29 percent.[4]

Beyond antitrust worries, the process of institutionalization contributed to the rapid spread of conglomerates. A whole merger industry comprising lawyers, tax consultants, and business analysts arose and gained a vested interest in pushing diversification, and especially conglomerate mergers forward. Wall Street investors early on rewarded conglomerates by bidding up their stock prices. Given the success of conglomerates like ITT, many established firms jumped on the conglomerate bandwagon, whether it was Coca-Cola getting into the cattle-feed business, Firestone Tire becoming a manufacturer of rifles, or Gillette razors selling pens. Indeed, the successful single-industry firm of the past was, in this new environment, a vulnerable target for conglomerate acquisition.[5]

As conglomerates came to dominate the economic landscape, a management philosophy emerged to justify their ascendance. With more and more managers professionally trained and in possession of MBAs, some analysts concluded that they now had the specialized knowledge that enabled them to manage any line of business. Furthermore, conglomeration created "synergies." This presumably meant that the interaction of formerly independent businesses produced an effect that was greater than the sum of the separate effects. But these were possibilities that only a new breed of manager could exploit.[6]

By 1970, most of America's major corporations had become conglomerates, with the largest two hundred now operating in 2,200 separate industrial categories. The merger wave also produced larger corporations and a greater degree of economic concentration than at any time in the nation's history. Between 1955 and 1970, the five hundred largest industrial firms increased their control of industrial assets (64 percent to 75 percent) and industrial sales (58 percent to 65 percent). They also employed 14.6 million workers, or 73 percent of all industrial employees (up from 64 percent in 1955). This group also captured 74 percent of all industrial profits. Yet another indicator of increasing size was the fact that eighty of the Fortune 500 largest industrial corporations in 1962 disappeared through merger by the end of the decade.[7]

Of course, while most major corporations now operated across industries, most major industries remained oligopolies at the end of the sixties. For example, the four largest firms controlled over 75 percent of domestic production of automobiles, synthetic fibers, aluminum, copper, cereal foods, typewriters, and rubber tires, among others. Furthermore, other governance structures and practices that benefited large corporations when they operated in single industries continued to benefit large corporations now that they operated in multiple industries. For example, it was large corporations—now frequently large subsidiaries of large conglomerates—that benefited from growth in private contracting that accompanied the expansion of the federal government as it fought a war on poverty as well as a war in Vietnam. By 1970, government contracting represented 25 percent of federal government expenditures. Similarly, it was now multinational conglomerates that were frequently associated with foreign direct investments that continued to grow, nearly doubling between 1963 and 1970 (from $40.7 billion to $78.1 billion).[8]

Large corporations now possessed greater economic power than at any time in US history, and they led an economy that continued to grow and dominate the world's economy. Some observers suggested that America had reached the economic end of time. In his 1967 best-selling book, *The New Industrial State*, Harvard economist John Kenneth Galbraith asserted that the imperatives of modern technology had produced a system of economic planning that had subsumed the market.[9] He argued that the large corporation was the only organizational form capable of managing production that required a massive commitment of time, money, and personnel.

Professional managers, it seemed, had finally succeeded in their long quest of taming the market.

Those who viewed the conglomerate as the pinnacle of development for the large corporation expressed similar sentiments. With so much economic power at their disposal, these corporate giants were now in the position to more fully rationalize their environments and thus control their destinies. Some, in fact, saw no end in sight for the process of conglomeration and, extrapolating from the merger trend of the 1960s, predicted that by the end of the 1970s all major corporations (those with assets over $10 million) would have been acquired by larger conglomerates. As a result, only two hundred large corporations would remain.[10]

—

Up through the first half of the 1960s, the American public did not seem at all troubled by these developments involving large corporations. As late as 1966, an Opinion Research Corporation survey found that 55 percent of the public had "a great deal of confidence" in the leaders of major corporations, a postwar high.[11] But this was about to change. Corporate stalwarts like General Motors were about to become targets of a renewed antipathy toward big business.

Ideological and Political Challenges: The Return of Antimonopolism

In 1963 Ralph Nader took a job as a part-time consultant to Assistant Labor Secretary Daniel Patrick Moynihan. His assignment was to write a report on highway safety. Nader had developed an interest in the safety of automobiles shortly after graduating from Harvard Law School in the mid-1950s, and he was particularly intrigued by the notion that automakers might be liable in cases of unsafe auto design. His growing interest and expertise helped him land a contract in 1964 to write a book on the subject. At about the same time, the newly elected and incoming chairman of the Executive Reorganization Subcommittee of the Governmental Relations Operations Committee, Senator Abraham Ribicoff, was casting about for an issue that might interest his fellow senators and engage his liberal leanings. Troubled by the growing number of fatalities on American roadways, Ribicoff announced hearings on automobile safety. As fate would have it, Nader became an unpaid advisor to the subcommittee.[12]

It was 1965, and the automobile industry had little reason to worry. After all, it was riding a wave of success in which it sold most of the world's cars. Given its central position in the US economy, it had largely been left alone by politicians in Washington. So while the first round of hearings generated enough publicity to prod President Johnson to announce in his 1966 State of the Union address that he would propose a bill to address the issue, the Highway Safety Act that he subsequently introduced to Congress was sufficiently weak to justify the industry's seeming lack of concern.

This time, however, business as usual did not prevail. Unhappy with the administration's bill, Ribicoff decided to reopen hearings. He was given greater ammunition with which to fight for a stronger bill with the recent publication of Nader's book *Unsafe at Any Speed*.[13] In the book, Nader catalogued engineering decisions that produced unsafe vehicles, especially during a car's "second collision," when passengers collide with unpadded dashboards and sharp knobs. Not surprisingly, Nader was promoted from advisor to witness.

But as compelling as Nader's testimony was on February 10, 1966, it is what happened afterward that improved the odds of passing a significant piece of regulatory legislation. After his appearance, news stories began to appear that GM was conducting surveillance on Nader, asking associates about his political and sexual preferences. Outraged, Ribicoff held a hearing to determine if Nader was being harassed, and with television cameras rolling, the president of GM apologized for the company's actions. With the story of a mighty and abusive Goliath attempting to squash an intrepid David serving as a backdrop, Congress passed the National Traffic and Motor Vehicle Safety Act, which authorized the federal government to both set and administer safety standards for cars and highways. President Johnson signed the bill into law on September 9, 1966.[14]

The passage of legislation promoting automobile safety was only the beginning. Over the course of the decade of 1965–1975, Congress passed a raft of legislation that required greater responsibility in a variety of forms, ranging from safer products to less pollution to more fairness in hiring decisions. Not only were these the strongest regulations aimed at corporations in the nation's history, they constituted social regulations, the type that had always been difficult, if not impossible, to enact. Underlying this burst of legislative activity was a revival of the reformist strain of antimonopolism that had not been much seen since the Progressive Era. This populist sentiment found expression in the congeries of social movements that came to define the period, from civil rights to public interest. By whittling the esteem with which the public viewed big business (confidence in large corporations plummeted from

220

55 percent in 1966 to 16 percent in 1975), an environment was created that was conducive to mandating that corporations meet higher standards of corporate behavior.[15]

The roots of this renewal of antimonopolism can be found in return of muckraking journalism and the negative attention that it brought to socially irresponsibly corporate practices. Early in the decade there were stories about the health risks of products. These included stories reporting the connection between smoking and cancer, and the link between the sedative Thalidomide and fetal deformities.[16] Nader's *Unsafe at Any Speed* not only exposed a safety hazard with the Corvair, but also assailed corporations like GM for the systematic negligence that regularly placed profits ahead of safety. Vance Packard wrote several best-selling books that criticized the American way of doing business and the corrupting influence of business values. In *The Waste Makers* (1960), he chronicled corporate practices, such as planned obsolescence and deceptive advertising.[17] There were also stories that highlighted the connection between corporate practices and pollution. The seminal work in this genre was Rachel Carson's examination of the link between corporate misconduct and environmental degradation in her best-seller, *Silent Spring* (1962).[18]

Scholarly critiques of large corporations also grew during this period. A growing line of attack was that large corporations had become private governments.[19] More importantly, the decisions made by those who ran large corporations were seen as increasingly consequential. As Wolfgang Friedmann noted, corporations had ceased to be private phenomena: "That they have a direct and decisive impact on the social, economic, and political life of the nation is no longer a matter of argument. It is an undeniable fact of daily experience."[20] Of particular importance in this analysis were investment decisions, since the decision to build a new plant, or close one down, "may well determine the quality of life for a substantial segment of society."[21] Comparing General Motors with the federal government, Peter Bachrach concluded: "It is on the basis of this similarity that General Motors and other giant private governments should be considered a part of the political sector in which democratic norms apply."[22]

But as these writers pointed out, there was no true democratic accountability for the private decisions of corporations. Corporate executives did not need to solicit the public's input, nor did such decisions require Congressional approval. In fact, the decision-making process of large corporations was usually insulated from the actual owners themselves. This was due to the separation of ownership and management of large corporations, which had continued to widen. The 44 percent of large corporations under "management control" that Berle and Means found at the end of the 1920s expanded to 83 percent by 1974.[23] As Nader and his coauthors pointed out in their *Taming the Giant Corporation*, incumbent management so fully controlled the proxy election process that in 1973 over 99 percent of board elections for America's largest corporations were uncontested.[24]

By the end of the decade and into the early 1970s, both journalistic and academic attention came to focus upon the conglomerate movement. Not only were conglomerates now criticized for having the same anticompetitive consequences as horizontal and vertical mergers, they were viewed as facilitating greater corporate secrecy, with accounting tricks used by a conglomerate's subsidiaries obscuring the truth about corporate performance. Instead of viewing them as the end state of some inevitable corporate progression toward greater efficiency, conglomerates were characterized as the creations of empire builders seeking power after power.[25]

These critiques helped to feed the social movements that demanded changes in corporate practices. But this begs the question of why these attacks resonated with the American public when they did. After all, there was nothing new about most of these practices. Furthermore, large corporations were dominant in the 1950s as well, and during that decade business leaders mostly inspired confidence. Then there is the fact that, as indicated above, big business still seemed to be delivering the goods. Between 1947 and 1966, the annual rate of economic growth averaged 4 percent per year. As a result, real family income doubled during this period, and the ranks of the middle class swelled.[26]

The seeming contradiction of demands for greater control of corporations in the face of their economic success can be understood, in part, as a manifestation of the "culture shift" that took place in Western societies in the latter decades of the twentieth century. Applying Maslow's notion of a "hierarchy of needs" to the level of society, political scientist Ronald Inglehart has argued that, having achieved economic security, members of newly affluent societies could now aspire to a set of postmaterial goals that place a greater emphasis on personal fulfillment and quality of life. This was especially true of their children, who grew up in an environment of abundance instead of scarcity. In addition to equal rights and a clean environment, one way that this shift in values revealed itself was in higher expectations for corporate behavior in relation to the full contingent of corporations' stakeholders. In a short span of years, Americans rendered their judgment that the leaders of America's corporations were not meeting these elevated standards.

At first, attacks upon large corporations were suffused within the social movements that came to define the decade of the sixties. During the civil rights movement, for example, a bright light illuminated the hiring practices of corporations, and in 1964 Bank of America, the world's largest bank at the time, became a target of demonstrations to protest employment discrimination. In the antiwar movement that followed, companies like Dow Chemical, the makers of napalm, became the objects of protest for their complicity in the war effort. Then, of course, there was the more diffuse countercultural movement of young people, where mainstream goals such as monetary success and pursuing careers within large corporations were summarily dismissed as base and unfulfilling. By the late sixties and early seventies three new social movements arose that placed the reform of corporate practices at the center of their agendas: consumers, environmental, and public interest.[27]

consumers movement: An important step in creating a national consumers movement occurred in 1967 when the Consumer Federation of America was founded as a coalition of 140 state consumer organizations and consumer cooperatives, together with a number of unions. In 1969 the National Consumers Union, with its 1.3 million members who read *Consumer Reports*, set up a Washington office. Consumerism was an emblematic middle-class movement, reflecting an increase in discretionary income and rising expectations for an improved quality of life.[28]

environmental movement: The environmental movement exploded onto the national scene between 1969 and 1970. While only 1 percent of Americans polled in 1969 listed pollution as a national problem, 25 percent did so a year later. By the end of 1970, a Harris poll showed that Americans considered pollution to be the nation's "most serious problem." Much of the credit for the new environmental awareness goes to the new environmental organizations that had formed since 1967 (the Environmental Defense Fund, Friends of the Earth, and the Natural Resources Defense Council), as well as the efforts of older groups, like the Sierra Club and National Audubon Society, that saw their memberships soar. The apex of the movement was achieved on April 22, 1970, when over twenty million Americans participated in Earth Day, a series of rallies and teach-ins that highlighted the need to restore and protect the environment.[29]

public-interest movement: Shortly after the passage of National Traffic and Motor Vehicle Safety Act, Ralph Nader demonstrated that he was not a single-issue entrepreneur, as he helped win passage of the Wholesale Meat Act of 1967. By the summer of 1968 he was ready for a bigger project. With his star rising, Nader was able to mobilize the talents of a group of idealistic recent graduates of ivy-league colleges to investigate the Federal Trade Commission. The 185-page report that they produced revealed, among other findings, that only one in every 125 consumer complaints resulted in action by the commission, and that it took an average of four years for a complaint to be investigated—after decades, the Commission was still chronically underfunded. Furthermore, instead of going after large corporations, with whom the commissioners frequently had cozy relationships, and for whom some would work after passing through the revolving door, the FTC tended to focus its efforts on small companies.[30]

By 1969 Nader was able to enlarge his group of would-be muckrakers, now dubbed Nader's Raiders, and give them an organizational home in the newly founded Center for the Study of Responsive Law, headquartered in an old mansion near DuPont Circle. As they say, the rest is history. By the middle of the 1970s, Nader had become his own do-good industry, establishing an array of groups, including Congress Watch, the Public Citizen Litigation Group, the Tax Reform Research Group, and the Corporate Accountability Project.[31]

Nader represented the vanguard of what came to be known as the public-interest movement. Emerging in the late sixties, it comprised a diverse set of lobbying groups, law firms, membership groups, research institutes and community groups, which sought a variety of collective goods. Importantly, most shared the common goal of curtailing the private power of business by demanding greater accountability and social responsibility. Like the environmental and consumer movements with which it was allied and subsumed, it sprang to life and proliferated rapidly.

The causes of this pervasive activism were many, including the weakening of political parties, which opened up new outlets for political demands; the rise of "political entrepreneurs" who were willing to assume the costs of mobilizing large constituencies; innovations in fundraising, especially direct mail solicitation; and the formation of liberal foundations with resources to fund public-interest groups. These various groups also benefited greatly from, and helped inspire, an influx of highly educated people (many of whom were lawyers) to the nation's capital wanting to work for a cause—and willing to work for little money.[32]

Like interest groups generally, many of the constituent groups of the public-interest movement relied upon lobbying as the main tactic for seeking reform. But in light of further revelations concerning captured regulatory agencies, reliance upon regulations alone was not enough. Some therefore pushed for reforms that would strengthen the regulatory agencies themselves, such as the proposal to close the revolving door by making it more difficult for regulators to take jobs in the industries that they oversee. From the Nader network came a proposal that called for the creation of a consumer protection agency that would represent the interests of consumers. Consumer-based organizations had bandied about the idea of such an agency since 1969, and in an interview published in 1971, Nader stated that he would happily trade in all pending consumer protection legislation for an agency dedicated to consumers. But this would be a regulatory agency with a difference. Instead of having direct authority over the private sector, a consumer protection agency would represent the interests of consumers before existing regulatory agencies; in effect, consumers would be empowered with their own captured agency.

By the mid-1970s, the Nader wing of the public-interest movement revived the idea, first proposed during the Progressive Era and briefly resuscitated during the Depression, of chartering corporations at the federal level. Instead of using charters to control corporations or at least ensure strong corporate governance, states had typically weakened their laws of incorporations in order to compete with other states in the contest of attracting businesses and collecting franchise fees—an age-old form of competitive federalism. Many years earlier, Delaware had won this race to the bottom, becoming the home to over half of the Fortune 500 corporations. The federal law proposed by Nader and company would, among other provisions, stipulate that each corporation's charter include a limit on that company's market share within an industry. In this way, competition would be assured and oligopolies destroyed.[33]

However, there were some in the movement who had no faith in either the ability of Congress to pass new reforms or the Executive Branch to enforce laws regulating corporate behavior. Instead, they pushed for a strategy that would rely upon the judiciary. Inspired by the constructive role of the courts during the civil rights movement, these reform leaders believed that the more insulated judiciary could be persuaded to expand the practice of judicial review to ensure that agency decisions were in compliance with regulatory mandates. It was probably no coincidence that such a strategy emerged within a movement that included a preponderance of lawyers in its leadership ranks. It is also true that, like their forbearers in the Progressive Era, this contingent of public-interest advocates not only mistrusted big business, they also mistrusted big government. They therefore hoped that judges would exhibit neutral independence, the quality that earlier reformers projected onto the commissioners constituting independent regulatory bodies like the Interstate Commerce Commission.[34]

But for the new interest group politics to actually bring about change, the political calculus of Washington had to change at the same time. This was facilitated first by Lyndon Johnson's landslide victory in 1964, and the huge Democratic majorities it produced (295 to 140 in the House and 68 to 32 in the Senate). Not only did this weaken the conservative coalition of Southern Democrats and Republicans, Congress also became younger and more liberal. In this political environment Johnson was able to pursue the ambitious legislative program of the Great Society, which legitimized a greater role for government. Other political changes encouraged congressmen to take the political initiative as well. For example, seniority rules had been weakened that allowed junior senators like Ribicoff to sponsor legislation. This possibility was further enhanced by increases in the size of congressional staffs and the number of subcommittees. Even the election of Republican Richard Nixon in 1968 did not quash the zeitgeist of reform.

One of the great strengths of this new brand of interest-group politics is that it helped to mobilize those animated by a single issue, whether it was the environment or consumer protection. This strength, however, was simultaneously a weakness. Though there were strongly articulated sentiments and ideas attached to any particular issue, there was no underlying philosophy that integrated the various streams of reform. Yet another weakness was that much of this new activism was "checkbook activism." Instead of building a grassroots network of organizations that engaged members at the local level, the various social movement organizations increasingly came to be headquartered in Washington; they tended to have little, if any, presence in local communities across the nation. Membership, as a result, tended to involve sending an annual check and receiving a periodic newsletter.

—

But these underlying weaknesses would become visible only in the long run. In the short term, the extraordinary political climate of the sixties and seventies produced an unprecedented number of strong mandates for corporations to act in a more socially responsible manner toward workers, consumers, communities, and the environment. For the first time in the nation's history of dealing with large corporations, government switched its focus from economic regulations, especially antitrust, to social regulations.[35]

Social Regulations and Welfare: A Wave of Mandates and the Promise of Health Care

consumer mandates: Even before there was a consumer movement, members of Congress found that consumer protection legislation was popular with the public. A controversy over Thalidomide helped the venerable antimonopolist Estes Kefauver push for the passage of the Food and Drug Act Amendments of 1962. As shown above, Senator Ribicoff helped stoke the public ire over automobile safety to win passage of the National Traffic and Motor Vehicle Safety Act of 1966. Once the consumer movement began to emerge, the volume of consumer protection legislation increased and included the Fair Packaging and Labeling Act, the Flammable Fabrics Act, the Wholesale Meat Act, and the Truth in Lending Law. In 1970 Congress passed the Consumer Product Safety Act that established the Consumer Product Safety Commission, which was given the broad-based charge of protecting consumers from unsafe products. That year also saw Congress pass the Cigarette Advertising Act, which ultimately led to the banning of cigarette commercials from radio and television.[36]

environmental mandates: Responding to demands for a cleaner environment, Congress passed several important bills, including the Clean Air Amendments of 1970, which greatly strengthened air quality standards, and the Federal Water Pollution Control Amendments of 1972, which did the same for water quality. The Federal Environment Pesticide Control Act of 1972 expanded the federal government's regulation of pesticide use. In 1970 President Nixon signed the National Environmental Protection Act, which yielded the "environmental impact statement," the requirement that all federal agencies consider the impact of impending decisions upon the environment. Later that year, the president, who was competing with Democrats in Congress for the mantle of environmental leadership, established the Environmental Protection Agency (EPA). The EPA brought together six thousand federal employees, working in three separate departments on fifteen different programs, into a new administrative agency charged with protecting the environment. Following the recommendations of the Ash Commission, the new agency would not be modeled on the independent regulatory agency, but instead have a single administrator appointed by and directly responsible to the president.[37]

workplace mandates: Well before the issues of consumer protection and environmental degradation placed corporate behavior in the media's spotlight, the civil rights movement had focused the public's attention on the discriminatory employment practices of corporations. During the early 1960s, especially as the movement spread to the North, dozens of businesses were the targets of pickets, boycotts, and other demonstrations in an effort to pressure the business community to hire more blacks. While these protests did produce some voluntary agreements to increase black employment, including one with the Bank of America, they also added to the momentum that was building toward passage of the Civil Rights Act of 1964. As a result, for the first time in the nation's history there was a law that explicitly prohibited employment discrimination based upon race, sex, religion, or national origin.[38]

The act also created an enforcement mechanism in the form of the Equal Employment Opportunity Commission (EEOC). The EEOC opened for business the following year with a budget of $2.25 million and roughly one hundred employees, and in just its first year, it received close to nine thousand complaints. With no authority to bring lawsuits, the commission would investigate such charges of discrimination; if they were found to have merit, an attempt would then be made to reach a voluntary settlement. The mission of the EEOC was reinforced when in 1965 President Johnson signed Executive Order 11246, which required all government contractors to take "affirmative action" to expand job opportunities for women and minorities.[39] Over the next several years, Congress expanded the scope of the EEOC and gave it litigation authority. By 1973 the EEOC had a budget of $43 million, two thousand employees in thirty-two district and seven regional offices. That same year the EEOC signed a consent decree with AT&T, the nation's largest employer, to eliminate the company's discriminatory recruiting, hiring, and promotion practices against women and minorities.[40]

Progress was also made in terms of workplace safety. For the first generation after World War II, workmen's compensation laws remained America's dominant approach to the problem of hazardous working conditions. These laws directly helped those who were injured, while indirectly promoting workplace safety by raising the costs of compensation for those employers with injured workers. However, by the end of the 1960s, fourteen thousand workers were dying annually in workplace incidents, and two million more were injured. Even so, strong employer resistance was enough to defeat a comprehensive workplace safety bill submitted by the Johnson administration in January of 1968.[41]

But with environmental consciousness rising at the end of the decade, the political climate for this issue changed dramatically. Congressional hearings in late 1968 revealed the magnitude of the problem and highlighted the growing problem of worker exposure to toxic chemicals as the result of the chemical revolution in manufacturing. Already seeking to solidify his support among blue-collar workers, the newly elected President Nixon in a message to Congress called for a bill that would "guarantee the health and safety of workers."[42] Congress ultimately passed the Occupational Safety and Health Act of 1970, which placed the power to set safety standards in the Department of Labor (in the form of the Occupational Safety and Health Administration), while creating an independent commission to enforce the rules (the Occupational Health and Safety Review Commission). This marked a significant milestone, since the federal government would now be empowered to protect the health and safety of over fifty million workers of the tens of thousands of firms, across all industries, involved in interstate commerce.

pensions: The push for workplace mandates extended to the fringe benefit of pensions as well. As private pensions expanded after World War II, there was increasing concern that three types of risk might prevent employees from receiving their pensions. The first of these was "default risk," or the risk that a pension plan might not have the funds to meet its obligations, such as when a company went bankrupt. "Agency risk" occurred when those administering a fund misused or stole assets, thus leaving the plan short of the funds needed to meet its obligations. Workers who changed jobs or who experienced a layoff were subject to "forfeiture risk." This was even true for workers with long job tenures, since many employers required twenty or more years of service before employees were fully vested.[43]

Efforts to address these problems stretched back to 1962 when President Kennedy formed a cabinet-level committee to study the role of private pensions in the economic security system of the country. It would take several years, however, for pension reform to gain traction. But in the new era of congressional mavericks, Republican Senator Jacob Javits of New York adopted the issue. The cause of pension reform received an inadvertent push from the Watergate scandal and the subsequent resignation of President Nixon on August 8, 1974. With a palpable feeling that Washington was broken, Congress sought to show that it could still work on the nation's ills, and within two weeks of the new Ford administration it passed the Employee Retirement Income Security Act of 1974 (ERISA). In addition to strengthening reporting and disclosure requirements for pension funds, ERISA set minimum standards for vesting and funding levels. It also created the Pension Benefit Guaranty Corporation (PBGC) to provide insurance for those whose plans terminate.[44]

One thing that the bill did not do, however, was actually mandate that employers offer pensions to their employees, which would have served to strengthen America's welfare state. They were only regulated *if* an employer offered them as a fringe benefit—which meant that they remained an item for both union negotiations and CSR. However, in the area of health care, the American welfare state seemed poised to finally assume the responsibility of ensuring universal coverage.

health care: Like social regulations, America's welfare state also grew during the 1960s, especially after President Lyndon Johnson declared war on poverty in his State of the Union address in 1964. In addition to patching holes in the nation's safety net, Johnson hoped to alleviate unemployment and expand the role of government in the areas of education and health care. Initiatives to help with the safety net included the Food Stamp Act of 1964, while employment and education proposals led to the creation of a number of programs, including Head Start and Job Corps.

In the case of health care, though the fringe benefit of medical insurance expanded rapidly after the war, there were glaring holes in coverage. In particular, most retirees and poor people were uninsured. Filling these holes became an early initiative of the Great Society agenda. But the success of employment-based health plans narrowed the policy options that were considered. A proposal to develop a national health care system was never considered. Instead, Congress established Medicaid, which would subsidize health care for welfare beneficiaries, and Medicare, which would provide hospital insurance for retirees. The latter would be funded, like Social Security, through a payroll deduction so that, like the public pension, it would represent a right that people had "earned."[45]

Energized by success, reformers decided to keep pushing for universal coverage. By early 1974, there were three competing proposals for health care reform, and while none proposed a government-run health care system, two featured an employer mandate. It therefore seemed that there was sufficient momentum that the question was not whether health care reform would pass, but which of the various proposals would become law. Instead, the initiative died in August. Causes of death included mounting opposition from a coalition of medical and business groups, scandals involving Wilbur Mills, the powerful chair of the House Ways and Means Committee, and, because of the Watergate scandal, a progressively enervated President Nixon. But an additional reason was that progressive groups held some of their fire. The impending resignation of the president led many to calculate that it was better to wait until after the 1974 elections, when Democrats would likely build their majorities in Congress and thus improve the climate for reform. This was especially true of organized labor, which hoped that earlier proposals to create national health care could be revived. So as of 1974, health care remained, like pensions, an item for either union-management negotiation or employer benevolence.[46]

—

By the mid-1970s, the federal government had passed a number of social regulations, and it had also assumed greater responsibility in the case of health care and seemed poised to assume more. The combined effect of these developments gave the strong impression that government was in the position to balance the political economy and strengthen the pillar of mandated responsibility of the nation's regulatory structure. Arguably, demands for more restraints upon large corporations were as strong, if not stronger, and certainly more varied than at any time since their emergence in the nineteenth century. Paradoxically, the union movement played a marginal role at best in securing this array of new mandates. It did, however, secure better contracts for its members.[47]

Negotiated Responsibility

It became clear early on that instead of reinvigorating the labor movement, the merger of the AFL and CIO in 1955 had produced an intense rivalry between AFL president George Meany and the CIO's last president, Walter Reuther. A plumber by trade, Meany proved himself to be cast in the old mold of a craft unionist, catering to the interests of skilled workers. Mistrustful of the politics of social mobilization, he continually stymied the efforts of Reuther to push the merged federation in the direction of greater social activism. A developing conservatism extended to union militancy itself, as Meany bragged in later years that he had never been on a picket line or led a strike. Aggressively organizing new members was not a priority. Ultimately, the leader of the AFL-CIO seemed content to enjoy the perquisites of power.[48]

By the early 1960s, Reuther, unable to reorient the AFL-CIO, refocused his energies back upon the UAW, and hoped to use it again as a vehicle to promote political unionism and social activism. In 1963 he walked arm in arm with civil rights leaders during the March on Washington, and the UAW threw its weight into the fight to pass the Civil Rights Act. Such a gesture led to the hope that unions, including the UAW, could overcome their own discriminatory practices, thus uniting the working class. In 1964, at his invitation, leaders of the Students for a Democratic Society were in attendance at the union's annual convention, having earlier used the union's summer education camp to draft the Port Huron Statement. In sync with Reuther's orientation to change, the student leaders viewed unions as the best candidates for the leadership position in movements for social change.[49]

While he dusted off his credentials as an agent for social change, Reuther was also able to put one foot into the halls of the establishment. This began with the election of John F. Kennedy, in whose administration he became a member of the newly established Labor-Management Advisory Committee. Sitting on the board with the likes of Henry Ford II and Thomas Watson of IBM, Reuther hoped to revive the notion of instituting corporatist bargaining in the United States. By now firmly established in Europe, the basic notion would involve setting up a structure for industries whereby prices and the distribution of profits would be subject to political negotiations among representatives of government, industry, and workers.[50]

It was with the Johnson administration, however, that Reuther got both feet in the door. After being sworn in as president, Lyndon Johnson reached out to Reuther, and Reuther returned the embrace. For his first State of the Union address in January 1964, LBJ sought Reuther's input, and ultimately incorporated several elements from the memo he received into his address. After declaring a "war on poverty," the president secured passage of the Economic Opportunity Act, which featured the Community Action Program. Modeled after a UAW program of training community leaders, CAP called for the "maximum feasible participation" of the poor in fighting poverty, a kind of community-level equivalent of a trade union local. After Johnson's landslide victory in November, Reuther enthusiastically endorsed the Great Society programs and was particularly instrumental in helping shape what became the "model cities" housing initiative. All of this seemed to add up to a progressive, social Keynesianism that would bring about the long-sought goal of full employment.[51]

But just as this window of opportunity opened for a resurgence of political unionism, it began to close. The war on poverty had hardly begun when the Vietnam War became Johnson's primary focus. Not only did this draw attention and energy from the domestic front, it meant that the former war would go underfunded. In the hopes that the Great Society initiatives could be saved, under the assumption that Johnson's escalation of the war would be short-lived, Reuther remained loyal to the president. This, in turn, contributed to the fissure that began to develop between the union movement and New Left, antiwar forces.

This fissure became an ever-widening gulf as the stalwart anticommunist George Meany placed the AFL-CIO squarely behind Johnson's efforts to contain the spread of Communism. This, in turn, contributed to divisions within the house of labor, as Reuther pulled the UAW out of the AFL-CIO in 1968 over the federation's focus on foreign-affairs issues and failure to commit sufficient resources to organizing new members. The hopes for working-class solidarity went up in flames in the race riots that followed the assassination of Martin Luther King, and members of the white working class were drawn to the racist populism of George Wallace. The death of Walter Reuther in a 1970 plane crash also seemed to signal the death of a broader vision of unions acting as the vanguard for social change.

By the end of the sixties, then, unions seemed out of step with the defining movements of the decade, including the revival of the reformist strain of antimonopolism. But this did not seem to matter, since American business unionism reached the apex of its success during this period. Collective bargaining between employers and unions produced an estimated 194,000 agreements by the end of the 1970s. Many of these were thick documents that covered issues ranging from wage and fringe benefit levels to work rules. To develop policy, conduct negotiations, monitor agreements, and handle grievances, unionized companies almost always had a labor or industrial relations (IR) department. While union avoidance would be assigned a higher priority by the 1980s, the top priority of labor relations staff during this period was to fashion the best agreement possible.[52]

Wages and Job Security

For unions, the focus upon pay, the hallmark of American business unionism, had literally paid off. In their thorough review of unions' impact in the 1970s, *What Do Unions Do?*, Harvard economists Richard B. Freeman and James L. Medoff found that union workers had wages that were 20 to 30 percent higher than their nonunion counterparts doing comparable work. Much of this reflected the success of unions in taking wages out of the arena of competition to achieve goals like establishing a living wage. Indeed, a Conference Board survey showed that finding the "industry pattern" was the chief criterion used by management in determining a wage target for negotiations—as opposed to "local labor-market conditions." This union wage premium was also found to be greater for less educated than more educated workers, younger than older workers, and junior as opposed to more senior workers. Together with the tendency for the wages of blue-collar workers to rise relative to the typical higher earnings of white-collar workers, collective bargaining tended to produce greater wage equality in the workforce.[53]

The union advantage was protected by the growing use of cost-of-living adjustments (COLAs). While roughly 25 percent of workers covered by major agreements (contracts covering over one thousand workers) had COLA protection in 1970, 61 percent were protected against inflation by 1977. Some of this proliferation signified unions' continued emphasis upon income security. Of course, in cyclical industries, this preference could come at the expense of employment security. When shifts in demand led to a reduction of available work, many union contracts called for temporary layoffs to preserve full-time work, as opposed to practices like work sharing, which protected employment at the cost of lower wages. As most temporary layoffs lasted less than a month, and since laid-off workers received unemployment benefits, unions judged this a reasonable trade-off. To provide some income protection beyond unemployment insurance, unions pushed hard for severance pay, and by 1975, 38 percent of workers under major agreements were covered by such a plan.[54]

This is not to say that unions did not seek job security for their workers. Union negotiators continued to bargain for work rules, such as mandatory crew sizes, that had the effect of protecting employment. Unions were also successful in winning contract clauses that limited the right of management to subcontract work, so as to protect against the option of employers attempting to shift work to nonunion workers. Some unions bargained for additional time off with pay as a means of reducing the length of the work year, as a way of forcing employers to hire more workers. Arguably the most important way that unions advanced the cause of job security was through the institution of grievance arbitration, which served to protect members from arbitrary discharge and discipline.[55]

That union workers actually experienced greater job security was reflected in studies that showed lower turnover rates for union workers compared with their nonunion counterparts. Some of this difference was no doubt due to the greater pay and benefits (see below) associated with union work. However, in analyses that held wages and other factors constant, union workers were still much less likely to leave their jobs than nonunion workers. Freeman and Medoff conclude that this clearly demonstrates a "voice effect." Because of the grievance and appeals options available in most union firms, workers there could securely voice dissatisfaction, instead of feeling that the only alternative was to "exit." Also contributing to job tenure was the further institutionalization of seniority. Aggressively pushed by unions as a way of reducing arbitrary treatment and favoritism in personnel decisions, seniority gave workers with the longest service the most secure jobs, as well as the first opportunity for the better jobs that became available.[56]

Of course, there were limits to unions' successes in winning secure employment for their members. For example, unions faced much stronger employer resistance when they sought protections for members against plant shutdowns. By the mid-seventies, only 11 percent of major agreements included provisions that gave employees of multi-plant employers the right to transfer in the case of a plant shutdown.[57] The lack of such protections would prove to be the Achilles heel of business unionism by the time corporate restructuring and downsizing entered the business vocabulary during the 1980s.

Fringe Benefits

While the late 1940s and 1950s were the years that witnessed major breakthroughs in fringe benefits like health insurance and pensions, the 1960s and 1970s represented the period when these benefits diffused widely across industries, and expenditure levels rose rapidly. Not surprisingly, a strong relationship was found between wages and benefits, such that the higher the average level of wages in an industry was associated with more comprehensive and generous fringe benefit provisions in union contracts. The latter, however, were increasingly expensive. By 1977, the cost of benefits averaged 35 percent of wages and salaries in firms surveyed by the Chamber of Commerce.[58]

In many ways, the growth in benefits reflected the desires and interests of both union members and employers. In the case of the former, a survey that asked members how much effort their union should devote to the areas of wages, fringe benefits, job security, and safety and health, found that fringe benefits were given the highest priority. Because older workers were more likely to use benefits like health and life insurance, they tended to assign them even greater importance, and because of seniority, the preferences of older union members tended to carry greater weight. For employers, whose greatest interest was protecting the prerogatives of ownership, improvements in fringe benefits could be traded for holding the line on demands for restrictions on layoffs or work assignments.[59]

Union firms continued to be the trend setters in providing fringe benefits, and union workers were much more likely to have them than their nonunion brethren. Data from the 1977 Quality of Employment Survey found that, controlling for characteristics such as wage level, firm size, industry, and region, unions increased the probability of fringe benefits being offered by an average of 19 percent. Union workers were thus more likely than nonunion workers to have medical insurance, life insurance, dental insurance, and an eyeglass benefit, among other benefits.[60]

Job Control

If the sixties and seventies were characterized by the diffusion and institutionalization of business unionism, the same can be said for the other face of US labor relations, job control. This was a byproduct of pressures from both sides of the "contested terrain" of the shop floor. For unions, work rules continued to serve as protection against arbitrary decision making and exploitation, and they served to protect jobs. For employers, work rules served to protect their decision-making prerogatives, and they embedded control within the bureaucratic, "ration-legal" structure of the organization, thus enhancing the legitimacy of management.

However, the proliferation of work rules and job classifications only reinforced the worst features of scientific management. More sophisticated techniques of job engineering, together with automated technology, left jobs even more fragmented and bereft of skill, autonomy, and decision-making authority. This, in turn, contributed to an uptick in labor militancy. Unauthorized, "wildcat strikes," increased during the latter years of the sixties, and the consensus of many analysts was that this reflected growing discontent with shop-floor issues. Such discontent was also directed at union leaders who negotiated such alienating conditions, as union members increasingly voted down agreements during the same period of time, even as they contained improved compensation packages. The symbol of what came to be labeled "blue-collar blues" was a three-week strike over assembly line speed-ups at the new GM plant in Lordstown, Ohio, in 1972.[61]

A growing number of employers also began to express concern about the effects of such "workplace contractualism." On the one hand, high turnover rates in the context of low unemployment rates led some executives to worry about retention and its relationship to the structure of work. On the other, a decline in productivity growth by the early 1970s led others to blame inefficient and inflexible work rules. Ultimately, there was sufficient concern on both sides of the bargaining table concerning current workplace practices that the Secretary of Health, Education, and Welfare, Elliot Richardson, commissioned a task force of social scientists in 1971 to write a report on the quality of working life. Their *Work in America* report published in 1973 declared Taylorism an anachronism.[62] The authors concluded that a major reason for this was that there was that there was a growing mismatch between the rising expectations for meaningful work, especially among younger, more educated workers, and the alienating conditions of much manufacturing work. Their major recommendation was job redesign, a trend that will be examined below.

—

In sum, the pay, benefits, and security of union workers continued to grow steadily through the sixties and into the seventies. There was a looming problem, however. While the number of union workers also continued to grow, reaching a record high of over 21.5 million in 1974, the percentage of the nonagricultural workforce belonging to unions was declining; the unionization rate of that year was 25.8 percent, down from the record of 35 percent in 1955. One factor contributing to union decline was employer resistance to unions. For all of the talk of "labor peace," many, if not most, employers who finally had to bargain with unions still did not fully accept them. One indicator of a lack of harmonious relations was the level of strike activity. Instead of declining, as greater harmony and acceptance would predict, the number of work stoppages increased from 3,419 at the time of the Treaty of Detroit in 1948 to 6,074 in 1974.[63]

For employers, "labor peace" was more likely to mean tolerance of unions, not full acceptance. For reasons that will be explored in the next chapter, employers' tolerance level for unions was lowered as the 1970s progressed and many began to more actively avoid them. But while union avoidance would turn primarily nasty by the 1980s, during the sixties and seventies, many corporations remained nonunion by creating positive employment conditions so that employees would have little reason to join—in other words, many turned to the high road of CSR.

Voluntary Responsibility (CSR)

The Human Resources Alternative

In the quarter century after the Second World War, IBM became an icon of the high-tech firm located in the new industry of computing and information technology. Noted for having a strong corporate culture, the company encouraged both innovation and an unrivaled dedication to customer service. "Big Blue" was also known for its dedication to its employees. Very early in the company's history, founder Thomas J. Watson eliminated the position of foreman and felt, as one observer put it, "that the individual worker should have the biggest job possible rather than the smallest."[64] He backed his commitment to workers with a "no layoff" policy, and indeed, the company had never laid off an employee for economic reasons, even going back to the Depression. As seen by the company's vice president of personnel, Walton Burdick, IBM's approach to personnel was governed by a set of core policies, including: *individualism*, where the focus was on the individual employee and maximizing his or her career potential; *staffing and employment*, in which the company stressed employment continuity, promotion from within, and encouraged the assumption that a career was being offered at the time of hire; *compensation policy*, where all employees were paid on a salary basis; *fringe benefits*, where the company paid 100 percent of a generous array of benefits, and all employees received the same benefits; and *communication*, in which the company encouraged direct communication through an "open door" policy.[65]

IBM was also a nonunion shop. Together with companies like Motorola, Delta Airlines, and Burlington Mills, it was the vanguard of large nonunion corporations that developed what was now called the human resources (HR) alternative to the industrial relations model. To understand such firms better, Fred Foulkes interviewed top executives in twenty-six large, predominantly nonunion firms (twenty were Fortune 500 firms) in the latter half of the 1970s, which resulted in *Personnel Policies in Large Nonunion Companies*. Framing his study as the beginning of a "theory of nonunionization," Foulkes found that all nonunion companies in his study "devote substantial time, effort, and money to the management of human resources." This manifested itself in personnel departments that were able to exercise considerable power. In over half of the companies, the vice president for personnel or human resources reported directly to the chief executive officer. With an increasingly professionalized staff, these departments employed a variety of techniques to satisfy three common functions: involve employees in the problems of the business, offer employees the opportunity to voice complaints or make suggestions, and create a climate where it was legitimate for employees to seek help for personal problems.[66]

Following in the footsteps of successful nonunion companies in earlier eras, the corporations in Foulkes's study placed employment security at the center of the program of treating workers well. Indeed, nine of the companies reported never having had a layoff. Connecting employment security to a company's nonunion status, one vice president for personnel with direct experience stated: "Of all the union organizing drives that I have ever participated in, one way or another the manner in which management created this feeling of job insecurity seemed to be basic to every one of them." This was corroborated by a Conference Board study of unionization drives among white collar that was published in 1970: "Next to dissatisfaction with salaries, the most frequently cited cause of union interest among employees is concern with job security. . . ."[67]

To prevent layoffs in the face of cyclical swings in the marketplace, many employers in Foulkes's sample used a common set of "buffers," including the use of temporary employees, overtime, subcontracting, and in some cases work sharing. But to truly engender job security, many large nonunion employers created a system of what was tantamount to lifetime employment. This meant that instead of hiring from without, these companies relied upon an internal labor market, and since these large corporations were typically steeply bureaucratic, career ladders were easy to build. The hoped for result was that workers would adopt an individualistic orientation to improvement, instead of the collective approach of unions.[68]

In order to solidify the bond between corporation and employee, the companies of Foulkes's study also coupled job security with generous pay and benefits. Almost without exception, executives paid close attention to what their competition was doing and adjusted their packages accordingly: "We are the top paying company in this area—we spend a lot of time tracking pay and benefits." Monitoring union settlements was particularly acute. The corporate director of employee relations at one firm clearly expressed the practical impact of the union threat: "The company pays a slight premium in its nonunion plants over the wages paid in the general geographic area for similar work at union plants."[69] In keeping with the desire to nurture an identity of interests, benefit plans tended to be applied equally to everyone in the company, whether janitor or president. Furthermore, to encourage a sense of common interests between management and employees, profit sharing remained the one fringe benefit that nonunion workers were more likely to receive than union workers.[70]

The role of union threat in the development of the HR system was also revealed in the motives articulated by management. As categorized by Foulkes, "doctrinaire" companies were those where remaining nonunion was the raison d'être:

> It is our policy to take all lawful steps necessary or desirable to operate on a nonunion basis. In effect, we have an implied, unwritten contract with our employees which says . . . that we will voluntarily take those steps which are necessary to ensure that . . . they will receive compensation and benefits which in their totality are competitive with the unionized companies in our field in this area.[71]

Even for the "philosophy-laden," those companies where the primary motivation for treating workers stems from core values, the stated commitment to treating employees with respect seemed to be conditioned by the threat of unions: "I don't think we will ever have to worry about our company becoming unionized. Our people are treated well. We have what the unions want."[72]

Other evidence also supports the premise that union threat benefited workers in large nonunion firms. In data examined by Freeman and Medoff in *What Do Unions Do?*, the authors conclude that the presence of unions raised the wages of workers in large nonunion firms by 10 to 20 percent and contributed to more generous benefits for these workers as well. Furthermore, in partially unionized firms, the pay and benefits won by union workers tended to be extended to the company's nonunion employees. Finally, nonunion workers frequently benefited, even when efforts to organize them failed. A NICB study of white-collar unionization showed that in 23 percent of cases where unions lost the election, workers experienced improvements in their fringe benefits.[73]

Job Redesign

The HR alternative began to take shape in the 1950s, when CSR employers began to adopt "human relations" practices, such as user-friendly leadership styles. By the late sixties and early seventies, a number of these large nonunion firms began to add "job redesign" to the model. With the focus on improving employee motivation by changing the structure of work itself, job redesign embraced several strategies, including 1) *job enlargement*, in which the central task of a job is expanded to include a variety of related tasks, 2) *job rotation*, in which an employee is rotated through a series of jobs or departments, typically for short periods of time, and 3) *job enrichment*, in which a job is expanded to include traditionally managerial functions, such as planning and organizing the work. A 1974 survey of three hundred firms on the Fortune 1000 list of leading industrials showed that 29 percent had experimented with some form of job redesign, while an additional 24 percent planned to do so in the near future.[74]

The movement to change the design of work had several roots. In the latter years of the 1960s, low unemployment and high turnover rates led some manufacturers to worry about worker retention. The increase in the percentage of workers with at least some college education led many analysts to conclude that, reflecting the broader "culture shift" to non-material values like self-expression, workers had rising expectations concerning the experience of work. Furthermore, the increase in labor militancy involving workplace issues at union establishments, together with growing frustration with the rigidity of work rules and job classifications, led some chief executives to rethink the assumptions of Taylorized work. As a result of this confluence of trends, a number of executives became receptive to new strains of psychological theory that challenged the prevailing view that workers naturally resisted work and were motivated primarily by material incentives, especially pay. Building upon the foundation of the human relations school's focus on the social aspects of work, theorists such as McGregor and Herzberg argued that workers were inherently motivated by work that was challenging, whether this involved performing a variety of tasks, having autonomy to make decisions, or experiencing the opportunity to learn new skills.[75]

Early on, efforts at job redesign were as likely to occur in unionized firms, like General Motors and Ford, as they were in nonunion firms, like Honeywell and Citibank. Over time, however, such experiments became concentrated in nonunion companies. Part of the reason for this is that job redesign did not fit well within the framework of collective bargaining. First of all, US labor law did not require that management bargain over the design of jobs, and in their growing frustration with workplace contractualism, managers were interested in keeping the reengineering of jobs fully within the purview of managerial preroga- tives. Furthermore, even where union cooperation was sought, the basic thrust of job redesign did not conform to the template of strict work rules and narrow job classifications, in which workers had gained some protection from unilateral managerial rule. Unions were also concerned that job redesign was just one more top-down, managerial initiative aimed at circumventing unions, both in terms of negotiation and in loyalty of employees. At least some of the suspicion of labor leaders was justified.[76] The personnel director of nonunion Texas Instruments reported liking schemes like job enrichment because they had the potential effect of making employees "adjuncts to management—and people do not organize against themselves."[77]

While the HR system was well established by the end of the 1960s, it began to spread more broadly among nonunion firms in the early 1970s. This seemed to be connected to the growing resistance to unions noted above. One clear indicator of this trend was the growing number of consulting firms that specialized in advising companies how to remain union free. While the following chapter will show how much of this activity eventually focused on negative, union-busting tactics, at least early on, the dominant advice in the face of the threat of unionization was for companies to adopt positive, preventative measures that would preempt union organizing. In books like *Making Unions Unnecessary*, this meant adopting a HR system of employee relations.[78]

—

By the mid-1970s, welfare capitalism had grown into a robust alter- native to the union workplace. At the same time, a growing segment of the public felt that corporations had broad responsibilities to the public at large that went beyond those that were mandated. In a

1970 survey conducted by the Opinion Research Corporation, two-thirds of respondents believed that business had a moral obligation to help society achieve social progress, even if this lowered a firm's profits. In this environment, it was reasonable to expect that the public's raised expectation would translate into greater corporate philanthropy.[79]

Corporate Philanthropy

At first glace, corporations did not seem to respond to growing pressures to do more good works. Though the total amount of corporate philanthropy rose, as a percentage of pretax income it actually decreased from 1966 to 1973 (from 0.96 percent to 0.75), and it remained well below the 5 percent level that the law allowed. In fact, a 1972 survey of 475 large corporations showed that the rate of giving actually declined with the size of a corporation. Furthermore, much of corporate giving came through individual corporate employees contributing to federated drives, like United Way, as opposed to budgetary expenditures by the corporation itself.[80]

A closer look, however, reveals that corporations actually adopted a great number of socially responsible practices, but many of these did not fit neatly into the traditional category of corporate philanthropy. For example, in 1969 alone, corporations invested $1.5 billion in air and water pollution control, which was nearly 50 percent higher than total corporate philanthropy for that year. However, these voluntary actions to improve the environment appeared on balance sheets as capital expenditures, not social giving.

Another area that would not have registered as corporate philanthropy was corporate involvement with urban problems. Judging by the titles published by the Conference Board (*Business Amid Urban Crisis, Business and the Development of Ghetto Enterprise*), there was also plenty of evidence that corporations were engaged in socially responsible initiatives to address the various afflictions of American cities.[81] One area of concern was lack of diversity in employment. In response, a survey of 247 companies found that 44 percent had minority-hiring programs.[82]

As was true in the past, the underlying motives for corporate philanthropy were varied. Given what was going on in Congress, some of the increase in philanthropic activity was no doubt a preemptive attempt to ward off further regulation. For example, much of the early spending on pollution reduction in the late 1960s came as the government was debating stronger regulatory legislation, and was thus an effort (ultimately unsuccessful) to demonstrate that regulations were not needed. The subsequent increases in environmental spending during the 1970s came largely as a result of new government mandates.[83]

Just as the threat posed by unions propelled many nonunion corporations to adopt CSR at the workplace, the growing threat of government regulations prompted many large corporations to engage in greater CSR activities in the broader community. In its 1971 policy statement, *Social Responsibilities of Business*, the Committee for Economic Development (CED) recommended that

> By acting on its own initiative, management preserves the flexibility needed to conduct the company's affairs in a constructive, efficient, and adaptive manner. And it avoids or minimizes the risk that governmental or social sanctions, produced out of a crisis atmosphere, may be more restrictive than necessary.[84]

In some cases, the dominant motive was self-interest. For example, the array of war on poverty programs included a number of public-private partnerships that represented profitable activities that had socially responsible results.[85] As one executive put it several years later, "Urban affairs is a new market for us. . . . Because of the poverty program, we bagged some government contracts for the first time."[86] In the Conference Board's study of urban affairs programs, one eighth of those interviewed stated frankly that their interest in getting involved was to make a profit.

In essence, enlisting large corporations to help with social problems represented an extension of the model of government contracting with the private sector to accomplish legislated goals. While government could engage large corporations to build infrastructure or munitions, it could also commission large corporations to help achieve social goals. For example, there was the JOBS (Job Opportunities in the Business Sector) program, in which the Labor Department would reimburse private businesses for the costs of educating and training of the hard-core unemployed in inner cities. In the case of housing, the Federal Housing Authority offered rent supplements to landlords so as to increase the profitability, and hence availability of low-income housing. All in all, the federal government provided an array of incentives, from contracting to subsidies to tax benefits so as to encourage the greater involvement of business in solving social problems.[87]

corporate campaigns and the new CSR: The expansion of the voluntary adoption of socially responsible practices, as well as the expanding turf of CSR, were also the result of what came to be called "corporate campaigns." In 1970 the small group of lawyers comprising the Project for Corporate Responsibility (PCR) called a press conference to announce that they would be using their twelve shares of General Motors stock to submit nine resolutions to the company's shareholders that dealt with the issues of corporate governance and social responsibility. Campaign GM marked the birth of the public-interest proxy proposal. It also marked the beginning of efforts on the part of activists in the 1970s to politicize corporations, a strategy consistent with the critique that corporations operated as private governments. As was true in the case of automotive safety legislation, GM made for a large, Goliath-like target. The decisions that its professional managers made on behalf of its 1.3 million shareholders touched the lives of millions of stakeholders. Yet the only power that shareholders had was to buy or sell shares of stock, while the only recourse of the company's stakeholders was to buy a GM car or not.[88]

By making direct appeals to corporations to act responsibly, activists were attempting to make corporations more democratically accountable. This was an increasingly important emphasis of the reformist strain of antimonopolism, which, as seen earlier, helped to animate the debates that yielded an impressive array of social regulations for corporations. However, since most of these appeals of groups like the PCR involved corporations voluntarily adopting practices that dealt with the broader society and environment, activists were also essentially demanding a more robust, democratic form of CSR.

Before 1970, shareholder-sponsored resolutions were rare and never made it to the proxy statements that corporations sent to their shareholders. Since managers could invoke SEC rules that allowed them to exclude proposals aimed at promoting social causes, they were well insulated from owners. This time around, however, while the SEC allowed GM to exclude seven of the nine PCR proposals, it ruled that two had to be included. The first of these would create a Committee on Social Responsibility, whose members would be chosen by GM management, the PCR, and the United Auto Workers. The second proposal would enlarge the board of directors by three seats to be filled by "public representatives."

The following year the PCR was able to place three additional proposals on the company's proxy statement. Thus began a trend. Given their potential for influencing public opinion, the number of public-interest proxy resolutions increased from 37 in 1972 to 105 in 1974. Among the issues addressed by these proposals were the corporations' environmental impact, the political activities of corporations, investments in undemocratic nations, and employment opportunities for women.[89]

In addition to seeking direct participation in corporate decision making via proxy proposals, some public-interest groups pursued the strategy of forcing greater disclosure by corporations of information that could show the degree of compliance with public-interest goals. For example, the Council on Economic Priorities, founded in 1969, published research reports ranking firms in the areas of equal employment, the environment, military contracts, and foreign operations. The hope was that shining a bright light on the social performance of corporations would help to nurture the practice of ethical investing. Harkening back to the approach of the National Consumers League during the Progressive Era, there was also the hope that with greater disclosure, especially if it was regularized in the form of "social audits," consumers would weigh a company's record as corporate citizens before consuming its products.[90]

If one looks only at the votes for these shareholder resolutions, the politicization of corporations did not seem to work to encourage greater corporate social responsibility. In the case of Campaign GM, each of the original proposals was soundly defeated with less than 3 percent of the shares that were cast. In fact, over the course of the next several years, none of the shareholder resolutions passed. But, then again, winning was never the goal of the PCR. Instead, the goal was to generate publicity, engender debate concerning the social responsibilities of corporations, and have an impact on corporate policy. Here, arguably, the campaign showed some success. In the case of Campaign GM, not only did 130 reporters attend the next GM annual meeting, the company published a twenty-one-page booklet to all of its shareholders highlighting the progress it had made on auto safety, pollution abatement, and social welfare, thus legitimizing the public's demands for greater CSR.[91]

The politicization of corporations no doubt added to the pressures on corporations to act benevolently. In *The Conscience of Corporations*, a 1970 study of the urban affairs programs of 201 Fortune 500 financial and industrial corporations, one-third of the executives interviewed indicated that they adopted programs in order to discourage threats to their company's well-being, such as consumer boycotts. And whether it was theirs, or the damaged reputations of corporations generally during this period, four-fifths of the executives interviewed mentioned that strengthening their corporate image was a key objective.[92]

Some employers claimed loftier motives as well. For the CED, because corporations were treated as legal persons, they had "the same obligation as all citizens to participate in and contribute to the general welfare, and to treat human beings humanely."[93] Like the vanguard of business leaders after World War II, some saw greater social responsibility on the part of corporations as the logical next step in their history. For example, Louis B. Lundborg, the retired chairman of Bank of America, saw "the business system of America evolving into more socially oriented, humane and responsible institutions—more beneficial to the society, to the employee and to the shareholder."[94]

—

The corporate campaigns of the 1970s reflected the diverse goals of the public-interest groups that were demanding CSR, whether it was environmental or good-government activists. This period of time also signaled the appearance of what would become the "new CSR" of the twenty-first century, in which the beneficiaries of CSR practices shifted from employees and local communities to the environment and the policies of developing countries.

Summary

Having achieved a level of acceptance after the war, the large corporation entered the 1960s presumably secure in its dominant place in America's political economy. By the end of the decade, however, the large corporation was once again a contested institution, its legitimacy challenged to a degree not seen since the Depression. This time, however, the loss of esteem was the result not of declining economic fortunes, for which the large corporation was assigned blame. Instead, it was the rising fortunes delivered by an economy dominated by large corporations, and led now by conglomerates. The improved standard of living that millions experienced fostered rising expectations that corporations should do more, whether it was consumer groups demanding safer products, the environmental movement demanding a cleaner environment, or civil rights and women's groups demanding the end of discrimination in the workplace.

Consequently, during the decade from 1964 to 1974, each pillar of the regulatory structure for controlling large corporations was significantly strengthened. From consumer safety to the environment, occupational safety to hiring, this period produced the strongest array of social regulations mandating corporate social responsibility in the nation's history. The decade also witnessed unions achieve a record-high number of members. The institutions of industrial relations and collective bargaining yielded more expansive and generous contracts, thus strengthening the pillar of negotiated responsibility.

In the face of threats of government regulations and unions, welfare capitalism expanded as well. In the face of union threat, nonunion employers attempted to match their union counterparts in pay, benefits, and job security. But the nonunion, HR alternative now also featured the redesign of work, aimed at simultaneously increasing productivity and the bond between company and employee. Among the CSR vanguard there was also a growing recognition that corporate obligations extended beyond the firm's legal owners and included the stakeholders of employees, consumers, and the local communities in which they resided.[95] Some of this was the result of efforts to politicize the large corporation and expand the meaning of philanthropy.

Of course, CSR was revealing its limits as well. On the one hand, the underlying competition between the union and nonunion employment models resulted in an expanding system of private welfare in which the vast majority of employees of large corporations were provided with health care and pensions. A 1974 Conference Board study of mostly large employers found 86 percent offered major medical plans, almost all offered life insurance, and 87 percent offered pensions. On the other hand, a report by the Social Security Administration in 1976 showed that among all workers, only 67 percent had regular medical insurance, and only 44 percent were eligible for a pension.[96] While all of these numbers were up from 1965, they were not up dramatically, indicating the system might be reaching a plateau. Furthermore, beyond the workplace, the expectations for CSR could be shown to have outstripped its potential. As was true of high hopes assigned to corporate philanthropy in the past, the more attention paid to the social problems that corporations were being asked to voluntarily address, the more likely was the conclusion that the scale of problems was simply too great for corporations to solve.

Even so, by the middle of the decade of the 1970s, America's regulatory structure for large corporations had achieved a new peak of effectiveness. Each pillar had grown substantially in strength, and the immediate forecast was that each would continue to do so. Furthermore, with the rapid proliferation of new social regulations on corporate behavior, it appeared as though government was finally beginning to assume its long-hoped-for role as a counterweight to the power of business. Many believed that this role would soon be buttressed with a new wave of legislative proposals about to hit Congress. One of these would create a Consumers Protection Agency that would further empower government to better enforce social regulations, and it appeared likely to soon pass; another would nationalize or mandate health care, which would shift a critical responsibility from employers to the federal government. Labor leaders, having achieved electoral success in 1974, hoped that the return of a Democratic administration in 1976 would enable the passage of labor-law reforms that would lead to an uptick in organizing new members.

However, should the current trajectories of change in political economy and labor relations continue, a tipping point could be reached: continued growth of mandated and negotiated responsibility could obviate many of the current voluntary, socially responsible activities. The historic pattern of weak mandated responsibility, weak negotiated responsibility, and strong voluntary responsibility might be switched to strong, strong, weak.

Notes

1. C. Joseph Pusateri, *A History of American Business*, 2nd ed. (Wheeling, Illinois: Harlan Davidson, Inc., 1988), 364; John F. Winslow, *Conglomerates Unlimited: The Failure of Regulation* (Bloomington, Indiana: Indiana University Press, 1973), 118; Robert Sobel, *The Rise and Fall of the Conglomerate Kings* (New York: Stein and Dayl Publishers, 1984).

2. Richard J. Barber, *The American Corporation: Its Power, Its Money, Its Politics* (New York: E. P. Sutton & Co., Inc. 1970), 41.

3. Neil Fligstein, *The Transformation of Corporate Control* (Cambridge, Massachusetts: Harvard University Press, 1990), 201–202.

4. Ibid., 193, 195; United States Bureau of the Census, *Statistical Abstract of the United States 1972*, 93rd ed. (Washington, DC: US Government Printing Office, 1972), 484.

5. Robert Sobel, *The Age of Giant Corporations: A Microeconomic History of American Business, 1914–1970*, Westport, Connecticut: Greenwood Press, Inc., 1972), 199, 204; Winslow, *Conglomerates Unlimited*, 3, xvi; Pusateri, *A History of American Business*, 364; Fligstein, *The Transformation of Corporate Control*, 260; Barber, *The American Corporation*, 36.

6. Louis Galambos and Joseph Pratt, *The Rise and Fall of the Corporate Commonwealth: United States Business and Public Policy in the 20th Century* (New York: Basic Books, 1988), 166.

7. Philip I. Blumberg, *The Megacorporation in American Society: The Scope of Corporate Power* (Englewood, New Jersey: Prentice-Hall, Inc., 1975), 25; Philip I. Blumberg, *Corporate Responsibility in a Changing Society*,

(Boston: Boston University School of Law, 1972), 60; Barber, *The American Corporation*, 39, 27.

8. Barber, *The American Corporation*, 23, 255, 253, 32, 251; Committee for Economic Development, Research and Policy Committee, *Social Responsibilities of Business Corporations: A Statement on National Policy* (New York: Committee for Economic Development, 1971), 55; Murray Weidenbaum, *Business, Government, and the Public*, 2nd ed. (Englewood, New Jersey: Prentice-Hall, Inc., 1981), chapter 9; United States Bureau of the Census, *Historical Statistics of the United States, Part 2, Colonial Times to 1970*, Bicentennial Edition, (Washington, DC: US Government Printing Office, 1975), 870.

9. John Kenneth Galbraith, *The New Industrial State*, 2nd ed. (New York: A Mentor Book from New American Library, 1971).

10. Winslow, *Conglomerates Unlimited*, 1.

11. Seymour Martin Lipset and William Schneider, *The Confidence Gap: Business, Labor, and Government in the Public Mind*, rev. ed. (Baltimore: the Johns Hopkins University Press, 1987), 50.

12. David Vogel, *Fluctuating Fortunes: The Political Power of Business in America* (New York: Basic Books, Inc., Publishers, 1989), 43.

13. Ralph Nader, *Unsafe at Any Speed: the Designed-In Dangers of the American Automobile* (New York: Pocket Books, 1966).

14. Vogel, *Fluctuation Fortunes*, 43–46; Justin Martin, *Nader: Crusader, Spoiler, Icon* (Cambridge, Massachusetts: Perseus Publishing, 2002), chapters 4–5.

15. Lipset and Schneider, *The Confidence Gap*, 50.

16. Morton Mintz, "'Heroine' of FDA Keeps Bad Drug Off Market," *Washington Post*, July 15, 1962.

17. Vance Packard, *The Waste Makers* (New York: D. McKay Co., 1960).

18. Rachel Carson, *Silent Spring* (London: Hamish Hamilton, 1963).

19. Earl Latham, "The Body Politic of the Corporation," in *The Corporation in Modern Society*, ed. Edward S. Mason, Cambridge (Massachusetts: Harvard University Press, 1959).

20. Wolfgang Friedmann, "Corporate Power, Government by Private Groups, and the Law," *Columbia Law Review* 57, no. 4 (April 1957).

21. Andrew Hacker, "Introduction: Corporate America," in *The Corporation Take-Over*, ed. Andrew Hacker (Garden City, New York: Anchor Books, Doubleday & Company, Inc., 1964), 9.

22. Peter Bachrach, *The Theory of Democratic Elitism: A Critique* (Boston: Little, Brown and Company, 1967), 102.

23. Edward S. Herman, *Corporate Control, Corporate Power* (Cambridge, England: Cambridge University Press, 1981), 58.

24. Ralph Nader, Mark Green, and Joel Seligman, *Taming the Giant Corporation* (New York: W. W. Norton & Company, Inc., 1976), 81.

25. Ibid., 225–226; Martin Mintz and Jerry S. Cohen, *America, Inc.: Who Owns and Operates the United States* (New York: Dial Press, 1971), 43.

26. Jeffrey Madrick, *The End of Affluence: America's Economic Dilemma* (New York: Random House, 1995), 34–35.

27. David Vogel, *Lobbying the Corporation: Citizen Challenges to Business Authority* (New York: Basic Books, Inc., Publishers, 1978), 26–30; Vogel, *Fluctuating Fortunes*, 56, 33, 54, 100.

28. Vogel, *Fluctuating Fortunes*, 38–39.

29. Ibid., 64–65.
30. Edward F. Cox, Robert C. Fellmeth, and John E. Schulz, *The Nader Report on the Federal Trade Commission* (New York: Grove Press, Inc., 1969).
31. Martin, *Nader*, 71, chapters 7, 11, 13.
32. Jeffrey M. Berry, *Lobbying for the People* (Princeton, New Jersey: Princeton University Press, 1977).
33. Nader, Green, and Seligman, *Taming the Giant Corporation*, chapter 4.
34. Vogel, *Fluctuating Fortunes*, 106–107, 229.
35. The government did, however, grow increasingly concerned about conglomerates, and in 1969 the Justice Department filed five suits that challenged recent acquisitions made by ITT and LTV. As analysts began to advise against conglomeration, the merger wave was dramatically slowed. The number of large-scale mergers was cut by more than half between 1969 and 1971, from 2307 to 1011.
36. Vogel, *Fluctuating Fortunes*, 39, 87.
37. Ibid., 64–67, 81–83.
38. Vogel, *Lobbying the Corporation*, 26–30.
39. Equal Employment Opportunity Commission, "Milestones in the History of the U.S. Equal Employment Opportunity Commission," http://www.eeoc.gov/abouteeoc/35th/milestones/, accessed May 22, 2013; Charles V. Dale, "Federal Affirmative Action Law: A Brief History," Congressional Research Service Report for Congress, September 13, 2005.
40. Equal Employment Opportunity Commission, "Milestones."
41. John H. Stender, "Enforcing the Occupational Safety and Health Act of 1970: The Federal Government as a Catalyst," *Law and Contemporary Problems* 38, no. 4 (Summer/Autumn 1974): 641; Vogel, *Fluctuating Fortunes*, 83–87.
42. Vogel, *Fluctuating Fortunes*, 85.
43. James A. Wooten, "A Legislative and Political History of ERISA Preemption, Part I," *Journal of Pension Benefits* 14, no. 1 (Autumn 2006): 31–35; Steven A. Sass, *The Promise of Private Pensions: The First Hundred Years* (Cambridge, Massachusetts: Harvard University Press, 1997), 180–190.
44. Sass, *The Promise of Private Pensions*, 221.
45. Edward D. Berkowitz and Kim McQuaid, *Creating the Welfare State: the Political Economy of the 20th Century Reform*, rev. ed. (Lawrence, Kansas: University Press of Kansas, 1992), 213–214.
46. Flint J. Wainess, "The Ways and Means of National Health Care Reform, 1974 and Beyond," *Journal of Health Politics, Policy, and Law* 24, no. 2 (April 1999); Jill Quadagno, *One Nation Uninsured: Why the U.S. Has No National Health Insurance* (Oxford: Oxford University Press, 2005), chapter 5.
47. Vogel, *Fluctuating Fortunes*, chapter 4.
48. Nelson Lichtenstein, *The Most Dangerous Man in Detroit: Walter Reuther and the Fate of American Labor* (New York: Basic Books, 1995), 333.
49. Ibid., 390.
50. Ibid., 361–362
51. Ibid., 389–403.
52. Thomas A. Kochan, *Collective Bargaining and Industrial Relations: From Theory to Policy and Practice* (Homewood, Illinois: Richard D. Irwin, Inc., 1980), 85, 28–29.

53. Ibid., 217, 381; Richard B. Freeman and James L. Medoff, *What Do Unions Do?* (New York: Basic Books, Inc., 1984), 46, 20.
54. Thomas A. Kochan, Harry C. Katz and Robert B. McKersie, *The Transformation of American Industrial Relations* (Ithaca, New York: ILR Press, 1994), 40; Freeman and Medoff, *What Do Unions Do?*, chapter 7; Kochan, *Collective Bargaining and Industrial Relations*, 356.
55. Kochan, *Collective Bargaining and Industrial Relations*, 348–359.
56. Freeman and Medoff, *What Do Unions Do?*, chapter 6; Kochan, *Collective Bargaining and Industrial Relations*, 370–373, 365.
57. Kochan, *Collective Bargaining and Industrial Relations*, 353.
58. Ibid., 326, 343.
59. Ibid., 168, 222–223; Freeman and Medoff, *What Do Unions Do?*, 129.
60. Kochan, *Collective Bargaining and Industrial Relations*, 343–344.
61. David Brody, *Workers in Industrial America: Essays on the 20th Century Struggle* (New York: Oxford University Press., 1979), 209.
62. James O'Toole, et al., *Work in America: Report of a Special Task Force to the Secretary of Health, Education, and Welfare* (Cambridge, Massachusetts: MIT Press, 1973).
63. Ibid., 250.
64. Robert Levering, Milton Moskowitz, and Michael Katz, *The 100 Best Companies to Work for in America* (Reading, Massachusetts: Addison-Wesley Publishing Company, 1984), 156.
65. Thomas A. Kochan and Thomas A. Barocci, *Human Resource Management and Industrial Relations* (Boston: Little, Brown and Company, 1985), 98.
66. Kochan, Katz, and McKersie, *The Transformation of American Industrial Relations*, 56; Fred K. Foulkes, *Personnel Policies in Large Nonunion Companies* (Englewood Cliffs, New Jersey: Prentice-Hall, Inc., 1980), 56–57, 297.
67. Foulkes, *Personnel Policies*, 120–121.
68. Ibid., 143.
69. Ibid., 150–151.
70. Ibid., 150–151, 253–254; Kochan, *Collective Bargaining and Industrial Relations*, 344.
71. Foulkes, *Personnel Policies*, 45, 53.
72. Ibid., 47.
73. Freeman and Medoff, *What Do Unions Do?*, chapter 10; Edward R. Curtin, *White-Collar Unionization, Personnel Policy Study No. 220* (New York: National Industrial Conference Board, Inc., 1970), 67.
74. Harold M. F. Rush, *Job Design for Motivation: Experiments in Job Enlargement and Job Enrichment* (New York: Conference Board, 1971), 12–13; Stephen P. Waring, *Taylorism Transformed: Scientific Management Theory Since 1945* (Chapel Hill, North Carolina: The University of North Carolina Press, 1991), 148.
75. Robert N. Ford, *Motivation Through the Work Itself* (New York: American Management Association, Inc., 1969), 12–13; Fred K. Foulkes, *Creating More Meaningful Work* (New York: American Management Association, 1969), 15–16.
76. Eileen Appelbaum and Rosemary Batt, *The New American Workplace: Transforming Work Systems in the United States* (Ithaca, New York: IRL Press, 1994), 197–198, 235.
77. Charles L. Hughes, *Making Unions Unnecessary* (New York: Executive Enterprises Publications Co., Inc., 1976), 71.

78. Ibid.
79. Committee for Economic Development, *Social Responsibilities of Business Corporations*, 15.
80. Blumberg, *The Megacorporation in American Society*, 59–60; Commission on Private Philanthropy and Public Needs, *Giving in America: Toward a Stronger Voluntary Sector* (New York: Commission on Private Philanthropy and Public Needs, 1975), 60.
81. Barbara F. Flower, *Business Amid Urban Crisis: Private-Sector Approaches to City Problems, Public Affairs Study No. 3* (New York: National Industrial Conference Board, 1968); James K. Brown and Seymour Lusterman, *Business and the Development of Ghetto Enterprise* (New York: The Conference Board, 1971).
82. Newsweek, "The American Corporation Under Fire," *Newsweek*, May 24, 1971.
83. Blumberg, *Corporate Responsibility in a Changing Society*, 10.
84. Committee for Economic Development, *Social Responsibilities of Business Corporations* 29.
85. Noble, *Welfare as We Knew It: A Political History of the American Welfare State* (New York: Oxford University Press, 1997), 95.
86. Jules Cohn, *The Conscience of the Corporations: Business and Urban Affairs, 1967–1970* (Baltimore: The Johns Hopkins Press, 1971), 7.
87. Noble, *Welfare as We Knew It*, 88; Committee for Economic Development, *Social Responsibilities of Business Corporations*, 51–54.
88. Vogel, *Lobbying the Corporation*, chapter 3.
89. Ibid.
90. Ibid., 131; Raymond A. Bauer, and Dan H. Fenn, Jr., *The Corporate Social Audit* (New York: Russell Sage Foundation, 1972).
91. Vogel, *Lobbying the Corporation*, 82.
92. Cohn, *The Conscience of the Corporations*, 6.
93. Committee for Economic Development, *Social Responsibilities of Business Corporations*, 28.
94. Newsweek, "The American Corporation Under Fire," *Newsweek*, May 24, 1971, 75.
95. Lee E. Preston, Harry J. Sapienza, and Robert Miller, "Stakeholders, shareholders, and managers: Who gains what from corporate performance," in *Socio-Economics: Toward a New Synthesis*, eds. Amitai Etzioni and Paul R. Lawrence (Armark, New York: M. E. Sharpe, 1991).
96. Mitchell Meyer and Harland Fox, *Profile of Employee Benefits* (New York: The Conference Board, 1974), 13; Alfred M. Skolnik, "Twenty-Five Years of Employee-Benefit Plans," *Social Security Bulletin* 39, no. 9 (September 1976): 6.

8

The Decline of Corporate Social Responsibility

After nearly a century of struggles between owners and challengers, the American regulatory structure for large corporations was stronger than it had ever been. But the continued success in controlling large corporations depended upon the continued success of large corporations in driving the economy to achieve healthy levels of growth. This was true for a couple of reasons. First, the high levels of growth experienced in the postwar generation produced a burgeoning middle class that not only expected more from corporations, but this segment of the labor force could also help to defray the costs of greater government regulations through the higher taxes they paid. Second, high growth yielded the higher profits that helped to underwrite the costs of both union contracts that featured greater pay and benefits and the two forms of corporate social responsibility, welfare capitalism and corporate philanthropy. Historically, however, growth and profits depended upon the effectiveness of governance structures, like oligopolies, that helped to limit economic competition. This effectiveness was about to be tested by the rise of global competition, as foreign economies finally recovered from the devastation of the Second World War.

Mandated Responsibility

Growth of Large Corporations: Economic Decline and the Role of Conglomerates

Large corporations led a triumphant American economy to new heights in the first generation after WWII. By the late sixties and early seventies, however, the economic fundamentals that promoted this growth were already changing. Most alarming to investors was the profit rate. After reaching a postwar record 12.6 percent in 1965, the after-tax profit rate for manufacturing firms declined steadily over the next decade, falling to only 2.7 percent by 1974—a drop of nearly 80 percent.[1]

As it turned out, the economic laws governing business cycles had not been permanently suspended. The abrupt end to the high-flying postwar years was brought about, in large part, by the return of America's competitors. It will be recalled that America's domination of the world's economy, and hence the effectiveness of its corporations' governance structures, was built upon an uneven playing field. The Second World War had severely damaged the economies of the other major economic powers, especially those of Japan, Germany, Great Britain, and France. But with significant assistance from the United States after the war, they all rebuilt, and by the 1960s Japan and Germany were particularly ready to take advantage of the free-trade policies adopted by the United States.

Ultimately, growing global competition revealed a number of factors that placed American corporations at a competitive disadvantage. For example, the new competitors typically had lower wage costs, they produced goods in brand new facilities with the newest technology, and they could take advantage of new infrastructure. Furthermore, complacency had set in during a quarter century of uncontested economic rule, and the quality of many domestic made consumer goods had slipped as a result. Secure in their dominant position, bloated bureaucratic organizations were slow to change. The bottom-line outcome of all of these factors was that more and more Americans purchased foreign-made goods that were not only cheaper, but frequently of higher quality as well, with the value of imports doubling in the single decade of 1969 to 1979.[2]

But it was not the rise of foreign trade, per se, that caused the precipitous fall in the profit rate, it was the strategic choices made by corporate executives that truly mattered. Before the 1970s, most large firms operated in oligopolies. As an effective governance structure controlling competition, manufacturers had the luxury of engaging in "mark-up pricing," in which prices could simply be raised to maintain, or even increase, a desired profit margin. With foreign competition undermining this practice, managers had to adapt, and in theory, there were a variety of options available to cope with the ensuing profit squeeze. Potentially the most important of these was investment in new plant and equipment, technology, and organizational design, so as to increase productivity.

Instead, the dominant options chosen by executives of America's leading corporations featured reducing capital investments, thus conceding to the competition; moving production to offshore sites with lower labor costs; shifting investments to more profitable ventures within a firm's portfolio of companies; and lowering the costs of labor by attacking unions. Though these were strategic options, and not inevitable adaptations to a changed environment, two main factors favored their selection. One was business unionism, which will be discussed later. The other factor was the conglomerate form of organization.

the conglomerate reconsidered: The conglomerate quickly became the dominant organizational form for large corporations in the 1960s. But the strategy of conglomeration represented a fundamental change in orientation of corporations. Up through the 1950s, the main orientation of corporate owners and managers toward their economic environments was one of control, especially through governance structures that served to restrain competition. These organizational innovations included horizontal and vertical integration, securing government contracts, and establishing a multinational presence. But the rise of the conglomerate marked the triumph of what Neil Fligstein has called the "finance conception of control." Firms now sought to adapt to their economic environments by minimizing risk with an extreme version of diversification. Of course, seeking to spread out risks through diversification was not new, as such, since the multidivisional firm and product differentiation had been around for decades. In the past, however, diversification served to complement a corporation's efforts to employ governance structures to minimize competition in a particular industry; with conglomeration, it now served as a substitute.[3]

In practice this meant that corporations were reconstituted as portfolios of assets that earn different rates of return. The task for the top management in such firms, which came to be dominated by those with finance backgrounds, was like that of a Wall Street investor: maximize the returns on your investment by moving your money around. For conglomerates, this translated into altering the mix of companies in the portfolio through merger or divestment, depending upon an individual company's prospects for profitable returns in the short run.[4] As a result, an important step had been taken toward the commodification of the corporation itself: a set of assets to be bought and sold, and not a social entity seeking immortality through continuous operation.

As shown in the last chapter, the conglomerate strategy and form seemed quite successful at first. Conglomerates like Litton and Beatrice became investor favorites. But as time passed, and upon closer examination, it appears that the economy's success in the 1960s, instead of being driven by the conglomerate, may have actually masked the form's flaws. As early as 1970, evidence appeared that suggested that the apparent success of conglomerates was a mirage. A Federal Trade Commission study concluded the claims of the advocates of conglomerates "warrant genuine skepticism," while a seven-volume report of the House Antitrust Subcommittee found scant evidence of greater organizational efficiency. Scholarly research also soon appeared that typically found that the post-acquisition performance of merged companies was worse than when the companies had been independent entities. *The Economist* concluded that the conglomerate was "the biggest collective error ever made by American business."[5] Yet, though the pace of conglomeration slowed, it remained popular through the 1970s.

Upon reflection, the problems with conglomerates should have come as no surprise. The key ingredient in economic success has always been growth in productivity, and this requires capital investments. But a conglomerate's cash-management approach to investment translated into investments in preexisting plant and equipment. As a result, investment in new plants and equipment between 1966 and 1970 failed to keep pace with the rate of inflation. Not only were these the peak years of the conglomerate merger craze, they also represented a time when American manufacturing was still dominant globally. One estimate suggests that if the money spent acquiring corporations in 1968 had gone into new plants and equipment, business investment would have been almost 50 percent higher than it was, and American manufacturers would have been better positioned to compete.[6]

Greater capital investment would certainly have helped American manufacturers compete in the face of declining market share. Instead, conglomerates responded to renewed global competition by shifting assets around, depending upon the performance of the particular product lines. For example, for a company's "dogs," (lines with low market shares and low growth rates), abandonment, and not reinvestment, was the recommended course of action. Instead of being plowed back, the profits of a company's "cash cows," (high market share, but low growth rates) were "milked" in order to support the acquisition of new companies with greater potential. Sometimes, the financial maneuvers of conglomerates amounted to nothing more than creative accounting. Such bookkeeping machinations increased as corporations, faced with a shrinking pool of retained earnings, became more dependent upon attracting investor dollars.[7]

Ultimately, then, American corporations did adapt to the new environment of global competition, but they did so in a way that fundamentally changed the American economy. In practice, many of the dogs and cash cows of conglomerates were manufacturing subsidiaries. In addition, many manufacturers, whether they were part of conglomerates or not, increasingly shifted investments abroad in the face of growing international competition—this will reviewed further in a later discussion of union avoidance.

Together, these strategic choices contributed greatly to America's rapid deindustrialization: "a widespread, systematic divestment in the nation's basic productive capacity." As a result, the US share of worldwide exports fell from 32 percent in 1955 to 18 percent in 1971, while imports of foreign-made imports soared. By 1981, America was importing 60 percent of its consumer electronics (televisions, radios, tape recorders, phonographs), 26 percent of its cars, and 25 percent of its steel. These were all industries where twenty years earlier American market share had been over 90 percent. To be sure, the process of deindustrialization predated conglomeration, as technological changes, together with an expanding middle class demanding services, led to a reduction in demand for manufacturing labor and an increase in service employment, respectively. There is no doubt, however, that the strategic decisions made by the management of conglomerates greatly accelerated the process.[8]

The problem is that these changes did not restore profit rates: the after-tax profit rate for manufacturing firms was 6.3 percent from 1975 to 1978, which was not a marked improvement from the 6.0 percent average for 1971–1974, and both of these figures were well below the postwar average of 8.5 percent. Profits continued to decline because conglomeration and deindustrialization hurt productivity growth. After averaging growth rates of 2.6 percent for the years 1948 to 1966, productivity growth slowed to 1.8 percent for 1966–1973 and a woeful 0.5 percent for 1973–1979.[9]

The growth in international competition, together with the dubious strategic decisions made by America's corporate executives, contributed to the recession of 1973–1975. Of course, these were not the only factors that produced the nation's worst economic downturn since the Depression. Especially significant among these was the "energy crisis" that followed the OPEC price increase of 1973, which quickly eroded yet another foundation of American economic supremacy—cheap energy. But even after the recession ended, America's economy continued to grow at a snail's pace: the average growth rate of GNP for the 1973–1979 period was a paltry 2.5 percent.[10]

—

The continued poor economic performance of America's leading corporations would ultimately leave the conglomerate vulnerable to the corporate takeover movement of the 1980s, discussed below. In the short term, however, economic decline had the impact of stalling the momentum toward greater social regulations.

Social Regulations and Welfare: Big Business Strikes Back

After making great progress in the late sixties and early seventies, efforts to further regulate business stalled when Gerald Ford assumed the presidency in 1974. More conservative, and closer to business than Nixon, Ford vetoed sixty-four bills and threatened to veto others. Understandably, when Jimmy Carter was elected president in 1976, leaders of the public-interest movement were extremely optimistic. Democrats now controlled both the Executive and Legislative Branches of government. Carter raised expectations further when he appointed more than sixty public-interest activists to positions within his administration.[11]

The prospects for creating a new consumer protection agency (CPA) seemed particularly good. During the election campaign, Carter not only endorsed the enabling legislation, he stated that if the bill was not passed in the current legislative session, he would make it "one of the first bills passed during the next Administration."[12] Early in 1977 Carter committed to lobbying for the legislation, and leaders of both the House and Senate vowed to seek its passage. *The National Journal* predicted that a bill creating the agency would be on the president's desk by April or May of the following year.[13]

But things did not go as planned, as the bill stalled for the remainder of the year. When it finally came up for a vote in February 1978, the bill lost by a vote of 189 to 227. Even more ominous, the defeat of the consumer agency legislation was only the leading edge of a number of failed efforts to rein in the power of big business over the next few years. For example, shortly afterward, the House defeated a conference bill that would have strengthened the FTC. Later in the year, the president supported a bill that would have raised the taxes on both capital gains and corporate income earned overseas; Congress instead passed a tax bill that reduced the capital gains tax and left overseas earnings alone. Finally, as will be reviewed below, efforts that would have strengthened the hand of labor unions were defeated.[14]

One reason for this string of legislative defeats was the poor working relationship that was established early on between Carter and the Congress of his own party.[15] But the more fundamental reason for the problems in passing further corporate mandates was that the economic climate of the mid-seventies was dramatically different than that of the mid-sixties. The new decade had given rise to the new economic malady of "stagflation," in which slow economic growth, marked by high unemployment, was combined with rising inflation. After Carter took office in 1977, the inflation rate continued to rise, reaching the low double digits during the last couple of years of his administration. As "bracket creep" pushed many Americans into higher tax brackets, a growing anxiety among many in the middle class dampened the optimism of the earlier era. Such anxiety was compounded by unemployment rates that remained high during Carter's four years, growing federal deficits, and the sight of more and more foreign-made goods on store shelves and showrooms.[16]

This, then, was an environment no longer conducive to post-material values like consumer protection. In the short term, Americans descended Maslow's hierarchy of needs and focused upon economic survival. It was in this economic environment that the initiatives of the incoming Carter administration stalled. But the stagnant economy did not automatically defeat the consumer protection bill or any other legislation. Instead, it represented an opportunity. Large corporations actively exploited it.

To understand this string of legislative defeats, it is important to go back to the 1960s. The business community had been taken by surprise by the wave of social regulations, and it took them a while to regain their political footing. Ultimately, they heeded the advice of corporate lawyer, and future Supreme Court Justice Lewis Powell, who in an influential 1971 memo to the Chamber of Commerce entitled "Attack on American Free Enterprise System," argued that corporations needed to organize, and fund on a grand scale, a political campaign to push back against regulations.[17]

By the mid-seventies, the business community pushed back with tremendous force on several fronts. First, so as not to be caught off guard again, the business community improved its ability to both monitor the political environment and influence legislation. More and more corporations established public affairs offices during the decade of the 1970s—by 1980, more than 80 percent of Fortune 500 companies had one. Most also established a physical presence in Washington, and they all hired lobbyists. Trade associations followed suit, and by 1978, 2,000 lobbyists were headquartered in the nation's capitol. All in all, the political resources marshaled by business mushroomed so that by the end of the seventies, there were 9,000 business lobbyists, 50,000 trade association personnel, and 1,300 public affairs consultants.[18]

It was superior resources such as these that were effectively brought to bear in the legislative struggles like that involving the creation of an agency for consumer protection. In this case, hundreds of trade associations and individual firms lobbied against the bill in the years leading up to its defeat. But in addition to the sheer volume of resources applied, the business community also spent more smartly, freely borrowing from the tactics of the public-interest movement itself. For example, corporations learned to form effective coalitions, a strategy where the newly founded Business Roundtable, which represented the interests of large corporations, played a particularly instrumental role. Ironically, this collaborative tactic was encouraged by the nature of the newer regulatory legislation itself, which instead of targeting particular industries targeted corporate behavior that cut across industries. In the case of the coalition that opposed the CPA, one observer noted that "For the first time in history, you had 'the coalition': National Association of Manufacturers, Grocery Manufacturers of America, the US Chamber of Commerce, National Federation of Independent Business. . . ."[19]

In yet another tactic borrowed from the left, businesses and industry groups engaged in grassroots campaigns where they visited legislators from their own districts. In the case of the CPA, those targeted included the many legislators who might be members of the relevant legislative committees, moderate legislators who had supported the bill in the past, as well as all newly elected House members. As it turned out, business groups, with their chapter-based organizational structure, were in a better position to exploit grassroots strategies than many Washington-based public-interest groups, since these typically lacked a federated architecture.

More broadly, the business community relearned the lesson that to quash new regulations and get the kind of legislation desired, there was no surer means of affecting legislation than having business-friendly legislators. In this regard, the influence of business was greatly enhanced by the Federal Election Campaign Act of 1971, which, for the first time since the Progressive Era, allowed corporations to make contributions to election campaigns through political action committees (PACs). In an era of weaker political parties and candidate-centered elections, and as campaigns became increasingly expensive, PACs of all varieties became an increasingly important source of funds. But business and trade association PACs had deeper pockets than any other organized interest, and the $10 million that they contributed during the 1976 election surpassed that of labor for the first time.[20] By 1980, business and trade PACs, including the 1,204 individual corporation PACs, contributed $24.9 million to congressional candidates alone, nearly double the $12.8 million contributed by labor.[21]

As important as its investment in political resources, the business community spent heavily to improve the climate of public opinion. After enjoying high levels of support from the public for the first twenty years after the war, business leaders were taken aback by the hostility that they faced from the mid-sixties on. Like their predecessors in the postwar period, these leaders embarked upon a campaign to change public opinion. Some of this involved hiring consultants to help them nurture a better relationship with the press. Advertising that burnished a corporation's image increased, as did "advocacy advertising," in which companies made their case on particular issues directly to the public. But the public opinion of business could not be improved by greater public-relations expenditures alone. Recognizing that there was a broader battle over ideas, the business community invested in intellectual resources as well. Corporations helped to fund the foundations that, in turn, helped establish or grow conservative, pro-business think tanks. For example, the John Olin Foundation endowed new chairs and fellowships at the American Enterprise Institute, as well as the newly founded Heritage Foundation.[22]

The prolific output of policy papers, research reports, and various other publications that increasingly made their way into pressrooms and legislative committees helped to win the battle. The consistent message was pro-market and antigovernment. The business community and its intellectual allies were particularly successful in reframing the efforts to regulate business during a period of economic downturn. Instead of improving the quality of life, the growing number of social regulations were weighing businesses down, squeezing profits, and making it impossible to compete in the global economy. In short, if Americans were now anxious about the increasing indicators of economic decline, they could now blame government.[23] What this revealed was not so much the return of America's native antigovernment posture, but instead "the liability of bigness."

The Liability of Bigness

The recession and stagflation of the 1970s represented the worst economic slide since the Depression. In this climate, not only was the business community able to stop the wave of social regulations, they were able to lay the blame at government's doorstep. But this begs a comparative question. During the 1930s, big business was blamed. Why, then, was government blamed during the 1970s, even though most evidence pointed to bad decisions made by corporate executives in a new environment of global competition, and not the extra costs associated with compliance to social regulations?

This difference can be explained by what can be called the liability of bigness: if one intervenes in the economy, one owns it, regardless of culpability of economic bad times or responsibility for good times. When government was small, the only thing it could be blamed for was not intervening quickly enough. The causes of the economic calamity in the 1930s were transparently economic in nature, and businesses, especially large corporations, were blamed. After World War II, however, government not only permanently grew, but it adopted various economic policies aimed at encouraging growth and keeping the economy on an even keel. These interventions ranged from tax incentives for investment to spending on infrastructure to tinkering with the monetary supply. Since the business community had successfully resisted efforts at more muscular economic interventions in the United States, the government's economic role remained circumscribed, always stopping at the border of managerial prerogatives. As a result, the key decisions that ultimately drive economic growth, especially those concerning investment, remained private.

In a democracy, accountability tends to be associated with visibility. The economic actions of government during the 1970s, including the adoption of new social regulations, were very public and transparent. In contrast, the economic decisions of the faceless professional managers of large, multinational conglomerates remained private and increasingly opaque. In principle, as government grows, it should have a greater ability to hold accountable those who make decisions that negatively impact the public. In practice, however, government may be held accountable for private decisions over which it has no input. This pattern was strengthened after the war as politicians increasingly ran for office on the performance of the economy and voters developed a stronger tendency toward economic voting, in which electoral choice is shaped, at least in part, by one's assessment of how well the economy is doing.

The liability of bigness represented a new advantage for large corporations in America's lopsided political economy that now featured bigger government, but one that had greatly circumscribed economic authority in relation to the structural power of business. The best evidence for this, and the signature victory in the political resurgence of big business, was the election of 1980.

The Reagan Revolution

By 1980, American politics was at an ideological crossroads. The campaign for greater corporate social responsibility of the previous decade was nearly spent. But on April 17, 1980, Ralph Nader and his public-interest allies organized Big Business Day, a day of mass demonstrations in 150 cities across the country. Leaders hoped to highlight the abuses of large corporations in America and thereby create a groundswell of support for a proposed Corporate Democracy Act, which featured the federal chartering of corporations. The proposed legislation would require that a majority of a corporation's board of directors be "independent" and that a given number be charged with monitoring a corporation's social responsibilities. The bill went nowhere, and in many ways Big Business Day was the last hurrah of the public-interest movement of the 1970s.[24]

The antimonopolist, public-interest forces proved to be no match for a politically resurgent business community. To begin with, the organizational infrastructure of the business community, especially its business associations, was much stronger than that of public-interest groups, which were mostly "checkbook" organizations that had no grassroots presence. The more atomized collection of consumers, environmentalists, and citizens generally, on whose behalf these groups lobbied, also had fewer discretionary resources to contribute as a result of the recession and weak economy. This only magnified the resource advantage that business interests inherently possessed.

More significantly, the political resurgence of business was part of a broader revival of conservatism that culminated in the election of the most conservative president in over fifty years, Ronald Reagan. To be sure, Reagan's victory was as much a repudiation of the incumbent as it was a positive endorsement of conservatism. For Jimmy Carter, it had been a tough four years. In the face of persistent economic woes, voters responded to Reagan's deft campaign question, "Are you better off today than you were four years ago?" with an emphatic "no."

Ironically, in the last couple of years of his administration, Carter had largely tacked to the right in economic policy, and in ways that foreshadowed the economic agenda of his successor. To cope with mounting deficits, there were proposed cuts to social programs. Any talk of new programs or agencies to address problems was replaced with the language of cost effectiveness, efficiency and lowered expectations for government. Most important for the ability to regulate corporations, it was the Carter administration that started the country down the road of deregulation, seen as helping consumers, and thus quickening the pace of economic growth. This included successful passage of the Airline Deregulation Act of 1978, which eliminated the authority of the Civil Aeronautics Board to regulate fares and routes, and the Motor Carrier Act of 1980, which removed the Interstate Commerce Commission from the business of setting interstate trucking rates. By the end of his term, deregulation extended to the financial sector as well. The Depository Institutions Deregulation and Monetary Control Act of 1980 removed a number of controls that had been in place since the Glass-Steagall Act of 1933, including interest rate caps on savings accounts and prohibitions against intrastate bank mergers.[25]

This marked an important turning point for liberalism, especially the New Deal-Great Society variety of using government to solve social problems. But even before the election, it appeared that the dominant ideology of the American left was moribund. The economic troubles of the 1970s had revealed liberalism's inherent weaknesses. For example, its embrace of social rights, like health care, had never been as strong as its embrace of civil and political rights. Furthermore, in contrast to the socialist or social democratic ideologies of the Continent, liberalism did not present an alternative vision of an economy operating in accordance with an alternative set of values. Instead, liberalism was ideologically aligned with America's native antimonopolism, which championed the virtues of a pristine capitalism. Jimmy Carter became the first Democrat to throw the older liberalism overboard for what came to be known as neoliberalism, which not only shared the conservatives' skepticism about the effectiveness of government programs, but also argued that the proper role of government was to create the conditions of a favorable business climate.[26]

But neoliberalism could not compete with the real thing, an ascendant and robust conservatism. Ronald Reagan became the face of this conservatism, which he made more attractive to American voters by offering it with the glow of optimism and the promise to restore America's greatness. It was a winning combination. With his insistent campaign claim that government was the source, and not the solution to America's problems, Ronald Reagan effectively flipped America's populist switch from antimonopoly to antigovernment. Instead of a privileged clique of big-business owners, it was the concentrated power of Washington's political class that became the target of populist resentment. This privileged elite was seen as inherently corrupt, concerned not for the greater good, but for the aggrandizement of their own power. The conservatives' goal, then, was to restore the golden past of minimalist government.

Reaganomics

Building upon the premise that growth in government had impeded economic growth, the Reagan program to restore American greatness involved reducing the footprint of the federal government and recovering the conditions of free-market capitalism. Reaganomics, as the president's economic policies came to be known, comprised three main planks. The first was to reduce federal spending for most federal programs, with the exception of defense. The second was to slash tax rates for both business and individuals. The third was to reduce government regulations. It was this third plank that targeted mandated responsibility.[27]

For Carter and Democrats, deregulation referred strictly to economic regulations as embodied in independent regulatory commissions, which were originally enacted to control big business in the public interest. During the Reagan years, however, deregulation came to mean a full-scale assault upon government regulations generally, instructed by the ideology of antigovernment populism. The biggest target of this campaign was the set of social regulations that had been passed during the previous fifteen years that were intended to promote greater social responsibility on the part of corporations. On the day that he was sworn in, the new president signed an order that imposed a hiring freeze on all federal agencies, including regulatory agencies. The next day he established the Task Force on Regulatory Relief, which was charged with reviewing all federal regulatory statutes with an eye toward revising or abolishing those deemed unnecessary. A week later he issued an order that forbade agencies from issuing any new rules. A few weeks after that, Reagan issued an executive order that required that any new rules first undergo a cost-benefit analysis, and which stipulated that the least costly version of any new rule be adopted. Finally, the White House centralized control over regulations by creating the Office of Information and Regulatory Affairs (OIRA).[28]

So as to ensure that his radical brand of deregulation was implemented, Reagan borrowed heavily from the old practice of appointing regulatory officials from the business community, thus upending the efforts of some in the public-interest community to close the revolving door between business and government. He also had the habit of appointing officials who held views diametrically at odds with the mission of the agencies that they came to head. For example, as head of the Environmental Protection Agency Reagan appointed Anne Gorsuch, who as a state legislator in Colorado vigorously opposed federal environmental regulations. To oversee the policy of deregulation as head of the OIRA, Reagan appointed a prominent critic of government regulation, James C. Miller III.[29]

With these various pieces of the regulatory assault in place, the budgets of a number of regulatory agencies were slashed by 1982. For example, the EPA's budget was cut by 9 percent for fiscal year 1982, while that of the Consumer Product Safety Commission was cut by 38 percent. This was matched by personnel reductions. After growing by over 300 percent between 1970 and 1980, the number of employees of the major regulatory agencies was cut by 4 percent in fiscal year 1981 and another 8 percent in fiscal year 1982. With smaller budgets and fewer employees, worksite inspections by OSHA declined by 15 percent between 1980 and 1982, while the number of administrative enforcement orders issued by the EPA declined by one-third. In short, the pathway of stronger social regulations was nearly erased before it had a chance to carve deeper ruts through institutionalization.[30]

Economic Regulations: Deregulation Across the Board

In addition to targeting the social regulations of the previous fifteen years, the new administration extended its policy of deregulation to antitrust enforcement, an area that even conservatives had typically viewed as a legitimate role of government. The president's appointee to head the Antitrust Division of the Department of Justice was William Baxter, a Stanford University law professor who had a background in the conservative economics of the University of Chicago. He led an effort that produced new merger guidelines for the division in 1982 that resulted in a more lenient stance toward mergers. Updated again in 1984, the guidelines stated that the results of mergers were usually "competitively beneficial or neutral."[31]

Reagan's selection for head of the Federal Trade Commission, the nation's chief regulatory agency charged with protecting the environment for economic competition, also revealed that deregulation would reign there as well. It was none other than James C. Miller III, who had just served as head of the OIRA. Consistent with the policy that he helped fashion in that office, Miller advocated a policy of industry "self-regulation," and followed through by reducing both the size and discretionary power of the agency. By the time he left the agency to become Reagan's budget director in 1985, the FTC had been reduced by 30 percent.[32]

—

Ultimately, the Reagan Revolution defanged both social and economic regulations with the policy of deregulation. By underwriting the revival of conservatism, the business community had achieved a tremendous political victory: one pillar of America's regulatory structure was now severely damaged. But as it turned out, it was a Pyrrhic victory, at least for many current heads of major corporations. The success that they had in Washington was not matched on Wall Street, where declining or stagnating profits, stock prices, and dividends left these same executives vulnerable to challengers from within the business community itself. Ironically, the same laissez faire ideology invoked by these executives to undermine government regulations came to be wielded against them by an emergent group of corporate raiders and shareholder activists.

Ideological and Political Challenges: Corporate Raiders Takeover

In October 1985, the buyout firm of Kohlberg, Kravis, and Roberts (KKR) announced its bid for Beatrice, one of the nation's largest conglomerates. At first the company resisted, making KKR's bid an attempt at a hostile takeover. Ultimately, the company's management relented, and in February 1986, KKR consummated the largest leveraged buyout (LBO) in American history to that point, totaling $6.2 billion, most of which was borrowed money. With no intention of running the company, KKR began to sell off the constituent parts of the conglomerate, and within eighteen months it realized a profit of over $3 billion. In

1990 the remaining parts of Beatrice were sold off, and the company, which only ten years earlier was listed as one of the five best-managed companies by Dunn's Review, ceased to exist.[33]

The story of Beatrice is a case study in the rise and fall of conglomerates. In 1965 the FTC, as part of its efforts to enforce the Celler-Kefauver Act, forced Beatrice Foods to divest itself of $35 million worth of recent dairy acquisitions. As one of the nation's largest dairies, Beatrice adapted to the decision by embarking upon a path of unrelated diversification, a path that it would frequently travel over the next decade and a half. By 1979 Beatrice was a multinational conglomerate that sold not only Tropicana orange juice and Hunt's ketchup, but also Playtex lingerie and Samsonite luggage. With sales over $8 billion and a workforce of nearly eighty thousand, the company operated in close to ninety countries. It ranked thirty-fifth in the Fortune 500. In just a few years, however, the fortunes of Beatrice changed dramatically. After thirty years of uninterrupted earnings growth, Beatrice's earnings plunged by more than one-third in 1983.[34]

Having become a behemoth during the conglomerate movement of the 1960s, Beatrice became an early casualty of the America's fourth merger wave in the 1980s, a decade in which $1.3 trillion worth of deals were done. Not only was this the biggest wave to date, it was qualitatively different. While most mergers were friendly in nature, many represented hostile takeovers, in which management, at least initially, resists an offer to merge—as was true for Beatrice. As testimony that this was a departure from previous waves, the standard reference that kept track of mergers and acquisitions did not report hostile tender offers before 1970 because their numbers did not warrant a separate category. But of *Fortune* magazine's list of the five hundred largest companies, seventy-seven were targets of hostile bids during the merger wave, and fifty-nine of these bids were successful. Even this underestimates the impact of hostile takeovers, since in some cases, "friendly" mergers were consummated in order to preempt anticipated hostile bids.[35]

Another distinguishing feature was that some of the largest takeovers were "bust-up" takeovers, in which acquired firms (Beatrice, yet again) were broken up and the component parts sold to the highest bidder. For example, when the wave crested in 1986 with 4,463 mergers valued at $1 million or more, 1,419 represented divestitures.[36] By the end of this turbulent wave, almost one-third of America's largest industrial corporations no longer existed as independent companies. This list included such prominent names as Gulf Oil,

General Foods, RCA, Nabisco Brand, Firestone Tire, and Southern Pacific Railroad.[37]

There were many factors that contributed to the nation's fourth merger wave, including the growth of capital markets, the creation of innovative use of financial instruments like junk bonds, and the Reagan administration's weakening of antitrust enforcement. But the chief precipitating factor was the poor economic performance of many of America's largest corporations during the 1970s and into the 1980s. At particular risk for a takeover bid were corporations whose market value (the true value of its assets) was much higher than their stock market valuation (the value of all of their outstanding stock). In fact, there was a gap for most corporations during this time, since stock prices stagnated throughout the 1970s, while the high inflation of that decade raised the price of a company's underlying assets. Because this gap was particularly large for conglomerates, as their increasingly poor performance turned investors away, these predators of the 1960s became prey during the 1980s.[38]

Eventually, takeovers spread and were institutionalized. As the "deal decade" wore on, targets for takeovers could be found in all sectors of the economy, and they could include even healthy firms. Part of this proliferation can be explained by the success and apparent quick profits demonstrated by upstarts like KKR. As a result, the number of takeover firms grew. Mergers also spread after established brokerage firms, banks, and law firms got involved, so as to get a piece of the growing pie of fees and commissions thrown off by the orchestration and consummation of merger deals. Not only did this help to legitimize controversial practices such as takeovers and the use of massive amounts of debt, it also created an industry of actors with a vested interest in perpetuating the wave of mergers. Ultimately, the merger mania of the 1980s, together with the corresponding rise of the financial sector of the economy, finished what conglomeration had started: the commodification of the corporation.[39]

The Raiders' Rationale

The combined impact of these factors was to create a favorable opportunity structure for challengers. However, because hostile takeovers represented such a radical, unprecedented measure, they also required a robust justification from those who initiated them. Two of the era's most notorious "corporate raiders," Carl Icahn and T. Boone Pickens, provided one with resonating potential. Icahn, best known for taking control of TWA in 1985, argued, "the problem we have in our managerial society is that there is no accountability because corporate democracy is a travesty." Instead of building wealth, they have built "fiefdoms" and created a "corporate welfare state."[40] Pickens, best remembered for his attempts to assume control of Gulf Oil and Texaco, believed that because CEOs generally are not significant owners of the corporations that they manage, they are oriented "to entrench themselves and preserve their empires."[41]

This line of argument was noteworthy in a couple of ways. For one, by invoking the need for greater accountability, Icahn and Pickens co-opted the democratic ideology of the public-interest movement, and thus the reformist strain of antimonopolism, which they broadly channeled. Not only had managers become unaccountable for their actions, they were also exploiting their position of power at the expense of the "average stockholder." This turned the prevailing consensus on managerialism on its head: the corps of professional managers, once championed by the proponents of large corporations, was now portrayed as a privileged elite.

The public musings of corporate raiders thus attempted to give their actions a populist patina, but they were grafted onto agency theory, an emergent perspective in finance economics that had grown in popularity in the previous two decades. Theorists in this tradition focus upon the problems inherent in the "principal-agent" relationship. These occur where an individual, the agent, is contracted to act on behalf of another individual, the principal. Problems arise when, as self-interested actors, agents are able to ignore the interests of principals and pursue their own.[42]

Agency theorists argued that such a scenario became the reality of corporate America. As agents with delegated powers, corporate managers effectively neutralized the formal structure intended to ensure accountability: the board of directors.[43] Unaccountable to owners, managers were then in a position to ignore the interests of owners, which center on the maximization of profit and shareholder wealth, and instead pursue their own, which were seen to consist primarily of self-aggrandizement and preservation. This produced risk aversion and satisfaction with profits that were merely adequate. Unfettered, these interests ultimately manifested themselves in an organizational structure that agency theorists view as inherently inefficient, and hence, doomed to failure, i.e., the conglomerate. They further argued that by the 1970s, the resulting corporate underperformance had become chronic, and investors had no recourse but to resort to takeovers to restore accountability.[44]

The large corporation was a contested institution once again. But there was an important difference. For the reformist strain of antimonopolism, public-interest groups had challenged corporations from the left and sought a greater public purpose and stakeholder orientation. In contrast, corporate raiders were contesting the large corporation from the right, and advocating that corporations be restored to their private purpose, which was making money for their shareholders.

The Rise of Institutional Shareholders

While increasingly popular within the financial sector, hostile takeovers were not well received by the public. In general, these transactions were very disruptive. Not only did they frequently lead to layoffs, it was not unusual for them to result in the closing of a facility or movement of a headquarters, and hence the loss of tax revenue. Hostile takeovers had the effect of forging an unlikely but powerful coalition of labor and management, which worked with state and local governments to pass legislation to protect in-state companies from unfriendly suitors. By 1991, forty-one states had such statutes, including twenty-nine that passed "corporate constituency" laws that explicitly authorized managers and directors to consider the impact of takeovers on a corporation's "stakeholders."[45] A second counter tactic pursued by managers involved pushing through "poison pill" resolutions, which had the effect of making takeovers less attractive.[46]

But while these tactics did in fact slow the trend of takeovers, they did not restore the status quo. The main reason for this was that a fundamental transformation had occurred in the nature of corporate ownership. For most of the twentieth century, the typical owner of America's major corporations was an individual, and the typical ownership stake was small. As late as 1965, individual holdings constituted 84 percent of stock of publicly traded corporations. The other 16 percent comprised institutional owners, such as banks, insurance companies, mutual funds, and pension funds. By 1980, the fraction of shares owned by institutions had risen to close to 30 percent, and by 1990 it was up to 46 percent. Ultimately, institutional owners played an important role during this merger wave, both by being major buyers of junk bonds and serving as investors in LBOs. This was consistent with their fiduciary responsibility, which required that fund managers work to enhance the value of their portfolios. This same responsibility made institutional investors receptive to takeover bids, since these typically raised the value of the stock of target firms.[47]

While institutional shareholders were passive participants during the surge in takeovers, providing huge sums of capital, they were pushed to become more active. This was partially due to the dawning realization that their dramatic growth gave them potential clout, especially if they organized. It was therefore significant when nineteen pension funds with over $100 billion formed the Council of Institutional Investors in 1985. With a stronger organizational base and identity, and with take-overs all but foreclosed as a tactical option, institutional shareholder activists changed tactics. Co-opting a strategy from the public-interest movement's corporate campaigns, institutional activists attempted to use their voting power as owners to submit both binding but mostly advisory resolutions concerning corporate policy. Early resolutions revealed a pragmatic alliance with corporate raiders, as they were aimed at preventing managers from adopting antitakeover measures, such as poison pills.[48]

Since most of these efforts were unsuccessful, institutional activists changed tactics yet again and targeted the issue of corporate governance, especially the lack of accountability, more directly. If the problem was that managers were insulated from the true owners of corporations, then the solution was to strip away the insulation through corporate governance reforms so that accountability could be restored. With "board independence" now as its goal and "accountability" as its rallying cry, institutional activists initially stuck to the strategy of drafting shareholder resolutions. From 1989 through 1991, the most popular shareholder resolution was one that asked companies to adopt confidential voting procedures.[49] Executive compensation also became an issue of corporate governance. To both enhance accountability and encourage executives and directors to think like owners, many institutional activists also advocated making at least part of compensation contingent upon performance.

In the vanguard of many of these efforts was the California Public Employees Retirement System, or CalPERS. With over $60 billion invested in portfolio companies by the beginning of the 1990s, they represented the proverbial nine-hundred-pound gorilla of the public pension fund industry. The fund's managers characterized their orientation to investing, and thus their fiduciary responsibility as the "sole purpose" doctrine: "CalPERS fiduciaries must act solely in the interest of members and beneficiaries. For this reason, CalPERS cannot base its corporate governance activities on social or political causes. Instead, it must focus on the 'bottom line' of enhanced shareholder returns."[50]

Though it was one of the early and heavy users of the resolution weapon, by the late 1980s CalPERS opened a second front, using less formal tactics to encourage independent action on the part of outside directors. Most significant here was a campaign begun in 1990 to shake things up at General Motors. This involved the pension fund writing letters and holding meetings with outside directors to discuss GM's poor performance, which they linked to governance issues. Such pressure contributed to a watershed event in corporate governance in the early 1990s. At the instigation of the company's outside directors, GM's chairman, Robert Stempel, was first demoted and then pressured to resign in 1992. Within the next year, the boards of American Express, IBM, Westinghouse, and Eastman Kodak ousted their CEOs, largely at the behest of those companies' institutional shareholders. The radical nature of these moves cannot be overstated. They were seismic events that sent shockwaves through the corporate community.

Over the course of the next several years, CalPERS and other institutional investors were able to press corporations to make significant changes in corporate governance. For example, by 1998 outside directors comprised an increasing percentage of all directors (82 percent for the average board), while in the case of the Fortune 1000, outside directors filled all seats on the audit, compensation, and nominating committees. With respect to efforts to tie executive compensation to corporate performance, a 1992 *Business Week* survey found that the exercise of stock options constituted over 50 percent of total CEO compensation.[51]

But even where traditional board practices remained intact, the corporate governance campaign succeeded in realigning the interests of management and owners. As proclaimed in its *Statement on Corporate Governance*, the Business Roundtable made it clear that "the paramount duty of management and of boards of directors is to the corporation's stockholders. . . . The notion that the board of directors must somehow balance the interests of stockholders against the interests of other stakeholders fundamentally misconstrues the role of directors."[52] Now, the only legitimate orientation for corporations was to maximize value for shareholders.

—

Ironically, pension funds, meant to secure the retirement years for workers, were used to undermine the legitimacy of a stakeholder orientation, where a corporation could at least weigh the interests of its non-owning constituents, with the primary one, of course, being its workers. In the face of this new shareholder storm, the forecast for negotiated responsibility was decidedly poor.

Negotiated Responsibility

The Rapid Demise of Business Unionism

On July 19, 1978 Douglas Fraser, president of the United Auto Workers Union, resigned from the Labor-Management Group. This association of union and business leaders had been formed only two years earlier to find common ground on economic issues like productivity and tax reform, and thus represented the latest effort at achieving some form of voluntary corporatist cooperation. In his resignation letter, Fraser angrily declared that

> leaders of the business community, with few exceptions, have chosen a one-sided class war in this country—a war against working people, the unemployed, the poor, the minorities, the very young and the very old, and even many in the middle class of our society. The leaders of industry commerce and finance in the United States have broken and discarded the fragile, unwritten compact previously existing during a period of growth and progress.[53]

Fraser was reacting to various manifestations of an antiunion campaign on the part of employers. For example, the number of complaints concerning unfair labor practices filed with the National Labor Relations Board more than doubled from 1967 to 1977. In 1977 alone, 42,802 complaints were filed, and many of these complaints involved tactics adopted upon the recommendation of antiunion consultants. By the end of the 1970s, approximately one thousand firms with revenue over $500 million collectively advised employers on how to keep union organizers and sympathizers out of the workplace, how to beat unions in representation elections, and how to decertify them where they existed. The relative success of this activity can be measured in the declining rate of victory in representation elections: from 61 percent in 1967 to 47 percent in 1977. The success of these aggressive tactics was also reflected in the fact that in 1978, unions lost three-quarters of the record eight hundred decertification elections.[54]

Precipitating Fraser's resignation was the defeat of labor-law reform legislation that would address some of these antiunion tactics. Labor leaders and the newly elected Carter administration had negotiated a package of reforms that included a provision to speed up union-certifying elections and increased penalties for violations of labor law. After its quick passage in the House, the bill became a target of an intensive and unified campaign on the part of the politically resurgent business community. Leading the charge was the Business Roundtable, whose membership included the CEOs belonging to the Labor-Management Group. But for the business community, the campaign paid off, as Republican senators successfully filibustered the bill in June of 1978.[55]

The more troubling and consequential manifestation of employers' resistance to unions involved strategic decisions concerning plant location and investment. Fraser singled out General Motors, which he claimed, "has given us a southern strategy designed to set up a nonunion network that threatens the hard-fought gains won by the UAW." What Fraser was alluding to was the fact that the giant auto manufacturer had opened thirteen new plants in the South in recent years, and only two had become unionized. But this practice was not restricted to GM. There were a growing number of unionized firms, including rubber and tire companies, opening new plants on a nonunion basis, frequently in right-to-work Southern states. A study of the plant location decisions of major corporations in the 1970s found that an antiunion climate was an important consideration, and that Southern states had the edge in the location of new plants. Not coincidentally, these comprised most of the states that had passed "right-to-work" laws in the wake of the Taft-Hartley Act a generation earlier.[56]

What the Southern strategy highlighted was that most of the nation's large corporations included separate divisions, subsidiaries, and multiple physical locations—a tendency that was only reinforced by the conglomerate form of organization. In the absence of corporatist pacts, or master agreements that covered entire industries, the Southern strategy also exposed a preexisting vulnerability for American unions: many unionized companies were actually only partially unionized. Furthermore, for all of the talk of "labor peace," many, if not most, employers who had to bargain with unions still did not fully accept them. This is evident in a survey conducted by the Conference Board (formerly the National Industrial Conference Board) in 1978 that asked company executives of unionized firms which was the more important role of labor relations in their companies, "achieving the most favorable bargain possible" (union acceptance) or "keeping as much of the company nonunion as possible" (union avoidance). The study found a strong inverse relationship: the less unionized a large corporation's overall workforce, the more likely it reported the importance of keeping the rest of their workforce nonunion.[57] The Southern strategy was yet another reminder of the dilemmas posed to unions by America's federalist structure and corresponding lack of corporatist arrangements.

Put into practice, union avoidance for some companies meant shifting work from a union to a nonunion facility, as illustrated by the Southern strategy. In the case of conglomerates, union avoidance also influenced the type of "portfolio" decisions discussed earlier, whereby a company divested in one industry so as to invest in a presumably more profitable or promising (and frequently less unionized) industry. In one classic example, Youngstown Sheet and Tube Company was used as a "cash cow" by its conglomerate parent, the Lykes Corporation, in which profits were extracted and invested in the company's non-steel concerns. Insufficient capital investment in the steel plant ultimately resulted in the closing of the mill in 1977 and the loss of over four thousand union jobs.[58]

For a multinational corporation, union avoidance reinforced decisions to move production offshore to countries that had lower labor costs. For example, beginning in the late 1960s, many American manufacturers began to open plants just south of the border with Mexico to take advantage of both the region's cheap labor and the Mexican government's recent decision to create a 12.5-mile strip along the border that would be nearly tax and tariff free for foreign-owned companies. By 1974, licenses from the "maquiladora" program, as it was called, had been issued for 655 plants to be operated by, among other US companies, General Electric, Motorola, Hughes Aircraft, and RCA. General Motors and Chrysler joined the trend by the end of 1970s. Of course, union avoidance was not the only incentive to locate plants abroad; another was to more readily serve foreign markets. However, the impact on American union workers was the same regardless of company motives, and the impact would be huge, since the total for all of the direct investments in foreign countries by American companies increased from $50 billion in 1965 to over $213 billion by 1980.[59]

Of course, all of this begs the question of why, beginning in the 1970s, corporations engaged in multiple forms of union avoidance. The short answer is that in an economic environment of increasing global competition, union avoidance was a strategic option available to American businesses. Put even more simply, businesses chose to avoid unions because they could. The success of America's business unionism depended upon sustained economic growth and profits. Its Achilles heel was sustained economic decline. As profit rates declined in the face of global competition, corporations were not required by either a corporatist arrangement or by law to consult with unions to consider other strategic options, such as capital investments or organizational changes to increase productivity. Such alternatives were more likely to exist in nations where the dominant orientation of labor was political unionism. The best that unions were able to achieve after WWII was the capital-labor accord, the unwritten pact in which labor had acceded to management's traditional prerogatives in exchange for better wages and benefits. Unions, as a result, were powerless to prevent corporations declaring the accord null and void.

The effectiveness of union avoidance showed up in the bottom line of a declining unionization rate. A closer look reveals, however, that greater employer resistance merely accelerated a trend that reached back over twenty years.

Declining Unionization

Right after the war in 1945 there were 14.3 million union members in the United States. For the next thirty-four years this number steadily grew, reaching an all-time high of twenty-one million members in 1979. But growth in numbers helped to obscure the fact that after reaching a high of 35 percent in 1954, the unionization rate had steadily declined, so that by the time Fraser wrote his letter of resignation in 1978, only 23 percent of American workers belonged to unions. In other words, unions' organizing of new members was not keeping pace with the growth in the labor force. During the fifties and sixties some of this decline was attributable to the success that nonunion employers had in staving off unions with a human relations alternative, with its job security and compensation package—in other words, the positive form of union avoidance (CSR) that evolved in reaction to the threat of unions.[60]

The most important factor, however, was the structural shift in the economy from manufacturing to services that had been ongoing during the period of US economic dominance, due in part, as seen above, to the divestment strategy of conglomerates, as well as union avoidance via the off shoring of jobs. Of course, the causes of deindustrialization also included technological displacement as a result of innovation and the greater demand for services that accompanied the rising living standards of American workers after the war. The result was that by 1970 only 27 percent of nonagricultural employees could be found in the manufacturing sector, down from 38 percent in 1945.[61]

The reason that this was consequential for unions was that union strength had always been concentrated in manufacturing industries. Furthermore, with few exceptions, unions had done a poor job in organizing service sector employees. The task of now organizing these workers was made more difficult still by at least a few factors: most new service jobs were being taken by women and minorities, groups to whom unions had historically paid less attention; service establishments tended to be smaller and located in more competitive industries, neither conducive to organizing; and a growing share of these service workers consisted of white-collar professionals, who tended to view unions with a higher status disdain.

Another factor explaining the decline in unionization was union complacency. With the final triumph of business unionism, unions came to focus more exclusively upon administering contracts and servicing current members. As they lost any semblance of fighting organizations, unions were increasingly bureaucratic, while union leaders were more and more seduced by the trappings of office holding. In short, in the quarter century after the war, unions became quite good at negotiating new and bigger contracts, building new buildings, and holding annual conventions. What they were not doing, however, was organizing many new workers. Moreover, for a long time most union leaders did not seem overly concerned by the decline in unionization rates. Indeed, when asked in 1972 if he was worried about the decline in AFL-CIO membership, George Meany responded, "Why should we worry about organizing groups of people who do not appear to want to be organized. . . . The organized fellow is the fellow that counts."[62]

Yet an additional reason for lower unionization rates was the hostile political environment created by the Reagan administration. In his first year in office, the new president fired the over eleven thousand members of the Professional Air Traffic Controllers Organization (PATCO), who though legally barred, went on strike over deteriorating working conditions that the Federal Aviation Administration had declined to address for a number of years. The union was formally busted when it was decertified on October 22. Many felt that the president meant to send a strong message to business that cracking down on unions was an acceptable business practice.[63] The orientation of the NLRB under Reagan's watch only echoed the message. Slow to appoint new members to fill vacant seats, complaints involving unfair labor practices piled up. When it did hear cases, it was much less likely to decide in favor of unions than in the past. For example, in cases involving complaints against companies arising from union organizing and election campaigns, the board decided against the union position 65 percent of the time in the in the years 1984–85, compared to only 35 percent of cases in the years 1975–76.[64]

As a result, unionization rates continued to fall, and by 1990 only 15.5 percent of workers belonged to unions. Furthermore, since 1979, the actual number of union members had declined as well, down to nineteen million. Because the effectiveness of business unionism ultimately depended upon robust economic growth and steady, if not increasing, membership rolls, as both of these factors weakened, so did union contracts, as revealed in the trend of union givebacks.[65]

Concession Bargaining

In 1979 Chrysler, having lost money for two years straight, had a total debt of $1.5 billion and eighty thousand unsold cars in inventory. Because it had no way of meeting the payment schedule for its debt, the company negotiated with the Carter administration for $750 million in loan guarantees so that the company could receive more credit from private banks. However, at the insistence of the banks and ultimately Congress itself, the Chrysler Loan Guarantee Act of 1979 required that the company's autoworkers grant $462 million in wage and benefit concessions. Accepting the premise that such givebacks were necessary to save jobs, the same Douglas Fraser led his UAW members in ratifying a new contract with concessions. The following year, Chrysler's new CEO, Lee Iacocca, asked for and received additional wage cuts. Because this meant that Chrysler's workers now made significantly less than auto workers at GM and Ford, the two larger auto manufacturers successfully demanded that their workers make contract concessions as well. In other words, the Big Three bargaining pattern, established after the war, was now reversed. Instead of each company following the others in granting increases in compensation, they now followed one another in demanding contract concessions from their workers.[66]

After automakers demonstrated that they could win givebacks from their unionized workers, concession fever spread. By the end of 1982, unions had granted concessions in in the meatpacking, airlines, grocery, and rubber industries, among others. Of course, the economic recession of 1981–1982 helped employers make their case that such concessions were imperative if jobs cuts were to be avoided. But economic duress was joined by economic opportunism in many negotiations. A survey of four hundred corporate executives conducted by *Business Week* in 1982 found that almost one-fifth replied positively to the statement "although we don't need concessions, we are taking advantage of the bargaining climate to ask for them."[67] Concessions remained common for the rest of the decade.

—

By the end of the 1980s the pillar of negotiated responsibility had weakened substantially. But since the threat of unions had served for decades as the main catalyst for growth in CSR at the workplace, unions' growing impotence reduced the odds of further growth. The pressures of institutional activists to enforce a shareholder only orientation on the part of the executives of large corporations lessened these odds even further.

Voluntary Responsibility (CSR)

The Fall of the Human Resources Model

During the 1980s most large corporations adopted what came to be seen as an organizational innovation. It could be found in practically every industry, whether steel (Bethlehem), autos (Ford), electronics (General Electric), banking (Citibank), hotels (Holiday Inn), computers (Intel), or insurance (Allstate). It could be found as well in the public sector, whether at the local level (Phoenix), county (Yolo, California), or federal (US Customs Service). And it could be found in both strongly union firms (General Motors) and quintessentially nonunion enterprises (IBM). What all of these organizations adopted was a "quality circle."[68]

The spread of quality circles was part of a larger trend of socially responsible workplace reforms that were initiated from the 1970s to the 1990s. The common thread that tied these varied reforms together was an effort to solicit employee input in order to make the work process more efficient, while improving the quality of the product. Practices ranged from problem-solving task forces that solicited employee ideas on an ad-hoc basis to self-directed work teams in which workers had continuous input into the work process. The most common form that these efforts took was, in fact, the quality circle, where a group comprising both supervisory and nonsupervisory personnel sought to improve the quality of the product or service. Some of these experiments were stand-alone projects, while others were part of holistic "quality of work life" or "total quality management" programs. By 1990, one study of large firms found that 70 percent had at least one employee-involvement practice in place, with 66 percent reporting the presence of at least one quality circle and 47 percent reporting at least one self-directed team.[69]

This trend of employee involvement can be understood in the context of the responses to growing global competition after 1970 that were discussed earlier. During the early years, the dominant response of American manufacturers was either disinvestment or moving production offshore. For many unionized concerns, the strategic choice frequently involved the use of harsh union-avoidance tactics, effectively breaking the capital-labor accord. While these were low-road responses, the growing use of worker-involvement practices showed that there was a high-road response to globalization, and one that also gained momentum in the 1980s.

Those taking the high road adopted the diagnosis that the increased flow of goods produced abroad exposed basic flaws with the mode of production of most American manufacturers. First, most of these establishments were built upon the foundational principle of scientific management, where workers had no input into the production process. As a result, those with the most direct experience of making a product or delivering a service represented an underutilized resource, and many good ideas were left off the table. Furthermore, the bureaucratic, "chain of command" mode of decision making was inefficient in a global marketplace that featured rapid change and which demanded new ideas and nimble decision making. These inefficiencies were most glaring in unionized plants, where struggles over the workplace resulted in a stalemate between management committed to protecting its prerogatives through scientific management and unions committed to job control.

Not surprisingly, then, it was a vanguard of unionized firms that followed the prescription that getting workers more involved would increase productivity and quality. In fact, it was companies like Xerox, Corning, and the Saturn division of General Motors that in many ways took worker-involvement experiments the furthest. For all three, unionized production workers were involved in the design of new work systems and in the selection of appropriate technology and machinery. Worker input was then regularized on an everyday basis in the form of autonomous work teams. In other union plants, joint labor-management committees attempted to normalize worker involvement.

From the beginning, however, many union leaders were skeptical about the purpose of such practices. Part of this was due to the fact that very early on, their use in nonunion establishments was part of a broader union-avoidance strategy, where managers attempted to convince workers that there was an identity of interests between owners and workers. This was in direct opposition with the industrial-relations model of collective bargaining, which was built upon an adversarial mistrust between owners and unions that had been reinforced throughout labor history, and perpetuated by an orientation of business unionism, where unions had been intentionally and consistently shut out of decision making. As time went on, the trust required to make cooperative, joint employer-employee groups work in unionized firms was frequently undermined by the broader environment of labor relations that was growing increasingly toxic with the use of the harsh tactics of union resistance.[70]

As a result, leadership in employee-involvement ultimately passed to nonunion firms, which viewed them as an additional means of forging a bond of loyalty between employer and employee. But here too there were problems. One was limited implementation. Instead of a comprehensive restructuring of the workplace, firms tended to adopt such practices piecemeal. Part of this was due to the fact that implementing employee-involvement programs required significant investments of time and money. This limitation would help explain the pattern that when such practices were adopted, they tended to affect a minority of a firm's employees. In a 1987 study of Fortune 1000 firms, while 61 percent reported having quality circles, in most cases, less than 20 percent of employees actually participated. Greater expansion and fuller participation was also slowed by the resistance of mid-level managers, who had a difficult time sharing power with employees in whatever form that it took.[71] By themselves, however, these obstacles seemed surmountable. Presumably, piecemeal would become comprehensive over time, and more workers would be covered. More time would also seem to be the remedy to break down managerial resistance.

This was potentially very significant, since employee-involvement represented the newest piece added to the human resources (HR) model, joining human relations (chapter 6) and job redesign (chapter 7) that were added in previous decades. In fact, better social relations, more challenging jobs, and greater participation now added up to an attractive alternative to the industrial relations model of unionized workplaces. This was particularly true in the context of the growing pay and benefits enjoyed by the employees of large, nonunion firms. Indeed, by some accounts, during the 1980s nonunion and union employers traded places, with the former now the leader and the latter the follower with respect to innovative workplace practices. This pattern held for compensation as well; by 1984, the rate of wage increases in nonunion firms surpassed the rate of unionized firms for the first time in decades.[72]

By the late 1980s, then, the tradition of CSR appeared to be at a critical juncture with respect to both its new practices and its workplace model generally. Would the trend of employee-involvement programs overcome its limitations and continue to diffuse? Was it possible that the HR model would become America's dominant, fully institutionalized form of a socially responsible workplace, fulfilling the long-held promise of American CSR?

Downsizing

It did not take long for the answer to be forthcoming, with a resounding "no" delivered in the form of the thousands of pink slips issued by companies downsizing their workforces. Between 1991 and 1994, many of the biggest names in corporate America announced substantial job cuts, such as those illustrated in chapter 1. This wave of corporate downsizing swelled during the late eighties and early nineties, hitting both nonunion and union firms. The American Management Association, which in 1987 began surveying its members (mostly large firms) about job elimination and job creations, found that from 1988 to 1989, 39 percent reported some downsizing, and that of these, 66 percent eliminated more jobs than they created. The year between 1990 and 1991, which included the beginning of a recession, marked a record high, as 55 percent reported reductions, with 79 percent representing net job eliminations. But even during the recovery of 1993 to 1994, 47 percent continued to eliminate jobs (65 percent were net eliminators). The Department of Labor found that during this same recovery year, 2.4 million workers permanently lost jobs that they had held for at least three years.[73]

The scale and pervasiveness of these job cuts had not been seen since the Depression. But the late 1980s did not constitute another depression. Also perplexing was the fact that many of the companies that were announcing job cuts were the very same companies that were attempting to forge an identity of interests with workers through employee-involvement programs. What, then, could explain the clear contradiction of companies attempting to simultaneously travel the high and low roads of labor relations?

The answer provided by those announcing or advocating job cuts was that downsizing represented a necessary, if painful, part of the "corporate restructuring" needed to make business competitive. Yet another new term introduced into the business lexicon during this period, corporate restructuring comprised a set of prescriptions for making business organizations more efficient, and one of these was job cuts. Of course, this was the very same diagnosis used to explain the prescribed remedy of worker involvement. But whereas the latter was presented as an enlightened choice, downsizing was presented as a mandatory move to make corporations smaller, nimble, and more efficient. With the enhanced worker productivity that would presumably be forthcoming, the smaller, leaner corporation would be better able to compete in the global economy, and profits would grow as a result.

Much has been published since this wave of downsizing. Particularly helpful in judging the various claims surrounding the trend is the 1996 special report of the *New York Times*, *The Downsizing of America*, and the 2003 comprehensive review of the evidence, *Downsizing in America*, by economists William Baumol, Alan Blinder, and Edward Wolff. First, downsizing was in many ways a continuation of the job reductions of the late seventies and early eighties in manufacturing. Indeed, the *Times* report indicated that between 1979 and 1994, forty-three million jobs were eliminated. Of course, there was still a net increase of twenty-seven million jobs, suggesting that there was a great deal of churning in employment. While downsizing was still more likely to occur in manufacturing than other industries, no industry was safe. But in contrast to mass layoffs of the earlier period, downsizing was no longer the exclusive experience of blue-collar workers, as many white-collar jobs were eliminated as well. Still, contrary to predictions concerning the creation of flatter hierarchies, managerial employees as a share of total employment tended to *increase* as firms downsized; in other words, the white-collar workers affected most were clerical and sales workers, not managers.[74]

Baumol, Blinder, and Wolff reviewed a number of hypotheses concerning the causes of downsizing and concluded that consistent with what many claimed at the time, the chief, immediate cause of much downsizing was a weakening of demand, mostly due to the increase in global competition. Significantly, however, the authors found no support for the hypothesis that downsizing led to increased productivity; in fact, they cite some evidence that found a negative relationship between downsizing and productivity instead. In light of the negative impact that downsizing has upon the morale of those who are retained after the job cuts take place, this should not be surprising.

However, Baumol, Blinder, and Wolff did find that, consistent with the claims of its advocates, downsized firms did typically become more profitable. At first glance, this would seem contradictory, since it means that stagnant, if not declining, productivity was coupled with increasing profitability. What the authors found, however, is that downsizing worked to depress workers' wages and hold down total compensation. They thus conclude, "a central effect of downsizing has apparently been a transfer of income from labor to capital—that is, from the workers to the owners." In other words, "the dirty little secret of downsizing" was that it "appears to have been largely a way to squeeze labor."[75]

The roots of these efforts to transfer income from labor to capital can be traced back to the hostile takeovers of the 1980s. The deals consummated by buyout firms usually featured high levels of debt financing—hence the expression "leveraged buyout." Once these deals were done, the acquired companies had to pay off the high interest associated with financial instruments, like junk bonds, that facilitated the purchase. Because labor typically represents the lion's share of operating costs, it became the largest target of cuts. In a review of hostile takeovers, economists Andrei Shleifer and Lawrence Summers argue that the post-takeover performance gains posted by these corporations were derived primarily from breaking the implicit contracts with long-term employees. In other studies of takeovers, much of the savings needed to finance debt was found in the layoffs of workers.[76]

Downsizing gained greater traction after shareholder activists assumed control of the corporate governance campaign and further enshrined shareholder value as the only legitimate orientation for management in the new era of "investor capitalism."[77] As reviewed above, this message was initially reinforced through the dismissals of a number of prominent CEOs during the early 1990s. Under pressure, especially at corporations where institutional shareholder owned large blocks of stock, managers embarked upon the path of corporate restructuring to streamline operations and enhance shareholder value. To show investors that they now meant business, such plans almost always featured the downsizing of a company's workforce. Reinforcing this pattern was the tendency for the announcements of restructuring plans that included layoffs to be rewarded by a rise in the price of a company's stock.[78]

Shedding workers thus became a way of both attracting investors and keeping shareholder activists at bay. It did not take long for downsizing to become institutionalized and to have its own set of vested interests, including management consultants that designed restructuring plans and employment counselors who helped the newly unemployed. Managers themselves began to benefit royally from the obsessive focus on shareholder returns. With stock options (offered as a means to "align the interests" of managers and owners) comprising an increasing share of their compensation package, top executives were paid an average of $19.5 million in 2000, up from $1.4 million in 1978 (both in 2011 dollars). Expressed in terms of the growing distance between executives and workers, the average CEO made 411 times as much as the average hourly worker in 2000, compared to 27 times as much in 1978.[79]

Since it was now legitimized, some companies seemed to downsize for no other reason than they could. This included long time stalwarts of CSR, such as Proctor & Gamble, which could trace its pedigree of socially responsible practices back one hundred years. In 1993, P&G announced a 12 percent job cut, or thirteen thousand workers. It is worth quoting at length the reasoning of the company's CEO, Edwin L. Artzt:

> The public has come to think of restructuring as a sign of trouble, but this is definitely not our situation. We have a healthy, growing business, a strong balance sheet, positive cash flow, state-of-the-art products and a well-stocked technology pipeline with plenty of opportunities for growth. However, we must slim down to stay competitive.[80]

The Recommodification of Labor

If the employee-involvement programs discussed earlier represented a wave, then downsizing was the tsunami that swamped them. After all, to be effective such programs require the cultivation of trust and cooperation between employers and their employees; they also require substantial investments of time and money. But nothing is more corrosive to trust than an atmosphere of doom created by a sword of Damocles in the form of a pink slip. Shareholders now laid exclusive claim to any surplus cash ("free cash flow" in the parlance of finance economists) as profits to be reaped, instead a source of investment in the workforce. Furthermore, while employment involvement entailed an investment that would pay off in the long term, shareholders typically demanded immediate returns on their investments. It became abundantly clear that the time horizon for shareholders of investor capitalism was much shorter than that of owners and managers during the reign of managerial capitalism.

Downsizing was even more consequential. It effectively undermined the foundation of the entire structure of the human resources model: job security. As the book has emphasized, the strength of the nonunion model of corporate social responsibility had always depended upon the strength of the unions. Therefore, at the time that the HR model seemed poised to become dominant, the union movement was moribund, allowing employers to fall back to the default, low road of labor relations. Now the price tag for lifetime employment was seen as too high. Instead of union threat undergirding a stakeholder orientation on the part of management, it was now the threat of investors that supported the shareholder orientation.

By treating workers as disposable, downsizing restored the treatment of labor as a commodity, as a cost to be vigilantly controlled. As the ascendant shareholder orientation sank deeper roots, the various offshoots of the new disposable worker, the ones illustrated in chapter 1, became visible.

- instead of secure steady jobs, declining job tenure and increasing contingent work, whether in terms of more temp jobs or independent contractors.
- instead of jobs with sufficient hours, more involuntary part-time work and workers holding multiple jobs.
- instead of jobs with a decent benefit package, a declining percentage of large employers—and employers generally—offering health insurance or private pensions.

Not surprisingly, the shareholder revolution impacted corporate philanthropy as well.

Corporate Philanthropy

In 1981 American Express got involved in the efforts to restore the Statue of Liberty. Introduced with a $6 million advertising campaign, the company promised a penny for each charge on an American Express card and $1 for each new card issued, among other incentives. Within three months, and after the use of its card increased by 28 percent, the company raised $1.7 million for the restoration fund. What came to be known as "cause-related marketing" (CRM) diffused broadly, as more and more large corporations partnered with nonprofit organizations and their causes, which ranged from increasing literacy to fighting breast cancer.[81]

At first, the increase in CRM coincided with an increase in overall corporate philanthropy, which, as measured as a percentage of pretax profits, reached a record 2.35 percent in 1986. However, while CRM continued to grow for the rest of the 1980s and through the 1990s, overall corporate giving began to decline, reaching a low of 1.1 percent in 1997.[82]

A number of factors can help to explain this change in corporate giving. For one, large corporations had traditionally concentrated their philanthropic initiatives in the local communities in which they were situated. As the number of factory closings increased, and as capital became more mobile generally, large corporations loosened their ties to these localities. Consequently, giving shifted to causes that were more national in scope.

Of greater significance was the impact of the shareholders revolution. As seen above, shareholder groups were making successful claims for a greater share of a company's profits, and at the same time strengthening corporate governance to ensure that managers conformed to the dictum that corporations had but one stakeholder—the shareholders themselves. With managerial discretion being more closely monitored, managers might have worried that spending on corporate philanthropy would be viewed as suspect, especially if the corporate gift was unconnected to a company's objectives. As a result, corporations appeared to pull back from more traditional forms of charity, while increasing strategic giving, like CRM, that could easily be justified on the grounds that it made money. Corroborating this interpretation is evidence that shows that during the 1990s, corporations with low levels of giving were more likely to have a higher percentage of their stock owned by large institutional investors—in other words, those owners who were more likely to closely monitor management's decisions.[83]

Of course, with greater purchases of a sponsor's product, consumers were providing direct proof of the profitability of being socially responsible. Just as the corporate campaigns of the 1970s had changed the beneficiaries of socially responsible practices, the shareholders revolution changed their purpose. Both signaled the rise of a new CSR.

—

The greatest decline in social regulations, unions, and CSR occurred during the twelve years of the Reagan-Bush administrations. If the problem was Republican rule, then there was hope that the regulatory structure for large corporations could be rebuilt if a Democrat was back in the White House. Democrats got their wish with the election of Bill Clinton in 1992.

The Clinton Years

Social Regulations and Welfare

The Reagan administration represented a radical departure from the path of greater government intervention that had been cleared by administrations from the New Deal forward. But the election of Bill Clinton as president in 1992 was a positive omen for restoring a positive role for government, including that of controlling large corporations. Not only was he the first Democrat elected president in twelve years, in 1996 he became the first Democratic candidate to win reelection in fifty-two years. A forecast for a liberal restoration was also supported by the economic climate, which improved dramatically during the decade, as the nation experienced the longest period of sustained economic growth in its history. Profits once again soared. The decade of the 1990s would therefore test whether the changes ushered in during the Reagan years were transitory or long-lived.

The first sign that such a revival was not in the offing was the lack of any critique of corporate behavior in the Democratic Party Platform of 1992: no mention of takeovers, downsizing, attacks upon unions, etc. By the end of the first year of the Clinton administration it became clear that the main thrust of its overall economic policy would be neoliberal, or in other words, a no-strings-attached effort to encourage economic growth, and this with a smaller government. This can be seen in several first year initiatives: the Clinton-Gore Deficit Reduction Plan, which made it clear that the focus of the government's economic policy would be deficit reduction; the North American Free Trade Agreement (NAFTA), which was a full embrace of the free-trade policy that had been negotiated by the Bush administration; and the Reinventing Government Initiative, which in an effort to make government more efficient, ultimately led to a reduction of 377,000 federal employees.[84]

Clinton, who likened his own economic team during his first year as acting like "Eisenhower Republicans," stayed a neoliberal course for the remaining seven years of his administration. Most notably, with two pieces of legislation he finished off efforts begun during the Carter administration to deregulate the financial industry by removing provisions of the Glass-Steagall Act of 1933. The first was the Interstate Banking and Branching Act of 1994, which allowed banks to merge and operate across state lines. The second was the Financial Services Modernization Act of 1999, which allowed commercial banks, investment banks, and insurance companies to combine operations. In his 1996 State of the Union address, the president summed up the approach of his administration with words that could have been spoken by Reagan himself: "the era of big government is over."

Of course, there were some positive developments. Importantly, the Clinton administration ended the Reagan-Bush efforts to gut social regulations. It also appointed personnel to regulatory agencies, such as the EPA, OSHA, and the FDA, who were committed to the underlying missions of these agencies. During its first year, the administration was also successful in passing the Family and Medical Leave Act, arguably the most significant social regulation passed in a generation. Even here, though, the victory was limited, as the act guaranteed only three months of unpaid leave and did not apply to employers with fifty or fewer employees—effectively leaving out a large percentage of the labor force.

The one initiative that would have strengthened America's welfare state was the Health Security Act. As the proposed legislation would have provided health insurance to nearly all Americans, it would have diminished the nation's reliance upon the voluntary provision by employers and fundamentally altered America's regulatory structure. By 1994, however, it joined the list of failed efforts to universalize health care in the United States.

Unions in the 1990s

Two changes in the 1990s gave unions some reason for hope that the tide against unions could be reversed. The first was that with the election of Bill Clinton, unions once again had an ally in the White House. The most important legislative goal of unions at the time was the passage of the Cesar Chavez Workplace Fairness Act. The bill would have designated the hiring of permanent replacement workers during a strike as an unfair labor practice. Though legal since a 1938 Supreme Court decision, the hiring of permanent replacements had been largely avoided by employers during the post-WWII years, since it was recognized as poisonous to long-term labor-management relations; it became another tacit provision of the capital-labor accord. However, as part of the broader union-avoidance strategy that had strengthened since the 1970s, the practice had gained greater traction among employers in the previous decade. It was therefore good news for labor when the new president threw his support behind the bill, and it passed the House in 1993. However, due to a threatened filibuster, it was dropped in the Senate. Then, after the Republican Party assumed control of both the House and Senate after the 1994 midterm elections, the bill never saw the light of day again. Though an Executive Order issued by Clinton in 1995 would have barred companies that hired permanent replacements from federal contracts, it was overturned by the Court of Appeals.[85]

The second change involved unions' leadership and strategy. An insurgent group of union leaders helped to elect John Sweeney as president of the AFL-CIO in 1995. Sweeney had overseen the dramatic rise in the membership rolls of the Service Employees International Union (SEIU), the union representing workers in the fast-growing service sector of the economy, where unions had been historically weak. To increase the membership of all unions, Sweeney quickly adopted a number of initiatives and followed through on a campaign promise to spend $20 million to hire and train new organizers. With a democratic administration now appointing labor friendly members to the National Labor Relations Board, hopes were high. When Sweeney assumed the presidency, only 14.9 percent of American workers belonged to unions, down from 16.1 percent at the beginning of the decade. It was therefore discouraging to union leaders that the AFL-CIO's new focus on organizing did not show positive results at the beginning of the new century; in 2000, union representation was down to only 13.5 percent of the labor force.[86]

Neither change, then, reversed the fortunes of unions in the 1990s, and this during a time of healthy growth in both the economy and profits, conditions under which business unionism had thrived in the past. Union avoidance was now fully entrenched, supported by a shareholder only orientation that viewed unions as anathema, and which made vigilance in containing labor costs a first principle.

Summary

Decades in the making, America's regulatory structure for large corporations experienced an unexpected and rapid collapse in the 1980s and into the 1990s. What was particularly surprising was that from the perspective of the 1970s, America seemed poised to fortify its ability to control large corporations and secure more socially responsible behavior: the continued growth of strong social regulations, approaching a point where government might effectively counterbalance big business; the continued growth of unions (if only in numbers and not rate), approaching a point where their acceptance by management might lead to at least soft forms of corporatism, as with the industry wide Labor-Management Group; and the growing adoption of the HR model in nonunion firms.

Instead of a more robust system of ensuring that corporations act in a socially responsible fashion, the economic decline of the 1970s helped to usher in both a political (Reagan) and economic (shareholders) movement that together undermined each pillar of the regulatory structure, revealing the shaky foundations upon which it was built. In the political arena, the business community took full advantage of a stagnant economy during the decade to attack social regulations, in effect knocking the country off the path toward greater regulatory strength. In the process, large corporations greatly expanded their infrastructure for political influence to ensure the political economy remained lopsided in the direction of business interests. By 1980, the business counterattack against government helped produce the Reagan Revolution, which halted progress on social regulations and more broadly delegitimized government for years to come.

Ironically, the same economic conditions that helped corporate managers stave off government undermined their positions at the helm of large corporations. This outcome had its roots in strategic decisions made by corporate management in the face of growing global competition, as corporate performance, whether in profits or market share, worsened. In response, conglomerates, steered by managers operating under the influence of the finance conception of control, largely abandoned efforts at creating governance structures that encouraged long-range investment and planning. Instead, they tended to divest and moved capital to what were viewed as more profitable ventures. As these decisions typically did not help, continued underperformance created opportunities for corporate raiders and institutional investors, who led a shareholders revolution resulting in a shareholder only orientation. This spelled disaster for the other stakeholders of corporations, especially employees.

Even before the shareholders revolution commenced, greater global competition and the corresponding decline in profits had led to

294

greater efforts at union avoidance. This was neither preordained nor an unavoidable result, but instead a strategic choice made available by—or an Achilles heel that accompanied—business unionism. The shareholders revolution had the effect of strengthening the avoidance of unions, thus knocking unions well off the path of greater acceptance and shared power.

The importance of an ascendant union movement, and its corollary, union threat was demonstrated fully by the suddenness with which CSR was vanquished. Stalwart members of the CSR vanguard, like General Electric, which had for decades cultivated good relations with both its employees and communities, readily abandoned both. At the critical juncture when CSR, especially the HR model, seemed fully formed and ready to diffuse more broadly, the long-held promise of the CSR alternative was emphatically broken.

—

America's regulatory structure for large corporations crumbled rapidly at the century's end. Ultimately, it turned out to be a fragile structure that placed too much weight upon what was an inherently weak pillar, CSR.

Notes

1. Daniel Holland and Stewart C. Myers, "Profitability and Capital Costs for Manufacturing Corporations and all Nonfinancial Corporations," *American Economic Review* 70, No. 2 (May 1980).

2. Jeffrey Madrick, *The End of Affluence: America's Economic Dilemma* (New York: Random House, 1995), 68; Bennett Harrison and Barry Bluestone, *The Great U-Turn: Corporate Restructuring and the Polarizing of America* (New York: Basic Books, 1988), 8.

3. Neil Fligstein, *The Transformation of Corporate Control* (Cambridge, Massachusetts: Harvard University Press, 1990), chapters 7–8.

4. Ibid., 15.

5. Martin Mintz and Jerry S. Cohen, *America, Inc.: Who Owns and Operates the United States* (New York: Dial Press, 1971), 43; Gerald F. Davis, Kristina Diekmann, and Catherine H. Tinsley, "The Decline and Fall of the Conglomerate Firm in the 1980s: The Deinstitutionalization of an Organizational Form," *American Sociological Review* 59, no. 4 (August 1994): 548; Michael E. Porter, "From Competitive Advantage to Corporate Strategy," *Harvard Business Review* 65 (May-June 1987); Frank Lichtenberg, "Industrial De-Diversification and Its Consequences for Productivity," Working Paper No. 3231 (Washington, DC: National Bureau of Economic Research, 1990); Mark J. Roe, "From Antitrust to Corporate Governance? The Corporation and the Law: 1959–1994," Working Paper #119 (New York: Columbia University School of Law, 1995), 15.

6. Barry Bluestone and Bennett Harrison, *The Deindustrialization of America: Plant Closings, Community Abandonment, and the Dismantling of Basic Industry* (New York: Basic Books, Inc., Publishers, 1982), 124.

7. Ibid., 149–151.

8. Ibid., 42, 113, 6; Madrick, *The End of Affluence*, 68; Stuart Bruchey, *The Wealth of the Nation: An Economic History of the United States* (New York: Harper and Row, Publishers, 1988), 214.

9. Holland and Myers, "Profitability and Capital Costs," 320–325; Samuel Bowles, David M. Gordon, and Thomas E. Weisskopf, *After the Wasteland: A Democratic Economics for the Year 2000* (Armonk, New York: M. E. Sharpe, Inc., 1990), 149.

10. Bowles, et. al., *After the Wasteland*, 149.

11. David Vogel, *Fluctuating Fortunes: The Political Power of Business in America* (New York: Basic Books, Inc., Publishers, 1989), 147–149.

12. Ibid., 160.

13. Ibid.

14. Ibid., 160–163.

15. Sean Wilentz, *The Age of Reagan: A History 1974–2008* (New York: Harper Collins Publishers, 2008), 81.

16. The unemployment rates from 1977–80: 7.1, 6.1, 5.8, and 7.1 percent.

17. Jeffrey Clements, *Corporations Are Not People: Why They Have More Rights Than You Do and What You Can Do About It* (San Francisco: Berrett-Koehler Publishers, Inc., 2012), 17–18.

18. Vogel, *Fluctuating Fortunes*, 118–119, chapter 8.

19. Ibid., 161.

20. The Supreme Court's 1974 Buckley v. Valeo decision overturned efforts to limit campaign expenditures.

21. Vogel, *Fluctuating Fortunes*, 118, 207, 203–204; United States Bureau of the Census, *Statistical Abstract of the United States 1984*, 104th ed. (Washington, DC: US Government Printing Office, 1984), 266.

22. Vogel, *Fluctuating Fortunes*, 213–227.

23. Ibid., 228–233.

24. Guy Halverson, "A Public Coalition Takes a Bead on Big Business," *The Christian Science Monitor*, February 15, 1980."

25. Louis Galambos and Joseph Pratt, *The Rise and Fall of the Corporate Commonwealth: United States Business and Public Policy in the 20th Century* (New York: Basic Books, 1988), 243; Vogel, *Fluctuating Fortunes*, 169–171.

26. John Ehrman, *The Eighties: America in the Age of Reagan* (New Haven, Connecticut: Yale University Press, 2005), 75–76.

27. Harrison and Bluestone, *The Great U-Turn*, 95.

28. Wilentz, *The Age of Reagan*, 140; Vogel, *Fluctuating Fortunes*, 247–248.

29. Vogel, *Fluctuating Fortunes*, 248.

30. Ibid., 248–249.

31. Linda Brewster Stearns and Kenneth D. Allan, "Economic Behavior in Institutional Environments: The Corporate Merger Wave of the 1980's," *American Sociological Review* 6, no. 4 (August 1996).

32. Ibid., 705.

33. George P. Baker, "Beatrice: A Study in the Creation and Destruction of Value," *The Journal of Finance* 47, no. 3 (July 1992); James Sterngold, "Shaking Billions From Beatrice," *New York Times*, September 6, 1987.

34. Baker, "Beatrice."
35. Andrei Shlezfer and Robert W. Vishny, "The Takeover Wave of the 1980's," *Science* 249, no. 4970 (August 1990), 745; Paul M. Hirsch, "From Ambushes to Golden Parachutes: Corporate Takeovers as an Instance of Cultural Framing and Institutional Integration," *American Journal of Sociology* 91, no. 4 (January 1986): 807; Gerald F. Davis and Suzanne K. Stout, "Organization Theory and the Market for Corporate Control: A Dynamic Analysis of the Characteristics of Large Takeover Targets, 1980–1990," *Administrative Science Quarterly* 37, no. 4 (December 1992).
36. More generally, 60 percent of conglomerate-type purchases that were made in the 1960s and 1970s were divested by 1989, with many sell-offs occurring in the 1980s—see Shleifer and Vishny, "The Takeover Wave of the 1980's," 746.
37. United States Bureau of the Census, *Statistical Abstract of the United States 1991*, 111ᵗʰ ed. (Washington, DC: US Government Printing Office, 1991), 540; Davis and Stout, "Organization Theory and the Market for Corporate Control"; Margaret M. Blair and Girish Uppal, *The Deal Decade Handbook* (Washington, DC: The Brookings Institution, 1993), 57–58.
38. Davis and Stout, "Organization Theory and the Market for Corporate Control," 612–613; Stearns and Allan, "Economic Behavior in Institutional Environments," 705; Robert Sobel, *The Age of Giant Corporations: A Microeconomic History of American Business, 1914–1992*, 3ʳᵈ ed. (Westport, Connecticut: Greenwood Press, 1993), 271.
39. Margaret M. Blair, "Financial Restructuring and the Debate about Corporate Governance," in *The Deal Decade: What Takeovers and Leveraged Buyouts Mean for Corporate Governance*, ed. Margaret M. Blair (Washington, DC: The Brookings Institution, 1993), 12.
40. Newsweek, "Confessions of a Raider," *Newsweek*, October 20, 1986: 51; Carl C. Icahn, "Leveraged Buyouts: America Pays the Price," *New York Times*, January 29, 1989.
41. Time, "High times for T. Boone Pickens," *Time*, March 4, 1985, 52; T. Boone Pickens, "Viewpoints: 1 Share, 1 Vote: Make it the Rule for all Exchanges," *Los Angeles Times*, January 18, 1987.
42. Steven A. Ross, "The Economic Theory of Agency: The Principal's Problem," *American Economic Review* 63, no. 2 (May 1973); Eugene F. Fama and Michael C. Jensen, "Separation of Ownership and Control," *Journal of Law and Economics* 26, no.2 (June 1983).
43. Jay W. Lorsch and Elizabeth MacIver, *Pawns or Potentates: The Reality of America's Corporate Boards* (Boston: Harvard Business School Press, 1989); Michael T. Jacobs, *Short-Term America: The Causes and Cures of Our Business Myopia* (Boston: Harvard Business School Press, 1991), chapter 3; Robert A. G. Monks and Nell Minow, *Power and Accountability* (New York: Harper Business, 1991).
44. Henry M. Manne, "Mergers and the Market for Corporate Control," *The Journal of Political Economy* 73, no. 2 (April 1965); Michael C. Jensen and Richard S. Ruback, "The Market for Corporate Control: The Scientific Evidence," *Journal of Financial Economics* 11, nos. 1–4 (April 1983); Michael C. Jensen, "Eclipse at the Public Corporation," *Harvard Business Review* (September-October 1989).

45. Michael Useem, *Executive Defense: Shareholder Power and Corporate Reorganization* (Cambridge, Massachusetts: Harvard University Press, 1993), chapter 6; Blair and Uppal, *The Deal Decade Handbook*, 30–33.

46. Robert A. G. Monks and Nell Minow, *Corporate Governance* (Cambridge, Massachusetts: Blackwell Business, 1995), 213.

47. Michael Useem, *Investor Capitalism: How Money Managers are Changing the Face of Corporate America* (New York: Basic Books, 1996), 25; Useem, *Executive Defense*, 30; Robert Sobel, *The Age of Giant Corporations: A Microeconomic History of American Business, 1914–1970* (Westport, Connecticut: Greenwood Press, Inc., 1972), 280.

48. Investor Responsibility Research Center, *Investor Responsibility Research Center Background Report—Confidential Voting* (Washington, DC: Investor Responsibility Research Center, 1994).

49. Ibid.

50. California Public Employees Retirement System, *Why Corporate Governance Today?* (Sacramento, CA: California Public Employees Retirement System, 1995), 3.

51. *Business Week*, "Executive pay," *Business Week*, March 30, 1992, 52–58.

52. Business Roundtable, *Statement on Corporate Governance* (Washington, DC: Business Roundtable, 1997), 3.

53. Kim Moody, *An Injury to All: The Decline of American Unionism* (London: Verso, 1988), 148–149; Douglas Fraser, "One-Sided Class War," in *Political Directions for Labor*, ed. Kim Moody (Detroit: Labor Education & Research Project, 1979), 29–30.

54. Vogel, *Fluctuating Fortunes*, 153; David Brody, *Workers in Industrial America: Essays on the 20th Century Struggle* (New York: Oxford University Press., 1979), 248; Bluestone and Harrison, *The Deindustrialization of America*, 178.

55. Vogel, *Fluctuating Fortunes*, 153–156; Brody *Workers in Industrial America*, 247.

56. Moody, *An Injury to All*, 149; Roger W. Schmenner, *Making Business Location Decisions* (Englewood Cliffs, New Jersey: Prentice-Hall, Inc., 1982); Bluestone and Harrison, *The Deindustrialization of America*, 165–166; Thomas A. Kochan, Harry C. Katz, and Robert B. McKersie, *The Transformation of American Industrial Relations* (Ithaca, New York: ILR Press, 1994), 67.

57. Audrey Freedman, *Managing Labor Relations* (New York: The Conference Board, 1979), 2, 5–6; a follow-up survey in 1985 found an increase in firms that stressed "union avoidance": Audrey Freedman, *The New Look in Wage Policy and Employee Relations* (New York: The Conference Board, 1985).

58. Bluestone and Harrison, *The Deindustrialization of America*, 152; Louis Uchitelle, *The Disposable American: Layoffs and Their Discontents* (New York: Vintage Books, 2007), 131–133.

59. Ibid., Bluestone and Harrison, *The Deindustrialization of America*, 170–178; Harrison and Bluestone, *The Great U-Turn*, 26–27.

60. United States Bureau of the Census, *Historical Statistics of the United States, Colonial Times to 1970, Part 1*, Bicentennial Edition (Washington, DC: US Government Printing Office, 1975), 178; Barry T. Hirsch and David A.

Macpherson, "Union Membership and Coverage Database from the Current Population Survey: Note," *Industrial and Labor Relations Review* 56, no. 2 (January 2003): 352.

61. United States Bureau of the Census, *Historical Statistics of the United States, Part 1*, 137.

62. Paul Buhle, *Taking Care of Business: Samuel Gompers, George Meany, Lane Kirkland, and the Tragedy of American Labor* (New York: Monthly Review Press, 1999), 196.

63. Ibid., 140–141.

64. David M. Gordon, *Fat and Mean: The Corporate Squeeze of Americans and the Myth of Managerial Downsizing* (New York: Martin Kessler Books, The Free Press, 1996), 210.

65. Melvyn Dubofsky and Foster Rhea Dulles, *Labor in America: A History*, 7th ed. (Wheeling, Illinois: Harlan Davidson, Inc., 2004), 398–399.

66. Moody, *An Injury to All*, 152–156.

67. Ibid., 168.

68. Olga L. Crocker, Cyril Charney, and Johnny Sik Leung Chiu, *Quality Circles: A Guide to Participation and Productivity* (New York: A Mentor Book, New American Library, 1984).

69. Eileen Appelbaum and Rosemary Batt, *The New American Workplace: Transforming Work Systems in the United States* (Ithaca, New York: IRL Press, 1994), 60.

70. Kochan, Katz, and McKersie, *The Transformation of American Industrial Relations*, 100–106; Appelbaum and Batt, *The New American Workplace*, 23, 136–137.

71. Appelbaum and Batt, *The New American Workplace*, 63.

72. Kochan, Katz, and McKersie, *The Transformation of American Industrial Relations*, 82; Dubofsky and Foster Rhea Dulles, *Labor in America*, 396.

73. John A. Byrne, "The Pain of Downsizing: What it's Really Like to Live Through the Struggle to Remake a Company," *Business Week*, May 9, 1994; William J. Baumol, Alan S. Blinder, and Edward N. Wolff, *Downsizing in America: Reality, Causes, and Consequences* (New York: Russell Sage Foundation, 2003), 5.

74. New York Times, *The Downsizing of America: Millions of Americans are Losing Good Jobs. This is Their Story* (New York: Times Books, 1996), 4, 12–13; Baumol, Blinder, Wolff, *Downsizing in America*, 232.

75. Baumol, Blinder, and Wolff, *Downsizing in America*, 261–262, 26.

76. Andrei Shleifer and Lawrence H. Summers, "Breach of Trust in Hostile Takeovers," in *Corporate Takeovers: Causes and Consequences*, ed. Alan J. Auerbach (Chicago: University of Chicago Press, 1988).

77. Useem, *Investor Capitalism*.

78. Peter Cappelli, *The New Deal at Work: Managing the Market-Driven Workforce* (Boston: Harvard Business School Press, 1999), 78–83.

79. Lawrence Mishel and Natalie Sabadish, "CEO Pay and the Top 1%: How Executive Compensation and Financial-Sector Pay Have Fueled Income Inequality," Issue Brief #331, Economic Policy Institute, Washington, DC, May 2, 2012, http://www.epi.org/publications/ib331-ceo-pay-top-1-percent/.

80. Michael Janofsky, "Proctor & Gamble in 12% Job Cut as Brand Names Lose Attraction," *New York Times*, July 16, 1993.

81. Welsh Marketing Associates, "American Express & The Statue of Liberty Restoration Fund," Cause Marketing Digital Library, accessed February 25, 2012, http://dlib.info/omeka/judith/items.show/194.

82. Reference for Business, "Corporate Philanthropy," Encyclopedia of Business, 2nd ed. (Advameg, Inc., 2013), http://www.referenceforbusiness.com/encyclopedia/Con-Cos/Corporate-Philanthropy.html.

83. Barbara R. Bartkus, Sara A. Morris, and Bruce Seifert, "Governance and Corporate Philanthropy: Restraining Robin Hood?," *Business and Society* 41, no. 3 (September 2002): 336.

84. Whitehouse.gov, "The Clinton Presidency: Eight years of Peace, Progress, and Prosperity," http://clinton5.nara.gov/WH/Accomplishments/eightyears-index.html.

85. Clifford Krauss, "House Passes Bill to Ban Replacement of Strikers," *New York Times*, June 16, 1993; Steven Greenhouse, "Clinton Won't Appeal Court Rebuff on Workers," *New York Times*, September 12, 1996.

86. Peter L. Francia, *The Future of Organized Labor in American Politics* (New York: Columbia University Press, 2006), chapter 1, 40; Hirsch and Macpherson, "Union Membership," 352.

9

Can the Beast Be
Re-Tethered?

The Large Corporation in the Twenty-First Century

The twentieth century project to make America's large corporations more socially responsible was decades in the making. But the regulatory structure that was created was, in the end, vulnerable to collapse. Its interconnected architecture was such that weakness in one pillar of the regulatory structure contributed to the weakening of the entire structure. Consequently, its decline was rapid. As will be shown below, the trends that marked the decline of corporate social responsibility at the end of the twentieth century have continued their downward trajectory in the twenty-first.

The final task of the book is to discuss the prospects of re-tethering large corporations to larger social purposes and what a new regulatory structure would look like. To complete this task it is important to look first at the current state of America's lopsided political economy. Establishing its contours will help inform a discussion of the types of reforms that are most needed; this will include a critical look at the "new CSR," where advocates claim that voluntary initiatives are still the answer. The review of political economy begins with a look at the continued dominance of large corporations in three sectors of the economy (financial, manufacturing, and retail), together with a brief examination of the practices that characterize their typically shareholder-only orientation.

Financial Corporations

The Great Recession of 2008–09 revealed what is perhaps the most consequential change in the composition of large corporations, the emergence of financial corporations. Ranked by revenue, the top twenty of the Fortune 500 list of largest corporations in 2011 included three banks (Bank of America, J. P. Morgan Chase, Citigroup), one mortgage company (Fannie Mae), and two conglomerates whose main lines of business were financial (General Electric, Berkshire Hathaway).[1]

Not only has the financial sector grown in size, ownership within its constituent industries has become more concentrated. In banking, the six largest banks had assets that amounted to 18 percent of GDP in 1995. In 2012, that figure was 63 percent, and the top six had assets of roughly $9 trillion. As impressive is how central the financial sector has become a source of profits in the American economy. While financial corporations accounted for between 10 and 15 percent of all profits during the 1950s and 1960s, they have accounted for roughly 30 percent since the mid-1980s, peaking at over 40 percent in 2001.[2]

In her book *Capitalizing on Crisis*, Greta Krippner refers to this growing dominance of financial sector corporations as the financialization of the American economy.[3] The causes of financialization are many and complex, with the most fundamental having their roots in the economic and political changes of the eighties and nineties. First, there was the deregulation of the financial sector, discussed in the last chapter. In the new, lax regulatory environment, financial corporations grew, as did the degree of concentration in the financial industry. But the ascendance of the financial sector not only required deregulation, it also needed a growing pool of capital to invest. Much of this came from institutional shareholding funds, which continued to grow; in 2009, institutional investors controlled $25.3 trillion, or 17.4 percent of all financial assets in the United States. As dramatic was the growth in foreign capital. For a variety of reasons, including the strong dollar and the increasing globalization of capital markets, America became the preferred destination of foreign funds seeking a high return. By 2008, the United States was the destination for 43 percent of all of the world's capital imports, with the surplus funds of China's state capitalism leading the way.[4]

Financialization played a large role in the economic calamities that befell the nation that year. With so much capital demanding higher and higher returns, the financial sector responded with a supply of increasingly complex financial instruments. While these investment opportunities offered high rewards, they also entailed higher risks, which spiraled upwards, leaving the overall economy more vulnerable to speculative bubbles and collapse. As the latter occurred, the large size of financial corporations made them "too big to fail," leaving the country with little choice but to bail out the troubled ones.

The implications of the rise of financial corporations for the prospects of restoring greater public purpose involve the changed nature of investment. Instead of representing an activity that targets the long-term prospects of particular companies, it has become a form of high-stakes gambling. In short, the financialization of the economy has reinforced the shareholder-only orientation of all corporations. With institutional investors, both domestic and foreign, demanding higher and higher returns on their growing pools of capital, and with so many opportunities competing for investor dollars, managers of many large, nonfinancial corporations have become more fully committed to the goal of increasing the price of their company's stock in order to attract investors' funds.

Krippner calls this the financialization of nonfinancial firms, in which corporate executives have increasingly shifted from capital investments to investments aimed at increasing stock prices, such as dividend payments and stock buybacks. By one estimate, the investments in financial instruments by nonfinancial corporations reached 50 percent of total investments by 2000, up from 28 percent in 1980.[5] This has contributed to the continued shrinking of the time horizon of corporate executives. While capital investments tend to pay off in the long term, investment in financial instruments tend to have a short-term effect on the price of stocks.

This investment myopia has been reinforced by two other factors. First, the trend toward the short-term ownership of stock continued, declining from an average of five years in 1980 to only one year by 2002; by 2011, the average holding period for stock on the New York Stock Exchange was only five months. Second, corporations continued to tie much of an executive's pay to the price of their company's stock, especially in the form of stock options. After suffering a hit as a result of the recession of 2008, executive compensation climbed back up to an average of $12.1 million in 2011. Of course, such short-termism is consistent with the shareholder-only orientation. A commitment to other stakeholders, whether employees or communities, requires long-term thinking.[6]

Manufacturing Corporations

A cursory examination of the Fortune 500 list of largest corporations leads to an unexpected observation. For all of the talk of deindustrialization, America still seems to be dominated by manufacturing corporations. Of the fifteen most profitable corporations for 2011, ten were in the business of making things. In addition to industrial stalwarts like Exxon and Proctor & Gamble, this elite list included the computer giants IBM, Intel, Microsoft, and Apple. To be sure, most of the business of IBM and Microsoft is in the business services sector. Apple, however, is the producer of a full array of computer and communication equipment. Not only was it ranked third in profits, but it also ranked first overall in terms of market value, at over $568 billion. Given the importance of manufacturing corporations during the years in which regulations, unions, and CSR were more effective, Apple's success might give reason for hope that manufacturing might lead the way in a revival of the sector. This hope is quickly dashed, however, when one looks at Apple's payroll. With only 63,000 employees (43,000 domestic), Apple does not even break into the top fifty employers.[7]

How can a company that sold seventy million iPhones, thirty million iPads, and fifty-nine million other Apple products in 2010 employ so few workers? The answer, in short, is outsourcing on a grand scale. Instead of manufacturing its products in foreign-owned divisions, Apple subcontracts the production (and sometimes design, sale, and delivery) of products that bear the company's brand. Tremendous advances in information and communication technology, including the Internet and mobile phones, have facilitated the rapid diffusion of the outsourcing model, since monitoring, inspection, and other modes of administration can now happen from afar. The result has been the construction of global supply chains, so that whether it is an Apple iPhone, a Hewlett-Packard printer, a Dell computer, or an Intel microprocessor, the chances are that these products sold by American-headquartered firms are actually manufactured and assembled by a network of subcontractors abroad. This has certainly contributed to the fact that only about one in ten Americans work in manufacturing today.[8]

The manufacturing strategy of outsourcing stands in stark contrast to the approach adopted by early manufacturers like Standard Oil. As demonstrated earlier in the book, in the highly competitive oil refinery industry of the nineteenth century, John D. Rockefeller pioneered the use of the governance structures, especially those of horizontal and vertical integration, to contain competition and help build the modern, large corporation. This approach was especially successful in those industries with high capital investments, and thus high entry costs, and where economies of scale could be achieved. The oligopolies in industries like auto and steel that arose in a mostly domestic economy provided predictable profits.

Computer industry innovators, like Apple's Steve Jobs, have faced a very different economic environment in the late twentieth and early twenty-first centuries. First, computer manufacturers arose in an economic environment that was global in nature, which has rendered competition nearly impossible to contain in most industries. As a result, governance structures have been less effective. Second, exponential rates of technological change in the industry make the "it" product of today obsolete tomorrow. This has placed a high premium upon rapidly developing new products in order to keep customers buying the brand. Third, due to the existence of freestanding manufacturers that can function as subcontractors capable of making a variety of products, the start-up costs for new entrants can be low. Consequently, if the structural imperative of the manufacturing corporation of the nineteenth and twentieth centuries was to control competition, the structural imperatives for manufacturers in the global economy of the twenty-first century, especially those in high-tech industries like computers, are to control costs and rapidly develop new products.

The history of Apple illustrates the dynamics of this new environment. After introducing its innovative Apple II and Macintosh computers in the seventies and eighties, Apple soared in popularity and profitability. Early on, much of Apple's production was domestic. By the mid-1990s, however, the company had lost market share to the Microsoft-driven PCs and was close to bankruptcy. Eventually, it regained its innovative edge with the development of its "i" products, starting with iPods. Given its earlier "near-death experience," however, Apple became hypersensitive to both speed and cost and decided to switch to an outsourcing producer.[9]

A closer look at the outsourcing model reveals just how difficult it has become to demand or expect socially responsible practices in the twenty-first century. On the one hand, Apple is a model employer, at least for those who work in its high-end, engineering jobs. These workers generally receive good pay and benefits. However, the same cannot be said of the over seven hundred thousand workers worldwide who make Apple products. For example, over two hundred thousand Chinese workers employed by the Taiwanese manufacturing giant Foxconn assemble the iPhone. At its Longhua plant on the mainland, known as Foxconn City, employees work as many as twelve hours a day, six days a week, and earn less than $17 a day. Many live in company barracks, four to six to a room. In essence, then, outsourcing represents an outsourcing of irresponsible corporate practices. Of course, it is these same practices that help to make Apple so profitable, and make it so attractive to pension-fund managers seeking high returns on investments.[10]

Retail Corporations

Stronger evidence for deindustrialization in the Fortune 500 rankings comes not from the list of the most profitable corporations, but from the changed composition of America's largest employers. In 1960, all but two of the top fifteen employers were manufacturers, including U.S. Steel, General Electric, and International Harvester. The biggest was General Motors, with nearly six hundred thousand employees. By 2010, all but two of the top fifteen employers were in the service sector, led by Walmart with its 1.4 million employees (2.1 million worldwide). Not only are the vast majority (79 percent) of Americans now employed by service-sector companies, a number of the leading large employers are retail corporations. In addition to Walmart, the top fifteen in 2010 included Target, Kroger, Home Depot, Sears, and CVS. In fact, in 2010 more workers were employed in the retail sector alone than in manufacturing generally (14.4 million vs. 11.5 million).[11]

This development has serious implications for tethering corporations to public goals. Retail industries are inherently competitive. Even before globalization, there was no such thing as a retailing oligopoly. The reason for this is that retail has relatively low start-up costs, lower still with the onset of online shopping. Economies of scale can, of course, be realized as retailers get larger through chain-store expansion, with key corporate functions centralized in a headquarters. Even so, profit margins remain narrow. Not only is a retailer's market position never fully secure, as an upstart pharmacy, home improvement center, or grocery can appear at any time, but new technology may render a store's main retail product obsolete. As a result, there is a long list of formerly successful big-box stores that ultimately failed, including, in recent years, Circuit City, Blockbuster, and Borders.

Consequently, retailers operate under the singular imperative to hold down costs, especially labor costs. No one has been more vigilant and better at controlling costs than Walmart. To be sure, the low prices it offers have benefited consumers. However, Walmart's unwavering focus on reducing costs has also resulted in a set of practices that have made it the poster child of corporate irresponsibility. Headline-making examples in recent years include selling jewelry and toys made of toxic substances, selling furniture made from illegally logged lumber, and bribing Mexican officials in order to obtain building permits.[12]

But most of the criticism of Walmart centers on how its practices affect workers, its own and others'. The company's impact upon workers not on its payroll stems from its tremendous purchasing power, which allows the company to set the prices it is willing to pay suppliers, frequently forcing these employers to lower the wages of their workers. In many cases, American suppliers have responded to Walmart's pricing benchmarks by moving some or all of their production offshore, especially China. This "Walmart effect" also occurs domestically. Several studies have shown that once a new Walmart opens, local retailers are forced to reduce labor costs in order to compete—others go under. It is this predictable impact that has led many communities, especially larger cities where unions still have some strength, to resist new Walmart stores.[13]

With respect to its own workers, Walmart is a low-wage employer that provides meager benefits. Though the corporation does not publish detailed figures on the wages it pays, and though estimates vary, assuming an average hourly wage of $10 an hour for a Walmart's associate in 2010 would have placed the company well below the median wage of $16.27 for all workers. Many Walmart employees earn considerably less, since somewhere between 25 and 35 percent of company's employees are part-time workers. Most of these employees would prefer full-time jobs. In fact, the company is in the vanguard of retail companies that rely more and more upon part-time workers. In 2012 the Bureau of Labor Statistics found that nearly 30 percent of part-timers would prefer full-time employment, up from 11 percent in 2006. Of course, the increasing numbers of involuntary part-time jobs was only one indicator of the continuing use of contingent, disposable labor by employers. The number of temp workers grew from 1.1 million to 2.3 million between 1990 and 2008, while the Department of Labor's high-end estimate of all workers in "alternative arrangements" (temp work, on-call work, independent contractors) was 4.1 percent in 2005.[14]

Heavy reliance upon part-timers helps Walmart hold down benefits costs, since most of these associates are not eligible for health or pension benefits. For full-time associates, benefit costs are kept down by low job tenure, as nearly 40 percent of Walmart employees turn over each year. The publication of a 2005 internal memo showed that less than half of the company's employees received health insurance, while the low wages earned by others entitled them to Medicaid coverage.

The benefits policies of Walmart are indicative of the continued decline in employer-provided health insurance and pensions. The percentage of private-sector workers with employer-provided health insurance declined from 70 percent in 1980 to 59 percent in 2000. By 2010 coverage was down to 53 percent. Private-sector workers covered by a company provided pension declined from 50 percent in 1980 to 48 percent in 2000, and only 43 percent were covered by 2010. Overall, the percentage of "good jobs" in 2010 (defined as jobs paying at least $18.50 an hour that offer both health insurance and a retirement plan) was down to 25 percent, a drop of 3 percent from 1979.[15]

Key to Walmart's ability to keep labor costs low has been its ability to keep all of its thousands of stores union free. Its success stems from very heavy investments in antiunion tactics. As documented in the Human Rights Watch report *Discounting Rights*, Walmart employs a number of tactics from its "managers toolbox," including forcing employees to attend antiunion lectures, threatening workers with harmful consequences if a union drive succeeds, and firing union supporters.[16] Walmart is in the vanguard of American corporations that together spend millions of dollars annually to avoid unions. Such efforts have contributed greatly to the continued decline in unionization. In 2012 only 11.3 percent of American workers belonged to unions. For those working in the private sector, only 6.6 percent belonged to unions, while the figure for retail workers was a meager 4.9 percent. At the same time it was vigilant on keeping labor costs down, Walmart returned a record $19.2 billion to shareholders in 2011 in the form of dividends and share repurchases.[17]

Corporations as Vehicles for the Transfer of Wealth

What is abundantly clear at the beginning of the twenty-first century is that America's leading corporations are guided by a shareholder-only philosophy. Whether it is a financial corporation developing new and exotic financial instruments, whether it is a nonfinancial corporation buttressing short-term stock prices at the expense of long-term capital investments, whether it is manufacturers outsourcing, or whether it is a retailer employing contingent workers, the large corporation has become a profit machine that operates for the exclusive benefit of their owners, investors, and executives. Lost in the make-up of the twenty-first-century large corporation is any semblance to a social entity that serves the public good by satisfying multiple stakeholder needs.[18]

There is no better evidence of this proposition than the changed relationships that now exist among productivity, profits, and employee compensation. In the first several decades after WWII, whether through technological advances or changes in organizational structure, positive incentives, or supervisory coercion, when worker productivity improved, both profits and compensation went up. In recent years, however, the pattern has been largely obliterated. From 1989 to 2010, productivity in the United States grew by 62.5 percent. Corporate profits also soared, more than doubling from $664 billion to nearly $1.7 trillion (in 2008 constant dollars). However, real hourly wages grew by only 12 percent in the same period. As a result, corporate profits in 2011 accounted for the largest share of GDP since 1950, while wages and salaries accounted for the smallest share.[19]

As it turns out, then, there is nothing automatic in these relationships. Unless there is a mechanism in place to dislodge them, the profits accruing from greater productivity tend to congeal at the top among owners and managers—the default relationship. This was certainly true during the period of the rise of the large corporation in the late nineteenth and early twentieth centuries. In the generation after WWII, strong unions and union threat functioned to pull down some of those profits directly in the form of contracts with greater wages and benefits, and indirectly in the form of greater CSR. As these mechanisms have withered with the rise of the shareholder-only corporation, the default position has been restored.

Also restored is the trend toward greater inequality in American society. The share of total income held by the top 1 percent of households increased from 9.7 percent in 1979 to 21 percent in 2005; the share of just the top 0.1 percent more than tripled, from 3.3 to 10.3 percent. Driving this growing disparity was the income that was being garnered by both executives of nonfinancial corporations, and those who worked for financial sector corporations in general. Combined, households headed by such individuals accounted for 58 percent of increased income of the top 1 percent, and 67 percent of the top 0.1 percent.[20]

———

At the beginning of the twenty-first century, the large corporation still dominates the economy and is now oriented toward a narrow band of shareholders. It should not be surprising that it still has outsized influence in the political arena as well.

The Political Clout of Large Corporations Today

Elections

As the last chapter showed, big business spent heavily in the last quarter of the twentieth century to refine the art of political influence, whether this involved elections, lobbying, or policy formation. The ability of large corporations to influence elections was given a huge assist by the Supreme Court's Citizens United decision of 2010. Invoking the old legal precedent of "corporations are individuals," and taking it to the logical conclusion that corporations are thus protected by the First Amendment, the Court held that the "government may not suppress political speech on the basis of the speaker's corporate identity." Ruling that the act's key provisions were thus unconstitutional, the Court's conservative bloc in a 5-4 decision effectively undid decades worth of laws, dating back to the Tilman Act of 1907, that had attempted to restrict the ability of corporations to use funds from the general treasuries for political purposes.[21]

"Super PACs" quickly became the main vehicles for making unlimited contributions. The impact of these decisions was clearly seen in the money raised during the 2012 election, which, with $6 billion spent, was the most expensive in American history. Super PAC money alone represented an infusion of over $700 million, which was over half of the $1.3 billion in total spending by all outside groups. The dominance of business in campaign fundraising is revealed by the fact that nearly three-quarters of all contributions of over $200 from whatever source, whether group or individual, were from those with a business affiliation. In contrast, less than 5 percent came from those with a union affiliation. Compared with labor groups, business interests outspent them by a ratio of about 15 to 1.[22] Of course, the full extent of business dominance in campaign contributions is currently impossible to document, given the existence of 501(c) organizations that are not required to reveal donor information.[23]

Lobbying

Lobbying was another area where big business continued to dominate. Between 1998 and 2012, a total of over $36 billion was spent on lobbying, with annual totals doubling during this period. The top five spenders, ranked by sector, were all business sectors: miscellaneous business, health, finance-insurance-real estate, communications, and energy. Collectively, they spent nearly $24 billion. In lopsided contrast, the total spending by labor, which ranked twelfth, was $528 million. It is also safe to say that most lobbyists, whose ranks swelled from 10,408 in 1998 to 14,840 in 2007, represented business interests.[24]

Particularly valuable as lobbyists are those who not only have expertise in policy areas germane to particular industries and businesses, but those who also have personal connections to those being lobbied. Congressional staffers who work for House and Senate committees fit this bill quite well. For the past decade, the Center for Responsive Politics has kept tabs on the revolving door between government and industry. The group found that hundreds of "staffers-turned-lobbyists" (revolving door) and "lobbyists-turned-staffers" (reverse revolving door) could be found after reviewing the biographies of the personnel of Congress's most powerful committees, such as the Senate Finance Committee and the House Ways and Means Committee. Since the pay is much higher in the private sector, revolving-door staffers are frequently seen as "cashing in" on training provided by the public sector.[25]

As staff members nurture relationships with prospective employers, the ability of Congress to do the peoples' business is compromised. Even more damaging in this regard has been the recent trend of former members of Congress becoming lobbyists. In the decade of the 1970s, only 3 percent of former members of Congress became lobbyists. Today, more than a third pass through this revolving door. Former Republican members are particularly likely to follow this path, with roughly half of those leaving Congress between 2000 and 2004 working to lobby former colleagues.[26]

Of course, these particular revolving doors are only the latest examples of the permeable wall that has existed between business and government since the nineteenth century when, due to weak administrative capacity, new regulatory agencies, such as the ICC, drew upon the business sector to fill its personnel needs. But even as administrative capacity has grown, the practice of picking key administrators from the private sector continues. In the first administration of the twenty-first century, George Bush drew liberally from the business community to fill positions that are key to the effectiveness of social regulations. The new head of the Occupational Safety and Health Administration had worked many years for chemical producer Monsanto, while the new deputy director at the Environmental Protection Agency had worked for a law firm that fought tough regulatory standards.

Policy Formation

In the new century, conservative, business-friendly and funded think tanks and foundations continue to hold an advantage over their liberal counterparts, both in terms of sheer numbers and in terms of funding. During the Bush II administration, scholars from the American Enterprise Institute found their way into policy-making positions, while in Congress conservative white papers continued to inform Republican policy. One indicator of the broader influence of these organizations was the greater likelihood that their press releases and publications would be cited in the media: for the top twenty-five think tanks, citations of those with a conservative bent beat those with a liberal orientation, 33 to 20 percent.[27]

The ability of big business to affect policy is best illustrated by the billionaire Koch brothers, Charles and David. The brothers run Koch Industries, Inc., a family-owned oil and gas conglomerate with annual sales of over $100 billion, which makes it the second largest privately owned company in the country. From the mid-1990s through 2010, the brothers contributed more than $85 million to dozens of right-wing think tanks and advocacy groups—a who's who of the conservative movement. The common agenda of many of these groups is antiregulation, antitax. Of course, the brothers also spend heavily on elections, and they can take primary credit for providing the start-up funds for the Tea Party, channeled through their own Americans for Prosperity Foundation. In 2010, the $45 million it spent on Tea Party candidates helped elect sixty-two of the eighty-seven members of the GOP's freshman class.[28]

The influence of the business community on public policy can be found beyond Washington. The American Legislative Exchange Council (ALEC) provides large corporations with an avenue for helping to draft business-friendly legislation at the state level. Funded by corporate members such as Exxon Mobil, the Bank of America, Walmart, and Verizon, and conservative businessmen such as the Koch brothers, ALEC conducts its work through task forces that comprise both business representatives and state legislators (almost entirely Republican). These groups then craft model legislation to accomplish goals such as keeping taxes low, stripping workers of collective bargaining rights, and weakening environmental regulations. In 2009, ALEC claimed that 115 of the 826 model bills that in introduced were enacted into law.[29]

The Structural Power of Business

Beyond the advantage of tremendous resource, large corporations have the advantage of structural power, which gives them political clout. In short, corporations' decisions regarding investment and jobs have a tremendous impact upon the health of the economy, and consequently, the prospects for politicians' electoral well-being. In practice, corporations can use this power to threaten to withhold job-creating investment in order to get their way politically, or offer to create jobs if they are offered incentives, especially those that come with no strings attached. The greatest examples of the latter occur at the levels of state and local government, since competitive federalism gives corporations tremendous leverage as states compete with each other to attract businesses and their jobs. In recent years, states and localities have given at least $70–80 billion annually in "economic development" incentives to corporations in the forms of tax credits, cash grants, low-cost or forgivable loans, and subsidies for worker training expenses, among other forms of assistance, in order to lure businesses and their jobs. However, not much has been demanded in return. In a 2011 study of 238 of the most significant of these subsidies, it was found that only 57 percent had performance criteria that related to job creation, retention, or training; only 41 percent imposed a wage requirement; and only 21 percent mandated that the business offer health insurance to its employees, with only 13 percent requiring that the employer contribute to the cost of the premium. Furthermore, companies that received help were typically not required to commit themselves to a particular locale for an extended period of time, enabling them to shop for a better deal in another state or simply close down when it was in their interest to do so.[30]

Is the New CSR the Answer?

In sum, the continued dominance of large corporations in the twenty-first century economy, combined with the outsized influence of big business in American politics, adds up to a political economy that is in many ways as lopsided as it has ever been. In the absence of an effective regulatory structure, this condition continues to pose problems for American democracy, just as it did over a century ago. Whether it is the risky decisions of financial institutions that produce calamitous results, the movement of jobs and profits offshore, a proliferation of jobs that pay poorly and offer no benefits, corporations receiving government incentives without providing public benefits, or big business attempting to buy elections, the private decisions made by large corporations still have huge public consequences.

Given this state of affairs, is it possible to come up with a set of reforms that would result in corporations acting in more socially responsible ways? Before exploring what some reform proposals might look like, it is important to look at the one option that has gained some traction in the past ten to fifteen years: the revival of voluntary initiatives. The advocates of a "new CSR" argue that the twenty-first century has produced conditions that are now ripe for a new voluntarism that will usher in an era of greater corporate social responsibility. In light of the experience with CSR in the twentieth century, are these voluntary efforts up to the task of redirecting large corporations toward broader social goals?

The New CSR

There is a wide range of activities that comprise the new CSR, including:

traditional corporate philanthropy: donations to institutions or causes that are unrelated to a corporation's core business or strategy. For example, the McDonalds Corporation established and continues to donate to the Ronald McDonald House, which was established to provide a home-like environment to families of critically ill children receiving medical treatment away from home. The charity now operates in fifty-two countries. Then there is the Bill and Melinda Gates Foundation, with its clear association with Microsoft, the source of Gates' funding for the foundation. With an endowment of over $36 billion in 2012, the foundation spends hundreds of millions of dollars each year primarily on an array of programs to improve heath care, reduce extreme poverty, and expand educational opportunities

strategic philanthropy: contributions to issues or causes that also contribute to a corporation's business objectives. An example here is the Chrysler Corporation contributing to the education for workers in skills relevant to the automobile industry, some of whom may end up working for Chrysler. One subtype of strategic philanthropy is known as "cause-related marketing." This is illustrated by companies pledging to support a cause with a portion of the proceeds from selling those companies' products or services.

market for virtue: the sale of products or services that can make some claim to CSR. Examples are wide-ranging and include Starbucks selling coffee with the Fair Trade label, meaning that the beans they use were purchased from suppliers that abide by a set of socially and environmentally responsible standards; General Electric's Ecomagination product line that focuses upon renewable energy and low carbon emissions; and Ikea, which requires that its Indian rug suppliers prohibit the employment of child labor.

social entrepreneurship: for-profit corporations founded for the explicit purpose of using all or a substantial portion of a company's profits to address social problems. Two widely known and popular examples are Newman's Own, the company started by Paul Newman that dedicates 100 percent of it profits from the sale of its salad dressing, pasta sauce, and other food products to a wide variety of charities, and Tom's Shoes, the company that gives a free pair of shoes to impoverished children for every pair that it sells.

socially responsible investing (SRI): an investment strategy that seeks to do social good while simultaneously maximizing financial return. The strategies include "negative screening," where certain types of companies, like tobacco, are excluded from investment, and "positive screening," in which companies that satisfy certain environmental, social and governance (ESG) criteria are given preference in investment decisions. In 2010 over $3 trillion in assets were being professionally managed using SRI criteria.[31]

social accounting: with the growth of both ethical consumerism and socially responsible investing, there has been growth in efforts to certify that firms conform to some set of CSR standards. In addition to Fair Trade, listed above, other social accounting audits include the Fair Labor Association, Fair Wear Foundation, and the Social Accountability International's SA8000 standard. In conjunction with this trend, more and more companies also issue annual reports that cover their CSR efforts.[32]

At first glance, then, the new CSR of the twenty-first century seems both multi-faceted and widespread. How, then, does this robust palate of socially responsible activity jibe with the argument of declining CSR? One reason for this inconsistency has to do with a difference in stakeholders. Most of the examples of decline used in the book, including those in the updates above, concern what has historically been considered the main stakeholder and beneficiary of a corporation, its employees. In contrast, the central stakeholders of the new CSR are a corporation's consumers and investors, with the main beneficiaries of their more enlightened purchases and investments being the environment and workers in developing countries. The main problem of the

315

new CSR, then, is that it largely ignores the growing problems for many American workers, whether it is greater job insecurity, stagnating pay, or declining benefits.

Part of the explanation for the change in stakeholders reflects heightened concerns over dire environmental problems, especially global warming, and heightened awareness of the horrible working conditions in third-world countries. But the change of stakeholders is also due to the age-old desire of some large corporations to improve their tarnished CSR image by diverting attention away from questionable practices in one area to more responsible practices in another. For example, it is probably no coincidence that just as greater negative attention was being paid to Walmart's lamentable treatment of its employees, the company in 2005 adopted a number of initiatives aimed at promoting environmental sustainability, which it has since trumpeted in its annual Global Responsibility Report. However, given the decline in CSR experienced by American workers, merely changing the topic, or stakeholder, however worthy, does not eliminate the problems experienced by these workers.

What if we judge today's CSR on its own terms, with its own favorite stakeholders? Even the most optimistic forecast of the new CSR suggests it is no match for the scale of the underlying problems, whether it is the treatment of workers in developing countries or environmental problems like global warming. The problem lies in its central premise of the new CSR. Because CSR is now good for business, it will continue to grow, and, as a result, voluntary efforts alone will be able to solve major problems.

Of course, the idea that CSR is good for business is as old as the idea of CSR. Whether it was through the greater productivity of employees working in harmony with owners, or whether it was greater sales due to a better public image, proponents have always touted the bottom-line promise of good behavior. But in the twentieth century, owners and advocates also acknowledged other motives for their voluntary efforts. As shown earlier in the book, in the quarter century after WWII, many managers suggested that corporations had important social obligations to meet, regardless of their profitability. What distinguishes current discussions, then, is the nearly exclusive focus upon the presumed business advantages of CSR. With the exception of the category of traditional corporate philanthropy, all of the other types of CSR listed above share the claim, "good for business" as a common denominator.

However, the evidence that CSR is good for business is at best mixed: some studies show a positive effect, some show a negative effect, and some show no effect at all. This, then, is disappointing; since the hope is that a clear case for the profitability of CSR will contribute to its greater spread. Part of this inconsistency is due to the lack of methodological rigor that marks many of these studies and rankings. While some studies focus upon one dimension of CSR, like a company's environmental record, others look at multiple dimensions. In some cases, rankings on CSR are subjective, and quantitative data are frequently limited.[33]

But even if the reliability and validity of these studies were improved, it is still unlikely that a clear verdict that CSR invariably improves the bottom line of corporations would be achieved. After thousands of studies, success in business is, not surprisingly, a complicated affair involving many variables. Ultimately, neither the perfect mousetrap nor perfection in CSR guarantees success. Instead, multiple routes lead to profitability. Unfortunately, as has always been true, the low road to maximizing profits is as effective, at least in the short term, as the high road of corporate social responsibility.

There is also a problem with the underlying assumption that what is different about the new CSR is that sufficiently large numbers of educated, middle-class consumers and investors are now in place to drive it forward through "ethical consumerism."[34] But neither group is monolithic. Some consumers, no matter how smart or wealthy, will always prefer the lowest-priced goods and services, regardless of how they are produced or delivered. And, of course, some investors, however smart and wealthy, will prefer to put their money in those companies that generate the greatest return, regardless of how they are generated, as long as those companies are committed to the fiduciary dictum that only shareholders matter. Furthermore, even if the driving force of the new CSR was monolithic, it ultimately has limited horsepower. While there may now be a critical mass of educated, middle-class people globally, there simply are not enough of them to motivate more than a vanguard of large corporations to change their ways.

Yet another reason why the new CSR is not a sufficient solution to the problems of bad corporate behavior is the same reason that made it vulnerable in the previous century: it relies upon the voluntary actions of corporations. As the book makes clear, the problem with voluntary actions is that they can be easily withdrawn when the factors that encourage them falter. The CSR of the twentieth century declined when the threats of government mandates and unions abated. To the extent that the new CSR is dependent upon consumers able to afford the premium prices usually associated with the goods and services offered by socially responsible corporations, it is vulnerable to economic downturns and the shrinking pool of discretionary dollars available for such purchases.

In addition, voluntary standards are hard to monitor and enforce. Under pressure from critics of the sweatshop conditions in many developing countries, some large American retailers, like Walmart and the Gap, have set up certification procedures in order to be able to claim that they purchase apparel only from suppliers who comply with a set of socially responsible standards for the working conditions of their employees. However, deadly fires at apparel factories in Bangladesh and Pakistan in 2012 revealed serious shortcomings in the enforcement of these standards. For example, though an "ethical sourcing" officer at Walmart had cited the factory in Bangladesh for high-risk violations, the compliance protocol would punish a supplier with the suspension of Walmart orders only if three such violations were received in a two-year period. The factory fire in Pakistan that killed at least 262 workers had actually received the gold standard, SA8000 seal of approval. The SA8000 is the product of the Social Accountability International, an American-based NGO that is funded by membership fees from large corporations like the Gap, as well as by unions and other groups. Though the standards are stringent, enforcement is less so. In the investigation of the Pakistani fire, it was revealed that inspection and certification for the SA8000 is frequently delegated to subcontractors, who are often unsupervised and interested more in generating business than ensuring safe working conditions.[35]

But even if the new CSR could deliver on all of its promises, two major problems remain. First, like the old CSR, the new CSR is simply not up to the task. This is even truer today, as the issues targeted by CSR efforts today are global in nature. In 2011, total corporate philanthropy totaled $14.5 billion.[36] Though this is a conservative estimate of total CSR, since traditional measures do not capture much of entrepreneurial philanthropy, even doubling or tripling this figure would not come close to providing sufficient resources to take care of the problems that the new CSR hopes to solve. Second, to rely exclusively upon CSR to address the problems created by large corporations is to leave America's lopsided political economy untouched. In particular, the voluntary approach preserves the outsized political influence of big business. To rein in large corporations in the twenty-first century, they will need to be challenged, their purpose contested, and their behavior constrained.

There is certainly nothing wrong in encouraging CSR, new or old. In fact, an examination of the history of corporate social responsibility suggests that there is every reason to believe that it will produce good results. But the evidence is stronger in showing that reliance upon such voluntary measures alone will fall far short of the goal of re-tethering corporations to broader social purposes. As the main solution to the problem of corporate irresponsibility, CSR is simply not viable.

—

A fundamental flaw with the new CSR is that it perpetuates the old free-market fantasy of the invisible hand. In this rendering, consumer and investor demand will lead corporations, interested in maximizing profits, to do the right thing. Though the alchemy of economic exchange can certainly help to solve social problems, two hundred years of experience have proven that it is never enough. To believe otherwise is to engage in magical thinking. The fundamental problem, then, is ideological.

Recontesting the Large Corporation

The Ideological Groundwork

Controlling large corporations will require constructing a new regulatory structure with fortified pillars of government regulation and unions. Given the lopsided state of America's political economy, this is a daunting task. This task is made more daunting still by the fact in the past quarter century or more, the large corporation has not been subjected to serious challenge, nor have substantial reforms been advocated—at least not loudly enough to reach the threshold of gaining the sustained attention of the public. In contrast to the nineteenth century, there have been no calls for the breakup of large corporations and certainly no demands that big business be nationalized.[37] In contrast to the Progressive Era, there have been no calls to increase antitrust enforcement, nor has there been any advocacy of federal charters. In contrast to the Depression, there have been no demands for corporatist solutions involving big businesses or measures taken to rein in the risky decisions and concentrated power of the financial sector. And in contrast to the public-interest movement of the 1960s and '70s, there is no strong advocacy of new social regulations. Even in the wake of the largest financial crisis since the Great Depression, the Great Recession generated no proposals that would radically reorient large corporations.

In many ways, then, the main advantage that large corporations have in the political culture of the twenty-first century is ideological. Consequently, the first step in the ambitious project of rebuilding a regulatory structure is to once again contest the institution of the large corporation. In fact, there is reason to believe that Americans would be receptive to a renewed challenge. To begin with, according to a 2010 Gallup Poll, only 19 percent of Americans reported that they had "a great deal" or "quite a lot" of confidence in big business, while 38 percent reported having "very little" or "none." In a separate Gallup Poll taken the same year, nearly half of the public had a negative image of big business. A 2005 Hart Research Associates survey reported that 63 percent of respondents stated that corporations had too much power, while only 28 percent felt that the balance between corporations and workers was fair, and a paltry 4 percent thought that it was workers who had too much power. It is also the case that American voters rejected the message delivered by hundreds of millions of dollars worth of corporate funded ads and reelected President Obama in 2012.[38]

Furthermore, re-contesting big business does not mean constructing an ideological challenge from scratch. Instead, challengers need to tap into the available materials within America's political culture. The logical place to start is the rich tradition of antimonopolism. From the early appearance of large corporations in the nineteenth century, antimonopolists delivered a stinging indictment, which they continued to develop over time. The initial charges were that corporations were creatures of privilege and inherently corrupt. These were joined later by allegations that as they grew, the consequential decisions of corporations were unaccountable to the public, and thus a threat to democracy.

In fact, in 2011 the first signs of an antimonopolist revival appeared, in the form of the Occupy Wall Street (OWS) movement. What began as a protest in Zuccotti Park in the financial district of NYC, OWS rapidly spread across the nation and eventually became a worldwide phenomenon. The essence of the movement was captured by its slogan, "we are the 99 percent," a reference to the growing income disparity in the country. This was framed by an overall attack on greed and corruption, especially that which was manifested by large corporations, as well as the undue influence of the latter upon government.

But as rapidly as it spread, OWS quickly faded as a phenomenon commanding national attention. Part of the reason that it did not sustain itself was organizational. Founded upon the principles of participatory democracy, which for some included anarchism's constitutional disdain for leaders, the movement's endless debates neither produced an agenda nor congealed into a coherent organization that could survive the waning of participants' initial zeal. Instead of an agreed-upon set of demands, group energies focused on tactics that might keep the movement in the media's spotlight. As a result, beyond slogans, many in public did not know what the movement represented or demanded.

More fundamentally, OWS failed to reach its full potential because it was not animated by a broader discussion of values. Earlier appearances of antimonopolism resonated with the public because the particulars of the bill of charges against corporations were presented as threats to the core American values. For example, special or privileged treatment threatened the values of fairness, justice, and equality of opportunity, while corruption and unaccountability were corrosive to democracy. What was true then remains true now. Whether it is a renewed OWS or some other future challenge to corporations, advocates will need to make direct appeals to these threatened values.

By framing the attack upon large corporations as a battle to protect American values, challengers can simultaneously help to restore these values to their proper place, as goals to which society should aspire. Together they represent a progressive vision of a better society, one that strives toward greater justice, equality of opportunity, and democratic accountability. To realize this vision requires an active, legitimate government, which among its legitimate roles are those of addressing the social problems that corporations create and re-tethering corporations to public ends by, in part, ensuring that the rights of corporations' stakeholders are recognized and secured.

As any semblance of a progressive vision of society faded from sight, the ideological void was filled by the recycled vision of the invisible hand: the good society is the unintended byproduct of individuals pursuing their selfish interests in the market, including the artificial individual, the corporation, seeking to maximize the interests of its shareholders. But this view was buttressed by an extreme version of market ideology, one where there are markets for everything, whether it is the education of students, the incarceration of prisoners, the distribution of body organs for transplants, or the issuing of permits to pollute.

And of course, it was the ideology of free, unregulated markets that helped to rationalize unleashing corporations from societal restraints.[39]

The purpose of a restored progressive vision is not to oppose business or markets generally. Instead, countervailing values need to be refurbished in order to restore balance. For example, the value of profit making works best if it is tempered by value of fairness. More generally, markets work best when they operate within high containment walls of laws, norms, and countervailing values. Balance also refers to the different parts of society, which requires that markets be kept in their proper place: they work best for determining the distribution of private goods, like iPhones and detergent, and not as the decision rule for achieving public ends, such as the rehabilitation of criminals or saving lives through organ transplants.

The need for balance applies especially to corporations: they work best if tethered to social goals. After all, they are not natural entities, not individuals, in possession of a set of natural rights. Instead, it is wise to remember that corporations are legal constructs that provide investors with a set of benefits: limited liability, the ability to pool capital, and legal continuity, among others. Given that these are advantages bestowed by society, it is reasonable to expect that those who benefit have an obligation to act responsibly and provide society with a set of benefits in return, including employment, decent wages, and paying a fair share of taxes. In some ways, then, what is needed is a reversal of the status quo. Instead of institutions with rights and no responsibilities to society, corporations should be remade into entities with an agreed upon set of responsibilities, with no natural rights.

Ultimately, then, building a new regulatory structure begins with breathing life back into the antimonopolist critique of large corporations and making direct appeals to the values that their unfettered operation threatens. Of course, the solution favored by the first antimonopolists, the elimination of the large corporation, is not a realistic option. However, the reformist strain of antimonopolism that animated the most successful efforts to regulate big business needs only to be revived.

Proposals for a New Regulatory Structure: The Role of Government

Economic Regulations (Antitrust)

The ability to control large corporations starts with the ability to rein in financial corporations, since their short-term orientation has substantially spilled over to nonfinancial corporations and minimized their ability to act responsibly. Appropriately then, given the history of the antimonopoly movement, a new regulatory structure must draw from the antitrust, small is better, tradition for proposals. A good place to start is with banks. Simply put, since the gutting of the Glass-Steagal Act, banks have gotten too big, and the Dodd-Frank Act of 2010 did not include provisions that would stop, let alone reverse, the trend toward bigness. One reform proposal worth serious consideration is the Safe, Accountable, Fair, and Efficient (SAFE) Banking Act of 2012. This bill would place strict limits on banks' deposit and non-deposit liabilities, along with a leverage limit. Together with a provision that would require that banks hold more capital to buffer against losses, the impact of the bill would likely shrink the mega banks.[40]

Economic Regulations (Stock Ownership)

Of course, by itself, reducing the size of banks would not necessarily eliminate the financialization of nonfinancial corporations, which as discussed above, is not conducive to socially responsible behavior. A stakeholder orientation, especially where socially responsible practices are voluntary, requires a long-term time horizon on the part of a corporation's executives. This is less likely where the singular focus on the current price of a company's stock leads to the hyper mobility of institutional shareholders. It will be important, then, for fund managers to once again become long-term owners of large corporations. This is clearly a complicated question, and any solution will be multifaceted—and thus beyond the scope of this current review. In general terms, however, this will include changes in securities regulation and corporate governance. It would also help to increase the power of a corporation's chief stakeholder, its workers, a topic discussed below. In terms of taxes, the current structure should be changed to provide incentives for long-term ownership (e.g., lower capital gains tax rate for stock held for a longer period of time) and disincentives for more speculative, short-term ownership (e.g., much higher capital gains tax rate for stock briefly held).[41]

Social Regulations

In building a new regulatory structure, it is also important to avoid the fragility of the previous one. This suggests that a more stable regulatory structure begins with strengthening the pillar of mandated responsibility. What remains of socially responsible practices today, whether it is workplace or environmental protections, falls largely in the category of social regulations. Indeed, in the twentieth century, whether it was a shorter workweek, safer working conditions, cleaner air, or reclaimed waterways, government regulation deserved the lion's share of credit. This follows from the tendency that once regulations are passed, they are hard to rescind. While this is due in part to the fact that regulations acquire vested interests that over time protect them, the persistence of social regulations is largely attributable to their popularity with voters.

The case for an enhanced role for government is strengthened by the twenty-first-century economy. The long-term trend toward an increasingly global economy with greater competition appears to be irreversible. This fact only reinforces the case against the new CSR and its exclusive reliance upon voluntary initiatives, especially since the old CSR was in many ways dependent upon effective governance structures, especially oligopolies. These structures, in turn, allowed large corporations to control their economic environments and thus sustain profits over an extended period of time to fund CSR practices. This state of affairs is not likely to be reproduced, and the more uncertain economic environment that has replaced it will continue to tempt many to take the low road. It thus falls first to government to ensure greater responsibility.

In the political climate that has existed since the Reagan administration, new corporate mandates have been difficult to pass. However, the political climate has been known to change. This will become more likely if progress is made on the ideological front, and where the groundwork is laid over time to create pressure for new regulations. Starting from the premise that workers remain the main target and beneficiary of more responsible practices, workplace regulations, especially those that are family friendly, would be a good place to start—these have the additional benefit of allowing appeals to pro-family values. With the labor force participation at 71 percent for all mothers, and 61 percent for mothers with children under the age of three in 2011, parents continue to struggle to blend work and family and would be receptive to new regulations that would help them do so.[42] For example, while it took a long time for the United States to finally pass the Family and Medical Leave Act of 1993, which allows workers to take up to twelve weeks off at the birth of a child, it would be very helpful, especially for low-wage parents, if the United States joined the rest of its peer group of nations and required that some or all of this was paid. Another example involves part-time work. Because most part-time workers choose shorter hours to accommodate other demands, like family and education, which we also presumably value, most would no doubt consider it fair if such work was entitled to at least prorated employee benefits such as health insurance.

Another area in need of new proposals is the environment. In recent years, most of the discussion of issues like air pollution has been dominated by those advocating the use of markets to solve problems. Generally, recommendations center on establishing a market for the sale and trading of pollution permits. While market incentives may be a useful tool in the fight against pollution, much of this advocacy reveals an excessive faith in markets, the belief that they should exist for everything, and that they constitute a panacea for all problems. Given the strength of this market ideology, some reformers support a market for permits largely because of the belief that it is the only proposal that stands a chance of overcoming business opposition.

It should be recalled, however, that cleaner air and clearer water resulted from regulations, not markets. While it has been and will probably always be true that businessmen will oppose any new regulation, advocates of governmental action need to make the case that not only are regulations needed, but that America has continued to prosper, even as the number of regulations has grown. One reason for this is that regulations place all businesses that are subject to them on the same, even playing field. If regulations increase the costs of production, all are in the same position; some of the increased cost will no doubt be passed along to consumers, but this would hold for all in an industry. Furthermore, increased costs also spur innovation and new non-polluting technologies, which generate new jobs.

To the extent that increased costs related to regulations will disadvantage American corporations with international competitors that are not subject to the same or comparable regulations, the advocacy of regulations will necessitate support for stronger international standards and enforcement. This is emphatically the case with respect to the problem of global warming. Hopefully, the support for greater mandated responsibility will help the country overcome the allergy it acquired in recent decades to international bodies and agreements, and allow the United States to reassume a position of world leadership on issues like pollution.

The Welfare State and Private Welfare

As the book has chronicled, the United States developed a unique system of private welfare, featuring health insurance and pensions that relied heavily upon CSR. What should be the role of private welfare in the twenty-first century? The Affordable Care Act of 2010 accomplished many things, and with its various provisions it brought the country closer to universal health care coverage. However, it neither established a single (government) payer system, nor did it include an employer mandate, opting for an individual mandate in its place. Instead, it requires employers with at least fifty employees that do not provide health insurance as a benefit to pay a fee for any employee who receives a federal insurance subsidy. Since the impact of this provision will take years to determine, it is still unclear how this will affect what basically remains a form of CSR. While one possibility is that the likelihood of paying huge fees will encourage more employers to offer health insurance, another is that some employers who currently offer health insurance will find that paying government fees is cheaper, and as a result, drop the benefit. Over the longer haul, it may be that between the expansion of Medicaid and growing numbers of employers opting to pay fines, employers will finally be relieved of the responsibility.

With respect to pensions, it was noted above that not only has there been a downward trend for corporations offering a pension, so that less than half of American workers are now covered by a private pension, but the typical plan offered by employers today is "defined contribution," in which the risk of a plan has shifted to employees. For a couple of reasons, the problem of adequate retirement income is likely to worsen in coming years. First, the leading edge of the baby boomer generation has reached retirement age, and the current debate over Social Security is almost exclusively about cutting benefits or raising FICA taxes, and not about raising benefits. In other words, the importance of having a private pension is only likely to increase. It will be important, then, to once again advocate reforms that would require employers to both offer, and make contributions toward, an employee's portable retirement account. One proposal worth resurrecting is the idea of a Minimum Universal Pension System (MUPS) that was recommended by the President's Commission on Pension Policy in 1981.[43] With funding to come from mandatory employer contributions, the Commission recommended a minimum 3 percent payroll contribution as the minimum benefit standard.[44]

Government's Role of Contractor

The government also has other tools at its disposal to engender socially responsible practices in corporations. One of these is the power of its considerable purse strings. As discussed in earlier chapters, America

326

has a long tradition of contracting with the private sector to provide the goods and services budgeted for, whether it is with an aircraft manufacturer to build a jet fighter, a construction company to build an interstate highway, custodial service to clean a public building, or an office supply company to provide desks and paper. In 2010, this type of federal spending added up to roughly $528 billion.[45] One way of encouraging greater CSR would be to give preference to contractors that meet a set of CSR benchmarks, or score higher on a list of preferred practices.

Of course, the precedents for this practice go back decades. The Davis-Bacon Act of 1931 required that federal contractors pay the local prevailing wage on public-works projects. Arguably the best precedent is the executive order issued by President Johnson in 1965 to use government contracts to encourage greater diversity in the companies' workforces. Though controversial, affirmative action has been very effective in reducing institutionalized racial, and especially gender, discrimination. There could be a point system whereby the government favors companies that adhere to a set of responsible practices. For example, companies could receive points if they provide health insurance and pensions to employees, pay their fair share of taxes, and maybe more radically, have some form of worker representation on the board of directors; points could also be subtracted for violations of FLSA, EPA, OSHA, and NLRA laws.

In anticipation of the likely business objection that this would be coercive, it can be argued that private companies are certainly not entitled to government work. They can choose not to accept government work and operate only with other private-sector customers. But if they do choose to accept government work, the government as consumer has a right to adopt ethical standards just like any other consumer. In fact, if anyone should be an ethical consumer, it is the government. Since in a democracy government is meant to represent all interests, it should act as both a model employer and consumer.

This use of the federal government's purse strings to encourage greater CSR would hopefully spill over to the local and state levels, where the criteria for receiving economic development incentives could come to include CSR standards. To be sure, unlike the federal government, states and localities are constrained by competitive federalism, which gives corporations the leverage to avoid CSR conditions on the benefits they receive. However, a number of localities (e.g., San Francisco, Santa Fe) have passed living wage ordinances, and these apply to all employers.

Federal Incorporation

The one reform that would arguably have the greatest impact upon containing corporations would be to federalize the incorporation process, thus replacing state charters, at least for corporations that operate in more than one state. Incorporation in the nineteenth century evolved from special charters issued by states, where a public purpose was usually articulated among other conditions, to general incorporation statutes, where states ended up competing to win a corporation's official headquarters. The practical result of this form of competitive federalism was a race to the bottom, where public purpose was bought off by incorporation fees and taxes earned by revenue-strapped states. This race was ultimately won by Delaware, which because of its low taxes and few regulations is now the legal home for over 50 percent of all publicly traded companies in the United States, including more than 60 percent of the Fortune 500. Of course, though headquartered there, most Delaware corporations have no operational presence in the state.[46]

As reviewed in the book, proposals for federal incorporation go back to the Progressive Era. As the harmful effects of state incorporation have long been recognized, federal incorporation has been promoted as a way of removing the leverage that corporations now have in playing states off one another in order to achieve the most business-friendly incorporation statute. Of course, opponents will argue that federal incorporation usurps the power of the states. But proponents will surely be standing upon firmer constitutional ground. As almost all large corporations operate across state lines, federal incorporation would clearly fall within the purview of the Commerce Clause of the Constitution, which gives Congress the power to regulate commerce among the states.

With federal charters, the government would be in a position to establish basic parameters to encourage greater social responsibility. This might begin with the basic statement that in exchange for the legal benefits that corporations render their investors and managers, they have an obligation to the public, not only to abide by laws and regulation of the land, but also to weigh the interests of all of a corporation's stakeholders in the pursuit of profit. With this one statement, the obsessive focus of the shareholder-only orientation would lessen. Over time, Congress could add further minimal standards regarding particular stakeholders, such as workers and local communities.

Rescind Citizens United

Of course, little progress in passing new regulations, or even proposing transformative reforms, is likely unless the role of money in elections, and especially corporate money, is reduced. Specifically, until the floodgates opened by the Supreme Court's Citizens United decision, through which corporate money now courses into American elections, are closed, strengthening government mandates for corporations will be very difficult. Since the thoroughness of the Court's majority opinion rules out small, or politically easy fixes, only two difficult options are available: a constitutional amendment or a new ruling in which the Court overturns itself. The degree of difficulty of each can be measured by the fact that after the first ten amendments were passed as the Bill of Rights, only twenty-seven amendments have been added in the nation's over 225-year history, while the Court, by one count, has reversed an earlier decision only seven times.[47]

In 2011, two resolutions to amend the Constitution were introduced in the Senate. The first, offered by Senator Bernie Sanders of Vermont, targeted corporations by adding language to the Constitution that states that corporations are not persons with rights equal to people, that they are subject to regulation, that they may not make campaign contributions, and that Congress and the states have the power to regulate campaign finances. The second, offered by Senator Tom Udall of New Mexico, makes no mention of corporations, but instead explicitly asserts that Congress and the states have the power to regulate the raising and spending of money in both federal and state elections. Though an attempt to amend the Constitution is obviously a long shot, it is important to try, not only because no other direct option is available, but because such an effort can serve as a rallying point in a new antimonopoly campaign against large corporations.[48]

The odds of the Supreme Court reversing itself are also slight. Furthermore, this is a course of action that relies upon individuals who are not directly accountable to voters and do not directly respond to appeals of reformers. However, one very public way of recontesting the large corporation is to place the Citizens United decision front and center in any future confirmation hearings for nominations to the high court. Questioning nominees about the ruling might not only be revealing about their orientation to corporations and the business sector generally, a side benefit would be greater publicity for the efforts to amend the Constitution.

Slowing the Revolving Doors of Government

As important as reducing the influence of big business on elections is the need to lessen corporations' ability to weaken regulatory enforcement. As the book has chronicled, the administrative capacity of the federal government has always lagged behind the ability of businesses to weaken and circumvent enforcement, if not capture regulatory agencies. This is both a funding issue and an issue of personnel. Not much can be done if and when Congress cuts funding for regulatory enforcement, other than changing the political climate that allows this to happen. However, the caliber of regulatory personnel can be strengthened through efforts to slow, if not halt, the revolving door through which regulators find employment with companies and in industries that had been within their oversight purview.

Before suggesting concrete reforms, it is important to recognize there are multiple revolving doors that connect public- and private-sector employment. In addition to the door marked "regulator to regulated," these include government officials engaged in contracting with the private sector who then gain employment with a government contractor, and millionaire businessmen who finance their own campaigns for public office. The one featured earlier in the chapter, the booming trend of former politicians becoming lobbyists for private concerns, is particularly troubling. Of course, since these are revolving doors, there is also the problem of private-industry personnel finding employment in regulatory agencies or congressional committees. The common problems that all of these transitions pose include regulators and politicians "cashing in" on their government service. This, in turn, raises questions about the quality of decision making by individuals in advance of such moves, the loss of needed government expertise, and increased instances of conflicts of interest. In short, these intersections between public and private compromise the ability of government to mandate socially responsible practices for corporations.

The overarching goal of revolving-door reforms is to thicken the walls between public- and private-sector employment. Fortunately, laws passed in the wake of scandals in years past, together with decades-long efforts to professionalize public service, have put in place reforms that can be built upon. One of these has been the inclusion of "cooling-off period" clauses in the employment contracts of both Executive Branch senior staff and politicians entering the private sector. These should be extended to include more years. For example, for the Executive Branch, the one-year cooling-off period for former senior staff representing the interests of their new private employer before members of their former department should be extended to two or more years. This clause should also be extended to more midlevel staff. Furthermore, a cooling-off period should also be enacted for senior staff engaged in formulating policy who then seek employment with contractors that may benefit from such policies. In the case of the Legislative Branch, the two-year period of no contact for Senators turned lobbyists should be extended to at least four years, while the one-year period for House members and senior legislative staff should be extended to at least three years and broadened to apply to lower-level staff as well. It will also be important to continue to upgrade the status and pay of government regulators, and servants generally, so that the temptation to enter a revolving door is lowered and the prospects of a career of public service are raised.[49]

Strengthening Ethics Offices

Given the probability that revolving doors cannot be removed but traffic only slowed, and given the fact that interfaces between government and the business sector will always exist, and thus pose the potential for conflicts of interest and corruption, it is important to strengthen ethics compliance for both the Executive and Legislative Branches. Fortunately, again, the building blocks are already in place. In 1989, the Office of Government Ethics became a separate agency with the task of overseeing ethics compliance for the Executive Branch. Giving it some enforcement powers could strengthen this office. For the House, the Office of Congressional Ethics was created in 2008. It could be strengthened first by extending its charge to include the Senate, and by giving it subpoena powers.[50]

Proposals for a New Regulatory Structure: The Role of Unions

It is hard to examine the prospects of reforming negotiated responsibility without becoming pessimistic. As reviewed above, only 11.3 percent of the labor force belonged to a union in 2012, and only 6.6 percent of workers in the private sector carried a union card. But given the institutional importance of unions as a counterweight to business, and given the important role unions have played in both directly writing responsible practices into contracts and indirectly promoting greater CSR through union threat, reformers have no choice but to try and rebuild this pillar of the regulatory structure for corporations.

There is also reason for hope, for while few American workers currently belong to unions, most express a desire to belong to one. In a 2005 Hart Research Associates survey, 53 percent of nonunion workers reported that they would vote for a union if given the chance. This is up significantly from the 30 percent nonunion workers who reported such an inclination in a comparable Harris poll conducted in 1984, and up as well from the 39 percent who did so in an earlier Hart survey conducted in 1994. In other words, just as CSR at the workplace has declined, the percentage of workers who express a desire for a union has increased. In fact, if all workers who wanted a union had one (nonunion workers who report a desire for a union plus current union members who would vote to keep the union they currently have), the unionization rate in the United States would be 58 percent.[51]

Reforming Labor Law

Clearly, there is a disconnect between the desire for unions and the current reality. Much of this gap can be explained by the business community's fervid commitment to union avoidance in the last thirty years. Spending millions of dollars each year, large corporations employ a full tool kit of tactics, many illegal, to keep unions at bay. These include threatening workers with dire consequences should an organizing drive result in a union election victory, firing union organizers, feeding their captive audience workforce with antiunion propaganda, using legal appeals to delay and contest elections, and stalling negotiations even when unions win a representation battle.

Current labor law has proved ineffective in the face of obdurate antiunionism. As a result, proposals that make it easier to translate the desire of union representation into reality have been at the top of the agenda for union leaders for years. One such proposal is the Employee Free Choice Act (EFCA), which was first introduced to Congress in 2007. The first of its three basic provisions would greatly simplify the election process. Instead of the law's current two-step process of organizing workers to first petition the NLRB, and then the board holding an election at a later time, the central provision of the act would give workers a "card check" option. This would automatically grant union recognition when a majority of workers sign a card indicating support for a union. The act would also strengthen what are currently weak penalties for employer violations. In addition to reinstatement and back pay for union supporters who are fired, the act would add triple damages, which could be applied to other labor-law violations as well. Lastly, the act would require arbitration when contracts are not hammered out within the first 120 days of recognition. While the bill passed the House that year, it was filibustered in the Senate. The bill was reintroduced in the following Congress in 2009, but encountered stronger opposition and was never voted upon. But because the simple changes of EFCA would likely help unions tremendously, reformers should continue to advocate that the bill be introduced and passed.[52]

An alternative approach to labor-law reform was proposed in *Why Labor Organizing Should Be a Civil Right*. Richard D. Kahlenberg and Moshe Z. Marvit argue that the right to organize a labor union, without employer discrimination, should be added to the protective cover of Title VII of the Civil Rights Act. After all, the First Amendment protects the freedom of association, while the 1948 Universal Declaration of Human Rights, to which the United States is a signatory, recognizes the right to form trade unions. As a nation that treasures its basic rights, appeals to fundamental rights have obvious ideological advantages, and given the track record of the Civil Rights Act in reducing employment discrimination on the basis of race, sex, religion, and national origin, the inclusion of those seeking union membership would surely help to reduce the current discrimination against union supporters.[53]

Either of these approaches to removing employer obstacles to organizing workers would likely provide the critical advantage needed to prevail in the most important ongoing organizing effort, the campaign to unionize the 1.4 million employees of Walmart. As seen above, Walmart is not only the model of a low-wage, dead-end job employer, but also in the vanguard of antiunion resistance. Successful unionization here would be tremendously significant. With a huge foothold in retail, a successful Walmart campaign would become a model for efforts to organize at other big-box stores. It would also reveal a hidden advantage to service-sector unionization generally. Unlike manufacturers who can avoid unions by relocating abroad or outsourcing, once unionized, a large retailer has no such option. The same is true for other large service employers, like fast-food restaurants and hotels. In short, service employers are tied to their locales and have nowhere to run, as success depends upon customers walking through domestic doors. Consequently, gains in this sector or the economy are more likely to remain permanent. Not surprisingly, in addition to the Walmart campaign, unions are currently involved in large-scale efforts to organize workers at McDonalds and Sheraton Hotels.

Political Unionism

Though institutionally weakened, unions still possess the organizational infrastructure that makes them the logical candidate to lead the movement to recontest the large corporation. Given the huge majority of Americans who believe that corporations have too much power, the time would seem ripe for unions to engage in ideological battle by crafting a message that unions represent the one institution that can give workers a democratic voice in the workplace and achieve the fair and just treatment of employees. As this would break unions out of the narrow confines of business unionism, it would put them back on a path of a broader political unionism, once represented by labor leaders like Walter Reuther, where unions show their solidarity and support for the progressive causes of all workers. In fact, many unions have already moved in this direction by demonstrating support for causes like immigration reform.

Unions also need to broaden their political activities. Of course, though business unionism became the dominant orientation of the American labor movement decades ago, American unions never really abandoned political unionism. Each election cycle, unions spend millions of dollars in an effort to elect labor-friendly politicians. At the same time they lobby Congress to pass both union and worker-friendly legislation, whether it is proposals like EFCA or raising the minimum wage. However, with a diminishing base, the funds available to unions cannot compete with the dollars spent by the business community to defeat both union and worker-friendly initiatives.

But unions could strengthen their ability to advocate within the halls of Congress. One way of doing this would be to create a lobbying organization that represents the interests of all workers, along the lines of an AARP, which represents the interests of all older Americans. Membership could comprise all of the members of sponsoring unions, as well as nonunion workers for whom a low-cost, individual membership is created. A promising model exists in Working America, the organization created by the AFL-CIO in 2003, which had grown to over three million members by 2012.[54] Like AARP, Working America offers a set of selective benefits for members, including auto insurance and credit counseling. However, unlike AARP, the vast majority of Americans had never heard of it. Again, using the AARP model, greater name recognition can be gained through newsletters, magazines, and advertising.

Work Councils

Unions also need to rethink political unionism at the level of the workplace. Currently, the NLRA makes it difficult for employers to establish employee participation committees, since the experience with company unions and employee representation plans during the 1920s and 1930s was that they were employer-dominated groups that were frequently adopted with the express purpose of avoiding unions. However, the institution of work councils, where employees elect their own representatives to joint labor-management committees in order to discuss not only issues of quality and productivity but also working conditions and employee well-being, are quite common in America's peer group of nations. A carefully crafted proposal could insist that any such employee-representation plan, whether in a nonunion or union establishment, involve employees choosing their own representatives. This would dovetail with the goal of promoting greater democracy in the workplace and legitimizing worker input into the decision-making process of corporations. It could thus serve as a slow but needed antidote to the absolutism of managerial prerogatives.[55]

Proposals for a New Regulatory Structure: The Role of CSR

Despite the earlier rejection of the new CSR as the sole solution to the problems of large corporation, CSR still has a place in the new regulatory structure being recommended. After all, both welfare capitalism and corporate philanthropy have long traditions. But it is very important to understand the more limited role these practices should play in any new structure. Controlling large corporations is just too important to leave to chance. While not a central role, CSR has an important support role to play, one that can be amplified through government incentives. For example, in the case of the market for virtue, the government can expand its efforts to provide incentives to consumers to purchase, for example, energy-efficient autos. As was discussed above, the government can also use the power of its purse strings to encourage socially responsible practices. In the case of socially responsible investing, the government, through federal charters can liberate corporations from the stranglehold of the shareholder-only orientation.

Re-tethering the large corporation will be a daunting task. None of the reform proposals just offered will be easy to legislate or implement, and the odds against each are high—at least for now. However, there is no reason to believe that we have reached some end state in our political culture where the large corporation is somehow inoculated from society's efforts to control it. Many responsible practices that are now taken for granted, whether it is the forty-hour week or hiring women in managerial positions, once faced extremely long odds. What is certainly true is that the large corporation will remain impervious to change unless demands for reform are made.

Notes

1. Fortune, "The Fortune 500," *Fortune* 165, no. 7 (May 21, 2012), F-31.
2. Greta R. Krippner, *Capitalizing on Crisis: The Political Origins of the Rise of Finance* (Cambridge, Massachusetts: Harvard University Press, 2011), 28.
3. Ibid.
4. Investopedia, "Introduction to Institutional Investing," Accessed March 4, 2012, http://www.investopedia.com/articles/financial-theory/11/introduction-institutional-investing.asp; Donald Tomaskovic-Devey and Ken-Hou Lin, "Income Dynamics, Economic Rents, and the Financialization of the U.S. Economy," *American Sociological Review* 76, no. 4 (August 2011): 543.
5. Tomaskovic-Devey and Ken-Hou Lin, "Income Dynamics," 546.
6. Ibid.; Raffaele Della Croce, Fiona Stewart, and Juan Yermo, "Promoting Longer-Term Investment by Institutional Investors: Selected Issues and Policies," *OECD Journal: Financial Market Trends* 2011, no. 1 (2011); Lawrence Mishel and Natalie Sabadish, "CEO Pay and the Top 1%: How Executive Compensation and Financial-Sector Pay Have Fueled Income Inequality," Issue Brief #331, Economic Policy Institute, Washington, DC, May 2, 2012, http://www.epi.org/publication/ib331-ceo-pay-top-1-percent/.
7. Fortune, "The Fortune 500," F-31; Charles Duhigg and Keith Bradsher, "How the U.S. Lost Out on iPhone Work: Apple's Experience Shows Why Jobs are Flowing to China," *New York Times*, January 22, 2012.
8. Gerald F. Davis, *Managed by the Numbers: How Finance Reshaped America* (Oxford, England: Oxford University Press, 2009), 12, 139–140, 155–156.
9. Duhigg and Bradsher, "How the U.S. Lost Out on iPhone Work."
10. Ibid.; Charles Duhigg and David Barboza, "In China, Human Costs are Built Into an iPad," *New York Times*, January 26, 2012.
11. Duhigg and Bradsher, "How the U.S. Lost Out on iPhone Work"; Richard Henderson, "Industry Employment and Output Projections to 2020," *Monthly Labor Review* 185, no. 1 (January 2012): 66.
12. Justin Pritchard, "Miley Cyrus' Toxic Wal-Mart Jewelry Still on Shelves," Associated Press, May 19, 2010, http://www.huffingtonpost.com/2010/05/19/mileys-cyrus-toxic-walmar_n_582020.html; Amy Westervelt, "Target, Walmart, Babies-R-Us Sued Over Toxic Baby Products," *Forbes*, December 6, 2012, http://www.forbes.com/sites/amy-westervelt/2012/12/06/target-walmart-babies-r-us-named-in-legal-action-for-selling-baby-products-containing-cancer-causing-flame-retardant/; Marcus Kabel, "Wal-Mart Blind to Illegal Logging," *Forbes*, December 12, 2007, http://www.corpwatch.org/article.php?id=14853; David Barstow,

"Wal-Mart Hushed Up a Vast Mexican Bribery Case," *New York Times*, April 21, 2012.

13. Ken Jacobs, Dave Graham-Squire, and Stephanie Luce, "Low Wage Policies and Big-Box Retail: How a Higher Wage Standard Would Impact Walmart Workers and Shoppers," Research Brief, University of California, Berkeley, Center For Labor Research and Education, Berkeley, CA, April 2011, http://laborcenter.berkeley.edu/pdf/2011/bigbox_livingwage_policies11.pdf.

14. Steven Greenhouse, "The Part-Time Life, as Hours Shrink and Shift," *New York Times*, October 28, 2012; Tian Luo, Amar Mann, and Richard Holden, "The Expanding Role of Temporary Help Services from 1990 to 2008," *Monthly Labor Review* (August 2010): 3; United States Department of Labor, Bureau of Labor Statistics, "Contingent and Alternative Employment Arrangements, February 2005," July 2005, http://www.bls.gov/news.release/pdf/conemp.pdf.

15. Lawrence Mishel, et al., *The State of Working America*, 12th ed. (Ithaca, New York: IRL Press, 2012), 200–201, 204, 333–334.

16. Human Rights Watch, "Discounting Rights: Wal-Mart's Violation of US Workers' Right to Freedom of Association," *Human Rights Watch* 19, no. 2 (G) (May 2007).

17. United States Department of Labor, Bureau of Labor Statistics, "Union Members—2012," January 2013, http://www.bls.gov/news.release/pdf/union2.pdf; Walmart, *Walmart 2011 Annual Report: Building the New Generation Walmart*, http://stock.walmart.com/annual-reports.

18. Some have used the economics concept of "economic rents" to suggest that those in charge of today's corporations operate to maximize their own rents, i.e., income above what would be expected in a competitive market, while destroying the rents of other actors, especially workers. See Tomaskovic-Devey and Ken-Hou Lin, "Income Dynamics."

19. Lawrence Mishel and Heidi Shierholz, "The Sad But True Story of Wages in America," Issue Brief #297, Economic Policy Institute, Washington, DC, March 14, 2011, http://www.epi.org/publication/ib331-ceo-pay-top-1-percent/; Tim Worstall, "Why Have Corporate Profits Been Rising as a Percentage of GDP? Globalization," *Forbes*, May 2, 2013, http://www.forbes.com/timworstall/2013/05/07/why-have-corporate-profits-been-rising-as-a-percentage-of-gdp-globalization.

20. Mishel and Sabadish, "CEO Pay and the Top 1%"; Timothy Noah, *The Great Divergence: America's Growing Inequality Crisis and What We Can Do About It* (New York: Bloomsbury Books, 2012), chapters 1, 9.

21. Jeffrey Clements, *Corporations Are Not People: Why They Have More Rights Than You Do and What You Can Do About It* (San Francisco: Berrett-Koehler Publishers, Inc., 2012); Roger Parloff, "Why the Outcry of 'Citizens United,'" *Fortune*, February 12, 2010, http://archive.fortune.com/2010/02/11/news/companies/supreme_court_citizens_united.fortune/index.htm.

22. Open Secrets, "Business-Labor Ideology Split in PAC & Individual Donations to Candidates, Parties, Super PACs and Outside Spending Groups" Open Secrets, Center for Responsive Politics, accessed May 28, 2013, http://www.opensecrets.org/overview/blio.php.

23. The Court upheld the requirement for public disclosure for contributions to PACs. As a result some corporations (and other donors), seeking anonymity,

have chosen an indirect route. Public disclosure is still not required for contributions made to what are called 501(c) tax exempt organizations. These "social welfare" and charity groups can receive unlimited contributions and engage in independent electioneering communication, as long they do not spend more than 50 percent of their overall budgets on politics.

24. Open Secrets, "Lobbying," Open Secrets, Center for Responsive Politics, Accessed May 8, 2012, http://www.opensecrets.org/lobby/incdec/php.

25. Revolving Door Working Group, *A Matter of Trust: How the Revolving Door Undermines Public Confidence in Government—and What To Do About It*, Revolving Door Working Group, October 2005, http://www.cleanupwashington.org/documents/RevovDoor.pdf.

26. Ibid., 44.

27. Michael Dolny, "Think Tank Spectrum Revisited: Conservatives Gain Within Still-narrow Spectrum," *Fairness & Accuracy in Reporting*, Accessed June 1, 2012, http://fair.org/extra-online-articles/think-tank- spectrum-revisited/.

28. Tony Carrk, "The Koch Brothers: What You Need to Know About the Financiers of the Radical Right," Center for American Progress Action Fund, April 2011, at http://www.americanprogressaction.org/wp- content/.../04/.../koch_brothers.pdf.

29. Mike McIntire, "Conservative Nonprofit Acts as a Stealth Business Lobbyist," *New York Times*, April 21, 2012; People for the American Way, "ALEC: The Voice of Corporate Special Interests in State Legislatures," People for the American Way, http://www.pfaw.org/rww-in-focus/alec-the-voice-of-corporate-special-interests-state-legislatures.

30. Philip Mattera, et al., "Money for Something: Job Creation and Job Quality Standards in State Economic Development Subsidy Programs," Good Jobs First, *December 2011*, http://www.goodjobsfirst.org/moneyforsomething.

31. Social Investment Forum, "Report on Socially Responsible Investing Trends in the United States, 2010," Social Investment Forum Foundation, http://www.ussif.org/files/Publications/10_Trends_Exec_Summary.pdf.

32. Social Accountability International, Social Accountability 8000, Social Accountability International, 2008 version, http://www.saint.org/index.cfm?fuseaction=Page.View/PageID=1458.

33. David Vogel, *The Market for Virtue: The Potential and Limits of Corporate Social Responsibility* (Washington, DC: Brookings Institution Press, 2006), chapter 2.

34. A corollary assumption is that there is a critical mass of educated employees that expect or demand to work for a socially responsible corporation.

35. Declan Walsh and Steven Greenhouse, "Certified Safe, A Factory in Karachi Still Quickly Burned," *New York Times*, December 12, 2012.

36. Center on Philanthropy at Indiana University, *Giving USA 2012: The Annual Report on Philanthropy for the Year 2011*, 57th Annual Issue, Giving USA Foundation, 2012, http://www.alysterling.com/documents/GUSA2012ExecutiveSummary.pdf.

37. The Justice Department's unsuccessful antitrust case against Microsoft in the 1990s was not driven by popular protest against large corporations.

38. PollingReport.com, "Major Institutions," PollingReport.com, accessed December 8, 2012, http://www.pollingreport.com/institut.htm; Richard B. Freeman, "Do Workers Still Want Unions? More than Ever," Issue Brief

#182, Economic Policy Institute, Washington, DC, February 22, 2007, http://www.sharedprosperity.org/bp182.html.

39. Robert Kuttner, *Everything for Sale: The Virtues and Limits of Markets* (Chicago: University of Chicago Press, 1999); Michael Sandel, *What Money Can't Buy: The Moral Limits of Markets* (New York: Farrar, Straus, and Giroux, 2012).

40. Sherrod Brown, "Brown Introduces Bill to End 'To Big to Fail' Policies, Prevent Mega-Banks form Putting Our Economy at Risk," Senator Sherrod Brown for Ohio, Press Release, May 9, 2012, http://www.brown.senate.gov/newsroom/press/release/brown-introduces-bill-to-end-too big-to-fail-policies-prevent-mega-banks-from-putting-our-economy-at-risk.

41. Croce, Stewart, and Yermo, "Promoting Longer-Term Investment by Institutional Investors"; Gert Wehinger, "Fostering Long-Term Investment and Economic Growth: Summary of a High-Level OECD Financial Roundtable," *OECD Journal: Financial Market Trends* 2011, no. 1 (2011).

42. United States Department of Labor, Bureau of Labor Statistics, "Women in the Labor Force: A Datebook (2008 Edition)," December 2011, http://www.bls.gov/cps/wlfdatebook2011.htm.

43. The Commission was convened by President Carter, and the report was delivered to President Reagan.

44. Social Security Bulletin, "Report of the President's Commission on Pension Policy: Executive Summary," *Social Security Bulletin* 44, no. 5 (May 1981).

45. Ralph Nader, *The Seventeen Solutions: Bold Ideas For Our American Future* (New York: Harper, 2012), 181.

46. Ibid., 143.

47. Ed Grabianowski, "10 Overturned Supreme Court Cases," How Stuff Works, http://money.howstuffworks.com/10-overturned-supreme-court-cases.htm.

48. Bernie Sanders, U.S. Senator for Vermont, "A Petition to Support Saving American Democracy Amendment," Bernie Sanders, Senator for Vermont, Newsroom, July 24, 2012, http://www.sanders.senate.gov/newsroom/recent-business/saving-american-democracy; Charles P. Pierce, "Tom Udall's Bold Solution to Overturn Citizens United," *Esquire*, accessed December 29, 2012, http://www.esquire.com/blogs/politics/tom-udall-citizens-united-amendment-14761989.

49. Revolving Door Working Group, *A Matter of Trust*, 52–58.

50. Ibid.

51. Freeman, "Do Workers Still Want Unions?"

52. Lawrence Mishel, Richard B. Freeman, and Frank Levy, "The Employee Free Choice Act is Needed to Restore Balance in the Labor Market," Economic Policy Institute, Washington, DC, February 24, 2009, http://www.epi.org/publication/prominent_economists_call_for_passage_of_the_employee_free_choice_act/.

53. Richard D. Kahlenberg, and Moshe Z. Marvit, "A Civil Right to Unionize," *New York Times*, February 29, 2012.

54. Working America, "About Working America," Accessed December 28, 2012, http://www.workingamerica.org/membership/about,.

55. Freeman, "Do Workers Still Want Unions?"

Bibliography

Abrams, Frank W. "Management's Responsibilities in a Complex World." *Harvard Business Review* 29, no. 3 (May 1951): 29–34.

Appelbaum, Eileen and Rosemary Batt. *The New American Workplace: Transforming Work Systems in the United States.* Ithaca, New York: IRL Press, 1994.

Arnold, Thurman W. *The Folklore of Capitalism.* New Haven, Connecticut: Yale University Press, 1937.

Auerbach, Jerold S. *Labor and Liberty: The La Follette Committee and the New Deal.* Indianapolis: The Bobbs-Merrill Company, Inc., 1966.

Bachrach, Peter. *The Theory of Democratic Elitism: A Critique.* Boston: Little, Brown and Company, 1967.

Bailey, Stephen Kemp. *Congress Makes a Law: the Story Behind the Employment Act of 1946.* New York: Columbia University Press, 1950.

Bakan, Joel. *The Corporation: The Pathological Pursuit of Profit and Power.* New York: The Free Press, 2005.

Baker, George P. "Beatrice: A Study in the Creation and Destruction of Value." *The Journal of Finance* 47, no. 3 (July 1992): 1081–1119.

Barber, Richard J. *The American Corporation: Its Power, Its Money, Its Politics.* New York: E. P. Sutton & Co., Inc. 1970.

Barstow, David. "Wal-Mart Hushed Up a Vast Mexican Bribery Case." *New York Times,* April 21, 2012.

Bartkus, Barbara R., Sara A. Morris, and Bruce Seifert, "Governance and Corporate Philanthropy: Restraining Robin Hood?" *Business and Society* 41, no. 3 (September 2002): 319–344.

Bates, J. Leonard. "The Teapot Dome Scandal and the Election of 1924." *American Historical Review* 60, no. 2 (January 1955): 303–322.

Bauer, Raymond A. and Dan H. Fenn, Jr. *The Corporate Social Audit.* New York: Russell Sage Foundation, 1972.

Baumol, William J., Alan S. Blinder, and Edward N. Wolff. *Downsizing in America: Reality, Causes, and Consequences.* New York: Russell Sage Foundation, 2003.

Beard, Charles A. "A Five Year Plan for America." *Forum* July 1931.

Bellamy, Edward. *Looking Backward.* New York: Magnum Books, 1968— originally published in 1888.

Berkowitz Edward D. and Kim McQuaid. *Creating the Welfare State: the Political Economy of the 20th Century Reform.* Rev. ed. Lawrence, Kansas: University Press of Kansas, 1992.

Berle, Adolf A. and Gardiner Means. *The Modern Corporation and Private Property*. New York: Macmillan, 1932.

Bernstein, Irving. *The Lean Years: A History of the American Worker, 1920–1933*. Baltimore: Penguin Books, 1960.

———. *Turbulent Years: A History of the American Worker, 1933–1941*. Boston: Houghton Mifflin Company, 1970.

Bernstein, Marver H. "Independent Regulatory Agencies: A Perspective on Their Reform." *The Annals of the American Academy of Political and Social Science* 400 (March 1972): 14–26.

———. *Regulating Business by Independent Commission*. Princeton, New Jersey: Princeton University Press, 1955.

Berry, Jeffrey M. *Lobbying for the People*. Princeton, New Jersey: Princeton University Press, 1977.

Bittelman, Alexander, "Outline for a History of the Communist Party in America." (circa 1923) Published as "Hynes Exhibit No. 4" in *Report of the Special Committee to Investigate Communist Activities*. Washington, DC: Government Printing Office, 1930.

Bittlingmayer, George. "Regulatory Uncertainty and Investment: Evidence from Antitrust Enforcement." *Cato Journal* 20, no. 3 (Winter 2001): 295–309.

Blair, Margaret M. "Financial Restructuring and the Debate about Corporate Governance." In *The Deal Decade: What Takeovers and Leveraged Buyouts Mean for Corporate Governance*, edited by Margaret M. Blair, 1–17. Washington, DC: The Brookings Institution, 1993.

Blair, Margaret and Girish Uppal. *The Deal Decade Handbook*. Washington, DC: The Brookings Institution, 1993.

Blough, Roger M. *Free Man and the Corporation*. New York: McGraw Hill Book Company, Inc., 1959.

Bluestone, Barry and Bennett Harrison. *The Deindustrialization of America: Plant Closings, Community Abandonment, and the Dismantling of Basic Industry*. New York: Basic Books, Inc., Publishers, 1982.

Blumberg, Philip I. *Corporate Responsibility in a Changing Society*. Boston: Boston University School of Law, 1972.

———. *The Megacorporation in American Society: The Scope of Corporate Power*. Englewood, New Jersey: Prentice-Hall, Inc., 1975.

Bowen, Howard R. *Social Responsibilities of the Businessman*. New York: Harper and Row, 1953.

Bowles, Samuel, David M. Gordon, and Thomas E. Weisskopf. *After the Wasteland: A Democratic Economics for the Year 2000*. Armonk, New York: M. E. Sharpe, Inc., 1990.

Bowman, Scott R. *The Modern Corporation and American Political Thought: Law, Power, and Ideology*. University Park Pennsylvania: The Pennsylvania State University Press, 1996.

Brandeis, Louis D. *The Curse of Bigness: Miscellaneous Papers of Louis C. Brandeis*. Edited by Osmond K. Fraenkel. New York: Viking Press, 1934.

———. *Other People's Money and How the Bankers Use It*. Edited by Richard M. Abrams. New York: Harper Torchbooks, 1967—originally published in 1914.

Brandes, Stuart D. *American Welfare Capitalism, 1880–1940*. Chicago: University of Chicago Press, 1970.

Brands, H.W. *The Reckless Decade: America in the 1890s*. Chicago: University of Chicago Press, 1995.

Brecher, Jeremy. *Strike!*. Boston: South End Press, 1972.

Bremmer, Robert H. *American Philanthropy*. 2nd ed. Chicago: University of Chicago Press, 1968.

Brinkley, Alan. *The End of Reform: New Deal Liberalism in Recession and War*. New York: Alfred A. Knopf, 1995.

———. *Voices of Protest: Huey Long, Father Coughlin, and the Great Depression*. New York: Vintage Books, 1983.

Brody, David, ed. *Industrial America in the Twentieth Century*. New York: Thomas Y. Crowell Company, 1967.

———. *Workers in Industrial America: Essays on the 20th Century Struggle*. New York: Oxford University Press, 1979.

Brown, James K. and Seymour Lusterman. *Business and the Development of Ghetto Enterprise*. New York: The Conference Board, 1971.

Brown, Sherrod. "Brown Introduces Bill to End 'To Big to Fail' Policies, Prevent Mega-Banks form Putting Our Economy at Risk." Senator Sherrod Brown for Ohio, Press Release, May 9, 2012. http://www.brown.senate.gov/newsroom/press/release/brown-introduces-bill-to-end-too-big-to-fail-policies-prevent-mega-banks-from-putting-our-economy-at-risk.

Bruchey, Stuart. *The Wealth of the Nation: An Economic History of the United States*. New York: Harper and Row, Publishers, 1988.

Buder, Stanley. *Pullman: An Experiment in Industrial Order and Community Power, 1880–1930*. New York: Oxford University Press, 1967.

Budgett Meakin, Budgett. *Model Factories and Villages: Ideal Conditions of Labour and Housing*. London: T. Fisher Unwin, 1905.

Buhle, Paul. *Taking Care of Business: Samuel Gompers, George Meany, Lane Kirkland, and the Tragedy of American Labor*. New York: Monthly Review Press, 1999.

Burns, Arthur Robert. *The Decline of Competition: A Study of the Evolution of American Industry*. New York: McGraw-Hill Book Company, Inc., 1936.

Business Roundtable. *Statement on Corporate Governance*. Washington, DC: Business Roundtable, 1997.

Business Week. "Executive pay." March 30, 1992.

———. "The Pain of Downsizing." May 8, 1994.

Butler, Arthur D. *Labor Economics and Institutions*. New York: The Macmillan Company, 1961.

Byrne, John A. "The Pain of Downsizing: What it's Really Like to Live Through the Struggle to Remake a Company." *Business Week*, May 9, 1994.

California Public Employees Retirement System. *Why corporate governance today?* California Public Employees Retirement System, Sacramento, CA., 1995.

Campbell, John L., J. Rogers Hollingsworth, and Leon N. Lindberg, eds. *Governance of the American Economy*. New York: Cambridge University Press, 1991.

Cappelli, Peter. *The New Deal at Work: Managing the Market-Driven Workforce.* Boston: Harvard Business School Press, 1999.

Carrk, Tony. "The Koch Brothers: What You Need to Know About the Financiers of the Radical Right." Center for American Progress Action Fund, April 2011. http://www.americanprogressaction.org/wp- content/.../04/.../koch_brothers.pdf.

Carson, Rachel. *Silent Spring.* London: Hamish Hamilton, 1963.

Cashman, Sean Dennis. *America in the Gilded Age: From the Death of Lincoln to the Rise of Theodore Roosevelt.* 3rd ed. New York: New York University Press, 1993.

Center on Philanthropy at Indiana University, *Giving USA 2012: The Annual Report on Philanthropy for the Year 2011,* 57th Annual Issue, Giving USA Foundation, 2012. http://www.alysterling.com/documents/GUSA2012ExecutiveSummary.pdf.

Chamberlain, Neil W. *The Union Challenge to Management Control.* New York: Archon Books, 1967—originally published in 1948.

Chandler, Alfred D. Jr. *Scale and Scope: The Dynamics of Industrial Capitalism.* Cambridge, Massachusetts: The Belknap Press of Harvard University Press, 1990.

——. *The Visible Hand: The Managerial Revolution in American Business.* Cambridge, Massachusetts: The Belknap Press of Harvard University Press, 1977.

Chase, Stuart. "A Ten Year Plan for America." *Harper's Magazine,* June 1933.

Chernow, Ron. *Titan: The Life of John D. Rockefeller, Sr.* New York: Random House, 1998.

Clements, Jeffrey. *Corporations Are Not People: Why They Have More Rights Than You Do and What You Can Do About It.* San Francisco: Berrett-Koehler Publishers, Inc., 2012.

Cochran, Thomas C. *Basic History of Business.* Princeton, New Jersey: Princeton University Press, 1959.

——. *Business in American Life: A History.* New York: McGraw-Hill Book Company, 1972.

Cohen, Lizabeth. *Making a New Deal: Industrial Workers in Chicago, 1919–1939.* Cambridge, England: Cambridge University Press, 1990.

Cohen, Sanford. *Labor in the United States.* 3rd ed. Columbus, Ohio: Charles E. Merrill Publishing Company, 1970.

Cohn, Jules. *The Conscience of the Corporations: Business and Urban Affairs, 1967–1970.* Baltimore: The Johns Hopkins Press, 1971.

Commission on Industrial Relations. *Final Report of the Commission on Industrial Relations.* Washington, DC: Barnard & Miller Print, 1915.

Commission on Private Philanthropy and Public Needs. *Giving in America: Toward a Stronger Voluntary Sector.* New York: Commission on Private Philanthropy and Public Needs, 1975.

Committee for Economic Development, Research and Policy Committee. *Social Responsibilities of Business Corporations: A Statement on National Policy.* New York: Committee for Economic Development, 1971.

Commons, John R., David A. Saposs, Helen L. Sumner, E. B. Mittelman, H. E. Hoagland, John B. Andrews, and Selig Perlman. *History of Labour in the United States, Volume II*. New York: The Macmillan Company, 1926.

Cordiner, Ralph J. *New Frontiers for Professional Managers*. New York: McGraw-Hill Book Company, Inc., 1956.

Cox, Edward F., Robert C. Fellmeth, and John E. Schulz. *The Nader Report on the Federal Trade Commission*. New York: Grove Press, Inc., 1969.

Crocker, Olga L., Cyril Charney, and Johnny Sik Leung Chiu. *Quality Circles: A Guide to Participation and Productivity*. New York: A Mentor Book, New American Library, 1984.

Croly, Herbert. *The Promise of American Life*. Indianapolis: Bobbs-Merrill, Company, Inc., 1965—originally published in 1909.

Curtin, Edward R. *White-Collar Unionization, Personnel Policy Study No. 220*. New York: National Industrial Conference Board, Inc., 1970.

Cyphers, Christopher. *The National Civic Federation and the Making of a New Liberalism, 1900–1915*. Westport, Connecticut: Greenwood Publishing Group, 2002.

Dale, Charles V. "Federal Affirmative Action Law: A Brief History." Congressional Research Service Report for Congress. September 13, 2005. http://fpc.state.gov/documents/organization/53577.pdf.

Davis, Gerald F. *Managed by the Numbers: How Finance Reshaped America*. Oxford, England: Oxford University Press, 2009.

Davis, Gerald F., Kristina Diekmann, and Catherine H. Tinsley. "The Decline and Fall of the Conglomerate Firm in the 1980s: The Deinstitutionalization of an Organizational Form." *American Sociological Review* 59, no. 4 (August 1994): 547–570.

Davis, Gerald F. and Suzanne K. Stout. "Organization Theory and the Market for Corporate Control: A Dynamic Analysis of the Characteristics of Large Takeover Targets, 1980–1990." *Administrative Science Quarterly* 37, no. 4 (December 1992): 605–633.

DeLeon, Solon and Nathan Fine, eds. *The American Labor Year Book 1925, Volume VI*. New York: Labor Research Department of the Rand School of Social Science, 1926. http://www.marxists.org/history/usa/eam/other/cppa/cppa.html.

Della Croce, Raffaele, Fiona Stewart, and Juan Yermo. "Promoting Longer-Term Investment by Institutional Investors: Selected Issues and Policies." *OECD Journal: Financial Market Trends* 2011, no. 1 (2011): 1–20.

Democratic Party Platforms. "Democratic Party Platform of 1912." June 25, 1912. Online by Gerhard Peters and John T. Woolley, The American Presidency Project. http://www.presidency.ucsb.edu/ws/?pid=29590.

Denning, Steve. "Don't Blame Green for GE's Problems." *Forbes*, March 1, 2011. http://www.forbes.com/sites/stevedenning/2011/03/01/dont-blame-green-for-ges-problems/.

DiNatale, Marissa. "Characteristics of and Preference for Alternative Work Arrangements." *Monthly Labor Review* 124, no. 3 (March 2001): 28–49.

Dolny, Michael. "Think Tank Spectrum Revisited: Conservatives Gain Within Still-narrow Spectrum." *Fairness & Accuracy in Reporting*. Accessed June 1, 2012. http://fair.org/extra-online-articles/think-tank- spectrum-revisited/.

Donner, Frederic G. *The World-Wide Industrial Enterprise: Its Challenges and Promise*. New York: McGraw-Hill Book Company, 1967.

Dubofsky, Melvyn. *Industrialism and the American Worker: 1865–1920*. 3rd ed. Wheeling, Illinois: Harlan Davidson, Inc., 1996.

Dubofsky, Melvyn and Foster Rhea Dulles. *Labor in America: A History*. 7th ed. Wheeling, Illinois: Harlan Davidson, Inc., 2004.

Duhigg, Charles and David Barboza. "In China, Human Costs are Built Into an iPad." *New York Times*, January 26, 2012.

Duhigg, Charles and Keith Bradsher. "How the U.S. Lost Out on iPhone Work: Apple's Experience Shows Why Jobs are Flowing to China." *New York Times*, January 22, 2012.

Dulles, Foster Rhea and Melvyn Dubofsky, *Labor in America: A History*. 5th ed. Arlington Heights, Illinois: Harlan Davidson, Inc., 1993.

Editors of Automotive Quarterly Magazine. *General Motors: The First 75 Years of Transportation Products*. Detroit: General Motors Photographic, 1983.

Ehrman, John. *The Eighties: America in the Age of Reagan*. New Haven, Connecticut: Yale University Press, 2005.

Employee Benefit Research Institute. "Employee Databook on Employee Benefits, Chapter 4: Participation in Employee Benefits Programs." Employee Benefits Research Institute, updated July 2008. http://www.ebri.org/pdf/publications/books/databook/DB.Chapter%2004.pdf.

Equal Employment Opportunity Commission. "The Equal Pay Act of 1963." Equal Employment Opportunity Commission. http://www.eeoc.gov/laws/statutes/epa.cfm.

———. "Milestones in the History of the U.S. Equal Employment Opportunity Commission." Equal Employment Opportunity Commission. Accessed May 22, 2013. http://www.eeoc.gov/abouteeoc/35th/milestones/.

Fama, Eugene F. and Michael C. Jensen. "Separation of Ownership and Control." *Journal of Law and Economics* 26, no.2 (June 1983): 301–325.

Faragher, John Mack, Mari Jo Buhle, Daniel Czitrom, and Susan H. Armitage. *Out of Many: A History of the American People, Volume Two*. 2nd ed. Upper Saddle River, New Jersey: Prentice Hall, 1997.

Faulkner, Harold U. *The Decline of Laissez Faire, 1897–1917*. New York: Harper and Row, Publishers, 1951.

Feis, Herbert. *Labor Relations: A Study Made in the Proctor and Gamble Company*. New York: Adelphi Company Publishers, 1928.

Fine, Sidney. *Laissez Faire and the General Welfare State: A Study of Conflict in American Political Thought, 1865–1901*. Ann Arbor, Michigan: University of Michigan Press, 1964.

Fisher, Burton R. and Stephen B. Withey. *Big Business as the People See It: A Study of a Socio-Economic Institution*. Ann Arbor, Michigan: The Survey Research Center, Institute for Social Research, University of Michigan, 1951.

Fligstein, Neil. *The Transformation of Corporate Control*. Cambridge, Massachusetts: Harvard University Press, 1990.

Flower, Barbara F. *Business Amid Urban Crisis: Private-Sector Approaches to City Problems, Public Affairs Study No. 3.* New York: National Industrial Conference Board, 1968.

Foner, Philip S. *History of the Labor Movement in the United States: Volume I.* New York: International Publishers, 1947.

Forbath, William E. *Law and the Shaping of the American Labor Movement.* Cambridge Massachusetts: Harvard University Press, 1991.

Ford, Robert N. *Motivation Through the Work Itself.* New York: American Management Association, Inc., 1969.

Fortune. "The Fortune 500." 165, no. 7 (May 21, 2012), F-31.

Foster, William Z. *Toward Soviet America.* New York: Coward-McCann, Inc., 1932.

Foulkes, Fred K. *Creating More Meaningful Work.* New York: American Management Association, 1969.

———. *Personnel Policies in Large Nonunion Companies.* Englewood Cliffs, New Jersey: Prentice-Hall, Inc., 1980.

Francia, Peter L. *The Future of Organized Labor in American Politics.* New York: Columbia University Press, 2006.

Fraser, Douglas. "One-Sided Class War." In *Political Directions for Labor,* edited by Kim Moody, 29–32. Detroit: Labor Education & Research Project, 1979.

Freedman, Audrey. *Managing Labor Relations.* New York: The Conference Board, 1979.

———. *The New Look in Wage Policy and Employee Relations.* New York: The Conference Board, 1985.

Freeman, Joseph. *The Soviet Worker: An Account of the Economic, Social, and Cultural Statue of Labor in the USSR.* New York: International Publishers, 1932.

Freeman, Richard B. "Do Workers Still Want Unions? More than Ever." Economic Policy Institute, EPI Briefing Paper #182, February 22, 2007. http://www.sharedprosperity.org/bp182.html.

———. "The Effect of Trade Unionism on Fringe Benefits." *Industrial Labor Relations Review* 34, no. 4 (July 1981): 489–509.

Freeman, Richard B. and James L. Medoff. *What Do Unions Do?.* New York: Basic Books, Inc., 1984.

Friedmann, Wolfgang. "Corporate Power, Government by Private Groups, and the Law." *Columbia Law Review* 57, no. 4 (April 1957): 155–186.

Gage, Beverly. *The Day Wall Street Exploded: A Story of America in its First Age of Terror.* New York: Oxford University Press, 2009.

Galambos, Louis. *Competition & Cooperation: The Emergence of a National Trade Association.* Baltimore: The Johns Hopkins Press, 1966.

Galambos, Louis and Joseph Pratt. *The Rise and Fall of the Corporate Commonwealth: United States Business and Public Policy in the 20th Century.* New York: Basic Books, 1988.

Galbraith, John Kenneth. *American Capitalism: the Concept of Countervailing Power.* Boston: Houghton, Mifflin Company, 1956.

———. *The New Industrial State.* 2nd ed. New York: A Mentor Book from New American Library, 1971.

Ghent, W. J. *Our Benevolent Feudalism.* New York: The Macmillan Company, 1902.

Gilman, Nicholas Paine. *A Dividend to Labor: A Study of Employers' Welfare Institutions.* Boston: Houghton, Mifflin and Company, 1899.

Gordon, David M. *Fat and Mean: The Corporate Squeeze of Americans and the Myth of Managerial Downsizing.* New York: Martin Kessler Books, The Free Press, 1996.

Gorman, Joseph Bruce. *Kefauver: A Political Biography.* New York: Oxford University Press, 1971.

Grabianowski, Ed. "10 Overturned Supreme Court Cases." How Stuff Works. http://money.howstuffworks.com/10-overturned-supreme-court-cases.htm.

Green, Marguerite. *The National Civic Federation and the American Labor Movement 1900–1925.* Westport, Connecticut: Greenwood Press Publishers, 1973—originally published in 1956).

Greenhouse, Steven. "Clinton Won't Appeal Court Rebuff on Workers." *New York Times,* September 12, 1996.

——— . "The Part-Time Life, as Hours Shrink and Shift." *New York Times,* October 28, 2012.

Hacker, Andrew. "Introduction: Corporate America." In *The Corporation Take-Over,* edited by Andrew Hacker, 1–14. Garden City, New York: Anchor Books, Doubleday & Company, Inc., 1964.

Hacker, Jacob S. *The Divided Welfare State.* Cambridge, England: Cambridge University Press, 2002.

Hall, E. K. "The Spirit of Cooperation Between Employer and Employee." In *Industrial America in the Twentieth Century,* edited by David Brody, 87–94. New York: Thomas Y. Crowell Company, 1967.

Halverson, Guy. "A Public Coalition Takes a Bead on Big Business." *The Christian Science Monitor,* February 15, 1980."

Harrington, Christine B. and Lief H. Carter. *Administrative Law and Politics: Cases and Comments.* Washington, DC: CQ Press, 2009.

Harrison, Bennett and Barry Bluestone. *The Great U-Turn: Corporate Restructuring and the Polarizing of America.* New York: Basic Books, 1988.

Hawley, Ellis W. "Herbert Hoover, the Commerce Secretariat, and the Vision of an 'Associative State,' 1921–1928." *Journal of American History* 61 (June 1974): 117–140.

——— . *The New Deal and the Problem of Monopoly.* Princeton, New Jersey: Princeton University Press, 1966.

Hays, Samuel P. *The Response to Industrialism, 1885–1914.* Chicago: The University of Chicago Press, 1957.

Henderson, Richard. "Industry Employment and Output Projections to 2020." *Monthly Labor Review* 185, no. 1 (January 2012): 65–83.

Herman, Edward S. *Corporate Control, Corporate Power.* Cambridge, England: Cambridge University Press, 1981.

Hirsch, Barry T. and David A. Macpherson. "Union Membership and Coverage Database from the Current Population Survey: Note." *Industrial and Labor Relations Review* 56, no. 2 (January 2003): 349–354.

Hirsch, Paul M. "From ambushes to golden parachutes: Corporate takeovers as an instance of cultural framing and institutional integration." *American Journal of Sociology* 91, no. 4 (January 1986): 800–836.

Hofstadter, Richard. "What Happened to the Antitrust Movement." In *The Making of Competition Policy*, edited by Daniel A. Crane and Herbert Hovenkamp, 102–150. New York, Oxford University Press, 2013—revised version of article originally published in 1964.

Holland, Daniel and Stewart C. Myers. "Profitability and Capital Costs for Manufacturing Corporations and all Nonfinancial Corporations." *American Economic Review* 70, No. 2 (May 1980): 320–325.

Houser, Theodore V. *Big Business and Human Values*. New York: McGraw-Hill Book Company, Inc., 1957).

Hoxie, Robert Franklin. *Trade Unionism in the United States*. New York: D. Appleton and Company, 1923.

Hughes, Charles L. *Making Unions Unnecessary*. New York: Executive Enterprises Publications Co., Inc., 1976.

Hughes, Jonathan. *American Economic History*. Glenview, Illinois: Scott, Foresman and Company, 1983.

Human Rights Watch. "Discounting Rights: Wal-Mart's Violation of US Workers' Right to Freedom of Association." *Human Rights Watch* 19, no. 2 (G) (May 2007).

Hymowitz, Carol and Matt Murray. "General Electric's Welch Discusses His Ideas on Motivating Employees." *Wall Street Journal*, June 21, 1999.

Icahn, Carl C. "Leveraged Buyouts: America Pays the Price." *New York Times*, January 29, 1989.

Industrial Commission. *Final Report of the Industrial Commission*. Washington, DC: Government Printing Office, 1902.

Investopedia. "Introduction to Institutional Investing." Investopedia. Accessed March 4, 2012. http://www.investopedia.com/articles/financial-theory/11/introduction-institutional-investing.asp.

Investor Responsibility Research Center. *Investor Responsibility Research Center Background Report—Confidential Voting*. Washington, DC: Investor Responsibility Research Center, 1994.

Jacobs, Ken, Dave Graham-Squire, and Stephanie Luce. "Low Wage Policies and Big-Box Retail: How a Higher Wage Standard Would Impact Walmart Workers and Shoppers." Research Brief, University of California, Berkeley, Center For Labor Research and Education, Berkeley, CA, April 2011. http://laborcenter.berkeley.edu/pdf/2011/bigbox_livingwage_policies11.pdf.

Jacobs, Michael T. *Short-Term America: The Causes and Cures of Our Business Myopia*. Boston: Harvard Business School Press, 1991.

Jacoby, Sanford M. *Employing Bureaucracy: Managers, Unions, and the Transformation of Work in American Industry, 1900–1945*. New York: Columbia University Press, 1985.

——— . *Modern Manors: Welfare Capitalism Since the New Deal*. Princeton, New Jersey: Princeton University Press, 1997.

Janofsky, Michael. "Proctor & Gamble in 12% Job Cut as Brand Names Lose Attraction." *New York Times*, July 16, 1993.

Jefferson, Thomas. "The Present State of Manufacturers (1785)." In *The Philosophy of Manufacturers: Early Debates Over Industrialization in the United States*, edited by Michael Brewster Folsom and Steven D. Lubar, 15–18. Cambridge, Massachusetts: The MIT Press, 1982.

Jensen, Michael C. "Eclipse of the public corporation." *Harvard Business Review* 67, no. 5 (September-October 1989): 61–74.

Jensen, Michael C. and Richard S. Ruback. "The Market for Corporate Control: The Scientific Evidence." *Journal of Financial Economics* 11, nos. 1–4 (April 1983): 5–50.

Josephson, Matthew. *The Robber Barons*. San Diego: A Harvest Book, Harcourt, Inc., 1934.

Kahlenberg, Richard D. and Moshe Z. Marvit. "A Civil Right to Unionize." *New York Times*, February 29, 2012.

Kanigel, Robert. *The One Best Way: Frederick Winslow Taylor and the Enigma of Efficiency*. New York: Viking, 1997.

Katz, Michael. *In the Shadow of the Poorhouse: A Social History of Welfare in America*. New York: Basic Books, 1986.

Katznelson, Ira. *Fear Itself: The New Deal and the Origins of Our Time*. New York: Liveright Publishing Corporation, 2013.

Kaufman, Allen, Lawrence Zacharias, and Marvin Karson. *Managers vs. Owners: The Struggle for Corporate Control in American Democracy*. New York: Oxford University Press, 1995.

Kazin, Michael. *A Godly Hero: The Life of William Jennings Bryan*. New York: Anchor Books, 2006.

Keller, Morton. *Regulating a New Economy: Public Policy and Economic Change in America, 1900–1933*. Cambridge, Massachusetts: Harvard University Press, 1990.

Kennedy, David. *Freedom From Fear: The American People in Depression and War, 1929–1945*. New York: Oxford University Press, 1999.

Keyssar, Alexander. *Out of Work: The First Century of Unemployment in Massachusetts*. Cambridge, England: Cambridge University Press, 1986.

Kirkland, Edward C. *Industry Comes of Age: Business, Labor, and Public Policy, 1860–1897*. New York: Holt, Rinehart and Winston, 1961.

Kochan, Thomas A. *Collective Bargaining and Industrial Relations: From Theory to Policy and Practice*. Homewood, Illinois: Richard D. Irwin, Inc., 1980.

Kochan, Thomas A., Harry C. Katz and Robert B. McKersie. *The Transformation of American Industrial Relations*. Ithaca, New York: ILR Press, 1994.

Kochan, Thomas A. and Thomas A. Barocci. *Human Resource Management and Industrial Relations*. Boston: Little, Brown and Company, 1985.

Kolko, Gabriel. *The Triumph of Conservatism: A Reinterpretation of American History, 1900–1916*. Chicago: Quadrangle Books, 1963.

Krauss, Clifford. "House Passes Bill to Ban Replacement of Strikers." *New York Times*, June 16, 1993.

Krippner, Greta R. *Capitalizing on Crisis: The Political Origins of the Rise of Finance*. Cambridge, Massachusetts: Harvard University Press, 2011.

Kuttner, Robert. *Everything for Sale: The Virtues and Limits of Markets*. Chicago: University of Chicago Press, 1999.

Lamoreaux, Naomi R. *The Great Merger Movement in American Business, 1895–1904*. Cambridge: Cambridge University Press, 1985.

Landis, James M. Report on Regulatory Agencies to the President Elect, US Senate, Committee on the Judiciary, 86th Congress, 2nd session, December 1960. http://www.ratical.org/corporations/linkscopy/LandisRpt1960.pdf.

Latham, Earl. "The Body Politic of the Corporation." In *The Corporation in Modern Society*, edited by Edward S. Mason, 218–236. Cambridge, Massachusetts: Harvard University Press, 1959.

Lauck, W. Jett and Edgar Sydenstricker. *Conditions of Labor in American Industries: A Summarization of the Results of Recent Investigations*. New York: Funk and Wagnalls Company, 1917.

Lescohier, Don D. and Elizabeth Brandeis. *History of Labor in the United States, 1896–1932: Working Conditions, Labor Legislation*. New York: The Macmillan Company, 1935.

Leuchtenburg, William E. *Franklin D. Roosevelt and the New Deal, 1932–1940*. New York: Harper Torchbooks, 1963.

Levering, Robert, Milton Moskowitz, and Michael Katz. *The 100 Best Companies to Work for in America*. Reading, Massachusetts: Addison-Wesley Publishing Company, 1984.

Lichtenberg, Frank. "Industrial De-Diversification and Its Consequences for Productivity." Working Paper No. 3231, National Bureau of Economic Research, Washington, DC. 1990. http://www.nber.org/papers/w3231.pdf.

Lichtenstein, Nelson. "Labor in the Truman Era: Origins of the 'Private Welfare State.'" In *The Truman Presidency*, edited by Michael J. Lacey, 128–153. Cambridge, England: Cambridge University Press, 1989.

———. *Labor's War at Home: The CIO in World War II*. Cambridge, England: Cambridge University Press, 1982.

———. *The Most Dangerous Man in Detroit: Walter Reuther and the Fate of American Labor*. New York: Basic Books, 1995.

Lindsey, Almont. *The Pullman Strike: The Story of a Unique Experiment and of a Great Labor Upheaval*. Chicago: Phoenix Books, University of Chicago Press, 1964.

Link, Arthur. *Technological Change and Productivity Growth*. New York: Taylor and Francis, 1987.

Lipset, Seymour Martin and William Schneider. *The Confidence Gap: Business, Labor, and Government in the Public Mind*. Rev. ed. Baltimore: the Johns Hopkins University Press, 1987.

Lloyd, Henry Demarest. "Story of a Great Monopoly." *The Atlantic Monthly*, March 1881.

———. *Wealth Against Commonwealth*. Westport, Connecticut: Greenwood Press, 1976—originally published in 1894.

Lorsch, Jay W. and Elizabeth MacIver. *Pawns or Potentates: The Reality of America's Corporate Boards*. Boston: Harvard Business School Press, 1989.

Loth, David. *Swope of G.E.: The Story of Gerald Swope and General Electric in American Business*. New York: Simon and Schuster, 1958.

Lowi, Theodore J. *The End of Liberalism: The Second Republic of the United States*. 2nd ed. New York: W. W. Norton & Company, 1979.

Luo, Tian, Amar Mann, and Richard Holden. "The Expanding Role of Temporary Help Services from 1990 to 2008." *Monthly Labor Review* (August 2010): 3–16.

Madrick, Jeffrey. *The End of Affluence: America's Economic Dilemma*. New York: Random House, 1995.

Manne, Henry M. "Mergers and the market for corporate control." *The Journal of Political Economy* 73, no. 2 (April 1965): 110–120.

Marcus Kabel, Marcus. "Wal-Mart Blind to Illegal Logging." *Forbes*, December 12, 2007. http://www.corpwatch.org/article.php?id=14853.

Martin, Justin. *Nader: Crusader, Spoiler, Icon*. Cambridge, Massachusetts: Perseus Publishing, 2002.

Mattera, Philip, Thomas Cafcas, Leigh McIlvaine, Andrew Seifter, and Kasia Tarczynska. "Money for Something: Job Creation and Job Quality Standards in State Economic Development Subsidy Programs." Good Jobs First. December 2011. http://www.goodjobsfirst.org/moneyforsomething.

McCartin, Joseph A. "'An American Feeling': Workers, Managers, and the Struggle Over Industrial Democracy in the World War I Era.'" In *Industrial Democracy in America: The Ambiguous Promise*, edited by Nelson Lichtenstein and Howell John Harris, 67–86. Cambridge, England: Cambridge University Press, 1993.

McCraw, Thomas K. *American Business, 1920–2000: How it Worked*. Wheeling, Illinois: Harlan Davidson, Inc., 2000.

———. *Prophets of Regulation*. Cambridge, Mass.: The Belknap Press of Harvard University Press, 1984.

McIntire, Mike. "Conservative Nonprofit Acts as a Stealth Business Lobbyist." *New York Times*, April 21, 2012.

McIntyre, Robert S. Testimony of Robert S. McIntyre, Director of Citizens for Tax Justice. Hearing before the Committee on the Budget, United States House of Representatives, Waste, Fraud, and Abuse in Federal Mandatory Programs, Serial No. 108–9, June 18, 2003. http://www.ctj.org/html/corp0603.htm.

Meyer, Mitchell and Harland Fox. *Profile of Employee Benefits*. New York: The Conference Board, 1974.

Meyer, Stephen III. *The Five Dollar Day: Labor Management and Social Control in the Ford Motor Company 1908–1921*. Albany, New York: State University of New York Press, 1981.

Milkovich, George. "Union Role in Wage and Salary Administration." McGraw Hill Education Answers, 2013. http://www.answers.mhecucation.com/management/compensation/union-role-wage-and-salary-administration.

Millis, Harry A. and Royal E. Montgomery. *Organized Labor*. New York: McGraw-Hill Book Company, Inc., 1945.

———. *Labor's Progress and Some Basic Labor Problems*. New York: McGraw-Hill Book Company, Inc., 1938.

Mills, C. Wright. *The Power Elite*. New York: Oxford University Press, 1956.

———. *White Collar: The American Middle Classes*. New York: Oxford University Press, Inc., 1951.

Minor/Third Party Platforms. "Progressive Party Platform of 1912." November 5, 1912. Online by Gerhard Peters and John T. Woolley, The American Presidency Project. http://www.presidency.ucsb.edu/ws/?pid=29617.

Mintz, Morton. "'Heroine' of FDA Keeps Bad Drug Off Market." *Washington Post*, July 15, 1962.

Mintz, Martin and Jerry S. Cohen. *America, Inc.: Who Owns and Operates the United States*. New York: Dial Press, 1971.

Mishel, Lawrence, Jared Bernstein, and John Schmitt. *The State of Working America: 2000/2001*. Ithaca, New York: ILR Press, 2001.

Mishel, Lawrence, Josh Bivens, Elise Gould, and Heidi Shierholz. *The State of Working America*. 12th ed. Ithaca, New York: IRL Press, 2012.

Mishel, Lawrence and Natalie Sabadish. "CEO Pay and the Top 1%: How Executive Compensation and Financial-Sector Pay Have Fueled Income Inequality." Issue Brief #331, Economic Policy Institute, Washington, DC, May 2, 2012. http://www.epi.org/publication/ib331-ceo-pay-top-1-percent/

Mishel, Lawrence, Richard B. Freeman, and Frank Levy. "The Employee Free Choice Act is Needed to Restore Balance in the Labor Market." Economic Policy Institute, Washington, DC, February 24, 2009. http://www.epi.org/publication/prominent_economists_call_for_passage_of_the_employee_free_choice_act/.

Mitchell, Broadus. *Depression Decade: From New Era through New Deal 1929–1941, Volume IX, The Economic History of the United States*. New York: Harper Torchbooks, 1947.

Monks, Robert A. G. and Nell Minow. *Corporate Governance*. Cambridge, Massachusetts: Blackwell Business, 1995.

———. *Power and Accountability*. New York: Harper Business, 1991.

Montgomery, David. *The Fall of the House of Labor: The Workplace, the State, and American Labor Activism, 1865–1925*. Cambridge: Cambridge University Press, 1987.

———. "Industrial Democracy or Democracy in Industry?: The Theory and Practice of the Labor Movement." In *Industrial Democracy in America: The Ambiguous Promise*, edited by Nelson Lichtenstein and Howell John Harris, 20–42. Cambridge, England: Cambridge University Press, 1993.

Monthly Labor Review. "Senate Investigation of Welfare and Pension Plans," *Monthly Labor Review* 79, no. 7 (July 1956): 812.

Moody, Kim. *An Injury to All: The Decline of American Unionism*. London: Verso, 1988.

Morone, James A. *The Democratic Wish: Popular Participation and the Limits of American Government*. New York: Basic Books, 1990.

Morrell Heald. *The Social Responsibilities of Business: Company and Community, 1900–1960*. Cleveland: The Press of Case Western Reserve University, 1970.

Nader, Ralph. *The Seventeen Solutions: Bold Ideas For Our American Future* New York: Harper, 2012.

———. *Unsafe at Any Speed: the Designed-In Dangers of the American Automobile*. New York: Pocket Books, 1966.

Nader, Ralph, Mark Green, and Joel Seligman. *Taming the Giant Corporation*. New York: W. W. Norton & Company, Inc., 1976.

National Association of Manufactures. *Economic Principles Commission, The American Individual Enterprise System, Its Nature, Evolution, and Future*. New York: McGraw-Hill, 1946.

National Civic Federation. *Industrial Conciliation: Report of the Proceedings of the Conference*. New York: G. P. Putnam's Sons, 1902.

National Industrial Conference Board. *Effect of the Depression on Industrial Relations Programs*. New York: National Industrial Conference Board, 1934.

———. *Industrial Relations: Administration of Policies and Programs*. New York: National Industrial Conference Board, 1931.

———. *Industrial Relations Programs in Small Plants*. New York: National Industrial Conference Board, 1929.

———. *Personnel Practices in Factory and Office, revised, Studies in Personnel Studies, No. 88*. New York: National Industrial Conference Board, Inc., 1948.

———. *Personnel Practices in Factory and Office: Manufacturing, Studies in Personnel Policy, No. 194*. New York: National Industrial Conference Board, Inc., 1964.

———. *What Employers are Doing for Employees*. New York: National Industrial Conference Board, 1936.

Nelson, Daniel. *Managers & Workers: Origins of the Twentieth-Century Factory System in the United States 1880–1920*. 2nd ed. Madison, Wisconsin: University of Wisconsin Press, 1995.

Newsweek. "The American Corporation Under Fire." May 24, 1971.

———. "Confessions of a Raider." October 20, 1986.

New York Times. *The Downsizing of America: Millions of Americans are Losing Good Jobs. This is Their Story*. New York: Times Books, 1996.

Niebuhr, Reinhold. *Moral Man and Immoral Society*. New York: Charles Scribner's Sons, 1932.

Noah, Timothy. *The Great Divergence: America's Growing Inequality Crisis and What We Can Do About It*. New York: Bloomsbury Books, 2012.

Noble, Charles. *Welfare as We Knew It: A Political History of the American Welfare State*. New York: Oxford University Press, 1997.

O'Brien, Anthony Patrick. "Factory Size, Economies of Scale, and the Great Merger Wave of 1898–1902." *Journal of Economic History*, Vol. 48, No. 3 (September 1988): 639–649.

O'Toole, James, Elisabeth Hansot, William Herman, Neal Herrick, Elliot Liebow, Bruce Lusigman, Harold Richman, Harold Sheppard, Ben Stephansky, and James Wright. *Work in America: Report of a Special Task Force to the Secretary of Health, Education, and Welfare*. Cambridge, Massachusetts: MIT Press, 1973.

Olmsted, Victor. "The Betterment of Industrial Conditions." *Bulletin of the Department of Labor*, 5, no. 31 (November 1900): 1117–1156.

Open Secrets. "Business-Labor Ideology Split in PAC & Individual Donations to Candidates, Parties, Super PACs and Outside Spending Groups." Open Secrets, Center for Responsive Politics. Accessed May 28, 2013. http://www.opensecrets.org/overview/blio.php.

———. "Lobbying." Open Secrets, Center for Responsive Politics. Accessed May 8, 2012. http://www.opensecrets.org/lobby/incdec/php.

Ozanne, Robert. *A Century of Labor-Management Relations at McCormick and International Harvester*. Madison, Wisconsin: The University of Wisconsin Press, 1967.

Packard, Vance. *The Waste Makers*. New York: D. McKay Co., 1960.

Parloff, Roger. "Why the Outcry Over 'Citizens United.'" *Fortune*, February 12, 2010. http://archive.fortune.com/2010/02/11/news/companies/supreme_court_citizens_united.fortune/index.htm.

Patmore, Greg. "Employee Representation Plans in North America and Australia, 1915–1935: An Employer Response to Workplace Democracy." Paper presented at the Workplace Democracy Conference, Labour Council of NSW/Work and Organisational Studies, School of Business, University of Sydney, Sydney, Australia, June 2001. http://worksite.econ.usyd.edu.au/employer.html.

People for the American Way. "ALEC: The Voice of Corporate Special Interests in State Legislatures." People for the American Way. http://www.pfaw.org/rww-in-focus/alec-the-voice-of-corporate-special-interests-state-legislatures.

Perlman, Selig and Philip Taft. *History of Labor in the United States, 1896–1932, Volume IV*. New York: the Macmillan Company, 1935.

Perrow, Charles. *Organizing America: Wealth, Power, and the Origins of Corporate Capitalism*. Princeton, New Jersey: Princeton University Press, 2002.

Phillips-Fein, Kim. *Invisible Hands: The Businessmen's Crusade Against the New Deal*. New York: W.W. Norton, 2009.

Pickens, T. Boone. "Viewpoints: 1 Share, 1 Vote: Make it the Rule for all Exchanges." *Los Angeles Times*, January 18, 1987.

Pierce, Charles P. "Tom Udall's Bold Solution to Overturn Citizens United." *Esquire*. Accessed December 29, 2012. http://www.esquire.com/blogs/politics/tom-udall-citizens-united-amendment-14761989.

Piven, Francis Fox and Richard A. Cloward. *Poor People's Movements: Why they Succeed, How They Fail*. New York: Vintage Books, 1979.

Polanyi, Karl. *The Great Transformation*. Boston: Beacon Press, 1956.

PollingReport.com. "Major Institutions." PollingReport.com, Accessed December 8, 2012. http://www.pollingreport.com/institut.htm.

Porter, Michael and Mark R. Kramer. "The Competitive Advantage of Corporate Philanthropy." In *Harvard Business Review on Corporate Responsibility*, 27–64. Boston: Harvard Business School Press, 2003.

Porter, Michael E. "From Competitive Advantage to Corporate Strategy." *Harvard Business Review* 65 (May-June 1987): 43–59.

Preston, Lee E., Harry J. Sapienza, and Robert Miller. "Stakeholders, shareholders, and managers: Who gains what from corporate performance." In *Socio-Economics: Toward a New Synthesis*, edited by Amitai Etzioni and Paul R. Lawrence, 149–165. Armark, New York: M. E. Sharpe, 1991.

Pritchard, Justin. "Miley Cyrus' Toxic Wal-Mart Jewelry Still on Shelves." *Associated Press*, May 19, 2010. http://www.huffingtonpost.com/2010/05/19/mileys-cyrus-toxic-walmar_n_582020.html.

Pusateri, C. Joseph. *Big Business in America: Attack and Defense*. Itasca, Illinois: F. E. Peacock Publishers, Inc., 1975.

——. *A History of American Business.* 2nd ed. Wheeling, Illinois: Harlan Davidson, Inc., 1988.

Quadagno, Jill. *One Nation Uninsured: Why the U.S. Has No National Health Insurance.* New York: Oxford University Press, 2005.

——. *The Transformation of Old Age Security: Class and Politics in the American Welfare State.* Chicago: The University of Chicago Press, 1988.

Raucher, Alan R. *Public Relations and Business, 1900–1929.* Baltimore: Johns Hopkins Press, 1968.

Rayback, John G. *A History of American Labor.* New York: The Free Press, 1966.

Reference for Business. "Corporate Philanthropy." Reference for Business: Encyclopedia of Business, 2nd ed.: http://www.referenceforbusiness.com/encyclopedia/Con-Cos/Corporate-Philanthropy.html.

Revolving Door Working Group. *A Matter of Trust: How the Revolving Door Undermines Public Confidence in Government—and What To Do About It.* Revolving Door Working Group, October 2005. http://www.cleanup-washington.org/documents/RevovDoor.pdf.

Riesman, David. *The Lonely Crowd: A Study of the Changing American Character.* New Haven, Connecticut: Yale University Press, 1950.

Ritter, Gretchen. *Goldbugs and Greenbacks: the Antimonopoly Tradition and the Politics of American Finance, 1865–1896.* New York: Cambridge University Press, 1997.

Roe, Mark J. "From Antitrust to Corporate Governance? The Corporation and the Law: 1959–1994." Working Paper #119, Columbia University School of Law, New York, 1995.

Ross, Steven A. "The Economic Theory of Agency: The Principal's Problem." *American Economic Review* 63, no. 2 (May 1973): 134–139.

Roy, William G. *Socializing Capital: The Rise of the Large Industrial Corporation in America.* Princeton. New Jersey: Princeton University Press, 1997.

Rush, Harold M. F. *Job Design for Motivation: Experiments in Job Enlargement and Job Enrichment.* New York: Conference Board, 1971.

Salisbury, Robert H. *Interests and Institutions: Substance and Structure in American Politics.* Pittsburgh: University of Pittsburgh Press, 1992.

Sandel, Michael. *What Money Can't Buy: The Moral Limits of Markets.* New York: Farrar, Straus, and Giroux, 2012.

Sanders, Bernie. "Saving American Democracy." Bernie Sanders, United States Senator for Vermont, Newsroom July 24, 2012. http://www.sanders.senate.gov/newsroom/recent-business/saving-american-democracy.

Sass, Steven A. *The Promise of Private Pensions: The First Hundred Years.* Cambridge, Massachusetts: Harvard University Press, 1997.

Schatz, Ronald W. *The Electrical Workers: A History of Labor at General Electric and Westinghouse.* Urbana: University of Illinois Press, 1983.

Schlesinger, Arthur M. Jr. *The Crisis of the Old Order: 1919–1933, The Age of Roosevelt, Volume 1.* New York: Houghton Mifflin Harcourt, 2003.

Schmenner, Roger W. *Making Business Location Decisions.* Englewood Cliffs, New Jersey: Prentice-Hall, Inc., 1982.

Sellers, Charles. *The Market Revolution: Jacksonian America, 1815–1846.* New York: Oxford University Press, 1991.

Shierholz, Heidi and Lawrence Mishel. "The Sad But True Story of Wages in America." Issue Brief #297, Economic Policy Institute, March 14, 2011. http://www.epi.org/publication/the_sad_but_true_story_of_wages_in_america/.

Shleifer, Andrei and Lawrence H. Summers. "Breach of Trust in Hostile Takeovers." In *Corporate Takeovers: Causes and Consequences*, edited by Alan J. Auerbach, 33–61. Chicago: University of Chicago Press, 1988.

Shlezfer, Andrei and Robert W. Vishny. "The Takeover Wave of the 1980's." *Science* 249, no. 4970 (August 1990): 745–749.

Shuey, Edwin L. *Factory People and Their Employers: How Their Relations are Made Pleasant and Profitable.* New York: Lentilhon and Company, 1900.

Sinclair, Upton. *The Jungle.* New York: Penguin Classics, 2006—originally published in 1906.

———. "Outstanding Issues of the Forthcoming Campaign and the Fundamental Problems Confronting by Country Today." *Literary Digest*, October 13, 1934. http://www.sfmuseum.org/hist/sinclair.html.

Skocpol, Theda. *Protecting Soldiers and Mothers: The Political Origins of Social Policy in the United States.* Cambridge, Massachusetts: The Belknap Press of Harvard University Press, 1992.

Skocpol, Theda and Kenneth Finegold. "State Capacity and Economic Intervention in the Early New Deal." *Political Science Quarterly* 97, no. 2 (Summer 1982): 255–278.

Skolnik, Alfred M. "Twenty-Five Years of Employee-Benefit Plans." *Social Security Bulletin* 39, no. 9 (September 1976): 3–21.

Skowronek, Stephen. *Building A New American State: The Expansion of National Administrative Capacities, 1877–1920.* New York: Cambridge University Press, 1982.

Slichter, Sumner H. *Union Policies and Industrial Management.* Washington, DC: The Brookings Institution, 1941.

Slichter, Sumner H., James J. Healy, and E. Robert Livernash. *The Impact of Collective Bargaining on Management, Washington.* DC: The Brookings Institution, 1960.

Sobel. *The Age of Giant Corporations: A Microeconomic History of American Business, 1914–1970.* Westport, Connecticut: Greenwood Press, Inc., 1972.

———. *The Rise and Fall of the Conglomerate Kings.* New York: Stein and Dayl Publishers, 1984.

Social Accountability International. *Social Accountability 8000.* Social Accountability International, 2008 version, http://www.saint.org/index.cfm?fuseaction=Page.View/PageID=1458.

Social Investment Forum. "Report on Socially Responsible Investing Trends in the United States, 2010." Social Investment Forum Foundation. http://www.ussif.org/files/Publications/10_Trends_Exec_Summary.pdf.

Social Security Administration. "Social Security History: The Evolution of Medicare, Chapter 3: The Third Round 1943–1950." Official Social Security Website. http://www.ssa.gov/history/corningchap3.html.

Social Security Bulletin. "Report of the President's Commission on Pension Policy: Executive Summary." *Social Security Bulletin* 44, no. 5 (May 1981): 14–17.

Soule, George. *A Planned Society.* New York: The Macmillan Company, 1932.

——— . *Prosperity Decade: From War to Depression, 1917–1929.* New York: Holt, Rinehart and Winston, 1947.

Stearns, Linda Brewster and Kenneth D. Allan. "Economic Behavior in Institutional Environments: The Corporate Merger Wave of the 1980's." *American Sociological Review* 61, no. 4 (August 1996): 699–718.

Stender, John H. "Enforcing the Occupational Safety and Health Act of 1970: The Federal Government as a Catalyst." *Law and Contemporary Problems* 38, no. 4 (Summer/Autumn 1974): 641–650.

Sterngold, James. "Shaking Billions From Beatrice." *New York Times,* September 6, 1987.

Stevens, Beth. "Blurring the Boundaries: How the Federal Government Has Influenced Welfare Benefits in the Private Sector." In *The Politics of Social Policy in the United States,* edited by Margaret Weir, Ann Shola Orloff, and Theda Skocpol, 123–148. Princeton, New Jersey: Princeton University Press, 1988.

——— . "Labor Unions, Employee Benefits, and the Privatization of the American Welfare State." *Journal of Policy History* 2, no. 3 (1990): 233–260.

Temporary National Economic Committee. *Final Report and Recommendations of the Temporary National Economic Committee: Investigation of Concentration of Economic Power.* Washington, DC: United States Government Printing Office, 1941.

Time. "Corporations: One Merger Stopped." December 1, 1958.

——— . "High times for T. Boone Pickens." March 4, 1985, 52.

Tolman, William Howe. *Industrial Betterment, Monographs on American Social Economics.* New York: Social Service Press, 1900.

——— . *Social Engineering: A Record of Things Done by American Industrialists Employing Upwards of One and One-Half Million of People.* New York: McGraw-Hill Book Company, 1909.

Tomaskovic-Devey, Donald and Ken-Hou Lin. "Income Dynamics, Economic Rents, and the Financialization of the U.S. Economy." *American Sociological Review* 76, no. 4 (August 2011): 538–559.

Tomlins, Christopher L. *The State and the Unions: Labor Relations, Law, and the Organized Labor Movement in America, 1880–1960.* Cambridge, England: Cambridge University Press, 1985.

Tone, Andrea. *The Business of Benevolence: Industrial Paternalism in Progressive America.* Ithaca, New York: Cornell University Press, 1997.

Uchitelle, Louis. *The Disposable American: Layoffs and Their Discontents.* New York: Vintage Books, 2007.

Udall, Morris. "Military Spending—Let's Stop the Waste." Congressman's Report, October 12, 1961, University of Arizona Library Manuscript Collection, Tucson, Arizona. http://library.arizona.edu/exhibits/udall/congrept/87th/611012.html.

United States Bureau of the Census, *Historical Statistics of the United States, Part 1, Colonial Times to 1970.* Bicentennial Edition. Washington, DC: US Government Printing Office, 1975.

——. *Historical Statistics of the United States, Part 2, Colonial Times to 1970.* Bicentennial Edition. Washington, DC: US Government Printing Office, 1975.

——. *Statistical Abstract of the United States 1991.* 111th ed. Washington, DC: US Government Printing Office, 1991.

——. *Statistical Abstract of the United States 1984.* 104th ed. Washington, DC: US Government Printing Office, 1984.

——. *Statistical Abstract of the United States 1972.* 93rd ed. Washington, DC: US Government Printing Office, 1972.

United States Department of Labor, Bureau of Labor Statistics. "Contingent and Alternative Employment Arrangements, February 2005." Released July 27, 2005. http://www.bls.gov/news.release/pdf/conemp.pdf.

——. "Employee Tenure in 2000." Released August 29, 2000. http://www.bls.gov/news.release/history/tenure_08292000.txt.

——. *Trade Agreements, 1927, Bulletin No. 468.* Washington, DC, Government Printing Office, 1927.

——. "Union Members—2012." Released January 23, 2013. http://www.bls.gov/news.release/archives/union2_01232013.htm.

——. *Welfare Work for Employees in Industrial Establishments in the United States, Bulletin No. 250.* Washington, DC, Government Printing Office, 1919.

——. "Women in the Labor Force: A Datebook (2011 Edition)." December 2011. http://www.bls.gov/cps/wlf-databook2011.htm.

Useem, Michael. *Executive Defense: Shareholder Power and Corporate Reorganization.* Cambridge, Massachusetts: Harvard University Press, 1993.

——. *Investor Capitalism: How Money Managers are Changing the Face of Corporate America.* New York: Basic Books, 1996.

Vogel, David. *Fluctuating Fortunes: The Political Power of Business in America.* New York: Basic Books, Inc., Publishers, 1989.

——. *Lobbying the Corporation: Citizen Challenges to Business Authority.* New York: Basic Books, Inc., Publishers, 1978.

——. *The Market for Virtue: The Potential and Limits of Corporate Social Responsibility.* Washington, DC: Brookings Institution Press, 2006.

Voss, Kim. *The Making of American Exceptionalism: The Knights of Labor and Class Formation in the Nineteenth Century.* Ithaca, New York: Cornell University Press, 1993.

Waddell, Brian. *The War Against the New Deal: World War II and American Democracy.* DeKalb, Illinois: Northern Illinois University Press, 2001.

Wainess, Flint J. "The Ways and Means of National Health Care Reform, 1974 and Beyond." *Journal of Health Politics, Policy, and Law* 24, no. 2 (April 1999): 305–333.

Waldo, Frank. *Dawn in Russia.* New York: Charles Scribner's Sons, 1931.

Walett, Francis G. *Economic History of the United States.* New York: Barnes and Noble, Inc., 1954.

Walmart. "Walmart: 2011 Annual Report: Building the New Generation Walmart." Walmart. http://stock.walmart.com/annual-reports.

Walsh, Declan and Steven Greenhouse. "Certified Safe, A Factory in Karachi Still Quickly Burned." *New York Times*, December 12, 2012.

Walton, Clarence C. *Corporate Social Responsibilities*. Belmont, California: Wadsworth Publishers Company, Inc., 1967.

Waring, Stephen P. *Taylorism Transformed: Scientific Management Theory since 1945*. Chapel Hill, North Carolina: The University of North Carolina Press, 1991.

Weaver, Suzanne. "Antitrust Division of the Department of Justice." In *The Politics of Regulation*, edited by James Q. Wilson, 123–151. New York: Basic Books, 1980.

Wehinger, Gert. "Fostering Long-Term Investment and Economic Growth: Summary of a High-Level OECD Financial Roundtable." *OECD Journal: Financial Market Trends* 2011, no. 1 (2011): 1–21.

Weidenbaum, Murray. *Business, Government, and the Public*. 2nd ed. Englewood, New Jersey: Prentice-Hall, Inc., 1981.

Weingroff, Richard F. "Federal-Aid Highway Act of 1956: Creating the Intestate System." *Public Roads Magazine* 60, no. 1 (Summer 1996). http://www.fhwa. dot.gov/publications/publicroads/96summer/p96su10.cfm.

Weinstein, James. *Ambiguous Legacy: The Left in American Politics*. New York: New Viewpoints, 1975.

———. *The Corporate Ideal in the Liberal State: 1900–1918*. Boston: Beacon Press, 1968.

Welch, Jack with John A. Byrne. *Jack: Straight from the Gut*. New York: Warner Business Books, 2001.

Welsh Marketing Associates. "American Express & The Statue of Liberty Restoration Fund," Cause Marketing Digital Library. Accessed February 25, 2012. http://dlib.info/omeka/judith/items.show/194.

Westervelt, Amy. "Target, Walmart, Babies-R-Us Sued Over Toxic Baby Products." *Forbes*, December 6, 2012. http://www.forbes.com/ sites/amywestervelt/2012/12/06/target-walmart-babies-r-us-named-in-legal-action-for-selling-baby-products-containing-cancer-causing-flame-retardant/.

Weston, J. Fred. *The Role of Mergers in the Growth of Large Firms*. Berkeley, California: University of California Press, 1953.

White, Richard. *Railroaded: The Transcontinentals and the Making of Modern America*. New York: W.W. Norton & Company, 2011.

Whitehouse.gov. "The Clinton Presidency: Eight years of Peace, Progress, and Prosperity." http://clinton5.nara.gov/WH/Accomplishements/eight-years-02.html.

Whyte, William H. *The Organization Man*. New York: Simon and Schuster, 1956.

Wiebe, Robert H. *Businessmen and Reform: A Study of the Progressive Movement*. Cambridge, Massachusetts: Harvard University Press, 1962.

Wiener, Leonard. "The Tax Man Goeth," *U.S. News and World Report*. August 19, 2002.

Wilentz, Sean. *The Age of Reagan: A History 1974–2008*. New York: Harper Collins Publishers, 2008.

Winslow, John F. *Conglomerates Unlimited: The Failure of Regulation.* Bloomington, Indiana: Indiana University Press, 1973.

Woody, Carroll H. *The Growth of the Federal Government, 1915–1932.* New York: McGraw-Hill Book Company, Inc., 1934.

Wooten, James A. "A Legislative and Political History of ERISA Preemption, Part I." *Journal of Pension Benefits* 14, no. 1 (Autumn 2006): 31–35.

Working America. "About Working America." Working America. Accessed December 28, 2012, http://www.workingamerica.org/membership/about.

Worstall, Tim. "Why Have Corporate Profits Been Rising as a Percentage of GDP? Globalization." *Forbes*, May 2, 2013. http://www.forbes.com/timworstall/2013/05/07/why-have-corporate-profits-been-rising-as-a-percentage-of-gdp-globalization.

Zahavi, Gerald. "Negotiated Loyalty: Welfare Capitalism and the Shoemakers of Endicott Johnson, 1920–1940." *Journal of American History* 71, no. 3 (December 1983): 602–620.

Index